IBM

International Technical Sup

Planning and Managing the Deployment of WebSphere Commerce

June 2008

SG24-7588-00

Note: Before using this information and the product it supports, read the information in "Notices" on page xi.

First Edition (June 2008)

This edition applies to Version 6, Release 0, Modification 0.4 of WebSphere Commerce.

Contents

Notices

This information was developed for products and services offered in the U.S.A.

IBM may not offer the products, services, or features discussed in this document in other countries. Consult your local IBM representative for information about the products and services currently available in your area. Any reference to an IBM product, program, or service is not intended to state or imply that only that IBM product, program, or service may be used. Any functionally equivalent product, program, or service that does not infringe any IBM intellectual property right may be used instead. However, it is the user's responsibility to evaluate and verify the operation of any non-IBM product, program, or service.

IBM may have patents or pending patent applications covering subject matter described in this document. The furnishing of this document does not give you any license to these patents. You can send license inquiries, in writing, to:
IBM Director of Licensing, IBM Corporation, North Castle Drive, Armonk, NY 10504-1785 U.S.A.

The following paragraph does not apply to the United Kingdom or any other country where such provisions are inconsistent with local law: INTERNATIONAL BUSINESS MACHINES CORPORATION PROVIDES THIS PUBLICATION "AS IS" WITHOUT WARRANTY OF ANY KIND, EITHER EXPRESS OR IMPLIED, INCLUDING, BUT NOT LIMITED TO, THE IMPLIED WARRANTIES OF NON-INFRINGEMENT, MERCHANTABILITY OR FITNESS FOR A PARTICULAR PURPOSE. Some states do not allow disclaimer of express or implied warranties in certain transactions, therefore, this statement may not apply to you.

This information could include technical inaccuracies or typographical errors. Changes are periodically made to the information herein; these changes will be incorporated in new editions of the publication. IBM may make improvements or changes in the product(s) or the program(s) described in this publication at any time without notice.

Any references in this information to non-IBM Web sites are provided for convenience only and do not in any manner serve as an endorsement of those Web sites. The materials at those Web sites are not part of the materials for this IBM product and use of those Web sites is at your own risk.

IBM may use or distribute any of the information you supply in any way it believes appropriate without incurring any obligation to you.

Information concerning non-IBM products was obtained from the suppliers of those products, their published announcements or other publicly available sources. IBM has not tested those products and cannot confirm the accuracy of performance, compatibility or any other claims related to non-IBM products. Questions on the capabilities of non-IBM products should be addressed to the suppliers of those products.

This information contains examples of data and reports used in daily business operations. To illustrate them as completely as possible, the examples include the names of individuals, companies, brands, and products. All of these names are fictitious and any similarity to the names and addresses used by an actual business enterprise is entirely coincidental.

COPYRIGHT LICENSE:

This information contains sample application programs in source language, which illustrate programming techniques on various operating platforms. You may copy, modify, and distribute these sample programs in any form without payment to IBM, for the purposes of developing, using, marketing or distributing application programs conforming to the application programming interface for the operating platform for which the sample programs are written. These examples have not been thoroughly tested under all conditions. IBM, therefore, cannot guarantee or imply reliability, serviceability, or function of these programs.

Trademarks

IBM, the IBM logo, and ibm.com are trademarks or registered trademarks of International Business Machines Corporation in the United States, other countries, or both. These and other IBM trademarked terms are marked on their first occurrence in this information with the appropriate symbol (® or ™), indicating US registered or common law trademarks owned by IBM at the time this information was published. Such trademarks may also be registered or common law trademarks in other countries. A current list of IBM trademarks is available on the Web at `http://www.ibm.com/legal/copytrade.shtml`

The following terms are trademarks of the International Business Machines Corporation in the United States, other countries, or both:

AIX 5L™
AIX®
CICS®
ClearCase®
ClearQuest®
Cloudscape®
DataPower®
DataStage®
DB2 Universal Database™
DB2®
developerWorks®
Domino®
HACMP™
i5/OS®
IBM®
iSeries®
Lotus Notes®
Lotus®
Net.Commerce™
Notes®
OmniFind™
PartnerWorld®
POWER™
pSeries®
Rational Unified Process®
Rational®
Redbooks®
Redbooks (logo) ®
RequisitePro®
Requisite®
RS/6000®
RUP®
Sametime®
Storyboard™
System x™
Tivoli®
WebSphere®
Workplace™
Workplace Web Content Management™
z/OS®
zSeries®

The following terms are trademarks of other companies:

SAP, and SAP logos are trademarks or registered trademarks of SAP AG in Germany and in several other countries.

Oracle, JD Edwards, PeopleSoft, Siebel, and TopLink are registered trademarks of Oracle Corporation and/or its affiliates.

Photoshop, and Portable Document Format (PDF) are either registered trademarks or trademarks of Adobe Systems Incorporated in the United States, other countries, or both.

Oracle, JD Edwards, PeopleSoft, Siebel, and TopLink are registered trademarks of Oracle Corporation or its affiliates.

EJB, J2EE, Java, JavaScript, JavaServer, JDK, JSP, JVM, Solaris, Sun, Sun Java, and all Java-based trademarks are trademarks of Sun Microsystems, Inc. in the United States, other countries, or both.

Active Directory, Internet Explorer, Microsoft, MSN, Visio, Windows Server, Windows, and the Windows logo are trademarks of Microsoft Corporation in the United States, other countries, or both.

Intel, Pentium, Intel logo, Intel Inside logo, and Intel Centrino logo are trademarks or registered trademarks of Intel Corporation or its subsidiaries in the United States, other countries, or both.

UNIX is a registered trademark of The Open Group in the United States and other countries.

Linux is a trademark of Linus Torvalds in the United States, other countries, or both.

Other company, product, or service names may be trademarks or service marks of others.

Preface

We gathered a team of WebSphere Commerce experts together and asked them to write an IBM® Redbooks® publication, to explain how to transform a business to eCommerce using WebSphere Commerce. How do you plan and run an eCommerce project; what pitfalls can we help you avoid? Should you build the eCommerce team from within your own organization, or seek the help of solution or service providers? What advice can we pass on about how to work with IBM® and other service providers? What software do you actually get with WebSphere Commerce? What does it do? Can you tailor it to your business? What extensions do you need? Will it work with your existing business processes? We aim to help you answer all these questions, and more, as well as directing you to other sources of information for more technical information.

We should also say what you will *not* find in this book. We did not set out to write a book about how to run software projects. Of course we could not avoid questions about software development projects; deploying WebSphere Commerce is about managing software development, and if you do not have experience running software development projects, then our advice is unequivocal — go and get a service provider who does, to help you. If you have software development experience, you might find useful a companion book to this one, *Best Practices and Tools for Creating WebSphere Commerce Sites*, SG24-6699. It goes into a lot of detail about how to apply methods for software development to WebSphere Commerce.

Nor did we want to write a “handbook” about how to customize and extend WebSphere Commerces, for two reasons. First, our intended readership for this book are project managers, software architects, and lead designers, and not developers or programmers. Second, there are already sources of information about customizing and extending WebSphere Commerce in the Infocenter, in the WebSphere® Commerce Developer, and in a number of other Redbooks®[1].

Because WebSphere Commerce covers so much ground, to describe all its capabilities, and explain how to customize, extend, or configure them in one book, requires more basic skills than any single reader would possess, or would want to possess. In addition to this, the information would become dated in a matter of months. Detailed, and changing, technical information about such a wide variety of topics is best delivered in small chunks tailored to the needs of specific technical audiences.

[1] A full list of further reading is to be found at the back of this book, in the Appendix , “Related publications” on page 385

What you will find in this book is information we think is valuable if you are embarking, or thinking about embarking, on a WebSphere Commerce project. Our goal is to help the neophyte to WebSphere Commerce get familiar with its jargon and with the best practices people have evolved in working on WebSphere Commerce projects.

Armed with the information in this book, you are better able to get the most out of the product, as well as your engagements with WebSphere Commerce service providers, whether IBM, or IBM Business Partners.

How to read this book

The book is written for people who have been asked to plan how to introduce WebSphere Commerce to their organization. It should be useful in both the pre-sales and immediate post-sales phases of an eCommerce project. We have organized the book around the needs of people who have a software background, but have never worked with WebSphere Commerce before. The person to whom we hope the book is of most interest is the project manager who has the responsibility of setting up and running a WebSphere Commerce project. We hope it is also of interest of people who are setting up different parts of a WebSphere Commerce organization, and want to learn from the experience of people who have been there and done that before.

With this readership in mind, it is important to explain what eCommerce is, what WebSphere Commerce does, and how you need to extend WebSphere Commerce to build a really competitive eCommerce system. That is what Part 1 is about.

The next important topic to talk about is getting your project off to a good start. What do you need to do first and how should you organize a WebSphere Commerce project? Part 2 starts with these questions and talking about nine important challenges (or pitfalls) to bear in mind. We end Part 2 with a list of the ten most helpful suggestions that people who have trod this path before can offer as advice for a new WebSphere Commerce project manager.

Parts 3 and 4 get down to some of the planning tasks that you need to do and how to do them — such as planning the hardware and software you need, sizing the system, and what you need to do when the Web site is live, to keep it running and to troubleshoot problems. You need to plan and train people for these tasks, well before you *Go Live!*

What is in the book

The book is organized as follows:

- Part 1, "Know your eCommerce solution" on page 1 describes what kinds of eCommerce WebSphere Commerce is designed for, what the capabilities it provides are, and what additional software you can add to round out your eCommerce solution.
- Part 2, "Plan your eCommerce project" on page 123 discusses the project management aspects of setting up a WebSphere Commerce site and some of the technical factors that will make or break your eCommerce business. We consider the particular management challenges that building an eCommerce site presents, and how you should organize your project team to deliver your Web site.
- Part 3, "Plan your eCommerce infrastructure" on page 245 is a much more technical section, and discusses the hardware and software infrastructure you need to build to host WebSphere Commerce.
- Part 4, "Keep on running" on page 323 describes the day to day operations that you have to carry out to ensure that your Web site stays up and running. If there are problems, Chapter 12, "Troubleshoot your eCommerce site" on page 359, will help you with problem solving.

Which parts of the book are most relevant to you

We expect this book is of interest to project managers, architects, and lead designers. However, it can also be a beginners guide to WebSphere Commerce, so do not postpone reading it just because you are still waiting for that promotion! The book is not organized with chapters for project managers and chapters for architects: There are points all the way through for everybody. Perhaps you wonder if there are any short cuts to reading this book to get the message. For a quick read, we suggest the following sections:

1.1, "Electronic commerce" on page 5
1.2, "Factors that influence project scope and size" on page 10
2.1, "Business models" on page 22
2.3.1, "Business user tools" on page 69
4.2, "Level-setting" on page 128
4.3, "Setting goals and managing expectations" on page 130
4.4, "Business requirements" on page 132
4.7, "Project risks" on page 140
4.8, "Project scope" on page 144
4.9, "Project governance" on page 145
5.1.4, "Agile development and WebSphere Commerce" on page 176
6.1, "Requirements" on page 199

6.3, "Performance" on page 207
6.7, "Launch preparation and launch" on page 232
6.9, "Top ten tips" on page 238
9.1, "Sizing" on page 291
Chapter 11, "Running your Web site" on page 325

What to read next

"Related publications" on page 385 lists a lot of Web sites, articles, and books for further reading. But perhaps you are looking for one place to go. Then the WebSphere Commerce v6 InfoCenter, as well as providing probably far more detail than you want at this stage, also has a number of good introductions to different topics, for example:

- SOA and WebSphere Commerce, at:

  http://publib.boulder.ibm.com/infocenter/wchelp/v6r0m0/index.jsp?topic=/com.ibm.commerce.developer.doc/concepts/csdsoa.htm

- The store information model, at:

  http://publib.boulder.ibm.com/infocenter/wchelp/v6r0m0/topic/com.ibm.commerce.data.doc/concepts/cbm_imoverview.htm

- The online Infocenter that is shipped with WebSphere Commerce, at:

  http://publib.boulder.ibm.com/infocenter/wchelp/v6r0m0/index.jsp

The team that wrote this book

This book was produced by a team of specialists from around the world working at the International Technical Support Organization, Raleigh Center. Here we show some members of our team.

Left to right, top to bottom: Jennifer, Peter S., N Krishnan (Kitty), Charles, Peter W.

Peter Swithinbank is a Project Leader at the ITSO, Hursley Center. He writes IBM Redbooks and teaches IBM classes worldwide on Web services and building business integration solutions. Peter has worked for IBM for 29 years and has been with the ITSO for three years. He has a diploma in software engineering from Oxford University and an M.A. in Geography from the University of Cambridge.

Charles Ackeifi is a Principal at CourtBridge Consulting Group, an information technology company that specializes in Technology consulting and software development services in East Granby, Connecticut, USA and an IBM Business Partner. He has over 18 years experience in information technology and has written extensively on eBusiness and Internet development initiatives.

Jennifer Allan is a Staff Software Developer on the WebSphere Commerce support team. Based out of Toronto, Canada, she has been working with WebSphere Commerce since starting at IBM in 2004. She graduated with distinction from the University of Victoria, earning her Bachelor's degree in Computer Engineering, specialization: systems (2004). Her areas of interest include debugging performance problems and product documentation.

Christopher McCollum is a Director of Product Engineering at USi, an AT&T Company. He has been working with IBM WebSphere Commerce since it was called Net.Commerce™ v3.1. Before coming to USi, he spent over six years at IBM in Global Services and the ITSO. Chris has written extensively on WebSphere Commerce and related eCommerce topics. He holds an MBA in Technology Management and numerous industry certifications.

Nevine Helmy is a staff software engineer in Egypt. She has 6 years of experience in the e-Commerce field. She has worked at IBM for 8 years. Her areas of expertise include Enterprise Java™ programming, WebSphere Commerce and WebSphere Portal development and administration. She is an IBM certified Deployment Professional - WebSphere Commerce V5.5 and an IBM certified System Administrator - WebSphere Application Server Network Deployment V6.1. She has written on WebSphere Commerce architecture, configuration and migration.

N Krishnan (Kitty) is an IT specialist working at IBM India in India Software Labs. He has over nine years of experience in IT field. He was part of WebSphere Commerce development team and currently working as a consultant in IBM Software Services for WebSphere. He was also part of developing retail solutions in Retail EBO team. He holds a degree in Master of Computer Applications from Surathkal Regional Engineering College, India. His areas of expertise include design and development of e-commerce applications, retail solutions and message brokers.

Peter Woo is a Software Architect working for IBM Software Services for WebSphere (ISSW) at the IBM Toronto Lab, Canada. Peter has worked for IBM for 15 years. For the last nine years he has worked in eCommerce as a System Architect in ShopIBM and worked in the ibm.com Common Commerce Engine development team for 8 project releases. He is an expert in all aspects of Web site deployment using WebSphere family of products. He has a B.A.Sc degree in Engineering Science from the University of Toronto and a M.A.Sc. degree in Electrical Engineering from the University of Waterloo. He has written extensively on IBM SDE Workbench/6000 and software engineering on the Web.

Li Xie is an Advisory Software Engineer at ISSW in the United States. He has 14 years of experience in software development and services. He has worked at IBM for 5 years, mostly for WebSphere Commerce development and lab services. His areas of expertise include application integrations for SOA with MQ messaging and Web Services. He has written extensively on business models, OMS solutions, and sizing for software costs.

Acknowledgements

Shash Anand, who wrote the section on Analytics.

Polina Gohshtein, who wrote the section on developing Management Center customizations.

Jacques Leroy, who gave us valuable assistance planning the content of this book.

Craig Oakley, who leapt in at the last minute and helped us complete the section on Content Management.

Catherine Briscoe and Tamikia Barrow, who made our stay in Raleigh pleasant and well caffeinated; Linda Robinson for turning sketches into pictures for us; and Yvonne Lyon, for editing this book.

Become a published author

Join us for a two- to six-week residency program! Help write a book dealing with specific products or solutions, while getting hands-on experience with leading-edge technologies. You will have the opportunity to team with IBM technical professionals, IBM Business Partners, and Clients.

Your efforts will help increase product acceptance and customer satisfaction. As a bonus, you will develop a network of contacts in IBM development labs, and increase your productivity and marketability.

Find out more about the residency program, browse the residency index, and apply online at:

ibm.com/redbooks/residencies.html

Comments welcome

Your comments are important to us!

We want our books to be as helpful as possible. Send us your comments about this book or other IBM Redbooks in one of the following ways:

- Use the online **Contact us** review Redbooks form found at:

  `ibm.com/redbooks`

- Send your comments in an e-mail to:

  `redbooks@us.ibm.com`

- Mail your comments to:

  IBM Corporation, International Technical Support Organization
  Dept. HYTD Mail Station P099
  2455 South Road
  Poughkeepsie, NY 12601-5400

Part 1

Know your eCommerce solution

The first part of this book is devoted to describing the business of eCommerce:

- Chapter 1 talks about different forms of eCommerce, what forms WebSphere Commerce supports, and how WebSphere Commerce fits into your business.
- Chapter 2 describes the functionality provided by WebSphere Commerce, what it does for you "out-of-the-box", and what you can customize to suit your business.
- Chapter 3 talks about how to integrate WebSphere Commerce with other software in your business, and how to extend WebSphere Commerce with software from other solution providers to do tasks such as payment, fulfillment, click analysis, and better searches.

1

Identify your business context

In this chapter we discuss the business environment in which your electronic commerce channel is going to operate, its business drivers, and your objectives in conducting business online. Based on our own experience of eCommerce engagements, we characterize eCommerce Web sites as small, medium, or large based on various criteria affecting the implementation time and cost.

This should give you some idea about how large your ambitions for your Web site are. During the rest of the book, we use this sizing model to judge the appropriate architecture and implementation for your Web site. In Chapter 8, "Best of breed infrastructure" on page 271 we use the small, medium, and large characterizations of Web site to propose three different scales of infrastructure.

One of the goals of this book is to help you match your expectations for your Web site with how much you want to spend building and running it (Figure 1-1). At the start of an eCommerce project, thinking through what the relationship of it is to your business in all its aspects, is critical to making the right level of investment, and setting the right objectives for the different internal and external organizations you engage with to develop the eCommerce channel.

A common experience of external service organizations engaged to develop eCommerce solutions is often that you, their client, and the service organization start poles apart regarding the expected cost of the project. Perhaps you understand that the scope of the project is to build a Web site, and might have funded the project accordingly. It is an unwelcome shock to discover that to build the kind of Web site that you use frequently yourself on the Internet takes a lot more investment on other software than building some Web pages, loading a database server, and buying some hardware to run the solution.

A way to manage expectations and scope the project is to understand well the business context for the eCommerce solution. In this chapter we discuss using business context diagrams, and categorizing the scale of implementation as first steps in thinking about the type of eCommerce site you intend to build.

Figure 1-1 Fit your Web site to your wallet!

1.1 Electronic commerce

Today's business environment is undergoing dramatic change. Competitive pressure from traditional and non-traditional sources, the rapid emergence and growth of new channels, and increasing pressure to outsource selected business processes are all contributing to an ever growing pace of change.

Growth of one such channel is electronic commerce. As more and more businesses adopt electronic commerce, ways of doing business are changing dramatically and electronic commerce is proving invaluable for dealing with customers, suppliers and Business Partners. Electronic commerce is not limited to buying and selling of goods online; there is a lot more to it. Electronic commerce defines new forms of doing business, such as commerce on mobile phones and in-store kiosks, providing information about customers choices, and linking together different media and delivery channels in each transaction.

1.1.1 Business context diagram

A business context diagram is a useful way to look at a system from the outside, looking in. It defines the scope of a system by showing roles (people and services) and their interactions with the system.

Figure 1-2 is a business context diagram showing typical roles that interact with an eCommerce system. This is not the only context diagram you could draw of the system; for example, you could look at the it from the perspective of developing the system. The one we have drawn shows the roles and interaction involved in the day to day running of the system.

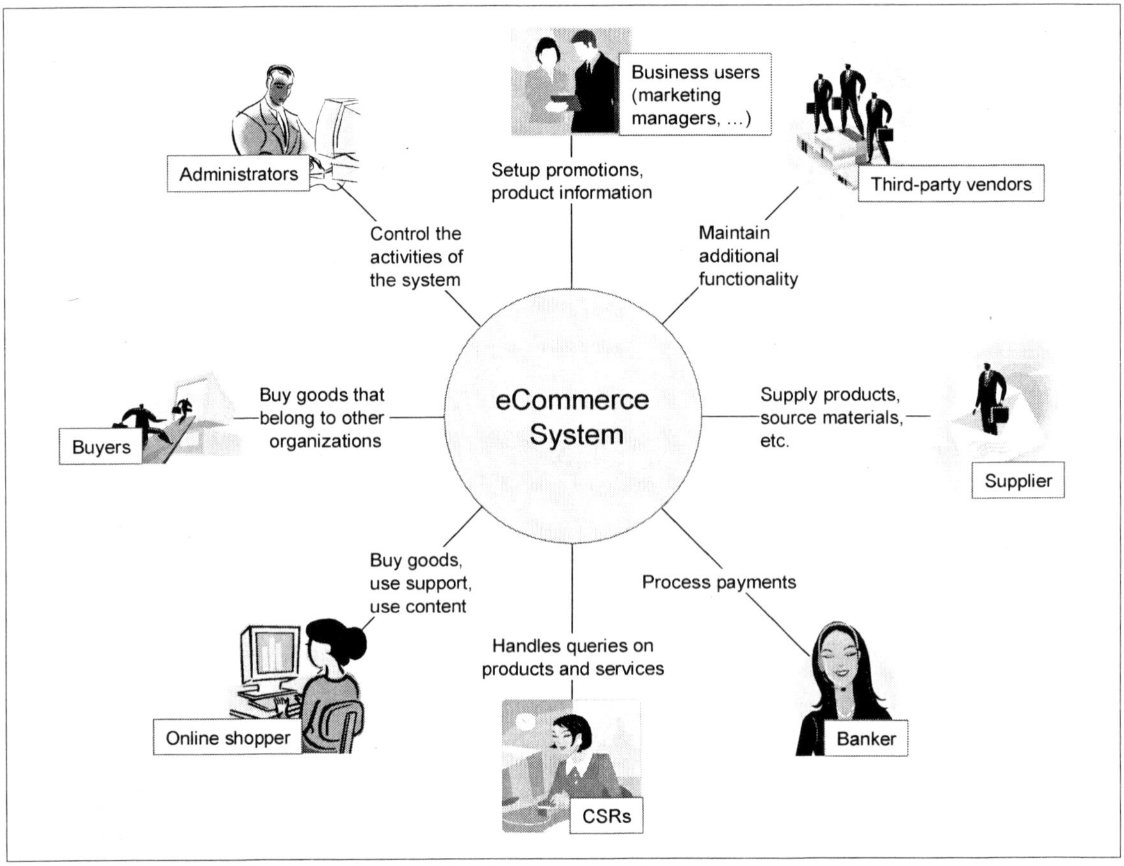

Figure 1-2 A typical electronic commerce business context diagram

Roles

The eight roles and their interactions are as follows:

Online shoppers An online shopper is an individual customer who browses a Web site and place orders for him or herself. Shoppers also use support services.

Buyers A buyer is like an online shopper except that a buyer places orders on an organization's behalf. For example, a software company employee uses the procurement portal set up by a major stationery vendor to buy stationery.

Administrators An administrator is a role representing people who maintain the Web site on a day-to-day basis. There are different ways the administration task can be organized and split up, depending on the organization of your business.

Bankers	A banker processes the payments submitted by online shoppers and buyers.
Suppliers	A supplier responds to purchase orders for products or source materials as a result of purchases on an eCommerce site. Alternatively a supplier participates in a private marketplace to offer products to buyers.
CSRs	A Customer Service Representatives (CSR) answers queries of shoppers and buyers.
Business users	A business user of the system is responsible for some of the content of the Web site. A business user creates promotions, makes product information updates, and updates the product catalog and price list, and so on.
3rd party vendors	Aspects of the Web site can be provided and maintained by third party vendors, for example, providing a chat room.

1.1.2 Types of eCommerce system

We categorize an eCommerce system by its scale and by what type of business or organization it is used in. A first approximation would be to predict the scale of eCommerce system you need to build based on the size of your business or organization. This turns out not to be a useful way of estimating the scale of eCommerce system you plan to build, partly because of the widely varying definitions of small, medium and large businesses, and partly because the scale of a business's eCommerce ambitions are not necessarily tied to the size of the business. However, large businesses might have the challenge of integrating eCommerce with the rest of their IT infrastructure, which tends to propel them to a larger scale infrastructure by virtue of its greater flexibility.

Businesses are broadly classified into small, medium and large depending on various criteria. Some of these criteria are number of people in the organization, yearly revenue, market capitalization. Four typical classifications you can find in use are shown in Table 1-1.

Table 1-1 Four classifications of business by size

Classifier	**Small**	**Medium**	**Large**
Revenue	<$100M	>$100M, <$1B	>$1B
Revenue	<$5M	>$5M, <$100M	>$100M
Employees[a]	<100	>100, <500	>500
Employees[b]	<50	<250	>250

a. Industry Canada - but numbers depend on sector
b. EU, but also depends on revenue

With the wide variation of criteria being used to classify businesses into sizes, often related to the purposes the classification is going to be put, we observe that investment in eCommerce is not just related to business size. So the size of your business is just not a good predictor of what scale of eCommerce deployment you need to plan to build.

In this book we have characterized eCommerce systems into small, medium, and large depending on size and complexity of the eCommerce implementation. Refer to 1.3, “Small, medium, and large scale implementations” for more details. The scale of an implementation can be judged by matching factors such as the volume of traffic you expect, the size of your product catalog, and the number and type of additional automation and integration features you require. From this rough survey, you can choose whether a small, medium, or large scale implementation is required and derive a ballpark guess of the cost of developing and maintaining your Web site, and the time that it is going to take to get the Web site into production. See 1.2, “Factors that influence project scope and size” on page 10.

Electronic commerce is adopted in various industries, including retail, electronics, automotive, telecommunications and manufacturing. Public sector and non-profit making organizations also engage in electronic commerce. Business processes for electronic commerce vary across the industries. Hence there are different types of Web sites depending on the kind of goods and services sold. For example, in telecommunications industries the emphasis on electronic commerce is self-care portals and purchasing of service plans, whereas in the case of retail, it is on products. If you look at medium and large Web sites by studying their URLs, you find they are often organized into different sub-sites, some parts specializing in eCommerce and using WebSphere

Commerce (typically with a URL such as "`.../webapp/wcs/stores/servlet`", and other parts using some other Web technology distinguished by a different URL path.

1.1.3 WebSphere Commerce

WebSphere Commerce provides a Web site framework for a company's eCommerce needs, scaling from a straightforward online store to a multi-channel sales network. It is a single platform to connect your business to your consumers and to your Business Partners, both in your supply chain, and also as your channel partners. It provides tools to customize content and promotions, for your client staff to help customers resolve problems finding or buying products on the Web site (Chapter 2, "What WebSphere Commerce provides" on page 21) and it integrates with tools such as Coremetrics for your business staff to analyze browsing and buying behavior (Chapter 3, "Complete your eCommerce solution" on page 89). This product is used by many enterprises and widely regarded as the industry leading eCommerce solution. Gartner, Inc. (Gartner Research "eCommerce Magic Quadrant, 4Q2006" by Adam Sarner, Eugenio M. Alvarez, January, 2007) recently evaluated the top vendors in B2B and B2C eCommerce and determined that IBM is a leader in eCommerce.

WebSphere Commerce:

- Provides cross-channel business processes (like order processing on the Web, through CSRs and kiosks) to give customers a single view of their orders with your company
- Provides multiple types of business model for B2C and B2B making it easier and quicker to set up international sites with language and cultural variation, and to support networks of partners using some common store components, and some specialized components
- Balances capabilities available out-of-the-box, with a framework that can be extended to integrate with your business needs
- Integrates with external systems through well defined extension points to work with commonly used systems, such as payment systems, and also integrates with other systems using both standard integration technologies, such as Web services, and widely used technologies such as WebSphere MQ
- Makes use of the WebSphere platform's scaling and caching capabilities, and integrates with content distribution network caching solutions such as Akamai, to meet your performance requirements for delivering rich media and large files
- Also uses WebSphere, and other platform technologies, to deliver high availability and recoverability, to meet your businesses requirements

- Is supported by many IBM Business Partners, IBM services, and a provides thousands of pages of in depth documentation to assist you build the Web site you need

Whether a small or mid-market firm or a large multi-national corporation, WebSphere Commerce has a solution for you. WebSphere Commerce comes with three editions catering to the small, medium, and large enterprise. WebSphere Commerce Express, Professional, and Enterprise are the three editions. Express and Professional editions generally cater to the small and medium businesses. Enterprise editions cater to medium and large businesses. Various business and technical factors influence the choice of edition to go for. Refer to 1.3, "Small, medium, and large scale implementations" on page 16.

Figure 1-3 shows how WebSphere Commerce is leveraged for processing of cross-channel business processes.

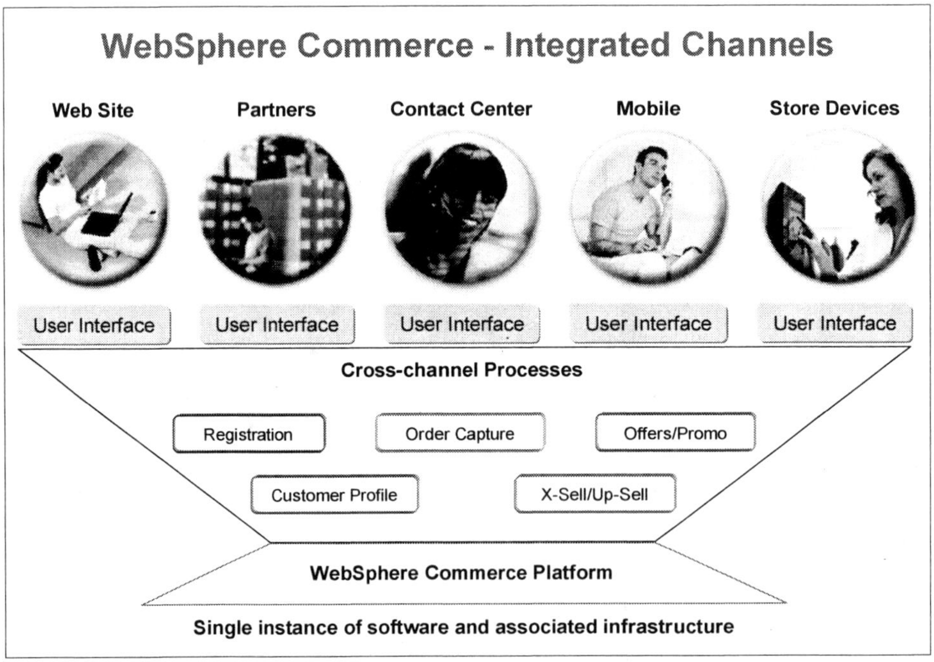

Figure 1-3 WebSphere Commerce as unified eCommerce platform

1.2 Factors that influence project scope and size

In this section, we discuss various business and technical factors that influence the project size and scope. Many clients have an expectation of the size of a WebSphere Commerce project based on looking at the project as solely a matter of building a set of Web pages, a database, and some of the hardware to host them. As we shall see, much more needs to be done to run an effective online business, for anything but small Web sites, and the sizings reflect this.

1.2.1 Business factors

Business factors include budget constraints, time to go to market, number of features planned, and anticipated growth.

Project time and costs

The information contained in the solution outline (Appendix A, "Solution Outline Template" on page 379) is the basis for the final estimates for the project. Be aware that the time and costs estimates from outside consultants are likely to start with the estimate for the entire WebSphere Commerce implementation life cycle, from conception to the post-launch support. Also be aware that the level of customization that is done to the WebSphere Commerce product — this of course translates into the number of tasks to be performed, which are evaluated for their duration, cost, and quality — will determine the time and cost of your implementation.

There is always a relationship between a project's time to completion and its cost. When you choose to use outside consulting help, the costs associated with such services are in direct proportion with the time it takes to finish the job. Costing is more complicated when you opt to use your own internal resources because you can schedule these resources on an as-needed basis. It is very characteristic of internally resourced projects that there are several combinations of time, cost, and quality goals based on the priority you assign to the project. Because of these two types of costs for internal projects, there is an optimal project pace for minimal cost and implicit quality or weighted quality goals.

Often, decisions relative to this time-cost-quality optimization are done on a hit or miss basis. In your project plan, generate and understand this time-cost-quality relationships, because these could be your only way to better predict the impact of changes (such as a schedule change or scope expansion) on the cost of your project so that better and more appropriate decisions can be made for any given situation, and the costs compared against those of an outside consultant.

Typically projects are not resourced wholly internally, or externally, but a combination of internal resources and outside consultancy and resources are used which best matches the objectives and skills of the business.

Number of features planned

If your online shopping Web site is to be built from scratch, then you have a couple of options as to how to build the Web site. One option is the "big bang" approach, wherein most of the requirements are taken into consideration for the go live date. The alternative is to have multiple releases, adding more features in later phases of the project. The business must decide which features are critical to the launch of the new sales channel and which ones can be deferred. This choice has a direct impact on the size of the implementation.

Within this overall release plan, you should also consider adopting an agile development approach, releasing features in an even more incremental fashion, perhaps with some features fully "Live" and others "On Trial" and perhaps incomplete.

The hallmark of an agile development is to break a project down into self-standing functioning deliveries, which can be developed, tested, and deployed as a smaller unit rather than as a complete release, and optionally made live, perhaps as a trial site. Look at the examples of phased geographical rollouts implemented by grocery stores or household furnishing outlets, for example. Built into an agile plan is the capability to learn from early experience and modify the Web site while there are fewer completed components to adjust to the design modifications.

Agile development might appear at first sight to increase the length of time to deploy a fully functioning Web site, and hence its costs, because of the additional overhead of managing multiple rolling releases. Where Agile development wins, is in better management of risk, earlier delivery of initial increments, and potentially implementing less function by relying more on customer feedback rather than on past experience in deciding what functionality is needed. This is the **YAGNI** principle, **Y**ou **A**in't **G**onna **N**eed **I**t — which has a strong software pedigree[1].

Growth

Growth plans influences the solution architecture and must strongly influence your decision of which edition of the product to choose.

You would not be entering the online retail business or switching your Web site investment to WebSphere Commerce unless you expected the investment to grow your business. So you must plan how your Web site is going to grow and adapt to the expected (and perhaps unexpected) trade generated by going online. It is important to think strategically, and build tactically.

It is possible to migrate from a lower end WebSphere Commerce edition to a higher one, while doing version migration (for example, from 5.6.1 to 6.0). The migration tool does this automatically.

1 `http://en.wikipedia.org/wiki/You_Ain't_Gonna_Need_It`

1.2.2 Technical factors

In the following sections, we discuss technical factors that strongly influence the size and scope of the project.

Volume

Browsing and transaction volume have a direct influence on the hardware infrastructure of the project. The greater the volume, the larger the infrastructure to support the traffic, while maintaining the quality of service in terms of response times.

At worst, if the site cannot scale to the volume of traffic, the site goes down. Peak volumes generate most of a business's profits. You cannot afford to plan for the average volume, you must plan for peak traffic. As you will see, this does not necessarily mean that you have to maintain all of your paid-for resource lying idle most of the time.

Volume can be:

- The number of page hits per unit time
- The number of orders that get placed in a period of time
- The number of registered customers in the Web site
- The size of catalog that you carry

Number of pages

The number of Web pages is directly proportional to the complexity of your business. Often complex business processes lead to a large number of Web pages in your site. This could mean more customization and integration with third-party software vendors to achieve the stated requirements. Review your business processes. Consider whether there are simpler business models to achieve your online trading goals with a lower number of pages.

Size of catalog

The size of your product catalog impacts the database choice and performance. As the catalog becomes larger, the complexity of the database design and configuration increases. Initial data load and subsequent updates to the catalog should be taken into consideration during the solution phase.

The numbers involved in product catalogs can be surprisingly large, and unexpected. It is not that unusual for catalogs to number in the hundreds of thousands. Multiply that by the data associated with each catalog entry, and you will appreciate that data loading, and coping with data errors, are not tasks to be taken lightly.

Geographic scope

If the business operates in more than one country or geography, often business processes become more complex to handle. For example, the taxation laws are different, shipping carriers and methods are different, payment integration is different, and differences in language, currencies and culture must be managed.

Converting Web pages to different languages is usually not a simple matter of arranging for translation. Aside from "technical" issues such as different languages taking up different amounts of page space, and that some languages do not run left to right, top to bottom on a page, cultural factors have a massive impact on such considerations as the campaigns you run, and their timings, and the content you select.

How do you choose where to host Web sites for different regions? Where do you do the work to customize the site, and to customize the content to cultural needs? What assistance can WebSphere Commerce give you to save money by providing a framework into which cultural variations can be worked? See 6.8, "Globalization" on page 234.

Scalability

Your goal should be to achieve linear scalability to cope with volume. Financially your hardware costs should grow at least no faster than the volume. If you achieve linear scalability, then your costs per transaction should fall. You will not achieve this goal unless you plan your software and hardware infrastructure for your expected future volume of traffic.

You can then purchase, or lease on demand, hardware as volume grows, and, if you are a large enterprise, you can plan to rotate load around the globe as demand follows the clock.

You need to architect and design software, and your software development processes, to address performance and scalability requirements from the earliest stage in your software development process.

Best practice in software development is to use profiling and performance measurements to direct efforts at improving performance where they have the most impact, and not to waste effort improving performance on code paths that are rarely or never traversed, or where performance is perceived to already be "good enough". Your performance team should be engaged early on to work with everyone on the project to adopt good practices for designing Web pages and interaction sequences, and to ensure that the Web site architecture is capable of tuning. To see how bad it can get, read *"Chapter 10, Case study: A DynaCache anti-pattern"*, in *"Mastering DynaCache in WebSphere Commerce,"* SG24-7393-00 at:

`http://www.redbooks.ibm.com/abstracts/sg247393.html?Open`

The study is not that unusual. It is based on what happened at a real live eCommerce site. An outside consultancy managed to implement some short term fixes to ameliorate the performance problems, but it took two additional releases to get the site to meet performance expectations. The good and bad news is that consultants are experienced in fixing performance problems, should they arise. But it is far better, and cheaper, to avoid performance problems by considering performance early and always during development. Every team must work on performance with the guidance from an expert performance team (Figure 1-4). You have to consider the resource necessary, not only in the performance team, but the impact on other teams, when sizing the effort required to create and operate the Web site.

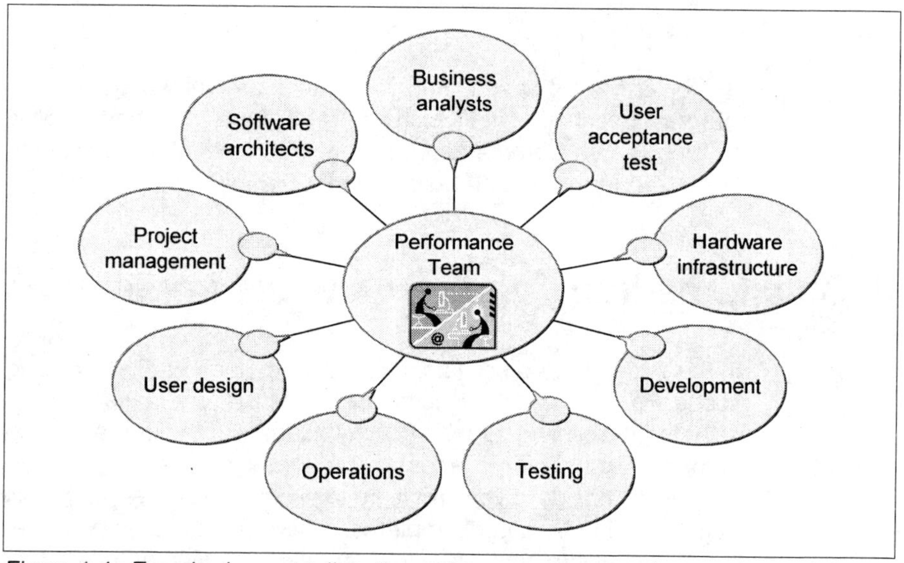

Figure 1-4 Everybody must talk to the performance team

Customization sizing

Outside consultants use "Fit/Gap" analysis to identify the customizations you need to build the Web site. In Fit/Gap analysis[2] the consultant compares your business processes with the functionality provided in WebSphere Commerce (see Chapter 2, "What WebSphere Commerce provides" on page 21) and proposes where you have to build customizations, or alternatively, where you might change your processes (see "Number of pages" on page 13).

2 Fit/Gap analysis is popular in WebSphere Commerce consultancy, because clients can compare the sample stores with their vision of their online store, see how well the sample stores fit their needs, and identify the gaps that must be filled by customization.

Sometimes, during fit-gap analysis, the customization effort predicted in implementing a Web site is significant. This occurs due to various reasons such as the nature of requirements, complex business processes to handle, and third-party software to integrate. In such cases, the customization effort impacts the size of the project very significantly.

Integration

Typically, eCommerce implementations of all sizes involve at least one or two integration points. Some integration points, such as payment processing, have well defined plug-in interfaces in WebSphere Commerce, others require much more significant effort tailoring the integration. The size of your project immediately becomes classified at least as medium, if your requirements can only be met by a tailored integration.

Use of standards based integration (such as Web services), or widely supported integration technologies (Such as WebSphere MQ), both of which are supported by WebSphere Commerce, are likely to reduce integration costs. This is discussed further in 7.3, "Integration" on page 258.

1.3 Small, medium, and large scale implementations

In this section, we discuss categorizing implementations varying in size and scope. For the sake of discussion in this book, we classify an eCommerce implementation engagement effort into small, medium, and large based on the number of hours of implementation effort. Implementation which takes about 3 months is considered as small, up to six months as medium, and anything above that is considered a large implementation. Table 1-2 on page 19 summarizes our classification into small, medium, and large implementations.

1.3.1 Small implementation

For a small implementation, the usability of the Web site, the competitiveness of the product offering, and the success with which the Web site connects with potential customers are the primary concerns. *Without success in these objectives, there is no point in spending money on a larger eCommerce Web site.*

In a typical small implementation, business processes are simple with some limited automation. A limited number of roles make up what drives such businesses. Online guest and registered shoppers, Web content providers, and administrators are main roles in the system. Cost, and in particular cash flow, is the main factor that drives the implementation size and scope. The hardware and software infrastructure is simple. The IT department is very small or non-existent.

Often the implementation and maintenance of such Web sites are outsourced. In many cases, the Web site is hosted in a third party hosting facility to eliminate the costs of maintenance, troubleshooting the hardware, dealing with software problems, and overall management of the system. Refer to the preferred small implementation architecture in 8.2.1, "Small infrastructure" on page 280.

As far as software capabilities are concerned, most of the out-of-the-box features are used. The choice of the edition of the product largely depends on the cost and the anticipated growth. If the online sales revenue is expected to grow rapidly and more features are planned, then it makes sense to invest in the edition which provides maximum capabilities and flexibility. Depending on present circumstances, and future plans, any edition of WebSphere Commerce, Express, Professional or Enterprise, could be employed.

Basic customization available in Express includes catalog creation, Web page design (branding) and possible integration with a payment system. Catalog creation involves creating a catalog and dividing the catalog into logical catalog groups or categories. Products are then assigned to catalog groups. The database schema that comes with the product is used to create the catalog. Catalog management tools are provided to create and maintain the catalog. Web page design involves the creation of graphics, static HTML pages, flash objects and JSPs to implement the layout of the Web site.

1.3.2 Medium implementation

For a medium size business, Web site usability, connecting with its target market, and the competitiveness of the product offering become relatively less important as critical success factors[3], and the ability to scale the Web site to deal with increasing business and be able to run the Web site and back office processes efficiently become relatively more important.

A medium implementation addresses the characteristics of businesses having well established business processes, and a small number of external systems with which they interact. The typical medium sized implementation might not be highly scalable but includes a moderate amount of customization. The time to build and customize the system would typically be around six months.

[3] The assumption is that a medium size business has a loyal customer base, which is cheaper to market and sell to, than attracting new customers, which is the main challenge and expense facing a small business.

The hardware and software infrastructure is moderately complex. Investment in hardware infrastructure is limited to having scalable application and database servers and some amount of network redundancy. In some cases the hosting of the system is outsourced to a third party hosting company. If the IT department is organized and experienced then system can be hosted in-house.

The software infrastructure includes Web servers, WebSphere Commerce instances, and integration servers such as WebSphere MQ. Depending on current and future requirements, choose either the Professional or Enterprise edition of WebSphere Commerce. Customization includes adding new business logic, custom data beans, schema extensions, third party software integration and other possibilities. Data feeds to the Web site can be large, and this requires data base load planning. Solution architecture is more complex to accommodate the integration with back-end and supplier systems. Often multiple payment methods are supported.

Refer to 8.2.2, "Medium infrastructure" on page 283 for more detailed analysis of the medium size implementation.

1.3.3 Large implementation

For a large sized implementation, especially a large enterprise implementation, new business objectives concerning the Web site increase in importance. The Web site might now represent a very significant proportion of the revenue and good will on the company's balance sheet. Major characteristics include:

- Coping with very large and "peaky" browsing and transactional loads
- Maintaining very high availability
- International stores
- Multiple stores, some run in alliance with partners on the supply or demand side of the business
- Integration of both existing and new IT initiatives

A large implementation addresses the characteristics of businesses having a high volume of users, number of orders, complex business processes, many external systems to integrate, and a complex internal and external organization.

A typical large implementation runs for nine months or more. The hardware and software infrastructure is typically complex, thereby making large demands on the IT department, necessitating a specialized eCommerce delivery organization and infrastructure. See 8.2.3, "Large infrastructure".

A large infrastructure is not simply a scaled up medium infrastructure, but includes additional proxy servers, perhaps an ESB or messaging integration bus, and possibly specialized hardware for hot failover, routing, and security. WebSphere Commerce Enterprise edition is the only choice for a large project.

Advanced customization includes database customization, configuration, and tuning; EJB™ development; and integration with external systems and with alternative client media such as voice response, mobile, and collaborative software. The large implementation handles multiple currencies and languages, has advanced search capabilities, provides custom promotions, and enables more complex data loads and many other possible features.

Many businesses wanting large implementations do not have in-house experience developing large software projects, or have not developed software that is going to be critical to the relationship the business has with its clients and which is so important in meeting its business revenue targets.

For this reason, many eCommerce implementations are either wholly or partly implemented by software services companies. These companies bring in the technical knowledge and experience in dealing with the managerial challenges in executing a integrated large Web site implementation. You need to think through — possibly with the assistance of an experienced consultant you engage to oversee the project — your relationship with the service companies you engage, and also the larger goals for the project as part of your business, beyond delivering the Web site.

Table 1-2 Key implementation size differentiators

Implementation size and duration	**Critical success factors**	**Characteristics**
Small 3-6 months	▸ Connecting with customers ▸ Usability	▸ Limited automation ▸ Simple IT or outsourced production site ▸ Mostly uses out-of-the-box features
Medium 6-9 months	▸ Scalability Efficiency	▸ integration with a limited number of external systems ▸ Moderately complex IT with scalable application and database servers, or outsourced production environment ▸ Moderate customization
Large > 9 months	▸ Performance ▸ Availability ▸ Integration	▸ Integration with a wide range of systems ▸ Complex IT with proxy servers, redundancy and specialized servers for security and routing ▸ Extensive customization to integrate with external software systems

1.4 Conclusion

In this chapter we have introduced thinking about business context and about the factors that influence the cost of implementation as a way for you to think about setting expectations for the Web site you intend to build. WebSphere Commerce has implementations for customers of all three types, with Web sites meeting their goals built and running, and with IT budgets to match.

You should think what the goals of your business are for eCommerce, and match investment and expectations for delivery, accordingly. Have another look at Figure 1-1 on page 4: Is your expectation for your Web site in line with the revenue it will bring to your company, and have you selected the scale of WebSphere Commerce implementation accordingly?

In the next chapter we shall look what WebSphere Commerce provides "out-of-the-box" for building an eCommerce solution.

2

What WebSphere Commerce provides

WebSphere Commerce is part of hundreds of successful business stories, each one different. In each one, WebSphere Commerce has been matched to the business requirements in a different way and has been integrated with other software to provide a better user experience, better management and exploitation of the Web channel, and better integration with software managing other business processes.

As demonstrated by those hundreds of Web sites built with WebSphere Commerce, transacting billions of dollars of Internet business a year, IBM aims to provide an eCommerce framework that can deliver a working eCommerce Web site cost effectively in months, and can be scaled to meet your needs as your Web site grows to meet the demands of a large complex and global e-Business.

In this chapter we look at what WebSphere Commerce provides for your business "out-of-the-box", and how it is configured to match your business model. At the end of this chapter we hope you have a better understanding of what WebSphere Commerce can do for your business, and are thinking about what gaps this leaves to be filled. In the next chapter we look at how you can extend WebSphere Commerce using other software to fill those gaps.

2.1 Business models

Helping businesses to succeed on the Web is the reason for the WebSphere Commerce platform to exist. It is not simply a tool for building a Web site, it is a framework for taking your business to the Web. It is built from examining the experience of businesses that operate in the Web marketplace (sometimes called the eMarketplace).

This experience has driven the design of the WebSphere Commerce suite since the late nineties when online shopping started. In those brief years, models for successful eBusinesses have been established, and WebSphere Commerce has incorporated those successful business models into the heart of its offerings. eBusiness continues to evolve, most recently in the way people interact with Web 2.0 applications, and as new patterns emerge from Web 2.0 that are relevant to eCommerce on the Web, they are incorporated into the WebSphere Commerce platform. In this section we describe the eCommerce business models that underpin WebSphere Commerce.

2.1.1 eCommerce business models

The Web is changing every aspect of our lives, but no area is undergoing as rapid and significant change, as the way businesses operate. As businesses incorporate Internet technology into their core business processes, they have been achieving real business value. Today, companies large and small are using the Web to communicate with their partners, to connect to their back-end systems, and to transact commerce. All these activities are part of eBusiness. eBusiness describes running key business processes using the Internet. eCommerce is a narrower term. It refers to all the activities concerned with buying and selling on the Internet.

For example, this is an eBusiness Web site:

`http://www.ibm.com/uk/en/`

This is an eCommerce Web site:

`http://www-304.ibm.com/jct03004c/businesscenter/smallbusiness/us/en/product`

Though any eCommerce solution is unique, it is generally possible to categorize it as business-to-consumer (B2C) or as business-to-business (B2B). Deviations can be understood as variations on the basic B2C and B2B models.

What does B2C mean in eCommerce?

B2C eCommerce is a model where transactions are between a company and consumers. B2C applies to any business or organization selling products and services to consumers over the Internet for their own use. In a B2C eCommerce solution, the focus is about enticing prospects and converting them into customers, and then retaining them as loyal customers by providing a good shopping experience and using information created during the shopping process to provide additional tailored services to get them to return to your Web site.

The ultimate goal is the conversion of shoppers into buyers, and from buyers into repeat buyers, and hence from online browsing to online order transactions as aggressively and consistently as possible. The transactions can include physical goods, digital media, or services. See Figure 2-1.

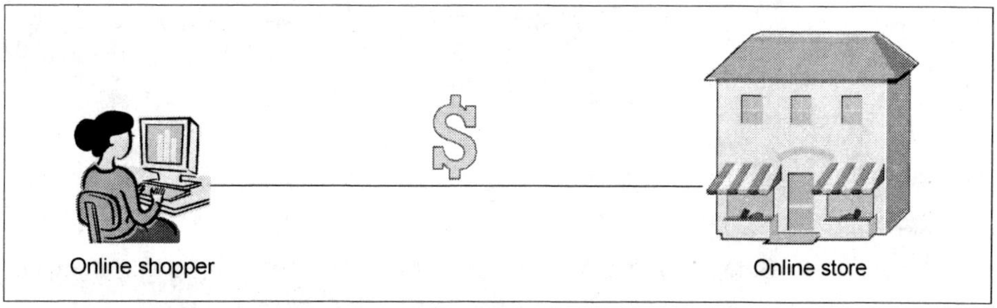

Figure 2-1 B2C eCommerce Business Model

Some key types of B2C eCommerce include:

- Auction
- Online stores
- Online services

Some key characteristics of B2C eCommerce include:

- Free to all-comers, an unorganized marketplace, only regulated (to some degree) by governments.
- User retention "stickiness" influenced by Web site characteristics. The Web site influence is especially true for Web channel only brands.
- For traditional retailers, the challenge is continuity between the Web site and the retailer's traditional brand values, and getting both sides of the business to reinforce each other to increase sales through both channels.
- Low conversion rates of browsing to buying
- Peakedness of usage, daily, weekly, and yearly

What does B2B mean in eCommerce?

B2B commerce is a model where transactions are between one company or business and another company or business. Simply put, B2B commerce can be loosely defined as "doing business electronically with others" over the Internet. It is most commonly associated with buying and selling information, products, and services via the Internet or through the use of private networks shared among Business Partners. B2B can also defined as exchanging of structured messages with other Business Partners over private networks or Internet to create and transform business relationships. See Figure 2-2.

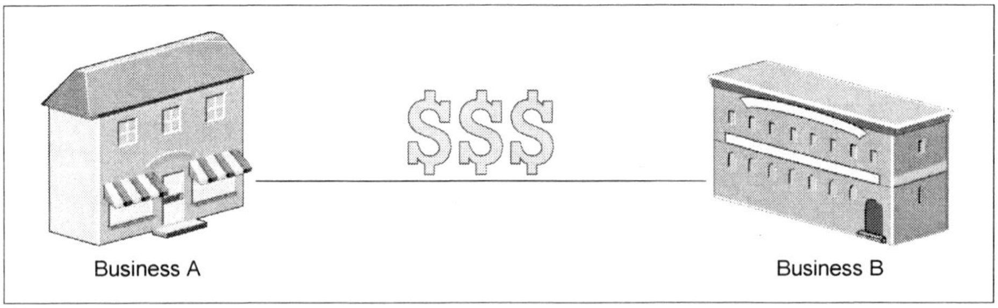

Figure 2-2 B2B eCommerce Model

Some key characteristics of the B2B eCommerce might include:

- Registered members and organized marketplaces
- User "stickiness" only slightly influenced by Web site characteristics
- Multi-channel management
- System integrations
- Performance and high availability
- Adaptability to changes

Discussion

It should be understood that this view of B2C and B2B is a contemporary view of eCommerce sites, emphasizing the importance of different characteristics rather than singling out a major difference in kind between B2C and B2B. Historically (if one can shrink history to a decade) then the single structural criteria to differentiate B2C from B2B, would have been the marketplace. B2C describes an (relatively) unregulated economic marketplace featuring consumers as customers and businesses as suppliers. The B2B marketplace is regulated, and only identified and authorized users participate. This distinction can no longer be said to be so black and white.

The distinction between B2C and B2B is illustrated in the treatment of "guest" customers in the B2C marketplace. In the B2C marketplace, it is important to choose the right moment to convert a guest user into an identified user, to increase the chance of converting a browser into a buyer. However, when a consumer becomes a known customer of an eCommerce B2C site, the customer's relationship with the site becomes more like a B2B relationship. For example, the site might offer different services to different types of customer (or even different individual customers). Differentiating services between customers is not vastly different to offering different services to different Business Partners.

So it turns out, from a technology perspective, that a B2C site is just the end point of a more sophisticated model, such as business-to-business–to-consumer (B2B2C) supply chain.

2.1.2 WebSphere Commerce business models

WebSphere Commerce provides the framework to create and support online businesses that fit into one of the following business models. The terminology matches that used in WebSphere Commerce publications. The models are listed here, and then each model is described in detail in the next sections. Note that the Direct sales models are the basic building blocks of WebSphere Commerce.

Direct sales

- Consumer direct (B2C)
- Business to business direct (B2B)

Scalable direct sales

- Extended Sites

Value chain

- Demand chain
- Supply chain

2.1.3 Consumer direct

WebSphere Commerce defines Consumer direct as the most commonly used B2C model. In a direct sales business model, the online business sells goods and services directly to the end consumer or to another business. Consumer direct supports commerce transactions involving products, services, or information between businesses and consumers. Consumers typically purchase goods or services directly from a supplier in a consumer direct scenario. See "Consumer Direct" on page 67 for details.

When do you need Consumer direct?

When you intend to sell goods, services, or digital media directly to customers from a single Web site, select Consumer direct. In typical cases, your customers are the end consumers, not resellers nor distributors.

The Consumer direct store can also contribute to part of the indirect sales models, such as value chain hub stores. We discuss these more complex scenarios in "Value chains" on page 32.

Objective

To allow the customer a variety of shopping experiences in an online retail store.

Means

The Consumer direct model helps consumers with the following shopping tasks:

- Finding products
- Ordering products
- Managing a wish list
- Using coupons and discounts
- Registering with the store
- Quick checkout using information stored for registered customers
- Receiving promotional material based on their profile information.

In addition, Consumer direct assists store owners with:

- Auctions
- Cross and up-selling using merchandise associations
- Email campaigns and promotions

2.1.4 B2B direct

WebSphere Commerce uses the term B2B direct to describe the B2B business model. B2B direct covers commerce transactions involving products, services, or information between two businesses or parties. Typical B2B direct transactions occur between buyers, suppliers, manufacturers, resellers, distributors, and trading partners. See "Business Direct" on page 67 for details.

Attention: Full B2B functions are available only in the Enterprise version of WebSphere Commerce. In the Express and Professional versions of WebSphere Commerce, the shipped B2B Direct store is simply the Consumer Direct store restricted to registered users. When a distinction is being made between the B2B stores the term Advanced B2B direct is used to refer to the additional, more sophisticated, B2B store shipped with Enterprise. The term B2B direct is sometimes used to refer to either B2B store, and sometimes specifically to the simpler kind of B2B store. You might have to be aware of the context for the meaning to be clear.

When do you need B2B direct?

When you are a selling enterprise, such as a wholesaler, a distributor, a manufacturer, or a retailer, who sells products, services directly to business buyers, you use the B2B direct model.

Organizations that are not traditionally considered businesses, such as governments, might sometimes implement sites based on the B2B direct business model. This occurs in such cases where governments provide goods and services directly to businesses.

Objective

To support commerce transactions in B2B marketplaces.

Means

The B2B direct model provides businesses with the additional capabilities to meet the needs of B2B marketplaces:

- Associate product catalog data with product presentational data.
- Manage relationships with a number of different customers (buyers).
- Differentiate product and pricing information between customers using contract management.
- Control inventory arrival rates and the location of inventory relative to their fulfillment centers.
- Quote prices on products and groups of products.
- Provide a mechanism to review and approve content and promotional updates prior to committing to the live Web site.

2.1.5 Extended Sites (eSites)

As an extension to the direct B2C and B2B, WebSphere Commerce also provides the Extended Sites, or eSites, business model. This model has gained popularity in recent WebSphere Commerce site deployments, and is frequently advocated because of its flexibility and extensibility.

Our recommendation is to consider starting with the eSites model from your first WebSphere Commerce deployment — it makes growth easier. But you should engage expert help for guidance: You might not recognize the benefits of the eSites model until you have had some experience with WebSphere Commerce.

What are Extended Sites?

The Extended Sites, or eSites, business model used to refer to "multiple stores with asset sharing". What this means is that the eSites model enables you to provide multiple customized stores, while sharing many of the assets from which the stores are built. This makes the model more scalable than the direct sales model when your business has the need, perhaps driven by globalization, or brand differentiation, to conduct business through multiple storefronts.

Figure 2-3 shows the conceptual comparison between Direct sales stores with no asset sharing and stores built using Extended Sites. The left side of the diagram shows each store, B2C or B2B, operating as separate businesses. All the catalogs, store administrator roles, and so on, are independent from one another. Operating costs increase linearly as the number of stores grows. The right side of the picture shows the same stores, now working together using the Extended Sites model. Economies of scale reduce the marginal costs of adding additional stores.

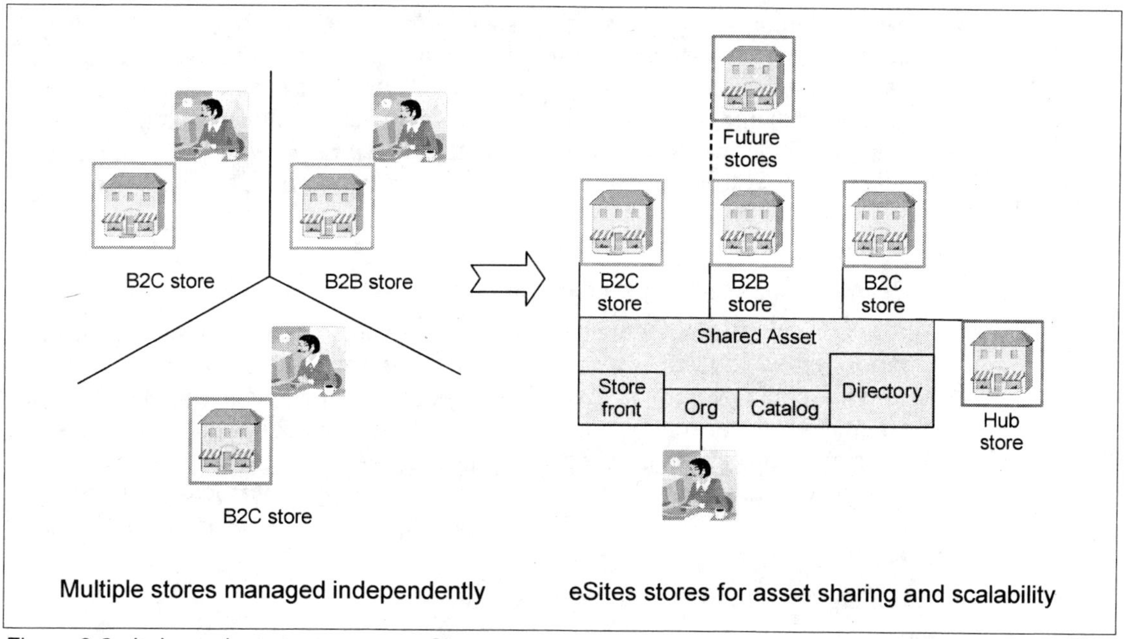

Figure 2-3 Independent stores versus eSites stores

Some of the capabilities offered by the eSites model are as follows:

Data sharing

Sharing data, such as catalog data, between multiple stores.

Presentation sharing

Web pages used by the stores can be shared. Some pages might be customized to a particular store to give it an individual look, and some Web pages and JSPs are shared to provide common features, like user registration. Changes to a common assets are propagated to all stores sharing this asset.

Ease of management

Lightweight stores are quick to create. A rich set of tooling is provided to make changes to distinguish one store from another. The changes are made in one location and are propagated to all stores.

Scalability

Given that there are less data and assets in the system, then compared to having multiple direct sales sites, the extended stores scale better.

Note: Managing your catalog is essential for an eCommerce business. It can also be labor intensive and time consuming, especially when you operate multiple online stores. It is not a good practice to duplicate common catalogs and product items on a per store basis. The eSites model eliminates duplication by keeping catalog management centralized among eSites stores, and yet each store still has the freedom to price and promote its products independently.

When do you need Extended Sites?

If you find your business matching the B2B or B2C direct sales model well to start with, and you want to look beyond that for ways to multiply your business without redoing everything over, the eSites model might be the right choice for you. In the most typical business scenario, extended sites is good for cases where there are multiple stores sharing the same catalog, with ability for each store to add products specific to them. To help you with practical business scenarios, any combination of the following scenarios can lead to the eSites implementation:

Multiple brands

Keep uniqueness by brand for sales strategy as well as look and feel.

Multinational sales

To comply with multiple languages, currency, tax and culture in a global eCommerce business.

Multiple retail geographies

To distinguish products and services by region within a country.

Multiple market segments

Honor your customers by profession, age, and other characteristics that are important to your business.

Enterprise account

Honor your large business customers with customization by business account.

Franchising

You run a retail franchise with multiple stores and each store is owned and run by a franchisee.

Partner sites

Hosting services for your partners who can participate in part of the site business.

Fast time-to-market for new stores with minimum IT involvement

Create new and updated stores in a matter of hours using asset stores.

Site hosting

Host WebSphere Commerce sites using the hub site archive which comes with extended sites to host sellers by using a partitioned catalog.

Objective

To reduce the time to create and maintain multiple eCommerce stores sharing some common assets.

Means

The eSites model is a componentized reusable store model. It has a set of asset "stores"[1], such as the Catalog asset store and the Store front asset store from which a real store is built by combining the asset stores, and adding or customizing the parts. After the asset stores are built, the creation of a new store only takes a matter of minutes.

This approach can be used to define stores in an on-demand fashion. For example, a business publishes quarterly sales catalogs. A new store for the next quarter is created by combining the existing store for the first quarter and a new Catalog asset store.

Things to consider

There are recommendations from the historical experiences of existing clients to consider regarding Extended Sites:

- Consider adopting the eSites model early in your solution design. Remodelling the existing direct stores, ConsumerDirect or BusinessDirect, to the Extended Sites model, incurs significant cost.
- The operational cost of the eSites infrastructure is small, if not negligible, when you have only a couple of stores. This should not be a concern when considering whether to adopt the eSites model for two or more stores, if you foresee opportunities to grow your Web site business in the future.
- There is a limitation when both Sales Catalog and Catalog filter are used in eSites. Ask your IT architects to work around the restriction.

[1] The WebSphere Commerce terminology is distracting. An asset store is not an online store; it has no online storefront; it is defined as a collection of reusable resources. But it is the terminology used in the Infocenter, so we accept it as the term to use.

You probably need expert help from IBM or an IBM Business Partner if you have stores to be remodeled to eSites. There is published material to help you; see *"Remodeling a Standard Store into the Extended Sites Model With WebSphere Commerce Business Edition V5.6.1"* REDP-4091-00, at:

`http://www.redbooks.ibm.com/abstracts/redp4091.html?Open`

2.1.6 Value chains

The phrase "Value chain" refers to set of companies working together to deliver a product to a customer. Some value chains are coordinated by a primary supplier, others are looser federations. WebSphere Commerce sets out to provide models of coordinated value chains to assist the primary supplier to build an integrated and efficient trading solution for the whole chain. Value chains are divided into two business models relative to the primary supplier: demand chain and supply chain as shown in Figure 2-4.

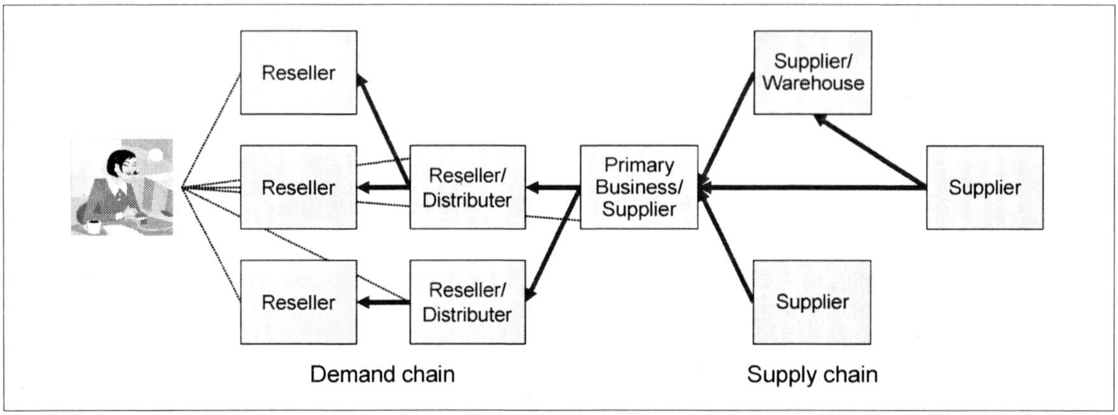

Figure 2-4 Schematic value chain with primary supplier

Value chains involve transactions between multiple enterprises or parties. Products, goods, services, or information are delivered through the parties of the value chain from producers to users. In addition to transactions passing between participants in a value chain, there are other administrative interactions between participants to manage the value chain. The primary supplier in a value chain must manage the two sides of their business: their customers and direct sales, and their channel partners and suppliers. Each side requires its own management channels and practices. The primary supplier uses WebSphere Commerce to offer services to help manage the value chain.

A WebSphere Commerce solution for value chains usually comprises a direct sales storefront for customers to purchase their goods or services directly and a hub store to manage relationships with partners and suppliers (Figure 2-5).

Value chain administrators manage the operational aspects of the value chain using the hub. Operations include enabling partners or suppliers to participate in the value chain by registering them, setting them up, and managing various partner and supplier operations. Partners and suppliers can also access the hub to do administrative tasks such as registering users and managing order status.

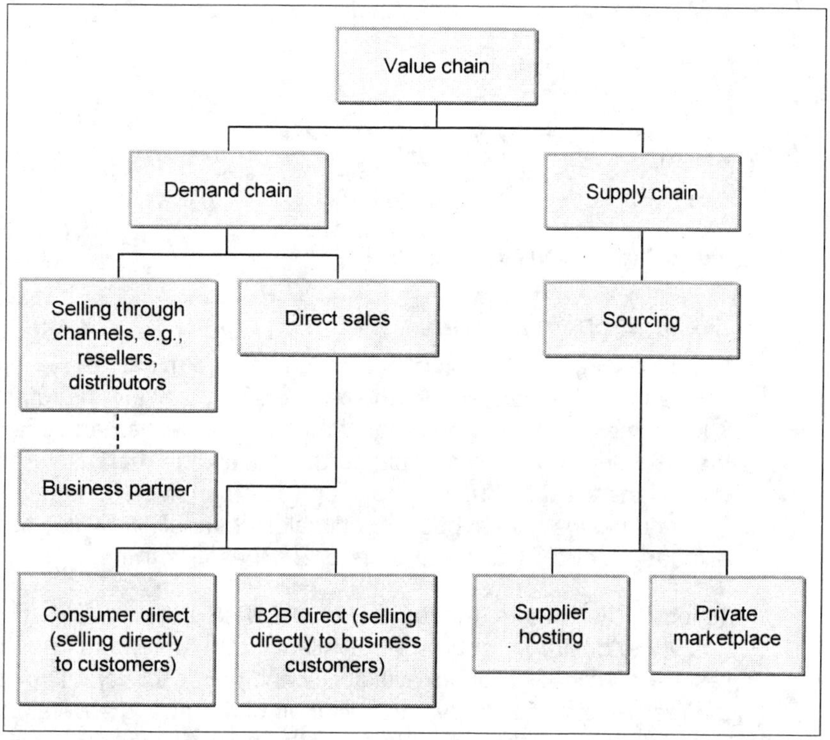

Figure 2-5 Value chain model

Demand chain business model

A demand chain is composed of the enterprises or trading partners that sell a business's goods or services The demand chain extends from the primary Business or supplier to end consumers; sometimes the partners are termed "downstream" partners.

From the suppliers' perspective, product moves through a demand chain in response to downstream "consumer pull". The partners exchange information, and finished goods flow through the network's physical infrastructure. The physical facilities include manufacturers' warehouses, wholesalers' distribution centers, retail chains' warehouses and retail outlets. A demand chain can include multiple business enterprises. As product flows through the network, the partners incur costs — but they also enjoy profit through added value, as the product changes ownership between business enterprises.

The Demand chain (Figure 2-6) is the business model defined in WebSphere Commerce as a framework for demand chain management. The emphasis is on enabling the Web channel downstream of the primary supplier, by providing Web sites and services to assist downstream partners sell the goods and services of the primary supplier more quickly and efficiently than if each partner had to create their own commerce sites and link them to the suppliers' infrastructure.

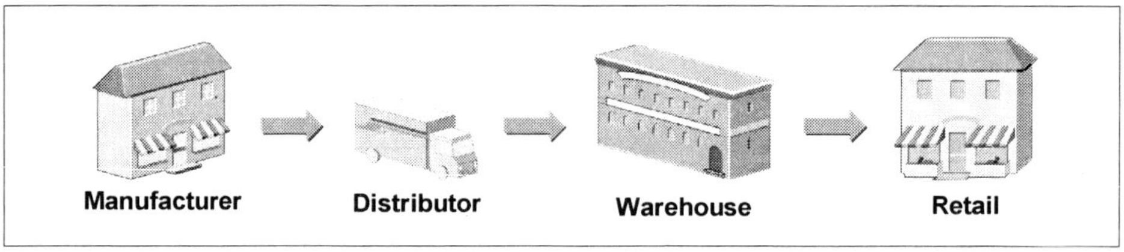

Figure 2-6 Demand chain concept

Demand chain business scenario

In a typical demand chain business, a scenario might consist of buyers who initiate the sales transaction, the resellers who sell the manufacturer's goods, and the manufacturer who creates the goods. The demand chain is composed of the resellers who sell a manufacturer's goods, the manufacturer who makes the goods, and the distributors who supply the manufacturer's goods to the resellers. Demand chains also support direct sales channels, in which the demand chain owner sells directly to consumers or Business Partners.

To locate distributors, the reseller can browse a product catalog in the private hub. If the desired products are available from more than one distributor, the reseller can check product availability and prices for various distributors. Then, if the reseller chooses, they can split their order among several distributors who complete the transaction and deliver the goods or services to the reseller. The reseller can then use these goods or services to fulfill its customers' orders.

The scenario details might change depending on the type of business being conducted. For example, if the enterprise is a manufacturer, the purpose of the hub might be to help the manufacturer's resellers locate the manufacturer's goods from several distributors. If the enterprise is a distributor, the purpose of the hub might be to help the distributor's resellers find goods or services from several different suppliers. In some cases, resellers can be agents. These agents are employees who have traditionally sold product by throwing parties where they showcase the products, or by going door-to-door to find customers.

When do you need the demand chain framework?

Many businesses are involved in trading relationship with resellers and distributors. If you intend to manage the trading relationships and provide Web sites for the trading transactions to take place, then you need to be the owner of a service such as an online hub store to manage your trading relationships and the transactions that take place.

The demand chain owner can create a site with stores for its channel partners, such as resellers or distributors. This reduces the infrastructure costs to the reseller or distributor who might not have the expertise or capital to create and maintain their own site. A reseller might use the site to sell goods from the catalog maintained by the demand chain owner, and also offer its own value-added products, services, or bundles from its own catalogs. The reseller or distributor in this case can also decide to administer his or her own store.

Demand chain stores

The demand chain sample site contains a channel hub and three collections of assets which are called asset stores by WebSphere Commerce. The asset stores are simply collections of shareable assets that the developer customizing the demand chain uses to build a complete store. The asset stores, to use the WebSphere Commerce term, in the demand change sample site are the distributor asset store, catalog asset store, and reseller storefront asset store (Figure 2-7).

The reseller asset store is either a Consumer direct or B2B direct store. Resellers choose the store type when they create the store. Note that the channel hub uses the catalog assets defined in the catalog asset store. The distributor has a so-called “proxy” store which allows the distributor to access WebSphere Commerce, for example to examine orders. The proxy store does not have a storefront and cannot be accessed by users. Distributor proxy stores are created by using the assets from the distributor asset store, while the reseller stores are created by using the assets from the catalog asset store and reseller storefront asset store. Resellers might choose to sell a subset of products defined in the shared catalog via the catalog asset store. They might also create their own products or bundles in their reseller store.

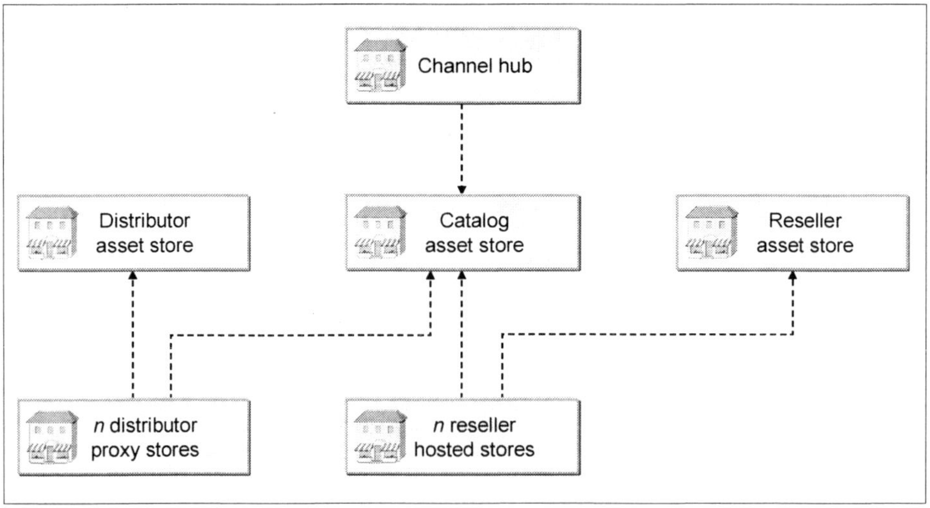

Figure 2-7 Demand chain stores

Supply chain business model

A supply chain is composed of the enterprises that provide services to the primary business, or supplier. The supply chain is a network of organizations, people, activities, information and resources involved in moving a product or service from suppliers to the primary business (or supplier) as consumer — sometimes termed the "upstream" value chain.

From the primary suppliers' perspective, product moves through the supply chain in response to a combination of suppliers "push" and the primary business "pull".

The Supply chain is the business model defined in WebSphere Commerce as a framework for supply chain management. The emphasis is on enabling the Web channel upstream of the primary supplier, by providing Web sites and services to assist upstream partners provision the primary supplier with goods and services more quickly and efficiently than if each partner had to create their own commerce sites and link them to the suppliers' infrastructure. The primary business can, for instance, define a common catalog, and then suppliers can offer the primary business goods and services from the common catalog.

There are two distinct supply chain models provided by WebSphere Commerce. In one model, the private stores model, the primary business creates stores for its suppliers, and the suppliers offer product or services to the primary supplier using their private store. Efficiencies come from the primary business replicating much of the Web infrastructure for different suppliers and having control over its catalog and interfaces to the stores. The other model is the private marketplace model. In the private marketplace model, the primary business sets up a Web site for suppliers to offer their goods and services for sale. Buyers in the primary business browse through different suppliers offers using the common catalog in the private marketplace and select the supplier or suppliers they wish to purchase from. Alternatively the buyers can request quotes from suppliers for goods and services in the common catalog (Figure 2-8).

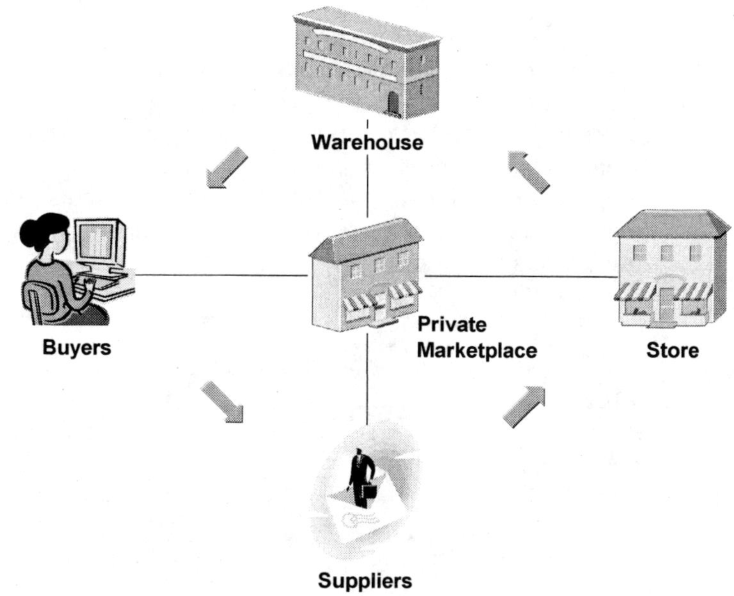

Figure 2-8 Supply chain concept

In Figure 2-8, the private marketplace created by the primary business manages the business relationships among buyers, suppliers, channel stores, and the warehouse. A buyer enters the primary business's hub store to browse and locate a supplier to trade with. The supplier directs the buyer to their managed channel store. After an order is placed, the warehouse / fulfillment center manages the order fulfillment and store replenishment. The primary business provides suppliers with sales data from the Web sites statistics to forecast the sales activities for the next business cycle.

When do you need the supply chain framework?

Many businesses are involved in trading relationship with suppliers and vendors. If you intend to manage the trading relationships with your suppliers then you need to own services such as the online private marketplace, or specialized private stores that use your parts catalog. Using these resources, you manage your trading relationships and the transactions which take place.

Note: You can also build supply chains in which each Merchant store manages its own catalog, and their own orders. Using the supply chain hub store provides an aggregated storefront, where one can search and view products from any merchant, but without the control of over the product catalog.

Supply chain stores

A supply chain hub store provides an aggregated storefront to search and view products from any merchant. The supply chain sample site contains a hub (supply chain hub) and two asset stores (catalog asset store and supplier asset store). Note that the supplier hub uses the assets defined in the catalog asset store. The suppliers are created by using the assets from the catalog asset store and supplier asset store. The model offers the ability to create additional merchant stores easily

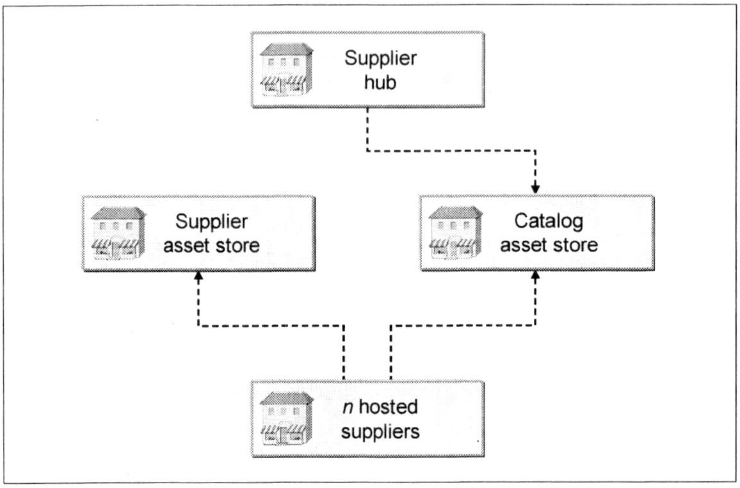

Figure 2-9 Supply chain stores

Note: You can host both supply and demand chain hub stores at the same time, though this is more commonly done using the Extended Sites model.

2.2 WebSphere Commerce components

WebSphere Commerce functionality is divided into components. Most of these components map directly to business processes and entities that exist in any retail scenario. In this section we name and explain WebSphere Commerce components.

The components described in the following sections are:

- 2.2.1, "Members" on page 39
- 2.2.2, "Catalog" on page 45
- 2.2.3, "Orders" on page 50
- 2.2.4, "Marketing" on page 53
- 2.2.5, "Payments" on page 57
- 2.2.6, "Gift registry" on page 59
- 2.2.7, "Scheduler" on page 60
- 2.2.8, "Staging" on page 61
- 2.2.9, "Workspaces" on page 62
- 2.2.10, "Contracts" on page 64
- 2.2.11, "Starter stores" on page 66

2.2.1 Members

In WebSphere Commerce, the member component handles the organization and security of online shoppers, as well as all other users in the system. The member component consists of users, user roles, member groups, and organizations. After a member is assigned a role, such as a buyer or seller, the access control component authorizes members to perform activities according to the access policy associated with the role and activity. Reflecting the richness of roles and activities in online commerce, there are more than 200 pre-built access control policies in WebSphere Commerce.

A member is a user, an organizational entity, or a member group. Each of these is discussed in the following sections. If you like to form a picture in your mind of what a member is, the diagram in Figure 2-12 on page 45 might be of some help to you. There is a lot to remember.

Users

Users are either online shoppers, or people who work in your business to maintain the Web site, such as business users or administrators. There are three different types of users: generic, guest, and registered.

Generic user

Online shoppers are automatically mapped to the "generic user" when they click on a WebSphere Commerce store for the first time. As a generic user, an online shopper does not have any personal information. They do not have a shopping cart, nor do they have any addresses associated with them. Because the generic user does not own any resources, there is only one generic UserId in the database. The generic user is there for first time shoppers that are browsing the Web site.

Guest user

When a generic user adds a product to their shopping cart they are automatically converted to a guest user. Each guest user has a unique UserId assigned in the database, and this is how their shopping cart is tracked. Since guest users are unique and can own resources, they have the ability to proceed through checkout and submit an order.

The UserId assigned to a guest user is maintained in the browser session. If the browser session ends, either by closing the browser session or if the session times out due to inactivity, then the guest UserId is lost along with access to its shopping cart. The online shopper cannot get this UserId back by going back to the store. If an online shopper submitted several orders as different guest users, there would be no way for that online shopper to see their accumulated order history. They would only be able to look up each order individually by the order number.

Registered user

A registered user has a permanent and unique UserId, associated LogonId, and password. A registered user also has a profile containing data such as addresses, order history, demographics, and so on. An online shopper can convert a guest user to a registered user at any point in their shopping session as shown in Figure 2-10.

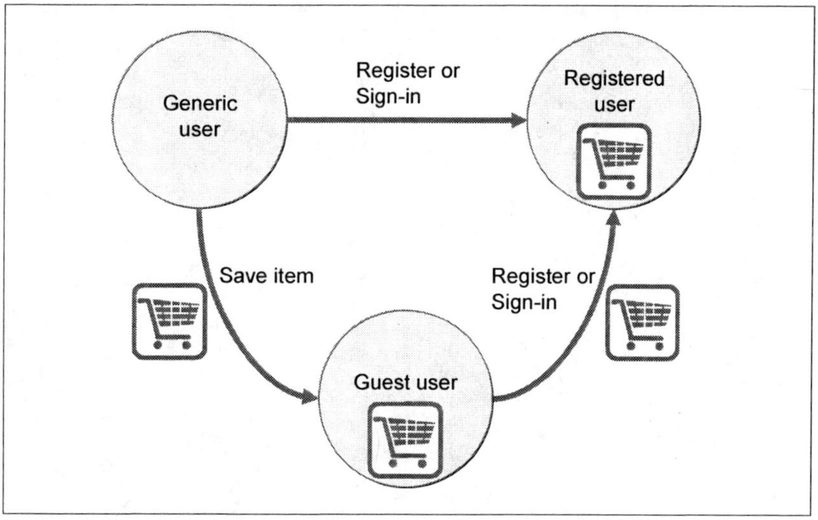

Figure 2-10 User states

Try it: Find a WebSphere Commerce site and add something to your shopping cart as a generic user, and then register or sign in.

All WebSphere Commerce business users and administrators are registered users.

Organizations

Within the database users are organized into a tree-like hierarchical data structure with organizations and organization units as the branches and the users as the leaves. You refer to organizations rather than individual users to apply access control policies. You can build your own organization structures from scratch, but it is recommended you start with one of the sample organizations and then amend it to suit your needs.

Figure 2-11 shows a simple example of an organization structure in an environment using the B2C business model. The three organizations: Root Organization, Default Organization and B2C Organization, are shown as blue ovals. The sample users are shown as orange boxes and the example B2C store is shown as a green triangle. The top level organization is the Root Organization. The Root Organization exists in all WebSphere Commerce implementations. By default, in a B2C scenario there are two child organizations: Default Organization and B2C Organization. In the B2C business model, by default, guest shoppers are assigned under the Default Organization. Store specific business users and administrators are assigned under the B2C Organization.

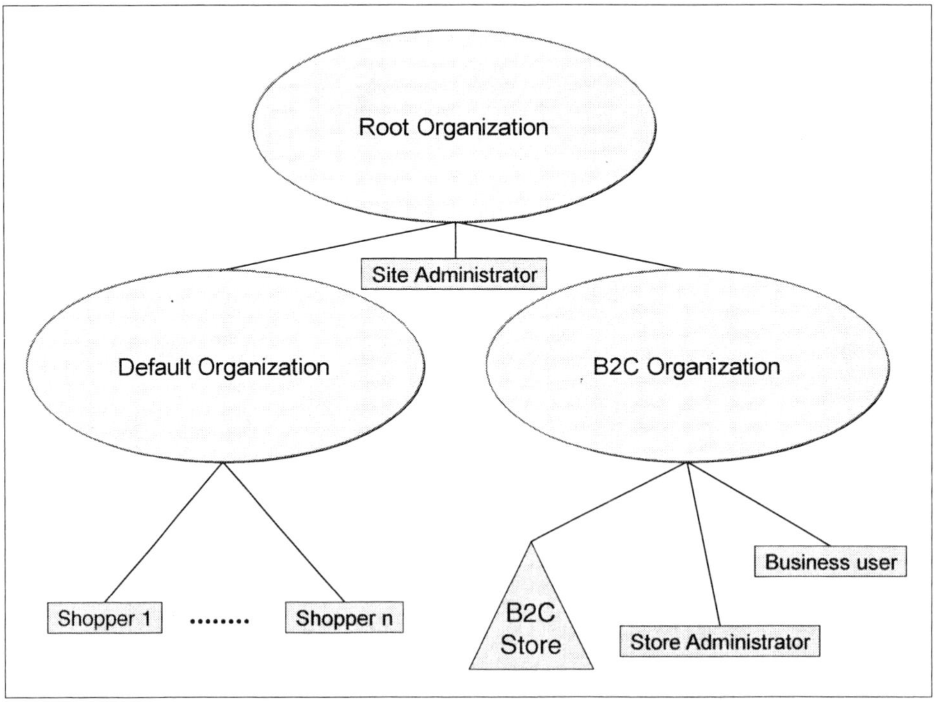

Figure 2-11 Example organization structure using the B2C business model

Member groups

A member group is a group of members (organization entities, users or other member groups) that is owned by an organization. It is used for various business purposes when it is convenient to have a specific group of users or organizations to be used for a particular purpose. There are two main types of member groups.

AccessGroups

AccessGroups are used for controlling access to different actions and resources within WebSphere Commerce.

CustomerGroups

CustomerGroups, for example customer segment groups, are groups of online shoppers that are organized according to some theme, such as demographics, that is useful for specific marketing and merchandising purposes. An example of a customer group might be a Customer Territory group. Customers are assigned to a Customer Territory group for a particular geography to assign them, as a group, to a particular customer service representative team. The assignment of a customer to a customer territory group might be explicit, or implicit.

Users are assigned to member groups either explicitly or implicitly. An implicit assignment is made on the basis of some rule — such as members sharing a common attribute. A user can also be assigned membership explicitly — and an implicitly assigned user can be de-assigned explicitly. A typical implicit member group assignment is by role, so that all users who are Seller Administrators are implicitly members of the member group Seller Administrators.

Member roles

Each member role covers a select set of actions that are performed on a particular resource by WebSphere Commerce tools (covered in 2.3, "WebSphere Commerce Tools" on page 69) or within the WebSphere Commerce stores (covered in 2.2.11, "Starter stores" on page 66).

WebSphere Commerce comes with many roles out-of-the-box. These default roles are grouped into the following categories (with some example roles listed below each category):

- Technical operations roles:
  - Site Administrator
- Marketing roles:
  - Marketing Manager
- Operational roles:
  - Seller, Logistics Manager, ...
- Customer service roles:
  - Customer Service Representative, Customer Service Supervisor
- Business relationship roles:
  - Account Representative, Sales Manager
- Product management and merchandising roles:
  - Product Manager, Category Manager,...

Each role is associated with one or more business models. Each member (user, organizational entity or member group) is associated with at least one or more member roles. For example, a role can be assigned directly to a user, or a role can be assigned to a member group — and if the user is part of the member group, the user implicitly takes on that role. Also, a role can be assigned to an organization that the user is a descendant of (direct or indirect descendant) and then again, the user inherits the role implicitly.

Access control

Access control allows authorized users to accomplish the tasks that they need to do on the resources that they need access to, and rejects access to all others. It can be divided into two sections: policies and runtime.

Policies

Access control policies are the rules that define actions and resources managed by the WebSphere Commerce system. They govern which roles can perform those actions on which resources, and also the mapping of roles to members. WebSphere Commerce comes with a comprehensive set of access control policies. This component is quite easily customizable because it usually does not require any Java code changes. The access control policies are implemented in XML files that can be loaded into the database. The loader utilities are discussed in 3.3.2, "WebSphere Commerce administration tools".

Runtime

Access control runtime is the part of the WebSphere Commerce runtime engine that evaluates the access control policies with each incoming Http request.

Summary

The member component is large and rich in function to give fine grained control over access control and performing actions on groups of entities. WebSphere Commerce has administrative functions in the member component to extend the sample organizational and member models and to make use of the functionality. Figure 2-12 shows some of the relationships between the entities we have described and how the relationships can be used to perform some action on a resource, like say, a shopping cart.

> **How to read Figure 2-12:** In this diagram, there are two types of arrow. A simple arrowhead " → " is an association, and the nature of the association is described in words (the so-called "role" of the association). The triangular type of arrowhead is a "kind of" relationship, for example, an Access Group is a kind of Member Group.

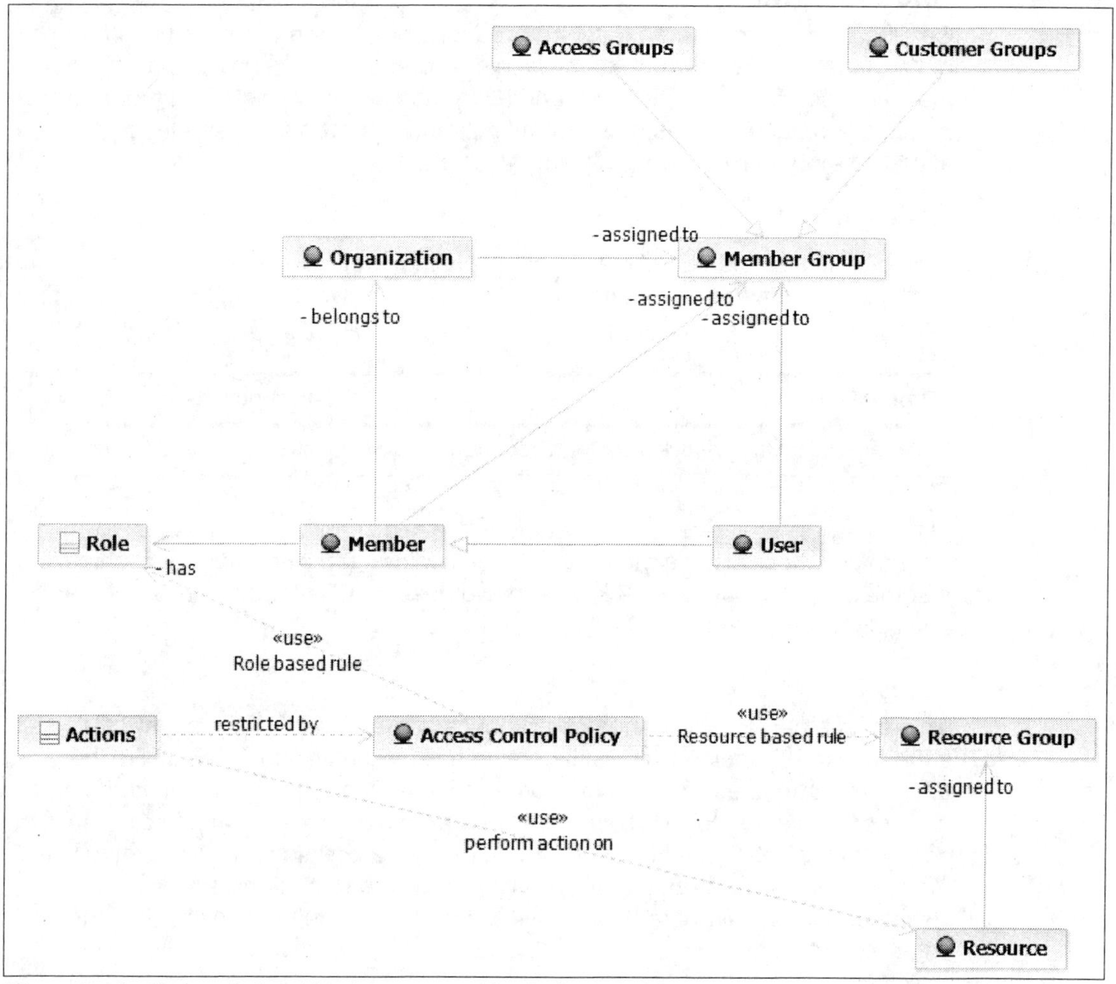

Figure 2-12 Some relationships between entities in the member component

2.2.2 Catalog

One of the most integral and essential parts of any retailing environment is the catalog. The catalog contains all of the products and variations on those products that are saleable or that the eCommerce store plans to sell. These products are divided into categories. Furthermore, the catalog is separated into different types of catalogs and sub-catalogs. In the subsequent sections, we review the different entities that make up the catalog component. Catalog data is input through the GUI or loaded in a batch form using the tools provided by WebSphere Commerce, as discussed in 2.3, "WebSphere Commerce Tools" on page 69.

Catalog entries

Catalog entries are for the most part products, but the term also includes groups of products that are sold together. Each catalog entry has a unique part number that is chosen by the administrator creating the catalog. It might be an arbitrary number or phrase, but it is more useful if the given part numbers reflect what the actual catalog entries are, as shown in Table 2-1.

Products

A product is a single unit of a saleable entity in the store. An example of a product is a women's cashmere v-neck sweater, shown in Table 2-1.

Table 2-1 Example product

Product	Part number
Women's cashmere v-neck sweater (Product A)	sweater style B 2007

The women's cashmere v-neck sweater shown in Table 2-2 has a couple of descriptive attributes: the material that it is constructed with, which is cashmere; and the shape, which is v-neck. These two descriptive attributes are combined and called style B 2007.

Items

An item is a particular instance of a product. It is commonly termed an SKU, short for Store Keeping Unit. An item also has attributes. However, unlike the descriptive attributes given to the women's cashmere v-neck sweater, items also have defining attributes. Defining attributes are characteristics that in different combinations define the item A versus item B for a certain product. Starting with the previously given example of Product A, a women's cashmere v-neck sweater, the items that are based on that product are defined by the size and color attributes, as seen in Table 2-2.

Table 2-2 Example product with corresponding items

Product or Item	Descriptive Attribute 1: material	Descriptive Attribute 2: shape	Defining Attribute 1: color	Defining Attribute 2: size	Part number
Product A	cashmere	v-neck	--	--	sweater style B 2007
Item A-01	cashmere	v-neck	red	small	sweater style B 2007 red sm
Item A-02	cashmere	v-neck	red	medium	sweater style B 2007 red md
Item A-03	cashmere	v-neck	red	large	sweater style B 2007 red lg
Item A-10	cashmere	v-neck	blue	small	sweater style B 2007 blue sm

Product or Item	Descriptive Attribute 1: material	Descriptive Attribute 2: shape	Defining Attribute 1: color	Defining Attribute 2: size	Part number
Item A-12	cashmere	v-neck	blue	medium	sweater style B 2007 blue md
Item A-13	cashmere	v-neck	blue	large	sweater style B 2007 blue lg

Bundles and kits

Bundles and Kits are configurable groupings of products or items that are sold together. A dynamic kit is a group of items that is created in real-time for the online shopper. An example of a dynamic kit might be a computer. The online shopper chooses the size and type of monitor, processor type and speed, and the type and size of memory their computer is to have. The selection is verified and assembled together by an external product configurator. Then the customer buys the computer as one single product composed of several items.

A static kit appears no different than a dynamic kit, except it is pre-assembled and loaded into the catalog, rather than assembled "on the fly". The components in a kit cannot be changed after the kit is assembled. The main purpose of a kit is to ensure that a customer buys compatible parts as a set, rather than mistakenly ordering the wrong type of memory when assembling a computer, for example.

Bundles are products or items that are grouped together by the business for the convenience of ordering. In one click a customer selects the whole collection of products in a single bundle. After selecting the bundle, the customer can modify the product selections. An example of a bundle might be a collection of accessories for a computer such as a carry bag, a printer, and a software package. After selection, the customer deletes the items they do not want.

Categories

Categories are groups of products within a catalog. We look at a department store as an example. The department store has different departments; in WebSphere Commerce, these departments are mapped as categories in the catalog as shown in Table 2-3.

Table 2-3 Categories and products

Category	Sub categories
Women's wear	Sports wear Casual wear Intimate apparel Elegant wear Shoes

Category	Sub categories
Men's wear	Sports wear Casual wear Underwear Suits Shoes
Kid's zone	Sports wear Casual wear Party clothes Shoes Toys

Master catalog

The master catalog contains all of the catalog entries of the store. There exists only one master catalog per store. In the master catalog, a product cannot exist in more than one category.

Sales catalog

Using sales catalogs enables you to divide, reorganize, and select from your master catalog, such that only part of the master catalog is displayed. Whereas there is only one master catalog per store, any number of sales catalogs can exist in a store.

Each sales catalog starts off empty. You copy in whichever catalog entries from the master catalog that you need to complete your sales catalog. You can create new categories and rearrange the catalog entries into these categories. Unlike the master catalog, a catalog entry can exist within multiple categories in a sales catalog.

Example: In a global business, using eSites for multiple stores in different countries, the one master catalog would contain your entire product catalog. Products in the master catalog contain images and descriptions appropriate to all countries, as well as images and descriptions designed for specific countries or regions. When you design the sales catalog for stores in different countries, you select the appropriate entries from the master catalog.

Sales catalogs are useful to divide your master catalog into different types of themes. For example, given a master catalog, you could create sales catalogs for each season that contain only the catalog entries that pertain to the respective season:

- Seasonal sales catalogs:
  - Spring
  - Summer
  - Fall sales
  - Winter sales

Another example using customer segments, as described in "Member groups" on page 42, you can control who sees the different catalogs. For example, suppose that you have different customer segments based on age and gender; you could then create eight different sales catalogs as shown in Table 2-4.

Table 2-4 Catalogs for eight different customer segments

Age range	**12-18**	**19-29**	**30-45**	**46+**
Male	Catalog 1	Catalog 2	Catalog 3	Catalog 4
Female	Catalog 5	Catalog 6	Catalog 7	Catalog 8

Merchandising associations

Merchandising associations are a mechanism that are used to suggest additional, different or replacement products based on the catalog entry that the online shopper is currently looking at. There are five different types of merchandising associations in WebSphere Commerce:

Cross-sell

You suggest different but somewhat related catalog entries based on the catalog entry that the online shopper is currently looking at. For example, you suggest a high-resolution color printer when a digital camera is purchased, or a particular type of battery when a flashlight is purchased.

Up-sell

You suggest a higher end catalog entry based on the catalog entry that the online shopper is currently looking at. For example, you suggest a higher quality television when a low-end model is selected.

Accessory

You suggest an accessory that compliments the catalog entry the online shopper is currently looking at. For example, you suggest an extra game controller when a video game system is selected.

Replacement

You suggest another catalog entry that is considered equivalent or competitive to the catalog entry that the online shopper is currently looking at. For example, if one type of brand name battery is sold out, you suggest a different brand name battery.

Custom

Create custom merchandising association types based on your requirements. For example, you might want to offer an own brand merchandising association to suggest a lower-priced catalog entry with a higher margin based on the selected catalog entry.

The different merchandising associations are configurable at the catalog entry level. Typically, the catalog entry suggested through the merchandising association is advertised with an eMarketing Spot. eMarketing Spots are discussed in “Marketing” on page 53.

2.2.3 Orders

Receiving orders is probably highest on the agenda for any eCommerce retailer. Essentially, all of the other functionality on the Web site has the objective of bringing in orders. WebSphere Commerce offers comprehensive order functionality. The Orders component is split up into four sub-components:

- Orders
- Inventory
- Taxes
- Shipping.

In the following sections we review each of these.

Orders

The WebSphere Commerce order component consists of an API used to capture, process, and manage orders. Examples of how to make use of this extensive API are demonstrated in the WebSphere Commerce starter stores (2.2.11, “Starter stores” on page 66).

Each order has a state and that state defines at what point in the order lifecycle it belongs to. When an online shopper adds an item to their shopping cart, a new order is created. While the customer continues to shop and browse the store, the order state is pending, “P”.

When the online shopper checks out their shopping cart, the order is submitted The next state of order depends on the type of inventory that is being used in your WebSphere Commerce store. This is discussed in the next section. When the order is finally approved, “M”, the order is shipped and the order is completed, “C”.

Inventory

WebSphere Commerce offers two types of inventory models: Available To Promise (ATP) and non-ATP inventory. These two inventory models, plus the option of no inventory tracking whatsoever, give you three options to choose from. WebSphere Commerce provides GUI tooling to manage and update the inventory (discussed in 2.3.1, "Business user tools" on page 69).

Non-ATP inventory

Non-ATP inventory is the simpler of the two types of inventory. With non-ATP inventory, what you have is what you get. The in-stock inventory is tracked in the WebSphere Commerce database. When an online shopper adds an item to their shopping cart, an inventory check is done to confirm that there is sufficient quantity in stock to fulfill the order. If there is insufficient inventory of the item, then a message is displayed to the shopper indicating that the item is out of stock.

With non-ATP inventory, after the order has been submitted as "M," if the order requires approval through the payments subsystem then it is accomplished here. This payment approval is configurable to be automatic (a programmatic check) or manual, depending on your particular scenario.

When the order has been approved, then it is up to you and your business team to fulfill the order. After you have shipped the order to the consumer you need to let WebSphere Commerce know that the order has been fulfilled by finalizing the order. A finalized order is represented in WebSphere Commerce as the completed, "C," state. This indicates that the order is complete (order has been shipped and payment has been captured).

ATP inventory

ATP inventory is designed to model a real fulfillment center. ATP inventory is a more complex type of inventory system. There are many different possible paths to get to the end target of a fulfilled, shipped order. In the following paragraph we review the most common order fulfillment scenario using ATP inventory, but be aware that it does not cover all possible order states and paths to order fulfillment that are possible using ATP inventory.

The in-stock inventory is tracked in the WebSphere Commerce database. When an online shopper adds an item to the shopping cart, an inventory check is done to confirm that there is sufficient quantity in stock to fulfill the order.

One of the places where ATP inventory differs from non-ATP inventory is that it is configurable to back-order items if there is insufficient stock. If an item is back-orderable, and the shopper tries to check out their order, and there is insufficient stock of that item in the shopping cart, then a message is displayed to the shopper indicating that the item is expected to ship at a future date and giving that date to the shopper. This conditional branch in the order life cycle makes for a more complicated order and inventory process.

With ATP inventory, after the order has been submitted, it will proceed to either the submitted state, "M," or to the back-ordered state, "B." If there is sufficient inventory, the state changes to "M," otherwise the order moves to the back-ordered, "B," state. The order then stays in the back-ordered state until the inventory comes into stock.

After WebSphere Commerce is made aware that there is sufficient inventory for the order to be fulfilled, then the order state moves to the submitted state, "M", which indicates that there is sufficient inventory. When the order is in the submitted state, "M", and any necessary approvals in the payments subsystem have been completed, then it is up to you and your business team to fulfill the order.

In the ATP inventory model, the fulfillment center is modelled in a lot more detail than in the non-ATP inventory model. The next step is to release the order for fulfillment which changes the state of the order to released, "R." When the order is in the released state, you must fulfill the order. WebSphere Commerce offers GUI based tooling to assist in the organization of fulfilling, packaging and shipping the orders. After the order is shipped, you let WebSphere Commerce know and the order moves to shipped state, "S." At this point, you must finalize the order (indicating that payment has been captured) and the order state changes to the deposited state, "D."

No inventory

With the "no inventory" option, no quantities of inventory of your products are maintained in the database. When adding a product to the shopping cart or checking out an order, WebSphere Commerce does not check to see if there is sufficient inventory. The order lifecycle using the no inventory options is the same as the Non-ATP inventory, but keep in mind that there is no inventory tracking or checking.

Taxes

Today's eCommerce retailers need to accommodate regional and federal taxes that differ across geographic and political boundaries. WebSphere Commerce has the ability to set up tax rules and the charging and collecting of taxes through the Orders component subsystem called Calculation Framework.

In the Calculation Framework, there is GUI-based tooling to configure taxes based on geographic jurisdictions such as zip code or postal code, state, or province and country. As taxes vary depending on the type of product or service purchased, the GUI allows you to assign taxes to different products or categories of products. Different taxes are frequently charged on shipping and handling, which are applied in conjunction with one another, or independently, depending on the specifics of the store and the consumer's personal information. In addition WebSphere Commerce offers integration with third-party tax calculation software. This is covered in Chapter 3, "Complete your eCommerce solution" on page 89.

Shipping

No eCommerce enterprise successfully operates without a sophisticated and highly configurable shipping component. WebSphere Commerce offers just such functionality. Setting up shipping rules and the charging and collection of shipping fees is handled by the Orders components subsystem called Calculation Framework.

Just as with taxes, the Calculation Framework provides GUI-based tooling to configure shipping based on geographic jurisdictions such as zip-code or postal code, state or province, and country. Shipping charges are selectively applied to whatever products or categories of products you specify and charged based on quantity or weight. Shipping services, offered by different carriers and varying levels of courier service, are selectable based on what you are able to offer to your customers. The combination of the geographic jurisdiction, product selection, carrier and carrier service offered (ground shipping, three day priority, overnight express, and so on) is called a shipping mode. In addition WebSphere Commerce offers integration points to third-party shipping calculation software such as TNT, UPS, or Fedex. This is covered in Chapter 3, "Complete your eCommerce solution" on page 89.

2.2.4 Marketing

WebSphere Commerce offers marketing tools, such as Commerce Accelerator, and the new marketing tooling included in Management Center which is released in Feature Pack 3 of WebSphere Commerce version 6[2] to implement marketing campaigns to attract and retain customers. Marketing campaigns include special Web page eMarketing spots, advertising and e-mailing, all of which you can target to customer segments using a variety of rules. There is more information about eMarketing spots and campaigns on page 55.

[2] See 11.5.2, "Applying WebSphere Commerce Feature Packs" on page 354

Promotions

Promotions give customers incentives to purchase. In WebSphere Commerce there are numerous types of promotions such as price promotions, including simple discounts, merchandise specials such as gifts with purchase, buy one, get one free (BOGOF), service promotions, which currently provide reduced shipping costs, and coupon promotions, which mimic paper coupons you might find in your local newspaper. Promotions are created and managed using the Promotions tool in the WebSphere Commerce Accelerator.

Promotions are built with a set of conditions, which if met, offer a reward. The actual promotions themselves are implemented in XML and are stored in the database. The promotions engine evaluates the promotions each time a change is made to the shopping cart such as when a product is added, removed or an order submitted.

Examples of the three main types of promotions: order level, product level, and shipping level, are shown in Table 2-5.

Table 2-5 Promotion examples

Promotion	Description	Condition	Reward
Order level	Order level promotions have conditions and rewards that are spread across the entire order	`IF the total of the order exceeds $75`	`THEN a discount of $10 is applied across the total of the order`
Product level	Product level promotions have conditions and rewards that are applicable to a single product, group of products, category or group of categories	`IF consumer buys product A and product B`	`THEN a discount of 50% is applied to product B`
Shipping level	Shipping level promotions have conditions and rewards that are applicable to a single shipping mode	`IF consumer chooses to ship order with mode A (carrier A using the overnight express option)`	`THEN a discount of $5 is applied to shipping charge applied when using shipping mode A (carrier A using the overnight express option)`

Within these three types of promotions, you can construct many variations of conditions and rewards. Conditions are usually based on quantity or the combination of product, the order total, the shipping type, or the number of items being shipped. Rewards consist of percentage off the products' order total, or shipping charge total, or a fixed discount off the products' order total, or shipping charge total, or free gifts, or free shipping. Promotions are offered to everyone or only to certain customer segments, or only via exclusive promotion codes.

WebSphere Commerce provides GUI-based tooling to create and manage the promotions listed in Table 2-6.

Table 2-6 Types of reward

Promotion	Reward
Product Level	Percentage off per item
	Fixed amount off per item
	Fixed amount off for all
	Buy X, get one or more items at a discount
	Free gift with purchase
Order Level	Percentage off
	Fixed amount off
	Free gift with purchase
Shipping	Free shipping
	Discounted shipping for an order using a selected ship mode
	Discounted shipping for all items using a selected ship mode
	Discounted shipping per item using a selected ship mode

Using the promotions engine, you can design an almost infinite variety of custom promotions. There is comprehensive documentation describing how to do this, but it is not a simple as using the pre-built promotions. Customizing the promotions engine and the GUI to support the customized promotions is not a trivial task.

eMarketing spots

The eMarketing spot is basic building block used for nearly all advertising specials. The eMarketing spot is an image, text, or video that is displayed on your WebSphere Commerce Web site in various possible locations on a page. It can be located in the sidebar, the header, the footer or even in the middle of the page if you want. The eMarketing spot is used to advertise a new product, feature a new category of products or highlight a promotion offered on a catalog entry, or what ever else you choose to market. The eMarketing spot is dynamic so that when the online shopper clicks on it, they are redirected to the page displaying the advertised entity.

Campaigns

WebSphere Commerce offers the ability to strategically organize your marketing content around central themes. Campaigns consist of a grouping of activities, usually displaying some kind of advertising in the form of an eMarketing spot and targeting an end product (suggestive selling), category or promotion (awareness advertisements).

The activities are generic or are configured to target a certain customer segment. There are two types of activities: Web activities and e-mail activities.

Web activities

Web activities have the marketing content displayed on the WebSphere Commerce Web site.

E-mail activities

E-mail activities consist of displaying the marketing content in e-mails that are sent out using mailing lists, usually based on customer segments.

Experiments

WebSphere Commerce also offers a feature called experiments. Experiments test the effectiveness of different marketing content, activities, and campaigns. Experiments report information such as the clicks-to-views ratio on eMarketing spots and the buys-to-clicks ratio on a featured product. Let us look at two example experiments, keeping in mind that these represent just a sample of the many other options that exist.

Example experiment A

You would like to test the effectiveness of the location of an eMarketing spot in attracting attention of your online shoppers. For the experiment you use eMarketing spot A and it targets promotion A. You configure the experiment that 50% of your shoppers view the eMarketing spot A in the sidebar of your page. The other 50% of your shoppers view the eMarketing spot A in the footer of your page. The experiment runs for 3 days. At the end of the experiment the number of clicks reported for the two different locations indicates which location is more effective.

Example experiment B

You would like to test the effectiveness of a promotion in converting sales. For the experiment you use two eMarketing spots. eMarketing spot B1 advertises product B. eMarketing spot B2 features a promotion on product B. 50% of your online shoppers see emarketing spot B1, and the other 50%, B2. The experiment runs for 3 days. The information reported gives you an indication how important the advertised promotion versus advertised product is in attracting the online shoppers attention based on the clicks-to-views ratio for the two different eMarketing spots, B1 and B2. Similarly, you are able to tell how important the promotion is by the buys-to-clicks ratio.

Note: The experiments feature is offered only in WebSphere Commerce Professional and Enterprise editions.

2.2.5 Payments

Payments is an integral part of any eCommerce system. Web sites offer various types of payment options. For example, using credit or debit cards, credit line and cash on delivery. This section discusses payment options and what WebSphere Commerce offers.

Payment service providers are typically banks, financial institutions or third- party merchants that provide credit card processing on behalf of credit card companies such as Visa and MasterCard. Payment gateways provide the infrastructure to process credit card payments submitted from Web sites.

The Payments subsystem is introduced for the first time with WebSphere Commerce version 6. Previous versions of WebSphere Commerce used WebSphere Commerce Multi-payment Framework. WebSphere Commerce Multi-payment Framework ran as a separate application and database. The new Payments subsystem is included as part of the WebSphere Commerce Server. The Payments subsystem connects to payment service providers using payment plug-ins (Figure 2-13).

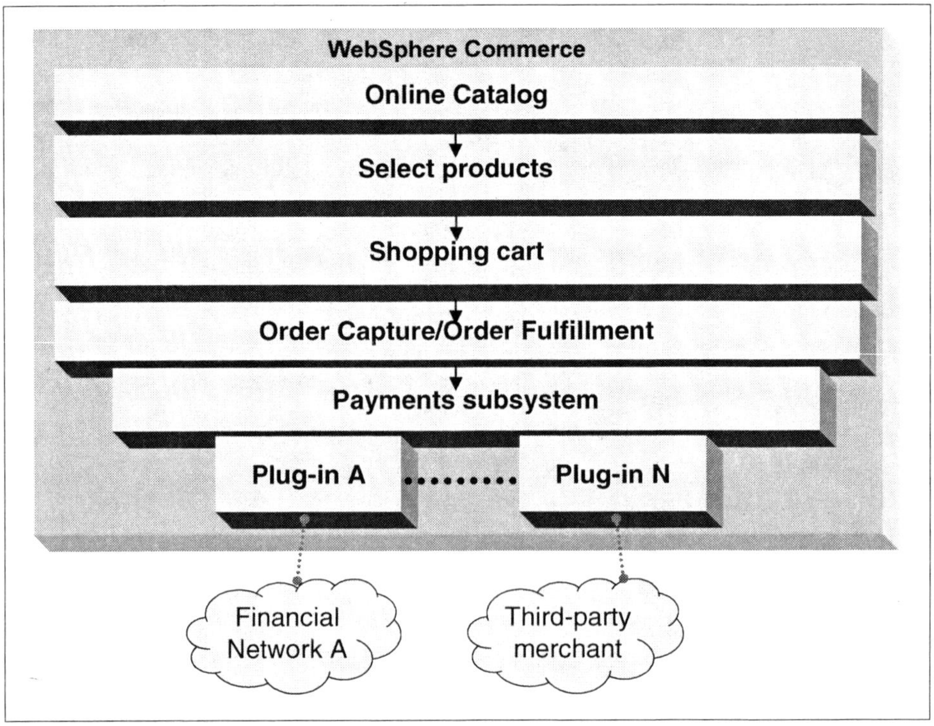

Figure 2-13 Payment subsystem

A *payment plug-in* is a self-contained software component that connects to a payment back-end system. A payment plug-in is responsible for six standard payment actions: approve, deposit, credit, reverse approval, reverse deposit, and reverse credit.

The following payment plug-ins are provided with WebSphere Commerce.

Paymentech

`http://www.chasepaymentech.com/solgat.do`

The Paymentech plug-in communicates with the Paymentech gateway. The Paymentech plug-in is a new feature introduced in WebSphere Commerce Feature Pack 2. There is more information about WebSphere Commerce Feature packs in 11.5.2, "Applying WebSphere Commerce Feature Packs" on page 354.

SimpleOffline

The SimpleOffline plug-in processes payments offline, or manually. Offline payments do not involve any direct communication with a payment back-end system. Instead, the SimpleOffline plug-in records events that have already happened outside of WebSphere Commerce. Transactions are recorded and maintained in the WebSphere Commerce database.

Line of credit (LOC)

With the LOC plug-in merchants can use lines of credit as a payment method. It enables buyers to delay the payment settlement for orders and is intended to integrate with accounts receivable systems used by customers. The LOC plug-in mimics the function of an actual line of credit. By default, it does not connect to an accounts receivable system. To connect to an account receivable system, you must write your own version of the plug-in.

WCPayments

The WCPayments plug-in acts as a bridge to the old WebSphere Commerce Payments Multi-payment Framework and enables the use of existing payment cassettes.

Custom payments

WebSphere Commerce provides these payments plug-ins. However, there are many scenarios and you might need to have your own custom payment plug-in created. WebSphere Commerce provides the Payment plug-in specification to enable developers to create custom plug-ins. The specification is located at:

```
http://publib.boulder.ibm.com/infocenter/wchelp/v6r0m0/index.jsp?topic=
/com.ibm.commerce.payments.events.doc/refs/rppppcspec.htm
```

Payment plug-ins are either simple in nature (serving as a proxy to a payment back-end system) or more complex, such as an interface to an accounting system, or some other system that serves a particular purpose, for example, a gift certificate processing system.

Custom payment plug-ins specific to popular payment service providers such as Paypal, Google checkout, and HSBC have already been implemented by IBM Business Partners as part of WebSphere Commerce projects. See 6.3.1, “Consultancy options” for more information regarding the third-parties that have created these payments plug-ins.

2.2.6 Gift registry

If you are from the United States, you are probably familiar with the concept of a gift registry. It is similar to Wish Lists on Amazon but it is a more structured implementation because it requires special registration. For an event where a person or a couple expect to receive many gifts, they often set up a gift registry with the store of their preference. From the store's catalog they make a selection of products. Then they let the invitees to their event know that they have a gift list registered at a particular store. The invitees then peruse the list of preferred gifts and buy one of them as a gift.

IBM Gift Center for WebSphere Commerce incorporates a gift registry solution into your WebSphere Commerce Web site. The IBM Gift Center for WebSphere Commerce can be configured for many types of occasions, it is often used for wedding, anniversary, baby or bridal showers, and birthdays celebrations. You could also suggest events such as starting a home together, or starting college.

Note: IBM Gift Center for WebSphere Commerce, an optional, chargeable feature, can be licensed to run only on WebSphere Commerce Enterprise Edition or WebSphere Commerce Professional Edition, not WebSphere Commerce Express Edition. IBM Gift Center software is installed using either WebSphere Commerce Enterprise or WebSphere Commerce Professional images, but you are required to first purchase separate licenses to use the IBM Gift Center component.

The Gift Center comes with a sample application using the gift registry in three different ways:

- Online Web channel
- In-store trained gift consultant
- In-store kiosk with hand-held scanners

Further information can be found online in the Infocenter article about the IBM Gift Center for WebSphere Commerce and gift registry feature, at:

```
http://publib.boulder.ibm.com/infocenter/wchelp/v6r0m0/index.jsp?topic=
/com.ibm.commerce.giftcenter.doc/concepts/cgcibmgiftcentercustomization
04.htm
```

2.2.7 Scheduler

In an eCommerce environment there are tasks that are best run in the background at scheduled times. In WebSphere Commerce these are called scheduled jobs. The scheduler component is used to automate the execution of routine tasks at specified intervals of time. Examples of scheduled jobs in a WebSphere Commerce store are jobs to process back-orders, inventory synchronization and cleaning the database. The scheduler component schedules and executes jobs both for the overall site and at individual store level.

2.2.8 Staging

Most online stores operate 24 hours a day, 365 days of the year, making it difficult to load new catalog items, new price lists, perform maintenance, or test changes to the system. To circumvent taking the production server down to make updates to a Web site's business content, WebSphere Commerce offers a staging server. To update the software or hardware in a production WebSphere Commerce site with minimal downtime, you also need a pre-production server. This is discussed in Chapter 10, "Development, test, and production environments" on page 307.

A staging server is a separate installation of WebSphere Commerce connected to your production environment. The staging server is used to test content updates such as updates to the catalog and marketing assets. Tests can be performed on the staging server before running special scripts to propagate the changes to the production server without halting the Web site.

Staging server environment

A WebSphere Commerce staging server is very similar to a WebSphere Commerce production server. In most cases, the staging server does not have as many nodes as the production environment.

Staging server data

In WebSphere Commerce there are two types of data[3]: configuration and operation.

Configuration data Configuration data consists of data such as stores, catalogs, catalog entries, languages, taxes, promotions and discounts.

Operation data Operation data consists of data such as shopper information, addresses, and orders data.

The staging server manages only tables that contain configuration data. Data in operation tables is not propagated or copied between the staging and production databases.

[3] There is a lack of uniformity in the terms used in WebSphere Commerce for data. During IT operations, such as development and deployment, the phrase Configuration Data is used to refer the tuning parameters for the IT infrastructure, and Operation data to the data in WebSphere Commerce databases, such as catalogs and prices. IT people refer to orders and other data that are generated by the operation of the store as "Dynamic Operation" data. In the business perspective, the meanings of Configuration and Operation data are as in our definition. You need to be aware of the context when you see the terms configuration and operation data used.

Note: When using a staging server, no manual updates should ever be made to configuration data on the production server. Otherwise, the data can become unsynchronized and future data propagations fail.

Delta data capturing function

The staging server uses a delta data capturing function to determine which data changed in the staging database and therefore, which data should be propagated over to the production environment. This function is used internally by the staging server, and no manual intervention is required. The delta data capturing function is a series of special database triggers on all tables that contain configuration data. Any changes that are made to those tables trigger an update to a special table (STAGLOG) that records all of the changes.

There are several tools provided by WebSphere Commerce to assist with propagation of files and configuration data from the staging server to the production server. These are discussed in 2.3.2, "WebSphere Commerce administration tools" on page 74.

2.2.9 Workspaces

Retailers need to make content owners (business users), not IT staff, responsible not only for the content on the Web site, but also how it should be delivered. Content differentiates your Web site from competitive stores. You need to empower business users to manage site content themselves, directly.

WebSphere Commerce puts complete control of creation, collaboration and management of content and user experience in the hands of business users through the workspaces component. A workspace is an isolated access-controlled work area that gives business users the ability to control site changes in the following ways:

- Assigning work
- Sending notifications
- Executing site changes to product, content, promotions and campaigns
- Previewing changes
- Approving changes
- Scheduling when changes go into production

Workspaces exist as a separate instance of WebSphere Commerce called an authoring server. An authoring server consists of several entities and roles. The main entities are:

Tasks

A task is an individual unit of work that contributes to the completion of an activity. For example, adding a new product to the store might consist of several tasks such as these: add the product to the catalog; add an image that can be used for advertisement of the product; create a promotion that features the product; create a campaign that features the product.

Task groups

A task group is a logical grouping of a number of tasks.

Workspaces

A workspace consists of a number of task groups.

The three roles used in authoring servers are:

Workspace manager

The workspace manager is responsible for the entire workspace. The workspace manager has the authority to create workspaces, create task groups, create tasks, assign workspace content contributors to complete tasks and assign workspace task group approvers to approve workspace task groups.

Workspace content contributor

The workspace content contributor is responsible for completing tasks assigned by the workspace manager.

Workspace task group approver

The workspace task group approver is responsible for approving the content created by the workspace content contributors for the task group.

In addition to workspaces, an authoring server provides all of the functions of a staging server including the staging utilities. Figure 2-14 shows workspaces in the context of an authoring server and production server.

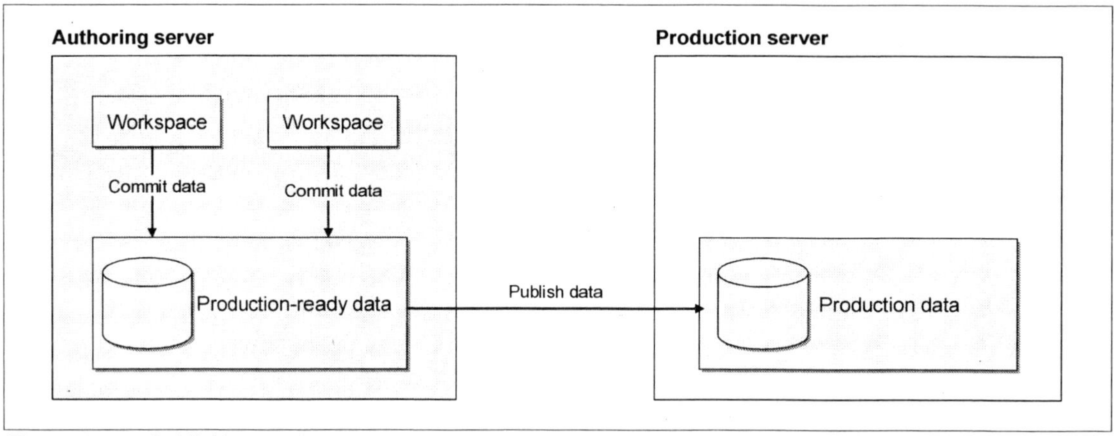

Figure 2-14 Publishing workspaces

Note: Workspaces are supported in WebSphere Commerce Professional and Enterprise editions only.

2.2.10 Contracts

In a typical B2B business model, the transactions between the seller and buyer organizations are managed through trading agreements. A contract is one such trading agreement. Contracts enable a buyer organization to purchase some or all products from a store at a specified price for a specified period of time under specific terms and conditions. Other trading agreements include auctions and request for quote.

To give an example, consider an office supply store (seller organization). At a high level there can be two types of shoppers to the office supply store, guest shoppers and shoppers from another organization (also called buyers from a buyer organization) with whom there is a trading agreement. The buyers shop at the office supply store under the trading agreement and hence they see a contract price, and product entitlement. The guest shoppers see the list price only.

One of the added values of WebSphere Commerce is the support of contracts. Managing a contract involves tasks from their creation to the end of the contract's life cycle. Just as an order has different states in an eCommerce system, a contract also got different states depending on what stage of the life cycle the contract is in (see Figure 2-15, which is taken from the Infocenter contract states topic). The states are used to help manage different contracts and contract activities that take place in a continuing business relationship.

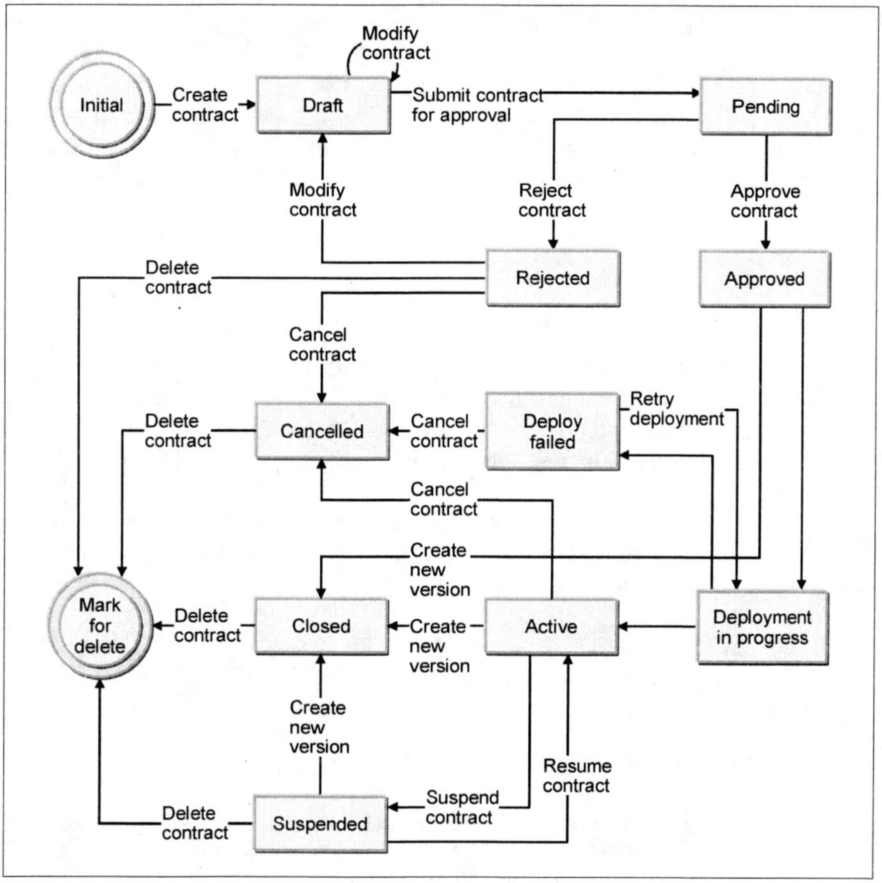

Figure 2-15 Contract states

Contracts are created in WebSphere Commerce either using the WebSphere Commerce accelerator tool or using XML files. A contract in WebSphere Commerce is made up of the following elements:

- Profile

  Every contract must have a unique name, a short description and a time period for which the contract is valid.

- Participants

  The contract participants are the buyer and seller organizations and their contacts

- Terms and conditions

  Contract terms and conditions are the rules that cover the actual implementation of the contract. Contract terms and conditions cover such information as product pricing, returns and refunds, payment, shipping, and order approval.

- Attachments

  Any information not covered by the previous elements such as file attachments that provide additional information about the contract and general remarks about the contract goes into an attachment which is referenced from the WebSphere Commerce stores using a Universal Resource Identifiers (URIs). The attachment is not stored by WebSphere Commerce.

- Reference

  A contract might refer to another contract to share its terms and conditions. For example, suppose contract A refers to contract B. Thus, a buyer who is trading using contract A is entitled to the terms and conditions in contract A, and the terms and conditions in contract B.

There are several ways to model your product and pricing entitlement in a WebSphere Commerce store. For more detail on contracts, refer to the online product documentation.

```
http://publib.boulder.ibm.com/infocenter/wchelp/v6r0m0/topic/com.ibm.co
mmerce.user.business.doc/refs/rctmodelling.htm
```

2.2.11 Starter stores

The starter stores in WebSphere Commerce are more than sample stores for demonstration purposes. They are functional (that is, working) stores for each business model and are fully tested before each new release. Most WebSphere Commerce implementations begin with a starter store because these reduce the time it takes to get your own Web store up and running.

In WebSphere Commerce, each functional store is built with one or more ***s***tore ***ar***chives, or ***sar*** files. Multiple sar files are grouped into a composite store. Each composite store archive contains all necessary assets to do business online. Publishing it makes the store live. The starter stores are pre-published in the Cloudscape® development database after WebSphere Commerce is installed.

Within a composite store archive, there are multiple component store archives. The typical components in a composite store are samples of an organization structure, predefined user roles, access control policy, storefront, and the related assets.

Consumer Direct

The Consumer Direct starter store is the basic B2C store model available for all editions. The ConsumerDirect.sar is the sample composite store archive containing the organization structure, predefined user roles, and necessary access control policies to create a consumer direct environment, plus a working store.

Additional Consumer Direct store archives are provided in Enterprise edition which is useful when there is a requirement to publish multiple B2C Web sites. Refer to the product online documentation for more details on publishing multiple stores on a single instance of WebSphere Commerce:

```
http://publib.boulder.ibm.com/infocenter/wchelp/v6r0m0/topic/com.ibm.co
mmerce.admin.business.doc/concepts/cbmmultiplestores.htm
```

Creating starter stores using the component asset store shared resources allows extensive manageable customization. After a composite store is published, the behavior of the store is defined by default, and any changes to the behavior would require the whole store to be redeployed. With the use of component asset store shared resources, if a change is needed to the store's behavior, you can change whichever asset store needs modification and there is no need to change the entire deployment. This modularization is a nice way to manage store assets and give you extensibility by building new stores based on an existing assets. as a template.

Business Direct

The Business Direct starter store is the basic B2B store model available for all editions. It is shipped as B2BDirect.sar. AdvancedB2BDirect.sar is the sample composite store archive containing the organization structure, predefined user roles, and necessary access control policies to create a B2B direct environment, plus a working store.

Additional Business Direct archives are available in Enterprise edition to construct multiple B2B sites.

Extended sites

The Extended sites starter store is the basic extended sites store model and is available only for Enterprise Edition. ExtendedSites.sar is the starter store composite archive, containing the organization structure, predefined user roles, and necessary access control policies to create an extended sites environment. It also contains the necessary assets to create a hub site, shared catalog, and seller storefronts.

Additional archives are shipped to create multiple sites from individual pieces of the extended site store.

Demand chain

The Demand chain starter store is the basic demand chain model and is available only for Enterprise Edition. DemandChain.sar is the sample composite store archive containing the organization structure, predefined user roles, and necessary access control policies to create a demand chain environment, plus the necessary assets to create a demand chain solution, including a channel hub site, shared catalog, and reseller and distributor stores.

Additional archives are shipped to create multiple sites from individual pieces of the demand chain store.

Supply chain

The Supply chain starter store is the basic supply chain model and is available only for Enterprise Edition. SupplyChain.sar is the composite starter store archive containing the organization structure, predefined user roles, and necessary access control policies to create a supply chain environment, plus the necessary assets to create a supplier hub site, shared catalog and supplier stores.

Additional archives are shipped to create multiple sites from individual pieces of the supply chain store.

Web 2.0 starter store

Starting from 6.0.0.2 with Feature Pack 2, WebSphere Commerce ships a sample Web 2.0 starter store called Madisons. With a few additional installation and store publishing steps, you have a new Consumer Direct based store featuring drag and drop user interactions, dynamic product finder, and hover tips.

Some of the features included in Madisons starter store are:

- The ability to drag items into the shopping cart, wish list and compare zone.
- eMarketing Spots with automatic scroll of items, products, categories and merchandising associations.
- Tool tip pop ups with product details when customers hover over items.
- A fast product finder where products are narrowed as the customer makes selections of attributes such as brand or price range.
- The ability to change product attributes directly on the shopping cart, such as color or fabric changes.
- Single page checkout.

- Coremetrics analytics integrated into the Rich Internet Application[4] (RIA) technologies.

Refer to the online product documentation for more details on the Web 2.0 starter store solution:

http://publib.boulder.ibm.com/infocenter/wchelp/v6r0m0/topic/com.ibm.commerce.web20storesolution.refapp.doc/concepts/csm_web20_intro.htm

2.3 WebSphere Commerce Tools

This section gives an overview of tools available as part of the product, what you can do and where and when to use them. Tools fall under the following categories:

- Business user tools
- Administrator tools
- Developer tools.

2.3.1 Business user tools

With business tools, business users create and edit the managed Web site data. Managed data overlaps somewhat with operational data, depending on whether the data is created by a customer (operational data) or by the business owner (configuration data). To give you an idea of what managed data includes, which the business owner has control over, this is an overview of managed data:

```
Catalog, prices, contracts, coupons, business policies, customer
segments, e-mail activities, fulfillment centers, inventory, sellers,
vendors, members, campaigns, orders, payment, promotions, supported
languages, currencies and units of measure, jurisdictions, shipping and
taxation.
```

WebSphere Commerce Accelerator

“I need to set up a winter sale,” or “I need to update product information”: These are some common business user activities. In WebSphere Commerce, making these changes is called *content delivery*. Content delivery includes the creation, management and placement of content. Business owners not only own the content of the Web site, but with the Accelerator are also able to deliver it without having to involve IT staff. They can take responsibility for managing the look and feel of the store, create and maintain orders and track store activities.

[4] RIA is the acronym used to describe enhanced user interface technologies in Web 2.0, such as AJAX.

WebSphere Commerce Accelerator is a Web browser tool that has an intuitive, role based interface for managing and maintaining online stores, hubs, and catalogs. The tool provides different roles for marketing, sales and service tasks. The tasks you are authorized to perform in your role are displayed on the WebSphere Commerce Accelerator home page menus. These tasks are based on your user role, authority level, the business model and the type of store. The user interface consists of several notebooks, wizards, dialogs, and lists to help you complete your tasks. For example, there are product management interfaces that allows business users to create, edit or delete products and to set up contracts in B2B stores.

To open WebSphere Commerce Accelerator:

1. Access the following Web address in your browser:

   `https://host_name:8000/accelerator`

   where *host_name* is the fully-qualified WebSphere Commerce Web server host name. The host name can be a virtual host name on the Web server.

   Log onto the WebSphere Commerce Accelerator as follows (Figure 2-16):

   – From the WebSphere Commerce Logon page, type your WebSphere Commerce user name and password.

   – Specify the name of the store you want to work with

   – Select the name of the fulfillment center associated with the store from the “Fulfillment center” list.

   – Select the language in which you want to administer the store from “Language to work with” list

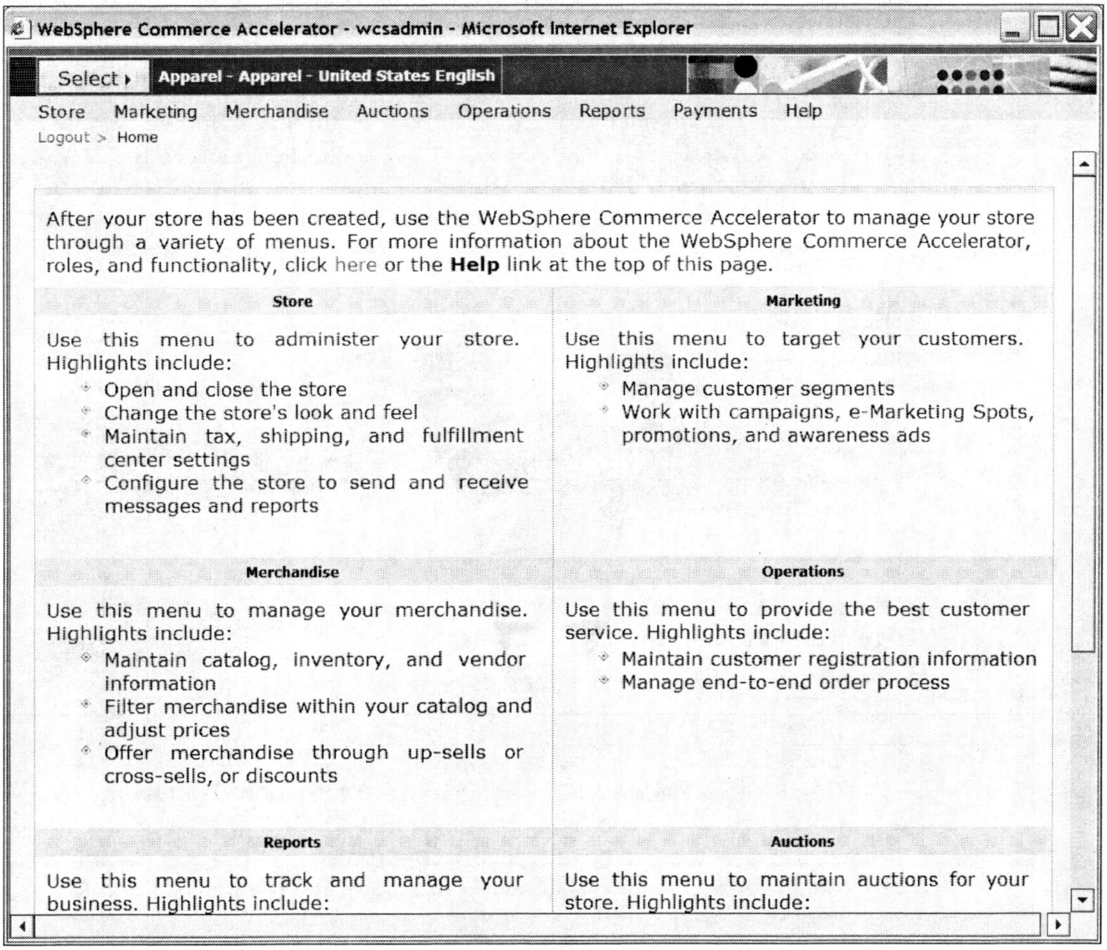

Figure 2-16 WebSphere Commerce Accelerator

Sales Center

IBM Sales Center is a WebSphere Commerce client application providing a high performance, information rich view for customer service representatives (CSRs) in a call center. The usage scenarios for the Sales Center are focused around managing customers and orders. It is not designed for a typical shopper where the shopper wants to browse through a store, check various categories that spark their interest and see graphically rich pages, The Sales Center is designed for customer service representatives who are typically called to assist a customer in placing an order or to resolve some issue such as finding an item, resolving an ordering or delivery problem or providing more information about an item which is for sale.

The Sales Center works as a client to the same WebSphere Commerce run time as customers are using with their browser interfaces. By using the same WebSphere Commerce runtime, the CSR is viewing the same products and business processes as customers are. This is important for existing businesses that are looking to protect their existing investment in a WebSphere Commerce Web site and have found a need to provide call center access. It is also important because in dealing with a customer, the CSR knows they are interacting with exactly the same system although their views are quite different, and any changes made by the CSR, or the customer, are by definition in synchronization.

Note: How many times have you phoned up a call center about a transaction initiated on the Web and found that the CSR does not have an up-to-date view of the system, including the transaction that is giving your problems? This is rarely a problem these days with retail companies who are using WebSphere Commerce, but still remains an issue for many financial services companies who have added Web sites after providing call centers for their customers.

The IBM Sales Center offers the following features for CSRs:

- Interact with WebSphere Commerce. The same store can receive orders from both the Web and an inbound call center.
- Perform the following customer service tasks:
  - Select and remove stores
  - Create, find, edit, and delete customers
  - Create, find, edit, cancel, prepare, save, submit, and view orders
  - Create, find, edit, copy, and cancel quotes
  - Add and view shipping instructions for orders
  - Add, remove, and edit payment instructions and methods for orders and quotes
  - Find, compare, and view products
  - Add products, prebuilt kits, dynamic kits, and merchandising associations
  - Add and remove ticklers[5]

In addition, WebSphere Commerce provides reports on CSR performance and activities, including revenue, sales, orders, price overrides, performance ranking, profit, quotations, customer organizations, and customer territories. These reports are available for individual Customer Service Representatives or a CSR team. You can access these reports in the WebSphere Commerce Accelerator.

[5] Ticklers are notes that are assigned either by the system or by a CSR to notify themselves, the CSRs, about an action - such as to return a call to a customer.

Management Center

Starting from WebSphere Commerce version 6.0.0.3 with Feature Pack 3, there is a new application for business users called the Management Center. It allows business users to perform merchandising (selling) and marketing tasks to create, update, and maintain merchandising (sales) and marketing assets in stores using the consumer direct and B2B business models.

The Management Center is a new, more usable, and intuitive tool for business users. It does not yet have the complete functionality of WebSphere Commerce Accelerator, but it is well worth using in preference to WebSphere Commerce Accelerator for tasks that it can perform, as it should prove more productive. The Infocenter has a table describing when to use the Management Center, which is reproduced in Table 2-7 for convenience. For other tasks, the business user should use the Accelerator.

Table 2-7 Management center tasks

If you are ...	You can use the Management Center to ...
Managing catalogs and merchandise	► Create and manage master and sales catalogs, including defining categories, creating products and SKUs, categorizing SKUs, and bundling SKUs ► Enrich and manage product content, and create merchandising associations
Managing marketing promotions	► Create and manage promotions for your merchandise ► Review and manage marketing promotions using the promotions calendar view
Managing marketing campaigns	► Design creative marketing campaigns containing Web and e-mail activities ► Define the flow of marketing activities using activity templates and change marketing activities through the marketing activity builder ► Review and manage marketing activities using the activities calendar view

2.3.2 WebSphere Commerce administration tools

The administration tools are divided into operations and configuration management tools.

Operations management

The operations management tools listed below are describing in the following sections.

- WebSphere Commerce Administration console
- WebSphere Commerce Organization Administration Console
- WebSphere Commerce Loader utility
- DBClean utility
- Staging utilities

WebSphere Commerce Administration console

The Administration console is a Web application tool that allows administrators to configure and control a commerce Web site or store. Administrative tasks include publishing and configuring stores, monitoring messages and setting up security policies.

Upon opening the administration console, you select the language in which you want to work.

To start the Administration Console:

1. Access the following URL in your browser:

   `https://host_name:8002/adminconsole`

   host_name is the fully qualified TCP/IP name of your WebSphere Commerce Server.

2. Log on with your site administrator ID and password

   If you are authorized to work with more than one store or language, the Administration Console Site/Store Selection page is displayed. If you are authorized to work with a single store and language, the Administration Console home page displays. Tasks that you are authorized to perform display in the Administration Console home page.

3. From the Administration Console Site/Store selection page, select the site radio button → **OK**.

The Site Administration Console home page displays as shown in Figure 2-17.

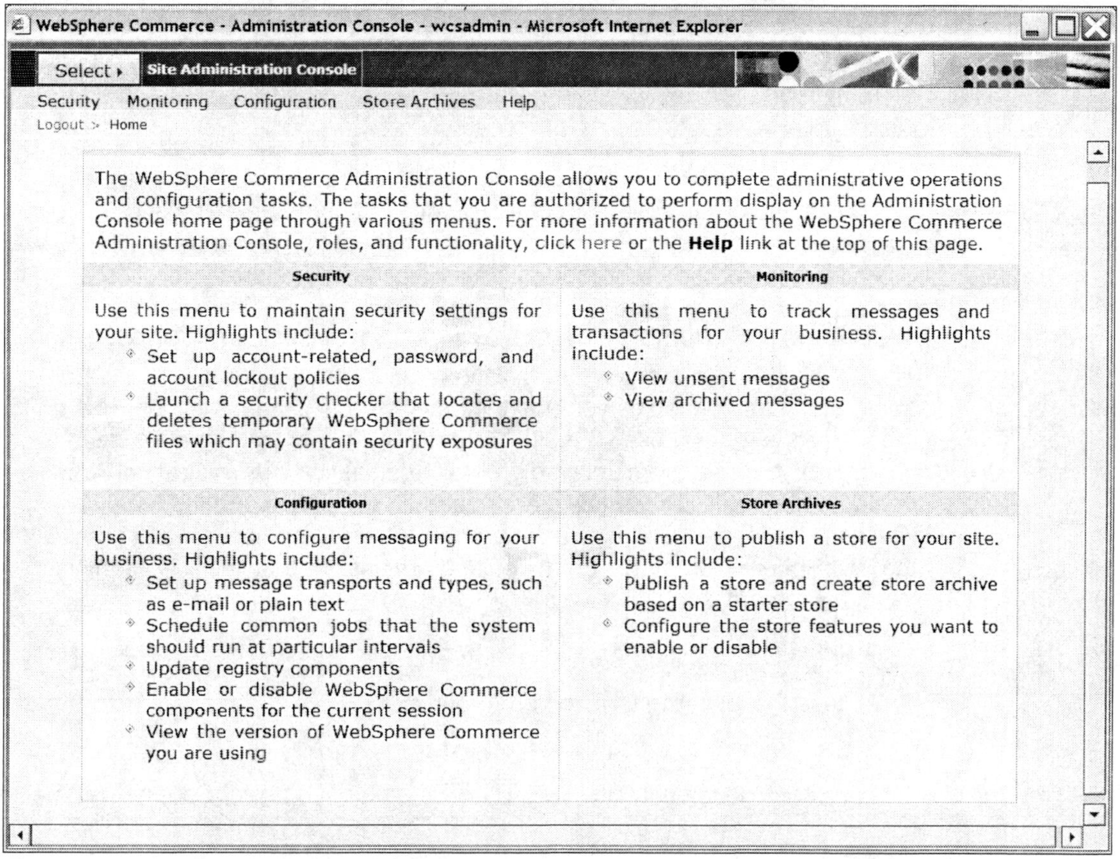

Figure 2-17 Site Administration console

The Site Administration Console provides several menus that contain the bulk of the functionality required to perform the site administrator role:

- Security

  Using the security menu administrators set up account policy. Account policy includes the password and account lockout policies for a particular type of user account. Password policies define the rules for passwords like minimum length of the password and maximum lifetime of the password. The account lockout policy includes rules like number of invalid logon attempts.

- Monitoring

  The monitoring menu lists unsent messages, and enables you to view and resend messages that have been sent previously.

- Configuration

  The configuration menu has various functions. You can list and configure transport methods, enable or disable different components, list jobs scheduled to run and list and refresh the registries which are used for caching runtime data.

- Store Archives

  The Store Archive menu is used to publish store archives. Store archives contain the organization structure, predefined user roles, and access control policies necessary for creating the environment for your store or site, as well as collections of assets used to create a catalog or storefront.

WebSphere Commerce Organization Administration Console

The WebSphere Commerce Organization Administration console is another Web application tool. It enables you and the buyer's administrators to control the organizations that access your site or store. Tasks that you are authorized to perform in your role are displayed on the Organization Administration Console home page menus. These tasks are based on user roles and authority levels, which are defined in XML files on your WebSphere Commerce system and within the WebSphere Commerce database and are assigned by the Site Administrator using the Organization Administration Console.

To start the Organization Administration Console:

1. Access the following URL in your browser:

   `https://host_name:8004/orgadminconsole`

   host_name is the fully qualified TCP/IP name of your WebSphere Commerce Server.

2. Log on with your site administrator ID and password.

   The Organization Administration Console home page displays as depicted in Figure 2-18.

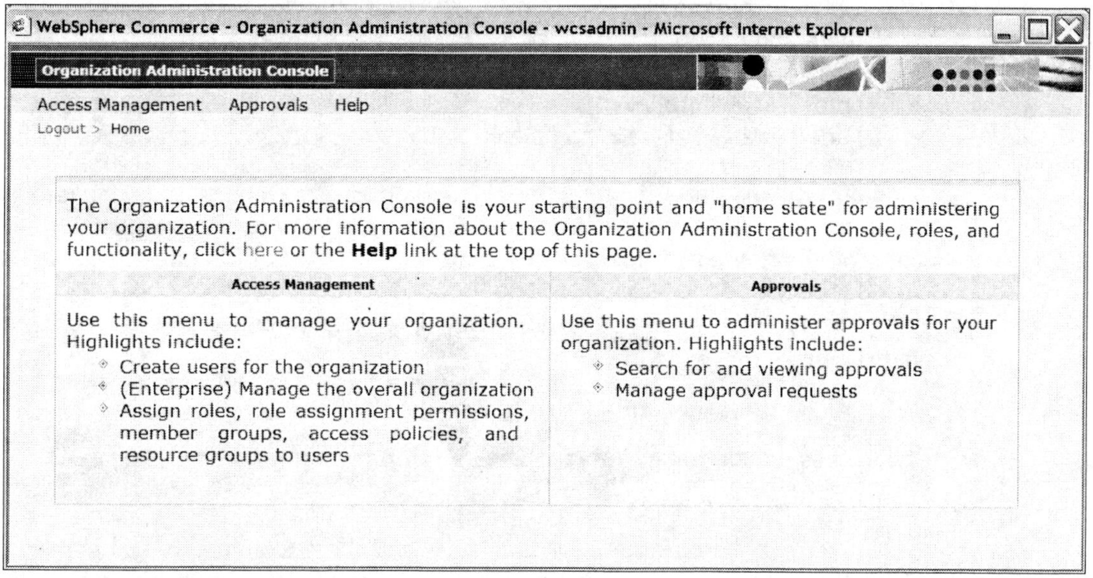

Figure 2-18 Organization Administration console

The Organization Administration Console contains two submenus for maintaining the access control environment within WebSphere Commerce:

- Access management

  The Access management menu is used to search for users, organizations, roles, member groups and add new users, organizations and member groups.

- Approvals

  The Approvals menu is used to search for approvals or list the approvals that are awaiting action from the user who is logged in.

Workspace Administration Tool

> **Note:** For details on Workspaces, refer to 2.2.9, "Workspaces" on page 62

The Workspace Administration Tool is a graphical user interface tool used to manage workspaces and workspace-related activities. It provides a single view across all workspaces and all tasks in the workspaces. Managers can see how work is progressing.

Using the Workspace Administration Tool, you can:

- Create and cancel workspaces, task groups, and tasks
- Assign approvers to task groups and content contributors to tasks
- Approve a task group
- Change a task's state to complete

Content contributors (Business users) use WebSphere Commerce Accelerator to perform the tasks that are assigned to them by the Workspace Administration tool. In performing their tasks with WebSphere Commerce Accelerator business users change the workspace content. Workspace content cannot be modified with the Workspace Administration tool; the administration tool is only used to administer workspaces.

To open the Workspace Administration Tool:

1. Access the following Web address in your browser:

   ```
   https://host_name:8000/workspaceadmin
   ```

   where *host_name* is the fully qualified WebSphere Commerce Web server host name. The host name might be a virtual host name on the Web server.

2. Logon to the Workspace Administration Tool with your WebSphere Commerce user name and password.

3. The Workspace Administration Tool home page displays as shown in Figure 2-19.

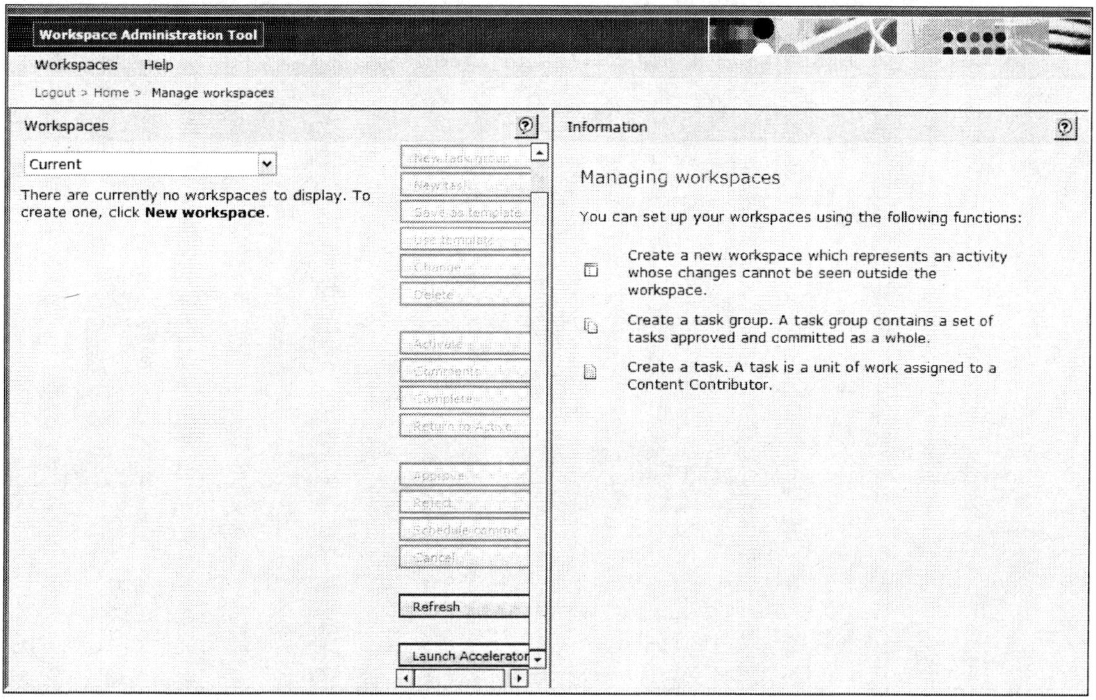

Figure 2-19 Workspace Administration Tool

WebSphere Commerce Loader utility

Use the WebSphere Commerce provides utilities (Table 2-8) for preparing and loading data into a WebSphere Commerce database.

Table 2-8 Massloader utilities

Utility	Purpose
txttransform	Transforms data between a character-delimited format and an XML data format
xmltransform	Transforms XML data into alternative XML formats
dtdgen	Generates a DTD based on the target database
idresgen	Generates identifiers for XML elements.
massload	Loads data into the WebSphere Commerce database
fileloader	Loads managed files into the WebSphere Commerce database
massextract	Extracts data from a database as an XML document

These utilities provide various functions that can be linked together in the required sequence to perform whatever your particular commerce data management tasks might be (Figure 2-20).

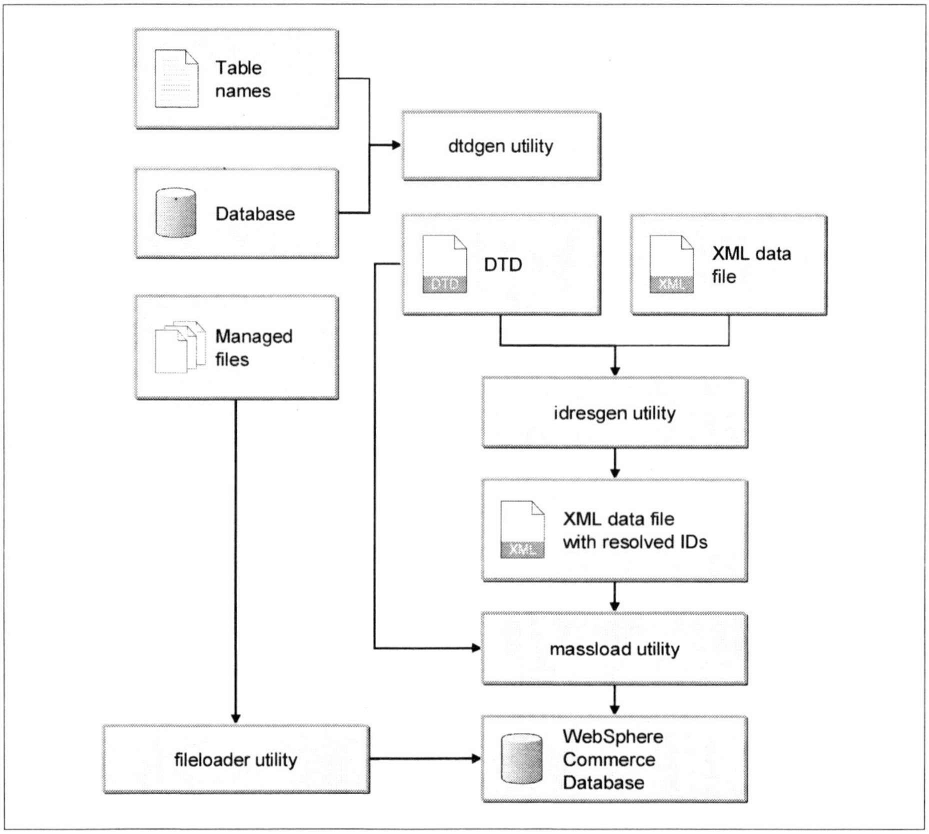

Figure 2-20 Data loading and extraction process

The loading utilities are flexible enough to handle customizations that are made to the WebSphere Commerce schema.

DBClean utility

One of the main advantages of having an electronic catalog is that it is dynamic. It means that different parts in the catalog are continually updated. For example, when new products are introduced, new product information is easily made available in the catalog by replacing the old information. But the new information does not literally replace the old information. The catalog is logically updated to point to the new information rather than the old. This leads to an increase in the database size that is not immediately a problem, but eventually might become so, especially with larger catalog sizes, and performance will deteriorate.

WebSphere Commerce has a utility called DBClean with which administrators delete unwanted objects from the database. Run this utility periodically to clean up the database and reduce its size. There is further information about this topic in chapter 11.1.4, “Maintaining the database” on page 332.

Staging Utilities

A WebSphere Commerce administrator uses the utilities in Table 2-9 provided with the staging server to manage publishing database changes from the staging server to the production server.

Table 2-9 Staging utilities

Utility	Purpose
stagingcopy	The stagingcopy utility copies data from the production database to the production-ready data on a staging or authoring server
stagingcheck[a]	The stagingcheck utility determines if there is a unique index key conflict between the production-ready data and the production database. Run the stagingcheck utility before the stagingprop utility to ensure successful publication
stagingprop	The stagingprop utility copies data and managed files from the production-ready data to the production server. This is the most commonly used utility
fileprop	The fileprop utility sends new and changed files to the production server.

a. Now deprecated

Configuration management

These configuration management tools are described in the following sections:

- WebSphere Commerce Configuration Manager
- WebSphere Application Server Administration Console
- WebSphere Application Server Cache Monitor
- WebSphere Commerce Migration utilities

WebSphere Commerce Configuration Manager

To enable and configure various components of WebSphere Commerce, such as creating a WebSphere Commerce instance, you use the Configuration manager. The Configuration manager is a Java application, which modifies configuration data stored in an XML file. Wherever possible, components should be enabled by logging on to Configuration manager rather than modifying the WebSphere Commerce configuration XML file.

To launch the Configuration Manager on Windows®:

1. Ensure that the IBM WebSphere Commerce Configuration Manager server process is running by executing the config_server command from a command window:

```
<WC InstallDir>\bin\config_server.bat
```

2. Start the configuration manager user interface by running **config_client** from a command window:

```
<WC InstallDir>\bin\config_client.bat
```

WebSphere Application Server Administration Console

WebSphere Commerce is a J2EE™ application that runs in WebSphere Application Server. Some of the WebSphere Commerce administration tasks managed in WebSphere Administration console are dynamic caching, trace and logging, database connection pool management, Java virtual machine heap management and more, depending on the configuration.

The WebSphere Commerce administrator needs to be familiar with using the WebSphere Application Server Administration Console. It is essential to optimize the configuration of WebSphere Application Server to get the best performance out of WebSphere Commerce. WebSphere Commerce uses the logging and tracing service provided by WebSphere Application Server and is configured using WebSphere Application Server Administration console. Refer to the online product information center for more details:

```
http://publib.boulder.ibm.com/infocenter/wchelp/v6r0m0/topic/com.ibm.co
mmerce.admin.doc/concepts/clslogging.htm
```

WebSphere Application Server Cache Monitor

WebSphere Application Server dynamic cache provides a built-in service for caching and serving dynamic content. The dynamic cache service includes servlet, JSP™, command caching and invalidation support to refresh cache entries. There is also edge side caching. Cache contents can be viewed and managed via the Cache monitor application. The cache monitor provides a GUI interface to refresh cached data manually, and to study the effectiveness of cache policies.

The CacheMonitor.ear file has to be installed manually from the `<WAS_HOME>/installableApps` directory using the WebSphere Application Server Administration console.

To start the cache monitor, type **`http://host_name:port/cachemonitor`** into a browser.

Refer to the IBM Redbooks publication, "*Mastering DynaCache in WebSphere Commerce*", SG24-7393, for information about many aspects of tuning the performance of WebSphere Commerce and how to plan and design for performance. You can find this book at:

```
http://www.redbooks.ibm.com/abstracts/sg247393.html?Open
```

WebSphere Commerce Migration utilities

WebSphere Commerce is a popular eCommerce product and has been in the market for several years. As such, many WebSphere Commerce implementations still run on previous versions of the product. When you decide to migrate to a new version of the product, perhaps to take advantage of new features, or to maintain a compatibility with other products or to run at a supported service level, careful migration planning is required to ensure minimal impact on your business.

WebSphere Commerce has the following migration utilities:

- Migration Wizard
- Command line scripts
  - migratedb utility (database migration script)
  - wcim utility (WebSphere Commerce Instance migration)
  - updateDB2 Configuration script

We recommend that you use the Migration wizard utility to perform migration. The wizard guides you through the complete migration process step by step.

The command line interface is for advanced users who are familiar with migrating WebSphere Commerce.

Your migration activity includes many of the following tasks:

- Migrating WebSphere Commerce Developer
- Migrating WebSphere Commerce Server
- Migrating WebSphere Commerce database
- Migrating WebSphere Commerce application
- Migrating Web servers
- Migrating WebSphere Commerce in a clustered environment
- Migrating LikeMinds Personalization Server
- Migrating from a previous payment implementation
- Any other component which is part of the your implementation that needs to be migrated

Refer to product information center on migration for more details

`http://publib.boulder.ibm.com/infocenter/wchelp/v6r0m0/topic/com.ibm.commerce.admin.doc/concepts/cmgmigrating.htm`

2.3.3 WebSphere Commerce development tools

This section describes the tools used to build a WebSphere Commerce Web site. Every Web site is unique and the out-of-the-box components are customizable to modify the sample stores into individual Web sites.

WebSphere Commerce Developer

Customization involves changing Web pages, adding new business logic and integrating with other systems. WebSphere Commerce Developer (commonly referred to as Commerce toolkit) is required to make these customizations. For each edition: Express, Professional, and Enterprise, a different WebSphere Commerce Developer is available. You must use the edition of WebSphere Commerce Developer that matches your edition of WebSphere Commerce.

WebSphere Commerce Developer uses IBM Rational® Application Developer for rapid development of JSPs, Web content, commands and EJBs to customize your store. Information about installing and configuring WebSphere Commerce Developer is located at:

http://publib.boulder.ibm.com/infocenter/wchelp/v6r0m0/topic/com.ibm.commerce.base.doc/concepts/covwheretofind.htm

Dojo toolkit for Web 2.0 starter store

Starting with WebSphere Commerce version 6.0.0.2, Feature Pack 2, a starter store based on Web 2.0 is available which provides an interactive and rich shopping experience. This Web 2.0 store, called Madisons ("Web 2.0 starter store" on page 68), uses the Dojo toolkit which is an AJAX javascript toolkit. Version 0.41 of Dojo toolkit is used to build the starter store. In order to customize this store, install Dojo toolkit in WebSphere Commerce Developer environment. Use this link to find the installation information:

http://publib.boulder.ibm.com/infocenter/wchelp/v6r0m0/topic/com.ibm.commerce.web20storesolution.refapp.doc/tasks/tsm_web20_install.htm

Management Center

The Management Center is a business user tool for managing online business tasks, introduced with WebSphere Commerce version 6, Feature Pack 3 (see "Management Center" on page 73). The Management Center application consists of two parts: the Management Center rich client application that runs on the browser side and the Management Center Web application that runs on the server side.

The Management Center client uses the OpenLaszlo open source technology (http://www.openlaszlo.org). Developing OpenLaszlo applications involves writing declarative XML with embedded JavaScript™. This source XML and JavaScript is compiled to Flash which is downloaded to the client browser and is displayed by the Flash Player. The Management Center client application communicates with the Management Center Web application using browser based HTTP requests. These request are mapped to Struts actions in the Management Center Web application which calls the SOA/SOI component services from WebSphere Commerce.

In Feature pack 3.0.1, there is an additional Web project in the WebSphere Commerce Developer workspace to customize Management Center assets. The project is called LOBTools. This project includes OpenLaszlo source files, images, HTML pages, properties files, Struts action classes, JSP files, configuration files and the ManagementCenter.swf file. All Open Laszlo source files, other than the ones located in the 'restricted' folder, can be customized.

The OpenLaszlo files are compiled by the OpenLaszlo compiler into the ManagementCenter.swf Flash file, which runs within the client's browser. Other files are part of the Management Center Web application that runs on the server.

For more information on the Management Center assets and on how to customize them, please refer to the Management Center Framework section in the WebSphere Commerce Information Center:

```
http://publib.boulder.ibm.com/infocenter/wchelp/v6r0m0/index.jsp?top
ic=/com.ibm.commerce.management-center_customization.doc/concepts/ct
fcmcframework.htm
```

You will also find the following Management Center customization tutorials useful:

- Tutorial: Adding new fields in the Catalogs tool:

```
http://publib.boulder.ibm.com/infocenter/wchelp/v6r0m0/index.jsp?top
ic=/com.ibm.commerce.management-center_customization.doc/tutorial/tt
fadpcat.htm
```

- Tutorial: Adding new search conditions in the advanced search of the Catalogs tool:

```
http://publib.boulder.ibm.com/infocenter/wchelp/v6r0m0/topic/com.ibm
.commerce.management-center_customization.doc/tutorial/ttfadsca.htm
```

- Tutorial: Adding a validation rule in the Marketing tool:

```
http://publib.boulder.ibm.com/infocenter/wchelp/v6r0m0/index.jsp?top
ic=/com.ibm.commerce.management-center_customization.doc/tutorial/tt
ftadval.htm
```

2.4 Editions

There are three editions of the WebSphere Commerce package: Express, Professional, and Enterprise.

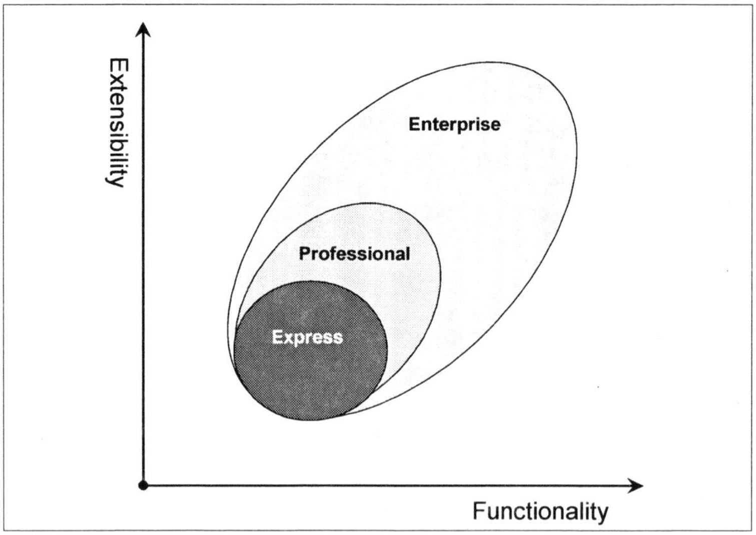

Figure 2-21 WebSphere Commerce editions

Express edition

"WebSphere Commerce-Express is an easily installed, affordable, yet complete solution designed to help growing mid-market companies do business on the Web. Start your online presence with the basics then grow with the industry leaders as your needs change. This edition provides the core capabilities growing firms need to get started or expand their eCommerce site at a minimum investment."

The typical features are listed here:

- Lightweight development
- Starter stores - Direct model
- Catalog import utility
- WebSphere Commerce business process models
- Sales catalogs
- Product configuration via Static and Dynamic Kit
- Streamlined installation
- Business user tools (such as Accelerator)
- eMarketing Spots to e-mail activity
- Manage e-mail
- Integration reference applications
- Migration wizard
- Payments plug-in controller
- Coremetrix Tag library
- Shipped with WebSphere Application Server Express
- Shipped with DB2® Express

Professional edition

"WebSphere Commerce Professional provides a comprehensive online selling solution for maximizing revenues, improving operational efficiencies, and increasing customer satisfaction and loyalty. This edition offers a robust online selling environment that enables companies to offer personalized, cross-channel shopping experiences. The product's infrastructure can support and integrate multiple sales channels and touch points, including Web, kiosk, point-of-sale (POS), call center and more."

In addition to the Express edition, the following features are (included but not limited to) supported in the Professional edition:

- IBM Sales Center Support
- Gift Center Support
- Buyer / Seller Administration
- Contract management
- Catalog Filtering
- Shipped with WebSphere Application Server ND
- Shipped with DB2 Universal Database™

Enterprise edition

"WebSphere Commerce Enterprise provides a powerful, flexible infrastructure based on a unified platform for running large, high-volume business-to-business and advanced business-to-consumer eCommerce Web sites for global e-businesses. It supports multiple sites, complex direct and indirect business models, workspace management, dynamic negotiations and role-based member management."

In addition to the Professional edition, the following advanced features are (included but not limited to) supported in the Enterprise edition:

- Workspaces
- Additional business models, such as Extended sites
- Business Relationship Management
- Sales center/CSR BI/operational reports
- Request For Quote (RFQ)
- Customer Service Representative (CSR) Price Override Approval

The packaging might be changed in future releases. You should refer to the release note for the most recent version available.

Choosing an edition

You must make a well advised decision on the right edition to fit your business growth and the budget. Our basic recommendation is to err on the side of trading up to a higher edition, if you can cost justify it.

You should determine the right edition of WebSphere Commerce for your business based on the factors including budget, business requirements for customizations, and future growth. Table 2-10 is a recommendation only.

Table 2-10 WebSphere Commerce editions and business profiles

Intended scale of WebSphere Commerce implementation[a]	Applicable WC Edition
Small	Express or Professional
Medium	Professional or Enterprise[b]
Large	Enterprise

a. See 1.3, "Small, medium, and large scale implementations" on page 16.
b. Further analysis is needed per scenario. However, upscale is better than downscale for future extensibility.

Note: WebSphere Commerce Developer is required in order to develop a custom solution for your business. For each edition mentioned — Express, Professional, and Enterprise — WebSphere Commerce Developer is available. You should use the edition of WebSphere Commerce Developer that matches your edition of WebSphere Commerce.

3

Complete your eCommerce solution

This chapter describes additional applications to complement an eCommerce solution.

First we discuss general integration approaches that you can use to attach WebSphere Commerce to your existing business processes and services, and also to attach to specialized commerce extensions provided by third parties.

In the second half of the chapter we discuss some of the commonly used extensions. In some cases, WebSphere Commerce provides specific extension points as part of the WebSphere Commerce product (for example, for payments), and in other cases, you have to customize WebSphere Commerce to attach it to a particular extension of your own.

3.1 Integration

In this section we review the methods that you can employ to integrate external systems with your WebSphere Commerce site. There are many points in WebSphere Commerce to integrate with third-party software such as payment systems to complete your solution. You can also integrate with back-end systems that perform tasks such as order management and order fulfillment.

First we review some Service Oriented Architecture (SOA) concepts and explain where WebSphere Commerce fits into the SOA paradigm. Then we discuss the most commonly used technologies for integration: WebSphere MQ, Web services, and WebSphere ESB.

3.1.1 Service Oriented Architecture (SOA)

SOA is an integration architecture approach based on the concept of a service. The business and infrastructure functions that are required to build distributed systems are provided as services that collectively, or individually, deliver application functionality to either end-user applications or other services. Applications collaborate by invoking each other's services. Services are composed into larger sequences to implement business processes. SOA requires a consistent mechanism for services to communicate. That mechanism should be loosely coupled and should support the use of explicit interfaces.

In SOA there is a life cycle that flows from gathering business requirements to maintaining the system. The first stage is to capture and model the components of a business, and the business processes the organization uses. These business processes carry out the activities the business components are responsible for. Some of these business processes are represented by process models, and the activities the processes perform modelled as services — either carried out manually, or performed by software.

If the process model is deployed as an IT process model, and linked to real activities that are carried out in the business, then the day-to-day operations of the business can be monitored and managed. This flow is what is known as the SOA life cycle of Model, Assemble, Deploy, and Manage. IBM provides tools to aid in activities performed at each stage of the life cycle, called IBM Foundation Tooling. For detailed exploration of IBM SOA see *"IBM SOA Foundation - An Architectural Introduction and Overview",* found at:

`http://download.boulder.ibm.com/ibmdl/pub/software/dw/webservices/ws-soa-whitepaper.pdf`

If you are new to WebSphere and SOA, see also:

`http://www.ibm.com/developerworks/WebSphere/newtosoa/index.html`

Implementing IBM SOA helps your company realize the following benefits:

- Alignment of business and IT
- Loosely coupled components and systems
- A network-based infrastructure, enabling geographically and technologically, diverse resources to work together
- Greater code reuse
- Better process standardization throughout the enterprise

IBM describes four phases for SOA adoption:

1. Implementing individual Web services:

   Creating services from tasks contained in new or existing applications.

2. Service-oriented integration of business functions:

   Integrating services across multiple applications inside and outside the enterprise to achieve a specific business objective.

3. Enterprise-wide IT transformation:

   An architected implementation enabling integration across business functions throughout an enterprise.

4. On Demand Business Transformation:

   Broad transformation of existing business models or the deployment of new business models.

WebSphere Commerce 6.0 supports the use of Web services as described in phase 1. With the use of the enhancements included in the WebSphere Commerce Feature Pack 1 for version 6.0, the WebSphere Commerce is enabled to phase 2: Service-oriented Integration (SOI).

WebSphere Commerce has enabled SOI scenarios specifically focused on back-office integration, especially on external order management systems (OMS) and with enterprise resource planning systems (ERP). Reference implementations for OMS and ERP scenarios are available as part of WebSphere Commerce Enhancements for version 6. For information about SOA Logical Architecture and WebSphere Commerce back-office integration, refer to:

```
http://publib.boulder.ibm.com/infocenter/wchelp/v6r0m0/index.jsp?topic=
/com.ibm.commerce.developer.doc/concepts/csdsoasoi.htm
```

WebSphere Commerce provides SOI support for these three components:

- Member
- Order
- Catalog

Incoming and outgoing commerce services are in the form of standardized XML messages. Http and JMS transports are supported. Integration between IBM WebSphere Commerce and a third-party application or back-end system is accomplished over an enterprise service bus, through WebSphere MQ channels or via Web services.

3.1.2 Enterprise Service Bus

The Enterprise Service Bus (ESB) is an architecture that provides different business applications the ability to communicate among themselves using a common service transport. An ESB removes the coupling between a service and the transport used to carry that service. The services are called and delivered in the form of standardized XML messages. This allows integration specialists to use the ESB as a platform to integrate applications that run on a variety of mainframe and workstation operating systems. IBM implements the ESB architecture with three main products: WebSphere DataPower® Integration Appliance, WebSphere Enterprise Server Bus (WESB) and WebSphere Message Broker. WESB supports communication over the following transports: JMS, WebSphere MQ, TCP/IP, SSL, Http(s).

For further information about ESB implementations, refer to the following Redbooks:

1. *"Connecting Enterprise Applications to WebSphere Enterprise Service Bus"*, SG24-7406, at:

   `http://www.redbooks.ibm.com/abstracts/sg247406.html`

2. *"Using IBM WebSphere Message Broker as an ESB with WebSphere Process Server"*, SG24-7527, at:

   `http://www.redbooks.ibm.com/abstracts/sg247527.html?Open"`

3. *"Patterns: SOA Design Using WebSphere Message Broker and WebSphere ESB"*, SG24-7369, at:

   `http://www.redbooks.ibm.com/abstracts/sg247369.html?Open`

4. *"IBM WebSphere DataPower SOA Appliances Part I: Overview and Getting Started"*, REDP-4327, at:

   `http://www.redbooks.ibm.com/redpieces/abstracts/redp4327.html?Open`

Figure 3-1 shows the general strategy of IBM to implement SOA using an ESB. The services currently offered by WebSphere Commerce support communication via the ESB between the Business Application Services and the Access Services.

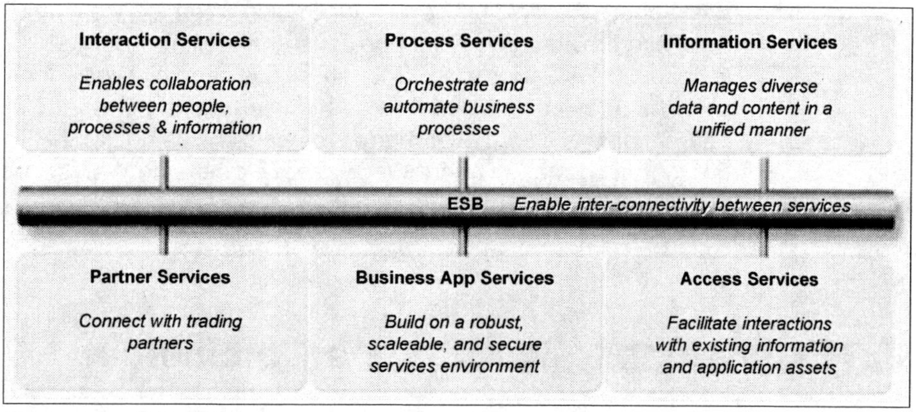

Figure 3-1 IBM ESB and Services

Further integration with the other components is discussed in the interesting IBM developerWorks® article, *"Migrating WebSphere Commerce to the SOA foundation tooling"*, at:

`http://www.ibm.com/developerworks/WebSphere/library/techarticles/0611_mohan/0611_mohan.html`

3.1.3 WebSphere MQ

Another method for communication with third-party and back-end systems is through messaging. WebSphere MQ is the market leader in messaging technology. WebSphere MQ can be used in conjunction with WESB to connect WESB to applications using WebSphere MQ or JMS over MQ. For more information about WebSphere MQ, see:

`http://www-306.ibm.com/software/integration/wmq/index.html?`

3.1.4 Web services (SOAP/Http and SOAP/JMS)

WebSphere Commerce uses the WebSphere Application Server engine to support Web services. Therefore, implementing a Web service in WebSphere Commerce is not much different from implementing Web services for any other WebSphere Application Server application. WebSphere Commerce acts as both a service provider and a service consumer. Following the W3C definition of Web services, the standardized XML messages used by WebSphere Commerce services or by customized services to integrate to third-party or back-end applications, are sent over many protocols, including JMS, Http(s) and MQ. For more information about WebSphere Commerce Web services, see:

`http://publib.boulder.ibm.com/infocenter/wchelp/v6r0m0/index.jsp?topic=/com.ibm.commerce.webservices.doc/concepts/cwvwc55webservicesguide08.htm`

3.2 Extensions to WebSphere Commerce

In the sections that follow, we explore the extensions that people commonly add to their WebSphere Commerce deployment. Many of the extensions, some of which involve third party software, are "pre-integrated" with WebSphere Commerce, in the sense WebSphere Commerce provides a framework, with extension points, into which it is relatively straightforward to plug the third party implementation.

Figure 3-2 illustrates the extensions that we discuss in the following sections:

- 3.2.1, "Catalog management" on page 95
- 3.2.2, "Content management" on page 99
- 3.2.3, "Advanced search" on page 101
- 3.2.4, "Order management system" on page 104
- 3.2.5, "Inventory management" on page 111
- 3.2.6, "Shipping" on page 114
- 3.2.7, "Tax calculation" on page 115
- 3.2.8, "Analytics" on page 115
- 3.2.9, "Payment processing" on page 118
- 3.2.10, "Call center integration" on page 118
- 3.2.11, "Collaboration" on page 119
- 3.2.12, "Member management" on page 121

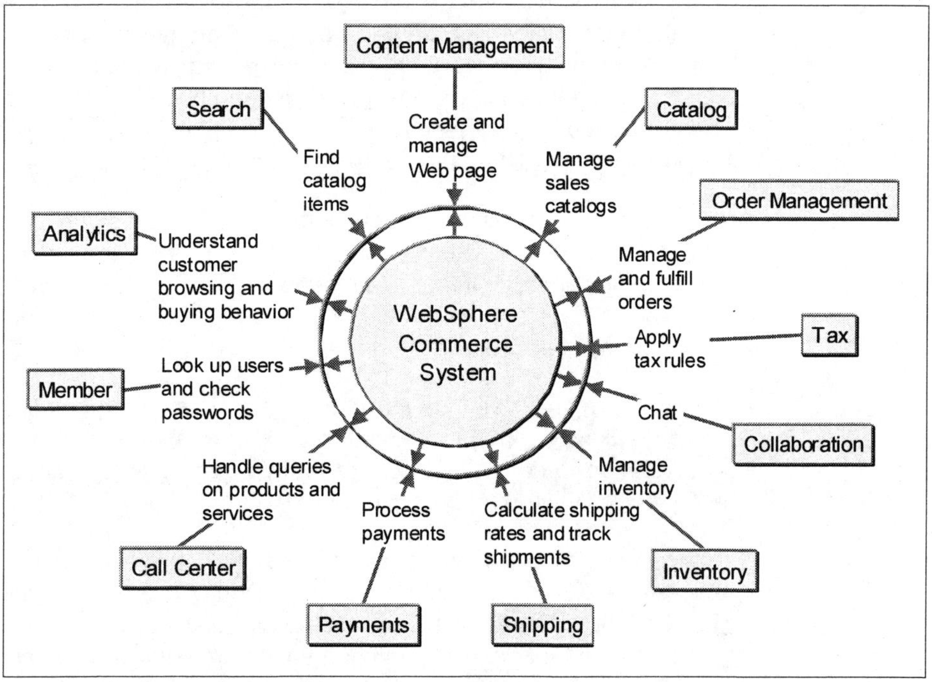

Figure 3-2 Extendable parts of a WebSphere Commerce system

3.2.1 Catalog management

In this section we discuss the value and added flexibility in sourcing catalog data from external systems, what you have to do in order to achieve a feature rich online catalog, and an example of integration with a product management information system.

Requirement for integration with external systems

Catalog management is the heart of any eCommerce system. The catalog contains most of the products and services that are saleable in a business. Businesses have their brands, products, and pricing content spread throughout the enterprise and sometimes even outside of it. This requires a complex data load process to update the contents of an eCommerce site.

There are many challenges in designing an electronic catalog to meet the requirements of a business. This often calls for an extension or modification of the catalog component that is provided in WebSphere Commerce for integration with external systems. Refer to 2.2.2, "Catalog" on page 45 for details on what is provided in WebSphere Commerce.

Today online shoppers use information in the catalog for extensive research before making a purchase. As such, the information in the catalog has to be accurate, up-to-date, and informative. Informative Web content is fast becoming a key communicator of brand image.

The complexity of the catalog depends on the nature and the volume of products and services. In small businesses, the product data feeds are limited to a single data source or none at all. Their catalog is relatively small, having fewer product attributes to manage. Business users who are contributing to the catalog are limited and often do not require a workflow or approval process. In the case of medium and large businesses, the catalog update process consists of product data feeds from multiple sources, incorporates many product attributes, many business users, and a complicated workflow. To deliver accurate and consistent catalog data to an eCommerce system requires efficient processes and products to automate those processes in a reliable and repeatable way.

What needs to be done

In case of medium to large businesses, you should first identify the systems that contribute to the catalog data. A typical scenario of aggregating and loading the data is show in Figure 3-3.

In case of small businesses, catalog data load is a one time activity from their existing system. Since the number of products are limited, sometimes the catalog data is entered manually.

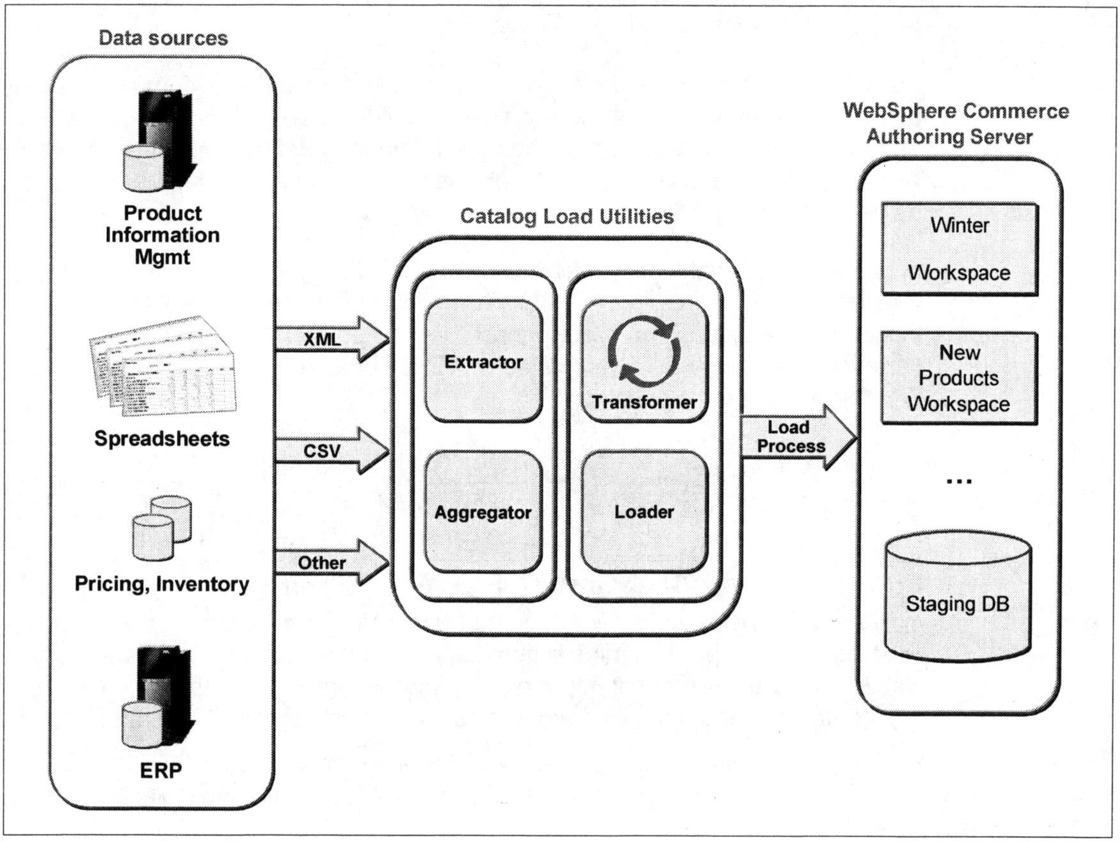

Figure 3-3 Typical catalog load process

WebSphere Commerce provides some catalog load utilities. Refer to 2.3, "WebSphere Commerce Tools" on page 69 for details on load utilities.

Apart from out-of-the-box utilities, there is an asset developed by IBM Software Services for WebSphere team to load massive amounts of data. This asset is called Business Object Data Load (BODL). Get in touch with your IBM contact for more information about the availability of the asset which is only provided as part of a service engagement.

Extraction and aggregation functionalities become very complex. Consider evaluating additional products that specialize in the extraction, transmission and transformation of data, for example, WebSphere DataStage® (now called WebSphere Transformation Extender. These products have extensive wizards and templates to simplify defining data transformation, aggregation and extraction functions that are much more maintainable than writing code to perform the same functions, and put in the hands of someone who understands the business requirements and data models removes the need to involve a programmer to create the transformations.

Since the structure and the elements that make up a catalog is complex, there is a need to extend the out-of-the-box schemas to support unique requirements. The best practice to extend the catalog schema is to define additional tables, though in some cases, the custom fields in the existing out-of-the-box tables can be used to meet the requirements at less expense.

In naming additional tables, WebSphere Commerce recommends always begin with letter X, for example, XATTRIBUTE to define extended attributes which are unique to the business. In WebSphere Commerce, each table has a corresponding entity EJB associated with it. So consider creating a new entity EJB for the new table defined.

Caution: Service providers usually consider modifications to tables to take a sizing to "large", which means from nine months in deployment effort.

Integration with WebSphere Product Center

In this section we discuss the integration with one of the "add-on" catalog data sources, that is, a product information management system. WebSphere Product Center is a popular product information management solution for the enterprise that centralizes and optimizes product data. Here are some of the features:

- Provides a single source of product information to various channels: eCommerce applications, printed documents and marketing collateral, kiosks and mobile devices.
- Synchronizes information internally with existing enterprise systems and externally with business and trading partners.
- Provides modeling of product attributes and categories, organizational structures, and related business processes.
- Work flow supports multi-department as well as multi-enterprise business processes enabling key users to introduce, authorize, maintain and enhance product information through standard business processes.

The integration with WebSphere Product Center combines the capabilities of WebSphere Commerce with the WebSphere Product Center's product information management features.

The integration involves designing WebSphere Commerce specific models in WebSphere Product Center such as categories, catalog entries (product, item, bundles, static kits), attributes, pricing, and merchandising associations. This is accomplished by use of WebSphere Product Center scripts.

Another aspect of integration is the ability to export the data from WPC, using the models defined above, in the form of XML. The XML data is then imported into WebSphere Commerce using the loading utilities.

Figure 3-4 pictorially depicts WebSphere Product Center powering various channels, including the eCommerce system.

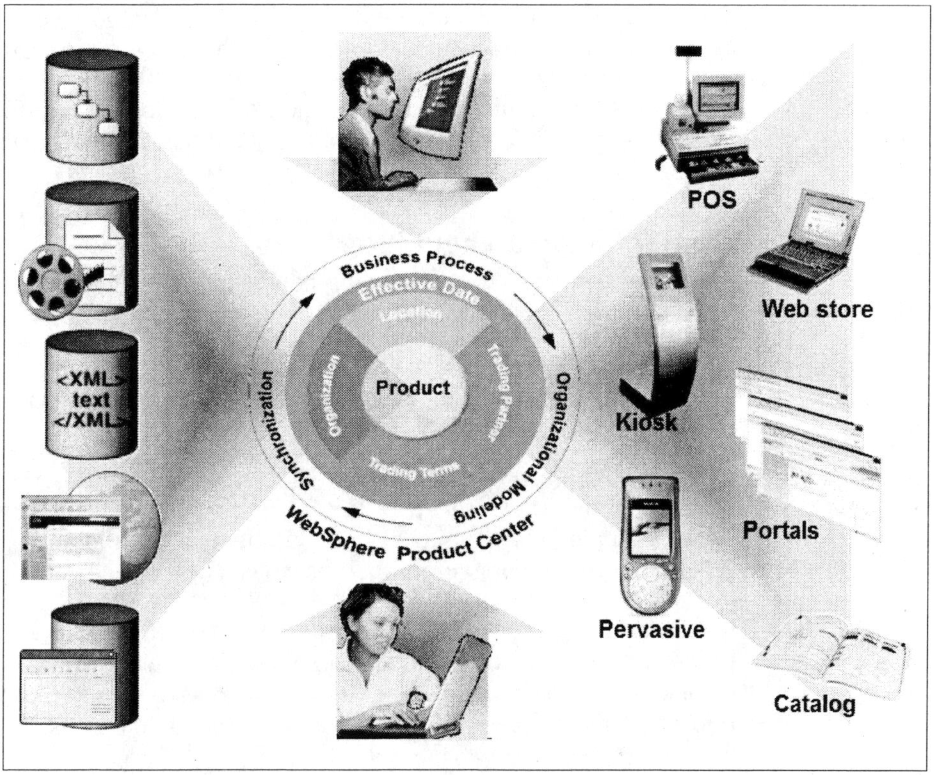

Figure 3-4 WebSphere Product Center Integration

3.2.2 Content management

Unless you have only a small Web site, you will have a team of business users creating content to be delivered to your Web site. To help them get the content right, they need tools to assist with content authoring and management of content — including versioning and processes to help review and publish content. Web content management tools generally provide:

- Role based access control to content (author, editor, reviewer)
- Authoring, using browser-based templates or conversion from a word-processing application.

- A content repository with library services, such as check-in/check-out and versioning.
- Review and approval workflow.
- Conversion to HTML or XML and support of templates for Web rendering.
- Managed delivery of content to Web servers or site management systems.

Since Web content management requires sophisticated business processes to be in place, it is usually considered by medium to large installations.

Web content management does not address catalog management issues, nor does it necessarily provide a repository of images to be associated with catalog items.

Content management interfaces

There are a number of interfaces to consider when integrating content management software with WebSphere Commerce:

- Common user repository for user authentication and authorization.
- Content management process flow interaction with WebSphere Commerce process flow.
- Content repository information access mechanisms.

For coordinated management of user authentication and authorization, see 3.2.12, "Member management" on page 121.

Content management process flow interaction with WebSphere Commerce process flow is too complex to discuss here in detail. In summary, business decisions have to be made as to how Web content creation, approval, and publishing integrate with the WebSphere Commerce process flow for catalog management and marketing publishing.

There are also business and technical choices on how to design Web site navigation through the content in the repository. Is the navigation authored along with the content in the content management system, or are the Web pages and navigation built with WebSphere Commerce tools? Do the pages then directly access content in the content management system using a proxy mechanism, or is the content transferred to the WebSphere Commerce database or file system?

Content management extensions

Should you need to integrate access control between the content management system and WebSphere Commerce, it needs careful planning. You can have one source of authentication, but the content management system and WebSphere Commerce retain their own authorization controls. Authorization of WebSphere

Commerce functions must remain within WebSphere Commerce. Authentication can be made to an external user repository through documented interfaces.

There are two ways to interface WebSphere Commerce to a content management system. Either make Web service calls to interact with WebSphere Commerce business flow, or alter the WebSphere Commerce Web interface to request content directly from the content management system.

The Web service interface allows the content management to interact with all aspects of the WebSphere Commerce System. In this mode, the content management system is in control of the user interface and makes decisions which commerce functions to call. The Web services interface is extendible with new calls, and there are new Web service capabilities in the feature packs for WebSphere Commerce v6.0.

Web interface integration between WebSphere Commerce and Web content management requires custom development. WebSphere Commerce retrieves content from the Web content management system then delivers the content as if it originated from the WebSphere Commerce system. The code required to integrate with the Web content management can be as simple as displaying flat pre-rendered Web content from the Web content management system, or as complex as dovetailing the Web content management business flow with the business flow of catalog management and marketing publishing.

Extension examples

WebSphere Commerce v6.0 Feature Pack 2 offers packaged integration with IBM's Workplace™ Web Content Management free through the support pages for WebSphere Commerce. See the description in the InfoCenter, at:

```
http://publib.boulder.ibm.com/infocenter/wchelp/v6r0m0/index.jsp?topic=
/com.ibm.commerce.wcm.refapp.doc/concepts/cwo_wcm_integrate.htm
```

The IBM Workplace Web Content Management™ integration with WebSphere Commerce uses the Web approach, rather than Web services, and couples the IBM Workplace Web Content Management content management flow with the WebSphere Commerce workspaces process flow. The solution uses custom WebSphere Commerce data beans to pre-render the IBM Workplace Web Content Management content on shared file storage and a custom servlet for the IBM Workplace Web Content Management instance to access the content.

3.2.3 Advanced search

In this section, we discuss several options for adding advanced search capabilities to WebSphere Commerce v6.0. While the search capabilities that are provided with WebSphere Commerce v6.0 are an improvement over prior releases, many online retailers find it essential to replace or augment the search with improved features. Some of the additional functions that are being requested include:

- Integration of catalog and site search capabilities
- Ordering search results based upon dynamic rule sets
- Integration of Web 2.0 technologies into the search process
- User driven dynamic filtering of the search results

Integration with WebSphere Commerce

Integrating advanced search capabilities into WebSphere Commerce is a four step process:

1. Select a product that best fits your requirements.

   There are quite a few on the market; we discuss three:

   - IBM OmniFind™ Discovery Edition
   - Endeca
   - Mercado

   Several products have an option of either purchasing the software or buying a service where the vendor manages the server and you pay a monthly fee. You have to determine which is right for your business.

2. When the server software is ready, integrate the server into your store.

   Do this by overriding the WebSphere commerce search commands with commands that call new server. You also have to modify the Java Server Pages for search and search results to incorporate features of your selected product. The integration work requires deep knowledge of WebSphere Commerce and the selected product. You need to get someone experienced to help you complete this task.

3. Configure the search.

   Do not underestimate this effort: You need to customize the logic and vocabularies of the search engine to your particular products and marketing strategies to get the best search results for your customers. It has to be an ongoing effort, as your product range and catalog changes.

4. Monitor the results of your customers' searches regularly.

   Ensure that the right products are being displayed. The more customers find the products they want, and the more they believe that the search has not overlooked what they are really looking for, the better your repeat business, and the better your conversion of browse into buy. These are the goals of an advanced search capability.

IBM OmniFind Discovery Edition

OmniFind Discovery Edition is built on a foundation of contextual understanding, adaptive presentation, tools for business users, and packaged market solutions.

- Contextual understanding combines a real-time understanding of user intent and application context to optimize relevance of information that is delivered:

  `When a user queries "what is Bluetooth" a definition is delivered.`

- Adaptive presentation guides the discovery process by presenting answers, navigational refinement options, and proactive guidance in a format that helps people take action.
- Business user tools allow organizations to continually enhance the self-service experience without reliance on IT. The bundled analytics guide to tuning workflow includes extending the vocabulary of the system, tweaking relevance, crafting targeted promotions, and modifying the page layout.
- Packaged market solutions provide industry vocabularies, configuration logic, and application UIs to speed implementation time and accelerate an organization's ability to realize ROI.

IBM provides a pre-built module to assist in the integration of OmniFind and WebSphere Commerce. It is called *"IBM Commerce Module for OmniFind Discovery Edition"* and is available to integrate with WebSphere Commerce v6.0.

In Feature Pack 1, WebSphere Commerce provided additional customization to speed up integration with Omnifind, called *"OmniFind Discovery Edition integration for WebSphere Commerce."*

You can find more information about OmniFind at:

`http://www-306.ibm.com/software/data/enterprise-search/omnifind-discovery/`

Integration with WebSphere Commerce is described at:

`http://www-306.ibm.com/software/data/enterprise-search/omnifind-discovery/commerce.html`

Specifically regarding the integration with Feature Pack 1, see:

`http://publib.boulder.ibm.com/infocenter/discover/v8r4/index.jsp?topic=/com.ibm.discovery.ds.commerce.doc/overview.htm`

For the enhancements in Feature Pack 1 of WebSphere Commerce, the integration includes:

- Automatic re-spelling, stemming, and vocabulary relationships such as synonyms and related terms to help the system understand the shopper's intent

- Navigation controls that allow users to narrow down the search results by using faceted navigation
- Automatic updating of the navigation options when new product categories are added to the product catalog
- Ability to perform search-based merchandising to provide targeted offers and information based on the shopper's specific interests and profile
- Business user analytics for monitoring shopper behavior and effectiveness of promotions
- User interfaces that provide an intuitive user experience
- Pre-packaged connector to acquire product catalog information and rapidly create rich search indexes, which:
  - Extracts product attributes such as size, color, brand, and price from the WebSphere Commerce catalog and uses these attributes to filter the search results
  - Supports WebSphere Commerce data modeling such as product bundling
- Support for WebSphere Commerce e-Sites and contracts

Endeca

Endeca has a great deal of experience in this space and should be considered. They have a professional services organization that performs the integration and assists in the product configuration to gain the best results and improve the ROI. More information about Endeca is found at:

`http://endeca.com/`

Mercado

Mercado offers both a perpetual license and an on-demand option. They also have a professional services organization to assist in the implementation and configuration of their products. More information about Mercado and their offerings is found at:

`http://www.mercado.com/`

3.2.4 Order management system

In an integrated solution, WebSphere Commerce provides Web and rich client user interfaces for the different sales channels. The Order Management subsystem is a component that provides shopping carts, order capture, order fulfillment, inventory, and payment function support. The Order Management subsystem provides a set of services that can interact with other systems, internal or external. These external services represent subsets of the functionality of the Order Management subsystem.

The integrated OMS in Figure 3-5 represents a generic order management solution on the WebSphere Commerce platform using the order management system components into WebSphere Commerce. The solution is a mixture of the WebSphere Commerce out-of-the-box order management subsystem and external components.

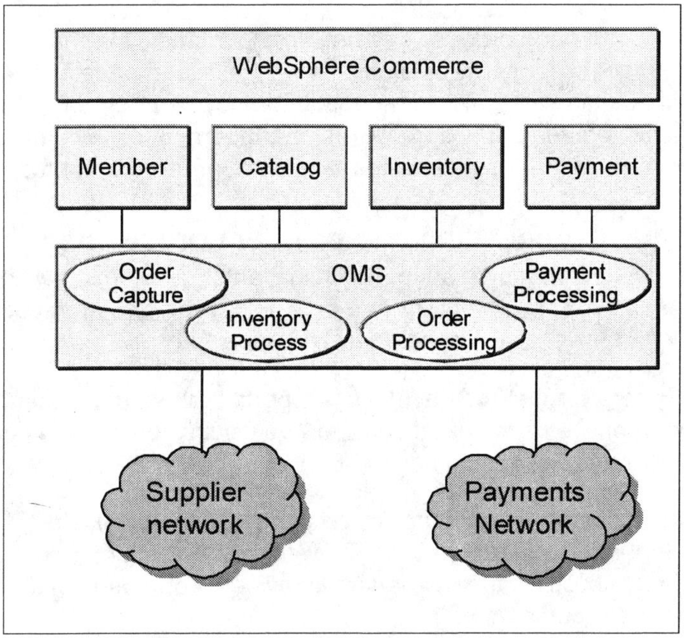

Figure 3-5 integrated OMS solution

Order management is broadly divided into four processes:

- Order capture
- Order processing
- Inventory processing
- Payment processing

Order capture and order processing

Order capture provides functionality such as sales quotes, requisition lists, and shopping carts, and order submission. With it, you can:

- Create, find, edit, submit, copy and cancel orders
- Create, find, edit, copy, and cancel quotes
- Add, edit, and remove shipping instructions for orders
- Add, edit, and remove payment instructions for orders and quotes

Order processing is responsible for the overall coordination of inventory allocation, payment processing, order fulfillment, and tracking order status and for driving the order life cycle through conclusion. For example, this involves the ability to present status and details of the order, drive fulfillment systems to process the order, track releases associated with the order, and interact with inventory and with payment systems.

Order capture and order processing are handled by internal WebSphere Commerce components as shown in Figure 3-5 on page 105. Also see "Integrating an external order management system" on page 106, where we discuss integrating an external order management system using the programming interfaces provided with WebSphere Commerce.

Inventory processing and payment processing

WebSphere Commerce supports four inventory systems: Available to promise (ATP), non-ATP, no inventory, and external inventory. We discuss the inventory solution in "Inventory management" on page 111.

WebSphere Commerce Payments supports the use of payment plug-ins for offline or online payment processing. We discuss payment processing in "Payment processing" on page 118.

The solution shown in Figure 3-5 on page 105 makes use of the ability of WebSphere Commerce to integrate with external inventory and payment systems to build a order management system composed of a mixture of internal and external components.

Integrating an external order management system

In an enterprise where orders are managed by a dedicated back-end system, WebSphere Commerce offers the ability to seamlessly integrate with the order management system using SOA, providing an integrated e-business solution that encompasses the entire order life cycle. Figure 3-6 shows the high-level view of the integrated solution with emphasis on multiple interfaces to external systems. In the following sections, we explain the means of connecting WebSphere Commerce to an external OMS.

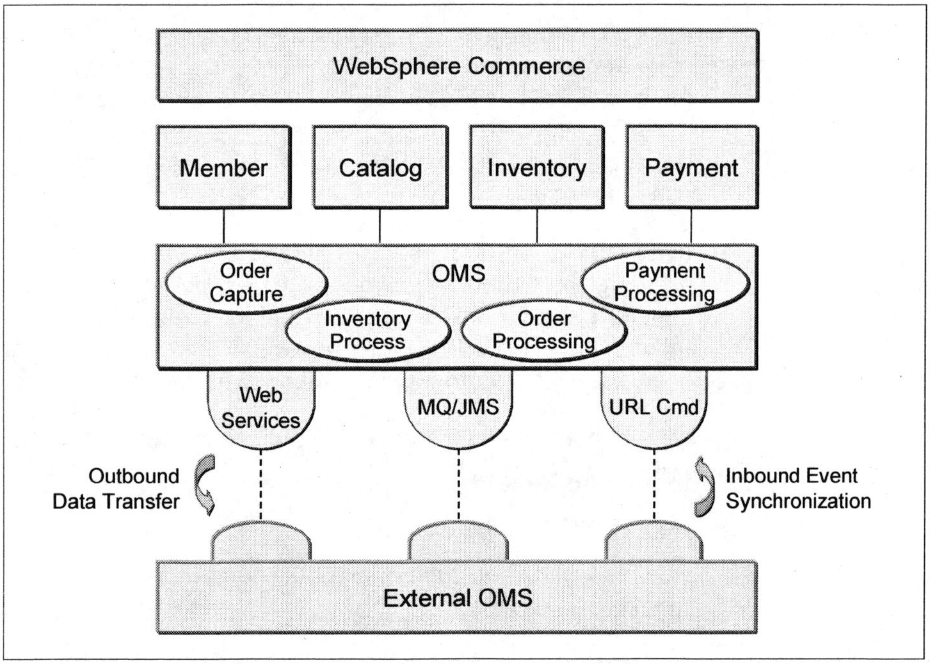

Figure 3-6 Order Management System Integration Interface

Packaged integrations

Feature Pack 1 of WebSphere Commerce includes pre-built integrations for SAP® and Sterling Order Management PCA built on top of the Web services integration which is also available in the Feature Pack. The additional integration features, available free of charge to WebSphere Commerce v6.0 customers, can be found at:

`http://www-1.ibm.com/support/docview.wss?uid=swg24013534`

Web services

WebSphere Commerce provides a set of Web services as a service provider itself and it can act as a service requester, or client, to external Web services.

The OMS processes, `OrderCreate` and `OrderStatus`, are examples of the Web services provided by WebSphere Commerce. When invoked, these services generate SOAP based XML messages that are consumed by the invoker. In the other direction, based on the known WSDL of an existing Web service, client code can be generated using WebSphere Commerce Developer to send Web service requests.

MQ / JMS messaging

Asynchronous messaging has been a key factor historically in integrating discrete applications into a common enterprise architecture. WebSphere Commerce OMS has WebSphere MQ messaging capability built-in. This capability is especially valuable for OMS integration with back-end systems that also use WebSphere MQ messaging in either native unformatted MQ or JMS message formats.

If your OMS system is not enabled for WebSphere MQ messaging, then there is a considerable worldwide pool of skill to help you write an adapter to WebSphere MQ, either by exploiting existing integration points in the OMS system, or by "piggybacking" on OMS import/export capabilities using file transfer, or perhaps by using the WebSphere MQ integration available for DB2 and Oracle®.

There are many types of messaging defined in WebSphere Commerce:

Outbound notification

- Report_NC_PurchaseOrder

  Notifies a back-end system of a new purchase order.

Back-end inbound notification

- Update WC Order Status

  Updates the status of an order that already exists in the WebSphere Commerce database.

Update WC Product Inventory

- Update WC inventory

  Updates the inventory for a product that already exists in the WebSphere Commerce database.

Outbound request and reply

- Update_WCS_ShoppingCartTransfer

  Shopping Cart Transfer Response to confirm a customer's shopping cart has been successfully transferred to an external system.

- Update_WCS_BatchAvailability

  Batch Inventory Availability Response to provide inventory availability information.

- Request_WCS_BE_ProductInventory

  Inventory Availability Check Response.

Inbound request and reply

- PriceAndAvailabilityRequest

  The originating request to get price, quantity, and availability information for product items of interest to customers. The message requests the price, quantity, and availability information about a list of items.

- Create_WCS_PickBatch

  To create a pick batch record in the WebSphere Commerce database. This message is ideal for instances when a fulfillment center manages the pick batch functions. The fulfillment center sends one of these messages to WebSphere Commerce to create a pick batch in the WebSphere Commerce database.

These sample messages are a portion of the defined messages in WebSphere Commerce. Add new or modified messages as part of your customization, if required.

URL commands

URL commands invoke integration tasks. There are defined URL commands for invoking OMS. The source of the Http request might be the external OMS, or from suppliers or fulfillment centers responding to events in the order fulfillment life cycle.

Here is an example of invoking a URL command:

```
http://myhostname/webapp/wcs/stores/servlet/ReturnProcess?RMAId=1&store
Id=1&URL=ReturnDisplay&URL2=ReturnListDisplay
```

We have listed OMS commands in Figure 3-1. The list is an example of what you can do with the commands packaged with the OMS framework in WebSphere Commerce. New commands can be added to meet your business requirements by customizing

Table 3-1 OMS URL commands

Category	Command	Description
Orders	DynamicKitConfigurationAdd	Configure dynamic kits. A kit contains multiple products, is ordered and returned as a unit, and has one price and one SKU. The information about the products contained in a dynamic kit is controlled by an external configurator.
	OrderCancel	Cancel the specified order by changing its order status to X, reversing any inventory allocations and canceling any backordered items.
	OrderCopy	Create, merge, or modify pending orders.
	OrderDisplay	Display the contents of the specified order.
	OrderList	Display a list of the customer's orders.
	OrderPrepare	Prepare an order by determining prices, discounts, shipping charges, and taxes for an order.
	OrderProcess	Submit an order. This invokes multiple commands including payment and so on.
	OrderCalculate	Determines a list of catalog items to be included in an Order, adds them to the Order by calling OrderItemAdd if they are not already in it, and recalculates specified CalculationUsages.
	OrderProfileUpdate	Create or update a customer's default billing and shipping addresses, shipping mode and payment information.
	OrderSchedule	Submit a recurring order, which will be processed by the scheduler.
	OrderUnlock	Unlock an order that was previously locked by the OrderPrepare URL.
	ScheduledOrderCancel	Cancel execution of a recurring order submitted by the OrderSchedule URL.
	SetOrderTemplate	Set or reset a "template" order or as a "current template" order.
	SetPendingOrder	Set a pending order as the current pending order.
OrderItems (specific products in an order)	OrderItemAdd	Add items or products to the list of items that are to be shipped.
	OrderItemDelete	Delete an order item from a pending order.
	OrderItemDisplay	List all order items which are in pending status.
	OrderItemMove	Split an order by moving order items from one order to another order.
	OrderItemSelect	Create or update order items in a quotation-selection order.
	OrderItemUpdate	Update order items in an order.
	InventoryAllocationCheck	Display a list of order items based on the status of the order items in specified orders.
OrderQuotation	OrderQuotationCheck	Check for quotation orders.
	OrderQuotationCreate	Create a quotation order.
	OrderQuotationDisplay	Display quotation information.
	OrderQuotationRequest	Submit request-for-quotation orders to quote-enabled stores.

Returns	ReturnCancel	Cancel a return merchandise authorization (RMA).
	ReturnCreditAndCloseScan	A scheduled URL designed to perform refunds.
	ReturnDisplay	Display the contents of the specified RMA.
	ReturnItemAdd	Add items to an RMA.
	ReturnItemDelete	Delete an item from an RMA.
	ReturnItemUpdate	Update information about a returned item.
	ReturnListDisplay	List all RMAs for a customer.
	ReturnPrepare	Prepare an RMA by calculating taxes to be refunded and rolls up the total credit to the RMA.
	ReturnProcess	Check to see if an RMA can be approved, and if so, the state of the RMA is changed to approved.
Requisition list	RequisitionListCopy	Copy an existing order or requisition list to a new requisition list.
	RequisitionListCreate	Create an empty requisition list.
	RequisitionListDelete	Delete one or more requisition lists.
	RequisitionListDisplay	Display one or more requisition lists.
	RequisitionListItemUpdate	Add, update, and delete items in a requisition list.
	RequisitionListSubmit	Submit a requisition list for order processing.
	RequisitionListUpdate	Change the requisition list type and update the billing and payment information.

3.2.5 Inventory management

A customer contacts you via one of your channels, perhaps by fax, and asks for a product that he wants immediately. Is your staff able to respond accurately to the customer's query? If the order is confirmed, are you making money from this deal? Compared with the bricks and mortar world, where the customer picks up the goods straightaway, the enemy in the eCommerce world is delayed gratification.

Mastering inventory is the big challenge. To fight the enemy, you want to fulfill the customer's order predictably and without delay. You need to organize your inventory to do so and to make money at the same time. This is the eFulfillment challenge and the holy grail of eCommerce.

Inventory management is one activity among others in eFulfillment. It ensures that orders are confirmed or promised with confidence and without excessive investment in inventory. The major goal of inventory management is to minimize the amount of cash tied up in stock and warehousing and to meet demand instantly.

The leanest way to do this is to practice just-in-time inventory management. But the leanest way is also a difficult way. You have to balance the cost of holding stock, the cost of replenishing the inventory, which varies with the size of stock delivery and the size of order you committed to the supplier, and the cost of shortage where there is not enough stock to meet demand.

WebSphere Commerce out-of-the-box provides your business with real-time inventory information that helps you to meet this eFulfillment challenge and operate your business efficiently. In WebSphere Commerce, inventory details are kept up to date for all your sales channels including Web, telesales, retail and distribution, so you can promise orders with a high degree of certainty that the stock is available. Added to this, WebSphere Commerce provides a framework to integrate fulfillment systems, automate workflow, and monitor the entire demand and fulfillment process. You need never be in the dark about the position of orders and inventories.

In WebSphere Commerce there are different types of inventory that are fulfilled. These are items, products, SKUs, bundles, and prebuilt kits. There are features such as kitting, serial number and lot tracking, multiple units of measure, and more, which give you the flexibility to manage inventory in a complex business environment and provide you with real-time information.

Product management tools

There are various Product Management wizards and notebooks in WebSphere Commerce Accelerator to manage products in your store's master catalog. Using the tools, you can track inventory, allow backorder, force backorder, release separately, and specify that a given product should not be returned.

You can update catalog entries directly using the Product Management dynamic table. Using the Product Management tools, you can work with the catalog assets shown in Table 3-2.

Table 3-2 Catalog entries

Catalog entry	Attributes	Description
Products	SKUs	Store Keeping Unit, See “Items” on page 46 and “SKUs” on page 339
	Bundles and Kits	See “Bundles and kits” on page 47 and on page 339
Categories		A category, also known as a catalog group, is used to group products and services offered by the store. You can create, find, list, change, and delete categories. You can classify products and under different parent categories

Catalog entry	Attributes	Description
Attributes	Defining	Defining attributes are attributes that are used to resolve SKUs (Key field)
	Descriptive	Descriptive attributes are attributes that provide additional descriptions but are not used to resolve SKUs.
Pricing		A price for a product or SKU, in one or more currencies, along with a set of conditions such as setting a price for different quantities (for example, 1 to 5, 6 or more), which must be satisfied in order to use the price. You can create, list, and change pricing associated with a product or SKU
Merchandising associations		Merchandising associations suggest additional, different, or replacement products based on a selected catalog entry. The merchandising associations are used as a product recommendation strategy to increase store sales
Track inventory	Track	Use WebSphere Commerce to track inventory
	Do Not Track	
	Externally Track	Use an external system to track inventory.

Inventory extensions

WebSphere Commerce provides several ways to integrate with back office processes to complete the entire order life cycle.

One important class of back office systems are Enterprise Resource Planning (ERP) systems. Integration between WebSphere Commerce and ERP systems combines the strength of WebSphere Commerce as an eCommerce system with the flexibility and power of dedicated ERP systems. The combination offers a competitive alternative to using the eCommerce offerings packaged by ERP vendors. The combination has the advantage of WebSphere Commerce's multi-channel sales integration and tools to manage the Web store, and also integrates with your existing ERP system for a single point of control for master catalog, inventory, and members.

Feature Pack 1 includes integration with the SAP ERP system. The ERP system provides the master catalog, inventory and member information system to WebSphere Commerce. It processes the orders and performs inventory management, and WebSphere Commerce presents rich content to the customers and captures the orders.

3.2.6 Shipping

A customer contacts you via one of your channels, perhaps by phone, asking for a different delivery date on a product that is wanted immediately, and the item has been logged in as a confirmed order. Can you promise a delivery date that is suitable to your customer? Can your customer track their order until it is delivered to them on your Web site? Or do you provide free marketing for a third party shipment company's Web site instead of bringing your customer back to your Web site, and lose opportunities for further sales? We know that shipping is one of the greatest influences on customer satisfaction — are you going to leave that for someone else to control!?

The WebSphere Shipping Module is tied into the order-fulfillment process and provides timely, accurate information when an item is shipped and the expected arrival date, the carrier shipping the item, and visibility into the carrier's network to track the item.

As explained in "Shipping" on page 53, the WebSphere Commerce Shipping Module also provides shipping rates calculation from different shipping carriers to the customer at checkout and enables you to add a variety of shipping charges to the customer's orders.

Shipping extensions

WebSphere Commerce provides several ways to integrate its shipping component with the external carriers that manage many of the order delivery and tracking processes to complete the entire order life cycle. See the Redpaper, *"Shipping Simplified: Integrating WebSphere Commerce with Third-party Shipping Providers"*, REDP-3910, at:

`http://www.redbooks.ibm.com/abstracts/redp3910.html?Open`

IBM service teams and IBM Business Partners have developed extensions for some of the major carriers. If you want to integrate the shipping component with a carrier's shipping network, you can either build it yourself or contact IBM or an IBM business partner to extend one of the solutions already built for these carriers:

- UPS
- FedEx
- USPS
- DHL
- ABF

3.2.7 Tax calculation

WebSphere Commerce provides tools for configuration and processing of taxes on products and shipping. However, uploading large sets of different tax codes for many different tax jurisdictions or products is cumbersome using the GUI based tools. In that case there is the option to use the WebSphere Commerce loader utilities, mentioned in 2.3.2, "WebSphere Commerce administration tools".

Using the loader utilities requires some technical expertise and in order to load the tax codes using the loader utilities, you need to generate all of the different tax codes, either manually or programmatically. As the number of variables increase (catalog size, number of tax jurisdictions the store sells to and so on) the complexity of generating these tax codes also increases. At some point the increased efficiency and convenience of integrating with a third-party tax calculation solution to calculate the taxes for each product and order is worth the extra effort and cost of setting it up.

The WebSphere Commerce orders component has to be configured to work with a third party tax calculation system. WebSphere Commerce has an application programming interface (API) for tax integration and either the third-party tax calculation software or an adapter needs to implement the API to enable communication between the two systems. When implemented, the tax calculations are diverted to the third-party system through the tax integration API.

The processing is as follows. The order component requests the tax amounts for an order and its order items to be calculated. The tax framework methods extract from the order all the information relevant to the tax calculation and pass the information through the tax integration API to the third-party tax calculation system. The tax amounts are returned by the third-party tax calculation system to the tax framework and the tax amounts added to the order and its order items. The tax integration API can also request the third-party tax calculation system to audit tax during order processing.

Taxware's TaxwareLink Package is an example of a third-party tax calculation system that has implemented the WebSphere Commerce tax integration API.

3.2.8 Analytics

Analytics is one of the most important parts of extending your WebSphere Commerce solution, because it provides in depth analysis and feedback on a site's performance and the customer's shopping experiences. In addition, your high traffic sites benefit from analytics, because it allows you to gain valuable insight on the effectiveness of each product and any marketing campaigns configured in your store(s).

For example, analytics might tell you:

1. I seem to be getting a lot of traffic on Tuesdays, Thursdays, and weekends. Perhaps I should put my promotions on those days to increase orders.
2. These products are getting a lot of browsing, but are not converting to sales. Perhaps I should offer them as a promotion.
3. I can see that customers for this geography are clicking on a lot of these items. Perhaps I should create a customer segment for them, and offer them further promotions on the products they are clicking on.
4. Customers do not seem to be going to the clearance section at all. Perhaps we should market it more heavily by featuring it in a marketing campaign.
5. A 30% discount seems to be a magic number, it pulls in far more sales than a 20% discount.
6. This e-mail campaign doubled our volume on the site last week and increased orders by 30%. A lot of registered clients are clicking on our e-mails.
7. Our big ticket item promotions seem to be quite strong, but our electronic product promotions are not effective.

What information could you collect using analytics to make these observations?

1. What is the daily volume of traffic on the site?
2. How many people placed orders and what did they purchase?
3. Where are people shopping at your store located geographically?
4. What were all the links the customer clicked on as soon as they got on the site, up to the time they left the site?
5. How many users saw and clicked on the "30% off all furniture" e-marketing spot been today compared to the 20% and 10% off spots?
6. How many users viewed and or clicked on the e-mail campaign we setup last week? And how many of those that clicked actually purchased something?
7. What are the promotions that people seem to be taking advantage of and which ones are not working that well?

How is the analytical data obtained?

Most of the data is gathered from the WebSphere Commerce database tables in a non-obtrusive way. For example, the `CatEntryId` of the product being purchased along with which category it falls under is required to report on what items are sold and what categories are people clicking on the most. The data is generated by the customer clicking through the site and is stored in a database.

With the data in the database, you can then perform queries against your database to find basic information, such as the number of orders, number of registered users and number of orderitems per order. Static data, such as these, collected after the user has placed the order is easy to gather by performing queries against the WebSphere Commerce database. There is much more value in being able to find out what the user did on your site to place that order. This is where analytics solutions play a vital role.

Analytics solutions typically take your data a step further by gathering further information about the Web site behavior of customers, correlating this with browser, account, and order information, and then analyzing the data and displaying the results in a useful way. You can then study the results to answer questions such as: "How many orders did we get on Saturday?" or "What demographic of users are buying on our site?" These reports are complex and provide detailed analysis of the data. In the case of third party analytic solution vendors, the reports offer suggestions on how to improve your site.

How do I get the data?

To get the data out of WebSphere Commerce, you can perform queries against the database and generate your own reports depending on your needs. This is not a recommended approach because you could be performing complex queries against your production system at peak times on the site, and this would affect performance on the site, while users are browsing and purchasing.

An alternative is to copy the data over to another database and view the reports from that database. This approach works, but is difficult to maintain, and you are still faced with investing in designing and implementing an easy to use system to query the data and create reports for business analysts. We recommend that you make use of a special purpose eCommerce analytics solution provided by an IBM business partner.

WebSphere Commerce has teamed up with Coremetrics to provide a cross-channel analytics solution. Coremetrics takes care of the entire back-end process on the running store with no additional hardware or database administrators required. Your role is to work with Coremetrics to instrument your Web pages and catalogs.

Coremetrics constructs a copy of your catalog to use with their analytics processing. You provide them with a copy of your product catalog, and keep them synchronized when you update your own product catalog. You also update each page on your Web site with a tag that passes information to Coremetrics each time the page is accessed. This sounds like a lot of work, and so there is a special Auto Tagging tool, in addition to a Catalog Definition File generator tool that helps to automate and simplify the implementation.

Using analytics data

The following WebSphere Commerce reports are provided out-of-the-box:

- WebSphere Commerce Campaigns Report
- e-Marketing Spot Report
- Marketing Experimentation Summary
- Promotions Summary
- B2B Contracts

With the Coremetrics solution, you can generate the customized reports we listed in the introduction, and these include cross-channel reports to correlate e-mail campaigns and direct sales from call centers.

Coremetrics identifies new customer segments based on the analytic data from your Web site, you can then transfer the customer segments from Coremetrics to WebSphere Commerce to implement targeted marketing campaigns.

3.2.9 Payment processing

WebSphere Commerce provides an extensive payment processing system that third party payment systems can be plugged into. Feature Pack 2 includes an example of a payment plug-in for PaymentTech. See 2.2.5, "Payments" on page 57 for more information about payment plug-ins.

3.2.10 Call center integration

Call centers are an integral part of the unified marketplace where eCommerce reigns, to provide answers to customer questions. Before eCommerce had begun to flourish, part of the sales benefit was to argue universally that eCommerce would reduce your call center costs by diverting traffic to a Web site.

This benefit is now much more finessed. In the case of some sectors and activities, on-line service is a quicker and better alternative to a call center, or physically visiting an outlet, and the call center volumes drop. In other sectors, particularly where trading never massively shifted from bricks and mortar to call centers, you can expect call center volumes to increase rather than reduce as a result of introducing eCommerce. If your revenue stream is made up of sales rather than subscriptions, you cannot afford to lose Web site customers through a poorly executed call center. In short, as eCommerce channels expand and extend, often so do the number of customers wanting to address their purchase and service issues through the call center.

Customers could call:

- To respond to online marketing campaigns
- For help navigating the Web site, interactive voice response (IVR), or a kiosk

- To purchase after speaking to a person, or to avoid using a credit card online
- To check on orders they placed at a Web storefront
- To follow-up on support issues that began in an e-mail dialog.

In any of these instances, customers expect customer service representatives (CSRs) to be aware of their situation and be ready to help. CSRs require immediate access to customers' previous activity. This translates to giving CSRs a fully integrated view of traditional and online marketing, sales, ordering and shipping functions.

The WebSphere Commerce platform supports fully integrated, multi-channel sales networks, and offers WebSphere Commerce Sales Center to give CSRs access to all the information integrated into the WebSphere Commerce Web site.

For details how to integrate, see *"IBM Sales Center With Computer Telephony Integration"*, REDP-4315:

`http://www.redbooks.ibm.com/abstracts/redp4315.html?Open`

3.2.11 Collaboration

Collaboration helps to bring together the various users of the WebSphere Commerce Web site. There could be several scenarios in which collaboration among users is required, such as when buyers and sellers need to discuss the terms of a sale, or when a shopper needs help from the Web site's customer service representative. There are two main collaboration features that WebSphere Commerce provides:

- Collaborative workspaces
- Customer Care

The distinction between collaborative workspaces and customer care is not only about whom the collaboration is between: Workspaces are for business users, and customer care is, naturally, for customers. The distinction is also about the style of interaction, which reflects what business users and customers want out of collaboration.

Business users can interact together quite well using the telephone or e-mail (or even face to face). What they want to do in addition is to work jointly on promotions or marketing campaigns, contracts, pricing, and other artifacts with colleagues — sometimes working together at the same time, and sometimes in tandem, reviewing changes and making changes of their own.

Customers' great frustration is being able to interact with a person in your business at all. What they want is to get and hold someone's attention on their problem, instantly. Customer care answers that need by providing instant messaging, or "chat".

Collaborative workspaces

Collaborative workspaces provide a tool to support business discussions between physically separated members of the eCommerce Web site. A typical scenario is for a seller to create a workspace and add buyers to it. This enables the seller and the prospective buyers to discuss and negotiate the terms and conditions of the sale using WebSphere Commerce Accelerator tool. The collaborative workspaces interface is provided using Lotus® Quickplace.

This feature is only available in the Enterprise Edition of WebSphere Commerce. In order to use it, you need to install Lotus Quickplace on a separate server from your WebSphere Commerce server. You also need to have your member data stored and managed on an LDAP server and not a relational database. The Lotus Quickplace server also needs to be on a separate machine from your LDAP server.

Collaborative workspaces are enabled in the advanced B2B direct starter store available with WebSphere Commerce Enterprise Edition, after an LDAP server and Lotus Quickplace are installed.

Customer care

As the name implies, customer care refers to the actions taken by the store to improve customer satisfaction by dealing with customer questions directly. In contrast to collaborative workspaces, customer care is about instant communication using live chats with a customer service representative and viewing the same page as the customer, their shopping cart, and the shopper's profile, all at the same time. The CSR can place orders on the customer's behalf, and also chat to other CSRs at the same time to get more eyes onto the problem.

In case of large anticipated shopper needs, queues are configured to direct the shoppers to the least busy queue.

The customer care feature is made available in WebSphere Commerce by installing Lotus Sametime® Server. Again, using Sametime requires the use of an LDAP server to store and manage users. However, unlike Quickplace, you do not have to use the same LDAP server as WebSphere Commerce. Your shopper data can be stored in a different repository from the one you use to store the data for the CSRs that have access to the customer care feature.

Customer care is enabled in the advanced B2B direct starter store available with WebSphere Commerce Enterprise Edition, after an LDAP server and Lotus Sametime Server are installed. This starter store provides the code that has to be present in your store's JSP files in order to enable customer care in your store.

3.2.12 Member management

In WebSphere Commerce, the member component manages the organization and security of online shoppers, as well as all other users in the system. We described member management in 2.2.1, "Members" on page 39. We told you that WebSphere Commerce uses either LDAP or information stored in the database supplied with WebSphere Commerce for authentication of members defined in the members component.

What if you already have a centralized user registry? Other applications use the shared registry, so why not WebSphere Commerce too? You do not wish to add another directory, just for authenticating WebSphere Commerce members. It would be much better for WebSphere Commerce to use the centralized registry that you already have in operation, rather than define a new registry just for WebSphere Commerce.

As an additional mechanism, WebSphere Commerce offers an interface to whatever kind of third party authentication you are using. You can use this interface to connect WebSphere Commerce to your existing registry. WebSphere Commerce also provides pre-built implementations of the interface to connect to seven commonly used directory technologies.

Authentication extension

Interfacing third party authentication to WebSphere Commerce is simple. The authentication extension is a Java interface:

```
com.ibm.security.commands.ThirdPartyAuthenticationCmd
```

It has two methods to set or verify the LogonId and Password.

To use the interface, select **third party authentication** using the WebSphere Commerce Configuration Manager, and provide an implementation of the authentication extension.

The interfaces that WebSphere Commerce has implemented are:

- IBM Directory Server for iSeries®
- IBM Tivoli® Directory Server 5.1 and 5.2
- IBM Tivoli Directory Server 6.0
- Active Directory® 2000
- Active Directory 2003
- Sun™ Java™ System Directory Server 5.2
- Domino® Directory Server 6.5.4

Part 2

Plan your eCommerce project

The success of any software project is not limited to the skills and capabilities of your programmers and other technical specialists. True, a brilliant user interface design specialist makes a difference, and a good programmer might code two or three times faster than a poorer one, with fewer bugs; but two aspects that really make the big difference in a software project are leadership and experience. With good leadership, you grow the skills and capabilities of all your programmers and specialists, along with the organization and processes to deliver, and keep delivering, a successful Web site.

The first steps you take are critical to building the organization and processes that you require, and Chapter 4, “First steps” discusses some of the important items to attend to when starting a new eCommerce project.

Chapter 5, “Organize your eCommerce resources” describes how to organize an eCommerce project, and describes the stages it goes through from inception to going live. We consider the critical success factors you must look out for.

An important recommendation of services teams who work on WebSphere Commerce deployments is that clients should aim to adopt an “agile development” approach. Perhaps more than in many kinds of software project, agile development is well suited to Web site development. The agile development approach is to release and evaluate functions bit by bit, rather than in one big bang. It is a better way to deliver a Web site on a surer schedule.

The final chapter in this part, Chapter 6, “Challenges and pitfalls” focuses on some of the challenges, such as security, performance, and usability, that can make or break your eCommerce business.

4

First steps

This chapter covers the "advancing-beyond-the-green-light" phase of a WebSphere Commerce project. Management has approved the implementation of an eCommerce site based on the WebSphere Commerce software. You have been given your marching orders by the chief executive and the board, "Get it done."

Your first few steps will make or break the project. You must gather enough information, organizational backing, and resource to take off. What are the initial steps that are vital to establish the ways and means to build an eCommerce site which meets the board's expectations?

The target audience for this chapter includes, but is not limited to, the project sponsor, decision-makers, stake-holders, and the project team.

Using a fictitious company as an example, we discuss how to establish the ways and means to get the most out of your WebSphere Commerce software. We lead you through the critical success factors to gain and sustain momentum for the development of an eCommerce site.

These critical success factors are:

- Gaining visibility and decision-making weight
- Support of your financial decision-makers
- Full participation of the all the stakeholders who are affected by the application, and who need to support it
- Setting goals and, most importantly, expectations and scope for the project
- Priority access to resources and support infrastructure (with many resources not under your direct control, this is essential to accomplish the project)

If you manage to set up your eCommerce organization with these success factors largely in hand, you are on your way to deploying a successful eCommerce site!

4.1 Featured case

ITSO Baby Magic, Inc. is a retail store based in Raleigh.

A number of years ago it decided to sell its products online to customers in the local area. Their eCommerce model was browse only. Customers who wanted to buy were redirected to call the closest Call Center, based on the customer address, to complete the sale off line. The board in ITSO Baby Magic soon realized the benefits of providing multiple sales channels for its customers even though sales were not completed on line. Over the past two years the company has grown from a relatively small store front serving the local Raleigh-Durham area into having a distribution network of over 50 retailers in 50 states. They are currently negotiating wholesale arrangements with companies outside the United States and securing a 20,000 square-foot office space for a call center.

The functionality of their current Web site is greatly limited. They have to make searching for and ordering easier through a simple and easy-to-use Web site. Their Order, Inventory, and Customer Service systems are loosely-coupled. There is a need to integrate these systems to provide better service by reducing errors and providing timely order status and acknowledgement. They want to move access to these systems to the Internet to allow customers to place orders more easily, and obtain the status of their orders, get quotes, view their current catalog and check available inventory to reduce overhead costs in call centers. Their overhead cost is out of control and they need to reduce cost wherever possible. They hope to increase revenues by making shopping online easier, and by being able to run marketing and merchandising campaigns.

In the Project Proposal, management defined the following objectives:

- Instead of redirecting buyers to a call center, lock in the buyer to purchase while browsing online.
- Reduce order lead time from 2.5 days to 4.5 hours.
- Improve order acknowledgement rate from 50 to 99 percent.
- Reduce order error rate from 25% to one percent.
- Enhance operating and business process efficiencies, visibility, asset structure and both customer and supplier satisfaction.
- Enable the creation of a value-based buyer pricing model that uses new buyer performance/buyer profile metrics.
- Enable the creation of a value-based supplier pricing model that uses new supplier performance metrics.
- Reduce operating risks due to optimization of buyer relationship profitability and lower error rates.

- Achieve ROI in nine months.
- "Go-Live" date MUST be November 25th, so called "Black Friday," the day after Thanksgiving.

4.2 Level-setting

You are a member of the project team at ITSO Baby Magic, Inc. and you have received your matching orders from the board to deliver their first eCommerce site based on the WebSphere Commerce software. What do you do next?

Armed with the project proposal document, your first task is to widen the visibility of the project within your organization. You also need to raise the awareness of the challenges and the pitfalls faced by the organization, and the changes and investments needed to realize the objectives proposed by the board.

Educating your stakeholders

As part of your plan to obtain the buy-in and cooperation of the ITSO Baby Magic stakeholders who are affected by the eCommerce plan, you should make a call to IBM to obtain collateral that IBM has prepared. This collateral helps you describe and explain the decision to use WebSphere Commerce. The collateral is a series of presentations geared towards education of your stakeholders about WebSphere Commerce. You can ask IBM for presentations on these topics:

- An overview of WebSphere Commerce.
- The capabilities and tools of WebSphere Commerce.
- Momentum and "Why IBM?".
- Technical Foundation of WebSphere Commerce.
- Customer Success stories.
- ISV Partnership extensions.

Your goal in this phase is to increase the knowledge of your stakeholders about WebSphere Commerce and set expectations about what WebSphere Commerce can do to develop the ITSO Baby magic business. This has two sides to it:

- Many in the audience have not thought about all the opportunities of introducing a Web sales channel. They are learning that eCommerce is not simply about creating a new Web page for customers to order items they have been browsing, but introduces a new marketing, sales, and distribution channel with the potential of changing many of the businesses processes for the better.

- Many more in the audience, for we are all Internet shoppers now, have had both good and bad experiences on the Web and want to repeat the best and avoid the worst of these in ITSO Baby Magic's Web site. These experiences translate into expectations about how the Web site will work. It usually comes as a surprise that many good features do not come "out-of-the-box" simply or cheaply, but require integration with other software and require changes to business processes.

You have a lot of expectation setting to do, as well as careful scoping and phasing of the project plan. One of the best pieces of advice customers who have been through this phase will give you is to adopt an ""agile" approach. Launch the Web site with the core capabilities you need to start with, and then add new capabilities as needs are demonstrated. Get people to agree that scope should not grow in response to vociferous advocates of some capability seen elsewhere on the Web, but should be based on what is demonstrably needed.

Changing the organization

The sales team have used a broad canvas to create for you a vision of what WebSphere Commerce can do for your business. But do not mistake the vision for reality. To continue the canvas metaphor, you now require hard working artists to turn the vision into reality. You need to appropriately identify, organize, and manage the artists to build the customized services that fulfil the vision and meet the needs of your customers. There is a lot of hard work and deep thought ahead to deploy a WebSphere Commerce solution.

You have to review your corporate goals and ambitions. You must take another look at what you do and the way you do it. You do have to look at what your competition is doing and try their Web sites to do better than the current best practices in your industry. You should perform fit-gap analyses, comparing what you do today with how you would like to do it tomorrow, and identify the gaps that need to be filled. Then you must determine the capabilities you have in-house and what investments you have to make in order to achieve your goals.

Start with a solution outline that maps your requirements to WebSphere Commerce "out-of-the-box" features, using the pre-built sample stores, and do a fit-gap analysis to determine what your company needs in the way of both human resources and hardware in order to successfully deploy WebSphere Commerce.

Your company could, as a result of the analysis, decide to build upon an in-house IT infrastructure and expand the IT organization. The organization requires managers, analysts, project managers, architects, developers, QA personnel, a content management team, and infrastructure support teams. You aim to combine the IT knowledge and experience of the new recruits, with that of your current IT and business staff.

You also need analyze the business processes that are required to support the site and recruit agents in both your organization and the departments or businesses running the processes you depend upon, to understand what changes have to be made, and make them happen.

You might decide to out-source some or all of this effort — but you need to understand and manage how the out-sourced processes are driven, and how they interact with your other business processes. Most WebSphere Commerce solutions are delivered through a combination of in-house and out-sourced projects with the assistance of consultants brought in early to help initiate, manage or review the deployment process.

Finally, leverage your champions! An eCommerce project touches on so many aspects of your business, it requires a critical mass and the iron will of your business behind it, to succeed. You need good political skills, and board level support, to obtain the organizational buy-in and management focus this project requires to foment the change and manage the colossal footprint it naturally creates. Understanding the organizational politics, understanding the politics of the project, and having a strong, capable communicator and consensus builder to manage this project ensures that this project is consistently on the radar screens of the decision-makers and the shareholders, and you can get their attention and help when you need it.

4.3 Setting goals and managing expectations

The great secret of eCommerce is that building an efficient operational site that reduces costs and increases return on investment, requires more thought and planning than money. Like most technologies, WebSphere Commerce though it promises enormous benefits, can get overly complicated — and there is nothing like complexity to drive up costs.

Do your homework. Talk to your user community and analyze your user behavior and environments to understand the business requirements and user expectations. Share this information with your teams and involve them as you plan out the process by which you can meet these requirements and expectations. Get the team to adopt an “agile” approach to requirements. Incorporate features that are demonstrably valuable to your users — to the customers and the business users who will run the site. Being clear about your goal setting and the expectations for the site will start your organization down the path of a responsive, customer-happy site.

Rationale and objectives for the project

Look back at the discussions, business objectives, and rationale that led ITSO Baby Magic, Inc. to purchase WebSphere Commerce. One rationale, among others, is:

"...to make searching for and ordering easier through a simple and easy-to-use Web site".

Your management have spelled out the business case for purchasing WebSphere Commerce in the project proposal document. In our featured case. management's answers to the question, "What do we want to achieve with WebSphere Commerce software?" effectively provided the project teams with the business's shared vision. The project teams' first task is to understand how to turn the vision into business requirements, milestones, deliverables, and to scope the project into a series of releases or increments.

It is a good approach to collect together all the ideas from the documents and notes that circulated during the software acquisition process about what your company wants to achieve with eCommerce in general, and WebSphere Commerce in particular, and summarize them in a "Business Vision Document". The business vision document is something for new team members to read and something for the team to refer to when requirements, scoping and priorities are considered. The Business Vision document is a template supplied with the IBM Rational Unified Process®[1].

The management mandate for the ITSO Baby Magic project has the following business goals:

- Customers are offered a new or an improved purchasing option.
- Customers experience improved customer service.
- Customers benefit from reduced ordering time.
- Business users benefit from less burdensome administration.
- Finances are improved by reducing the cost of receiving orders and improving cash flow.
- Sales are increased by the use of online marketing and promotional campaigns.

You should make sure that performance measures for these goals are agreed to and documented. If your project has not been sufficiently defined and documented, insist that this be done. It is essential to determine the business case against which your success is to be measured.

[1] A Microsoft® Word template is provided as part of the IBM Rational Method Composer. A summary of the vision document contents is provided in Appendix B, "Business Vision Template" on page 383.

4.4 Business requirements

Successful IT projects are driven by the joint goals of business strategy and business need. Only purchase new technology to meet business goals — and not just to "keep up to date".

Business requirements are the tasks that must be accomplished, or technology that must be delivered, to provide the values identified in the project goals. Obtaining all the business requirements for the project could span several business areas. You need to approach the task of identifying business requirements with as many requirement gathering methods as are available to you and above all, talk to all the stakeholders.

4.4.1 Questioning business goals

One approach is to discuss the business goals with stakeholders, by asking questions such as these:

1. Why are these business goals essential?
2. How do they change the way we do business?
3. How do they benefit my company financially?
4. How do you measure return on your investment?
5. How many users do you need to support?
6. What current processes and technologies can or cannot be changed?

You are not just looking for definite answers. Your questions should be open ended and start a continuing dialog between the project and the stakeholders that teases out what the project really can do to meet their business goals.

As an example, we identified some sample business requirements for ITSO Baby Magic, Inc., from its business goals:

- Why are these business goals essential?
  - We need to take this company to a new level, opening new markets and sales channels, to gain on the competition and increase profitability.
  - We need to have the system in operation in six months to take advantage of this year's Christmas sales.
  - We need the system to be integrated with our old order processing and inventory systems to provide us with a seamless order processing and order fulfillment system.

- How do they change the way we do business?
  - We need to exploit multiple sales channels to remain competitive
  - We need to increase sales without increasing our headcount, by deploying an eCommerce site.
  - We want to change our business from a largely bricks and mortar model to a multi-channel model, integrated for business process efficiencies, visibility, asset structure, and to be available to our customers 24/7 for viewing, ordering and checking the status of their orders.
- How do they benefit my company financially?
  - We believe that easy and ready access to our catalog will increase sales of our products.
  - We believe that ordering on the Web and a more efficient and integrated ordering system will reduce costs.
- How do you measure return on your investment?
  - We compare the revenue stream against the cost of receiving orders.
  - We review customer feedback, and measure how well we have recycled the feedback into our business.
- How many users do you need to support?
  - The site should be scalable! It must support a minimum of 10,000 concurrent users and a maximum of 80,000 concurrent users
- What current processes and technologies can or cannot be changed?
  - The Oracle back-end cannot be changed.
  - The Customer ID number cannot be changed.
  - All other systems and processes can be changed.

4.4.2 Business scenarios

Another approach is to create a number of business scenarios that you would like to see the Web site support. A business scenario is a set of activities that enact some aspects of the business vision and realizes one or more of the business goals or needs. By discussing each business scenario with the relevant stakeholders further business requirements are uncovered, and some might get adopted, and some rejected.

A typical business scenario to be discussed might be to upsell to a customer about to purchase a product. This scenario helps to realize the "increased sales" goal for the Web site. Discussing the upsell scenario with stakeholders leads to a number of questions and suggestions, which leads to further requirements.

For example:

- How do we identify an upsell alternative?
- How many alternatives should we present?
- How can we measure whether upselling is proving effective?
- How does the shopper compare the alternatives?
- Can we use customer reviews to push the upsell
- Can we use a promotion just for the upsell?

4.4.3 Use cases

When you have decided on a set of business scenarios to implement, writing use cases is another effective technique for eliciting requirements. Some project teams find it useful to divide use cases into Business Use cases, which describe the activities that are performed by the actors, or roles, you have identified in your business context diagram, and System Use cases, which are typically a lower level description of how Business Use cases are performed by the system, and often involve system components as actors. Dividing the use cases into the two kinds helps you to focus separately on what the business actor does, and what the system does.

Make sure you capture the non-functional as well as functional requirements when you are writing use cases. Write the happy path first, and then deal with errors separately to keep the basic use cases simple. The full details of the use cases need not be written at first, when the objective is on scoping the project requirements. Use case details can be elaborated in subsequent phases or iterations of the project plan. A tool such as IBM RequisitePro® keeps track of use cases and the use case scripts, and links them to business scenarios, to the business vision, and to phases of development, or release iterations. Use case diagrams are valuable to show how use cases and business scenarios are linked.

4.4.4 Welcome to the candy-store of features and scope creep

WebSphere Commerce projects tend to experience scope creep. You can see from the upsell scenario how easy it is to imagine new requirements for the store, all of which have the promise of closing more profitable sales. eCommerce is a candy-store of goodies, and when the capabilities of WebSphere Commerce are exposed to stakeholders for the first time, it results in an insatiable desire for features on the Web site. But you are aware of the other two members of the project triangle, cost and time; you have to deliver within time and budget constraints (Figure 4-1).

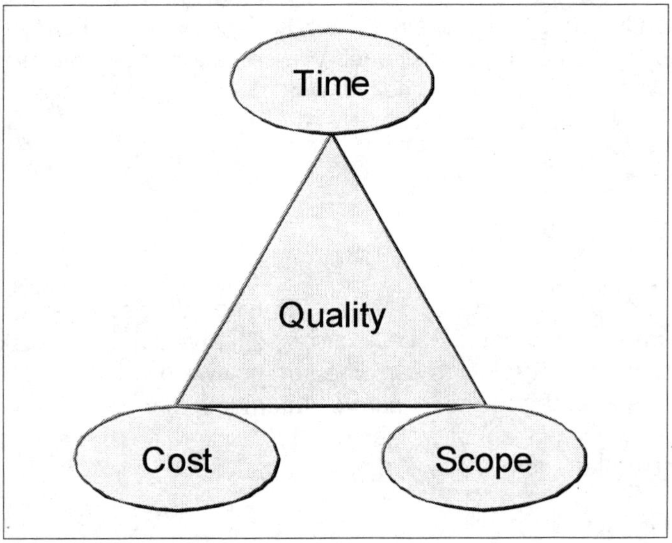

Figure 4-1 The golden project management triangle

You need to keep the scope of your project well-defined, documented, and signed-off. Spending time with stakeholders in the early stages establishing the goals of the project, and the process to be used to develop the Web site, are critical to maintaining control over costs and schedule. Tools such as IBM Rational RequisitePro help you to manage requirements, and link them to use cases, business scenarios and the business vision, and to organize them into releases. Rational Portfolio Manager helps you manage multiple releases, keeping track of the requirements, resources, costs and returns by release. You need to turn your business plans for multiple releases into a do-able development plan. Iterative, agile development methodologies are very suitable to manage projects with many incremental releases.

Keeping requirements well documented, and the process for reviewing and updating requirements transparent to all the stakeholders in the team, is an important part of effective management of requirements and avoidance of scope creep. The other major part is to deliver completed functionality incrementally, with release cycles measuring weeks or months, but not years. As well as providing a means to deliver regular improvements in response to customer requirements, a shorter release cycle gives you an acceptable means to defer requests for functional enhancements to the present release and address them in planned way in a soon to be delivered upcoming release, rather than risk the release under development with an unplanned extension.

The more you know and the more you can document about what your client specifically wants, and does not want, and the more your can offer a rapid release cycle, the better positioned you are to avoid scope creep and deliver a quality WebSphere Commerce site with high value to the client within the constraints you have.

4.5 Project objectives

With the help of the extended project team and your stakeholders, you should define and document project objectives so that they can be evaluated at the conclusion of the project to see whether they were achieved. The project objectives are the precise, concrete statements that describe what your project aims to achieve. Use these objectives to structure the project and validate success at the end of the project.

Project objectives are particularly important if you are out-sourcing or sub-contracting all or part of the project. Project objectives are part of the statement of work agreed between you and service providers in the contract materials. For internal teams, you should draw up project objectives as part of documents of understanding with other teams you are dependent on, but do not have full oversight of. You should also draw up overall project objectives as part of the package you prepare to report to your sponsor, or the board.

The project objectives must be clear. Each objectives statement describes the problem to be addressed by the WebSphere Commerce project and the proposed solution. At a minimum, the objectives must have these four elements; Each needs to be precise, detailed, measurable and time-bound.

Precise State in a straightforward unambiguous language what the project should achieve.

Detailed Provide a detailed description of the objective aimed at creating a better understanding between all parties.

Measurable Include a clear definition of how the success of the objective is to be measured.

Time-bound Work out a schedule for the delivery of the objective

4.5.1 An example of an objective statement

Here is an example of an objective statement:

```
“create a multi-language eCommerce site on a  WebSphere Commerce 6.0
platform  by November 25 to support contractual agreements that will
display merchandise to customers based on their specific contract”.
```

- The objective is very specific in its statement about creating an eCommerce site based on WebSphere Commerce 6.0 platform.
- The objective is comprehensive enough as it details the salient features of the site - multi-language support and support for contracts
- The objective is measurable in terms of what is displayed to a particular customer based on their contract and what the system should achieve.
- The objective is time-bound and should be completed by November 25, the day after Thanksgiving, to target the beginning of the Christmas shopping season.

The objectives of a project should link directly to deliverables[2]. In the previous example, the objective refers to the creation of:

"a multi-language eCommerce site on a WebSphere Commerce 6.0 platform"

It is easy for the project team to identify their deliverables:

- Create an eCommerce site.
- It must be one site that supports different languages.
- It must be on WebSphere Commerce 6.0 platform.

If you cannot get a sense for the deliverables required to fulfill the objective, the objective might be too vague and not measurable. On the other hand, if an objective describes the characteristics of the deliverables, it is too detailed and too specific and it runs the risk of becoming the requirements of the project.

4.5.2 How to create the objectives

You need to understand the goals of the project, the business case for the project and the key business requirements to be able to adequately identify the project objectives. You need to meet with the sponsor, to whom you are delivering the project, and with the stakeholder or business partner from whom you are receiving deliverables, to ensure that the objectives you have identified are understood, accurate, and complete.

In some cases the project objectives are already spelled out in the Project Proposal document, as is in the case with ITSO Baby Magic, Inc. You can use this as the starting point to refine your objectives. If in the end there are inconsistencies, go back to the other party to resolve the inconsistencies.

[2] Rational RequisitePro has the capability to create links between requirements and the development artifacts created by the tools in the Rational Application Developer, and also other Rational and WebSphere development tools. By clicking on a requirement, or an artifact, the tool navigates you to the other end of the link. A developer can immediately locate a requirement and vice versa.

4.5.3 Sample of objective statements

Using the questions above, let us develop our own sample business objectives:

- Create a new content delivery service to meet the growing demands of our online customers to gain on the competition and increase our bottom line.
- The content delivery service should be in operation within six months to take advantage of the Christmas shopping season.
- The new system should be integrated with our old order processing and inventory systems to provide us with a seamless order processing and order fulfillment system.
- Change our business from a largely bricks and mortar model to an integrated model whereby our catalog is available to the customer to view and purchase 24/7.
- Increase sales by 20% by providing multiple sales channels for our customers allowing them to order directly, by phone, online, and providing the option of home or in-store delivery.
- Decrease management cost by 30% and make the administrative task less burdensome.
- The site should support a minimum of 10,000 concurrent users and a maximum of 80,000 concurrent users.

4.6 Problem statement

As we have stated previously, when it comes to WebSphere Commerce and the suite of applications that compliment it, you are only limited by your imagination. Having said that, to be successful at implementing a WebSphere Commerce site does *not* mean that you have to solve every problem that the organization has identified that falls within the purview of eCommerce, at least not by the first release.

It is worth your while to identify and describe the problem or problems to be resolved by WebSphere Commerce in as much detail as possible. The problem statement is a clear and concise statement that describes the symptoms of the problem to be addressed. It provides the context for the project and typically generates questions which the project hopes to answer. A good problem statement allows you to identify what is in scope and what is not. It limits scope by focusing on some variables and not others. It also provides an opportunity for you to demonstrate why these variables are important. The problem statement is a heading in the Business Vision Document.

A good example of a problem statement is, "The current system requires that orders are phoned or faxed into the Call Center for operators to manually key in the orders. This leads to an operator and key entry error rate of nine percent."

The problem statement provides three benefits to the project teams:

- It creates a sense of problem ownership for the team.
- It focuses the team on an accepted problem.
- It describes the symptoms in measurable terms.

The problem statement is clear, concise, and well-written. Use the following four guidelines in creating a problem statement.

Define the problem

In the problem statement, team members define the problem in specific terms. Present facts such as the product type and the error made, For example, "The average time between when a *furniture order* is received by the sales department and when the client pays the *invoice is over sixty days*. That is not sustainable".

Identify where the problem is appearing

Identify where the problem is appearing as specifically as possible helps the team focus its improvement efforts. For example, "shoppers *order from catalogs that are outdated* causing delays or two to three weeks in order processing".

Describe the size of the problem

Describe the size of the problem in measurable terms. For example, "The lead time between when the order is received by the sales department and when the client pays the invoice is *two and a half days*".

Describe the impact the problem is having on the organization

Make the description of the problem's impact on the organization as specific as possible. For example, "The delays cost the company *one and a half million dollars a year*".

The more specific the statement, the better the chance the project team has of fixing the problem. Any problems that are deemed too large, too difficult, too expensive to fix should be identified as "Out-of-Scope". "Out-of-Scope" problems should be identified as exposures to the project achieving its goal, and the risks to the project evaluated. If the risk is significant, then the problems should be brought to the attention of the project sponsor[3] in a project review meeting.

[3] The project sponsor should have the authority to re-scope or terminate a project, and be answerable to the board for the financial impact.

Not only is the problem statement a valuable tool that demonstrates your knowledge of the issues at stake, it also focuses the project team on an acknowledged problem and describes the symptoms of the problem in measurable terms. The problem statement is a confidence-builder that should motivate the project team and establish a persuasive context for what follows in the Solution Outline or Project Definition document.

4.7 Project risks

What is the probability that something will go wrong with this project that has the potential to have an adverse effect on the WebSphere Commerce deployment and on the business? That probability is high. It is even higher if your organization has a history of project failures.

Rule 1: Be vigorously critical of your plan

Listen to the naysayers, and answer them. Listen to your development team. Believe even the most pessimistic development estimate is optimistic unless vigorously tested. If you choose to set a challenge, have a plan B. Identify as many risks as possible and early. This should start as the project is conceived and must continue through the life-cycle of the project. Knowing about such risks early in the life of the project and having enough relevant information about them allows you enough time to plan for them and manage them.

Rule 2: Be less ambitious

The deployment of WebSphere Commerce is complicated. Like other projects, the successful project manager is the person who is able to envision the entire project from start to finish and size up the job as much as possible. The project manager must also have the ability to communicate the task ahead to management and to the project team and help make necessary adjustments to ensure that this vision is realized.

Do not try to do more than it is necessary, especially in your first release. Walk through the length of the project with your team. Identify potential risks, evaluate them and with the help of your teams choose a path of risk avoidance or risk mitigation and management.

Rule 3: Restructure the project if risks are excessive

For example, if management is telling you to use internal resources who have never had an exposure to WebSphere Commerce development, tell them that is an excessive risk, you need to restructure the project. If you are told to go ahead anyway, you need to restructure the project to within acceptable levels of risk. Prepare the ground for a change of plan and monitor the risky areas so you can revisit management's decision with more data.

Rule 4: Avoid risks that do not offer the potential for gain

Continuously perform risk-benefit analysis and pursue paths that maximize your efforts. What might look like an unacceptable risk to one person, though, might rightly appear as an attractive challenge and opportunity to another; do not be completely risk averse if there is a big upside. If you can foresee a risk but with a great benefit, see it as an opportunity and a challenge. Go for it but evaluate it constantly.

The following sections describe some best practices in dealing with risks.

4.7.1 Risk management plan

First and foremost, have a risk management plan, which includes a regular series of status reporting and project review meetings. You chair the status reporting meetings, normally held weekly; and you expect to report to your sponsor in project review meetings, probably held monthly. Risk analysis should be a major agenda item in the project review meeting[4].

You need to establish a consistent month on month risk reporting format. A typical approach is to identify between six and twelve risk categories, and report risks within those categories. Quantify risks and assess the impact. Establish a risk severity scale: traffic lights are frequently used, where a Red light means your assessment is that without actions taken that require resources beyond the control of the project (hence outside your control), the project will slip.

[4] A thorough analysis of software risk management including software acquisition is to be found at the Software Technology Support Center, funded by the U.S. Air Force:
`http://www.stsc.hill.af.mil/resources/tech_docs/gsam3/chap6.pdf`

You should establish whole project checkpoints, relative to the project schedule and phasing (Figure 4-2).

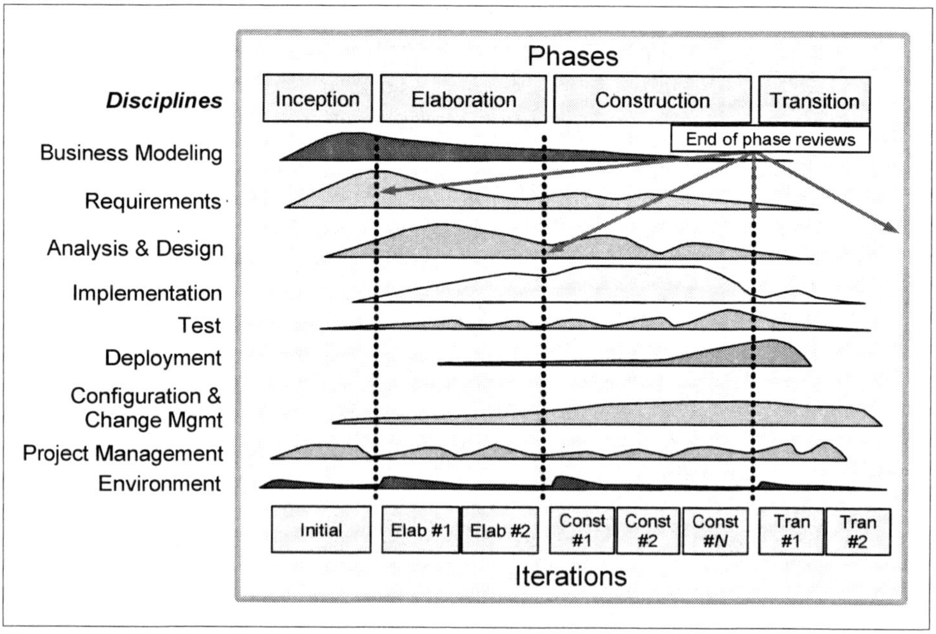

Figure 4-2 RUP® project phases

As an example, Table 4-1, adapted from *"Risk reduction with the RUP phase plan,"* Mark Akred, DeveloperWorks, November 2003, suggests how you should focus the risk analysis section of project checkpoint reviews on building the solution[5]. See the following URL for more details:

`http://www.ibm.com/developerworks/rational/library/1826.html`

[5] The table is just an example of questions to ask.

Table 4-1 Development RUP phase development activities and phase review questions

Phase	Inception	Elaboration	Construction	Transition
Tackles	Should we build it?	Can we build it?	Are we building it?	Have we delivered it?
End phase review risk questions for development	Is this the right project for the business to commit resource to?	Have we defined what we are building? Are we continuously designing and testing for performance and user acceptance? Have we sufficient resources? Have we agreements and contracts in place to manage dependencies?	Have we bit what we defined? Does it perform? What have we learnt from user acceptance tests? Have we trained operational and business staff? is the site ready to go live?	What are the results of the key performance measures of the Web site that we established as the objectives of the project? What performance issues have emerged? What are users reporting as problems? What new requirements are emerging?

4.7.2 Risk areas

What should you consider risky enough to put your project in jeopardy?

1. If there is *any* area under the purview of your project and the project manager does not have control, that area should be considered a risk area. Call it out to your sponsor and assess it for every project review.
   a. If you are aware of potential problems in an area you do not have control over this is termed a dependency. Potential problems are called "Dependency risks". If a dependency goes wrong, it will almost certainly be a red traffic light.
   b. If you do not expect problems with an area not under your control, this is usually termed a project assumption and should be clearly identified, so that if a change occurs to any of them, you are more likely to realize that you now have a dependency problem, than if you had not called out the assumption in the first place. A typical product assumption would be if you are expecting to ship the Web site on (say) WebSphere Commerce 6.0, Feature Pack 3.0, Service level 6.0.1.18. Any change to this assumption should trigger an action to review the change for its impact — for example, you might have to redo some build, test, or deployment tasks.

2. If there are items in the project plan that are important but have a cloud of uncertainty of any kind about them, they initially rate at least as Orange on the risk scale. Examples are:
   a. If the scope is not well-defined or is a moving target. Collect all possible requirements and have your teams help you prioritize them and then identify what is in scope and what is not, by release or iteration, and show both in your Project Definition document. There should be no project definition uncertainties at the end of the elaboration phase of an iteration.
   b. If the project approach is unfamiliar or if the development-to-deployment approach is pursued by an unproven or immature technical approach. You should contract outside services to mitigate this, or have downsize the first release, or plan for alpha and beta releases in the first iteration to check out the process.
   c. If there are known technical difficulties or complexities to the project. Engage a project mentor. We discuss this in Chapter 5, "Organize your eCommerce resources" on page 155. You do not need to go it alone; we have provided you with references of sources for help. Seek help when you need it.
3. If you are not periodically reviewing of the system design and project plans with out-sourcing teams.
4. Inexperienced personnel constitute project risks.
5. External interfaces cause risks because they can change and, even if they do not change, their descriptions or specifications might be inaccurate, or difficult to understand. Do not defer integration solely to an "integration phase" of the project. Have integration specialists test interface code before going into an integration phase with the whole project.
6. External organizational dependencies create project risks. You need to tackle these early with the help of the project sponsor. You need technical points of contact on each side of the organizational divide; you need representatives to be present in the project management meetings on each side, and you need sponsor representation where the organizations merge.
7. Incomplete planning or optimistic cost or schedule goals create risk. An organizational culture that has previously had problems executing projects is likely to repeat the same mistakes. These are organizational issues that you need to resolve with the sponsor before the rubber hits the road.

4.8 Project scope

The scope of a project is defined by specified boundaries that separate what is included in the project and what is not included. If the scope is too broad, you might not be able to deliver successfully. It is good practice (iterative or agile development) to break projects down into multiple releases or iterations, and revisit the scope of each iteration in the light of experience with the current iteration. For example:

1. Create a requirements review process to manage scope and releases.
2. Appoint a requirements analyst/coordinator.
3. Manage scope using a requirements management system, or at least create a scope document and "change control" it.
4. Clearly define what is and is not in scope.
5. Review and prioritize the scope items with stakeholders.
6. Organize prioritized scoped items into multiple iterations that form functioning systems.
7. Do what validation is necessary to obtain the approval of the project sponsor for the release plan, and approval of stakeholders who have management control or oversight of the project.
8. Revisit the scope and release plan during the inception phase of each iteration.

4.9 Project governance

As a rule of thumb, we recommend that you appoint a Project Sponsor and a Project Manager, and form two teams around these leaders to provide oversight and manage WebSphere Commerce deployment: the Project Leadership team and the Project Oversight team. The project manager should also meet with the project sponsor regularly.

In several places we have alluded to the fact that the success of a WebSphere Commerce project depends on how best to manage the decision-makers in your organization, spread out between stakeholders and IT teams, as well as how to maintain the balance between customer satisfaction and project controls.

You are engaged, more than usually for an IT project, in a juggling act between different groups with different temperaments and expectations and with different agendas, even though the overall end goals might be the same. By splitting the responsibility of dealing with the day to day business of managing the project from the responsibility of accounting for the success of the project to the business, you should be better able to acquire and maintain the active support of the business for the eCommerce project.

4.9.1 Project sponsor responsibilities

The project sponsor has a key role in creating the right climate for project risks to be managed effectively, and to enable the project team to bring their project in on time and in budget. Ultimately the project sponsor is responsible for initiating and terminating the project.

The project sponsor has another important role in that, by dealing with project matters outside of the project manager's control, the project manager is able to focus on making the project happen.

1. Select, develop, and mentor, or change, the project manager to achieve project goals. Other members of the project team have responsibilities in addition to the goals of the project. It is the project manager's responsibility to ensure that team members meet their part of the project goals.
2. Hold the project manager accountable for fulfilling the project's goals.
3. Require regular briefings and phase reviews.
4. Represent and advocate the project up the chain of command.
5. Support the project manager in obtaining resources and tools needed to manage and steer the project.
6. Obtain cross organizational support for the project.
7. Deal with exposures that the project manager cannot handle within the project's resource. Be prepared to radically change the objectives of the project or terminate it.

4.9.2 Project manager responsibilities

There are many books about the project manager's responsibilities. In brief, the project manager is responsible for ensuring that:

- The project is:
  - Well defined
  - Sufficiently resourced
  - Delivered on time
  - Within budget
  - Attains an agreed quality level
- Dependencies on external groups are effectively managed.
- Legal and corporate requirements are met.
- Project risks are assessed and unmanaged exposures are reported to the project sponsor.

To meet these objectives, the project manager needs a well motivated and organized team, following a well understood development process to perform all the tasks necessary to develop the solution, and to monitor the process effectively.

A good project manager has a clear understanding of all the tasks that take the project from initiation to completion, how they relate to one another, and whether they are being performed effectively and on schedule. The project manager continuously communicates with the team, not only to understand the status of the project, but also to understand when the project plan is broken in some respect or other.

For eCommerce projects, the project manager needs to focus especially on:

- Project scope and definition, with achievable cost, schedule, and performance goals
- Testing and user acceptance
- Performance

4.9.3 Project leadership team

The project leadership team typically includes the Project Manager (chair), IT Architect, and IT Technical Lead. Reporting to the team are representatives of functional areas, liaisons with IBM Business Partners, and assistants to the project manager. Typically the extended team members are:

- Project Manager
- Project Manager's assistants (Project office)
- Business Project Manager
- Merchandising or Marketing Project Manager
- Content Manager
- Architect
- Technical Lead
- Development
- QA
- Infrastructure liaison
- Help/Documentation liaison
- External IBM Business Partner or Vendor or their liaison
- Project Mentor

This team can be added to depending on the size of the project and who is involved. For example for a multi-national site, you can bring in the project managers of the different businesses, for example, the International Project Manager and the Domestic Project Manager. Where the design and implementation of infrastructure is part of the deployment, you can include the head of the infrastructure group on this team.

This team has a scheduled meeting weekly and might also have ad hoc meetings throughout the week. Their responsibilities include:

- Holding regular project status meetings to track the project plan, taking corrective action where necessary
- Reviewing the list of issues and deciding on risks that need to be escalated to the project oversight team
- Organizing phase reviews and deciding to Go Live when a project iteration is ready

4.9.4 Project oversight team

The Project Oversight Team, the extended team, is comprised of the Project Sponsor (chair), the Project Manager and any other decision makers in your organization who are accountable for the success of the project. These can be co-opted on an as-needed basis.

You need your oversight team to set the business climate for the project and keep it closely coupled to the overall strategy of the company. Where organizational policy allows, if you engaged a consultant, you are strongly advised to include the consultant in the oversight team to assist the project sponsor.

The project oversight team probably meets monthly. The responsibilities of the project oversight team are to assist the project sponsor with:

- Reviewing the outcome of project phase reviews
- Resolving exposures that require management decision making
- Signing off on any project decisions that have a significant impact on the business
- Keeping the project leadership team focused on achieving the project goals

4.10 Project estimating

The information contained in the solution outline (see Appendix A, "Solution Outline Template" on page 379) is a useful basis for the final "bottom up" estimates for the project. The time and cost estimates should include the entire WebSphere Commerce implementation life cycle, from conception to the post-launch support.

In developing estimates, pay particular attention to trading off in-house resource to using resources from IBM, or IBM Business Partners, or outsourcing some or all of the development.

The level of customization that is done to the WebSphere Commerce product, translates into the number of tasks to be performed. The number and duration of the tasks and the quality of their performance, more than anything else, determine the time and cost of your implementation.

In the following sections, we have tried to provide some guidance as to what types of customization prove more or less expensive by categorizing the skills needed into basic, intermediate, and advanced.

4.10.1 Customizing WebSphere Commerce assets

Each of the IBM WebSphere Commerce editions and corresponding IBM WebSphere Commerce Development editions include sample stores to speed application development. This section describes the types of application assets that you might have to customize using WebSphere Commerce Developer and provides a matching of skill levels needed for the customization.

Asset types

We have grouped the application assets into the following categories:

- Store front assets
- Back office assets (business logic)
- Data files

Store front assets

Store front asset customization is primarily done for the look and feel of the store pages. For example, if you started with the B2B direct sample store (ToolTech), you would most definitely change the store logo and headings on the store pages. This type of development is commonly performed by a Web developer (Web designer).

Store front asset types include the following elements:

- Static HTML pages
- JavaServer™ Pages (JSPs)
- Images
- JavaScript

Within WebSphere Commerce, these assets types are contained within the sample store archives.

Back office assets (business logic)

Back office assets (new or modified) contain the business logic. Examples of back-office asset types include:

- Commands
- Data access beans
- Data beans

Beans enable the store front JSPs (containing data beans) to interact with the instance database to allow for the storage, retrieval, and manipulation of data.

Data files

The sample store archives contain many XML data files. Some of the data files are used for site and store configurations for taxes, shipping, and so on. There are also many XML data files used to populate the WebSphere Commerce catalog. The sample stores include sample product catalog data that has to be updated or replaced to build your customized store.

Matching skills to customization needs

A commerce store can have varying levels of customization. The skills required depend on this level of customization. The level of customization affects both the development time and skills needed to develop a store. We have categorized the customization requirements into three levels: Basic, intermediate, and advanced.

For each level of customization, we describe the tasks involved and list the IT specialists' roles to complete the tasks.

Basic customization

Basic store customization normally involves the following tasks:

- Catalog creation:

  This task involves creating a catalog and dividing the catalog into logical catalog groups or categories. The store's products are then assigned to catalog groups (categories).

- Web page design:

  Web page design involves the creation of graphics, static HTML pages, and JSPs for a customized look and feel for the store using the existing WebSphere Commerce commands.

These tasks are performed by the site administrator and Web developer.

Intermediate customization

Intermediate store customization includes the elements of a basic customization plus the following tasks:

- Custom command development:

  Custom commands, which are Java classes, are used for flow control and to implement business logic. They extend existing commands or are created as new commands. WebSphere Commerce commands are developed in WebSphere Commerce Developer.

- Custom data bean development:

  The development of data beans is required to represent dynamic content to be displayed in JSPs. The dynamic content is populated at runtime most often from the database. Data beans are developed in WebSphere Commerce Developer.

These tasks are performed by the Site administrator, Web developer, and Java programmer.

Advanced customization

Advanced store customization includes the elements of an intermediate customization plus the following tasks:

- Database customization:

  The alteration of the existing database schema is needed to meet specialized needs of a business.

- EJB development:

  EJB development is the development of persistent Java objects to represent data in the database.

For example, if you need to add a table to the database, you must create an EJB to query and update that table. EJBs are developed in WebSphere Commerce Developer.

- Data access bean development:

  The data access bean is developed in Java and uses EJBs to access data from the database. Data access beans are developed in WebSphere Commerce Developer.

These tasks are performed by the Site administrator, Web developer, Java programmer, database schema owner, and database administrator.

4.10.2 Suggested estimating procedure

To obtain a detailed time and cost estimate after you have created an outline project plan, consider using this sample procedure as a template:

1. Determine the factors that affect the accuracy of your project time, cost, and implicit quality estimates.
2. Establish a top-down cost and time estimate for the project.

   Initially all team members should work independently to develop separate cost and time estimates.

   a. Develop a methodology for estimating the overall cost and time needed for the project without referring to the details of the Work Breakdown Structure (WBS) or work packages. What is the basis for your methodology? Write down your rationale, calculations, and estimates.

   b. Using the same or a similar methodology, all team members develop a cost and time estimate for each phase of the project they are involved in.

   c. Individual estimates should now be compared. Determine the average estimated time and cost. Determine the range or uncertainty in these estimates.

   d. Discuss these estimates, and arrive at consensus number as well as the average. Pay particular attention in discussions to outliers; they might point to erroneous assumptions.
3. Establish a bottom-up or micro cost and time estimate for the project:

   a. Complete the time and cost estimate for each work package. At least two independent estimates for each work package should be obtained.

   b. Compare the independent work package estimates, reconcile any differences, and obtain mean[6] values for the cost and time for each work package.

   c. Roll-up (sum) the work package values to obtain a cost and time estimate for the next higher level in the WBS. Roll-up these estimates to obtain the next higher level cost and time estimate.

   d. Continue the roll-up process until you determine cost and time estimates for each project phase.

   e. Roll-up the project phase results to obtain an overall cost and time estimate.
4. Compare your macro and micro estimates. What are the differences? List the potential reasons for these differences.

[6] You might prefer to bias towards the worst case, it is generally a better predictor.

5. Refine the bottom-up estimate:
   a. Identify which tasks in the WBS can be done in parallel.
   b. Refine your time estimates by taking into account these parallel tasks and identifying the critical path.
6. Compare your macro and micro estimates again. Reconcile any differences.
7. Record your final, detailed time and cost estimates.

Variables to consider

Here is a sample list of variables to consider:

- Development time
- Cost per feature based on high level design
- Time and Costs to produce estimates
- Project Management time and total cost per manager
- Costs for hardware, software, development, testing environment, and tools for each team member
- Time required for:
  - Research, requirements, and design
  - Prelaunch, launch and post-launch support
- Training time and costs for:
  - Project management team members
  - Development team members
  - Quality Assurance team and infrastructure
  - Content Management team members
  - Architecture team members
  - Infrastructure team members
  - Support team members

4.11 Conclusion

What was your highest expectation for your WebSphere Commerce project? A flawless implementation that results in a high quality customer-happy eCommerce site that meets or exceeds customer expectations, within time and cost estimates, and that is cheap to maintain and cost-effective to enhance?

High expectations are good because they give you something to aspire to. They keep you excited about the project and keep you motivated.

So how do you make it come true?

1. If you lack experience with WebSphere Commerce, engage an experienced person to help you, at least on a part time basis, in addition to other contracted development resources.
2. Be very clear about what you expect to deliver.
3. Communicate and document the goals of the project with the team.
4. Know what actions to take and when, and do them.
5. Break the project into iterations, and learn from each release.

WebSphere Commerce leads the marketplace in providing customized eCommerce sites built on a common store framework. It is complicated, time-consuming, and expensive to build a customized Web site, but WebSphere Commerce projects follow a well-defined path. Follow the path taken by other implementations and you will be successful as well.

5

Organize your eCommerce resources

The previous chapter gave you an introduction to the first steps you should take in setting up a WebSphere Commerce project. We talked about some of the critical success factors, and the risks, that accompany an eCommerce project. We stressed the importance of the Project Sponsor, and getting the full support of the business.

This chapter is addressed to the project manager: how the project manager should organize project resources to get the most out of them. First, we outline a roadmap to a successful WebSphere Commerce project implementation. Next, we list the roles involved in the project along with the skills needed to be present in the person taking that role to ensure all project tasks are efficiently completed. Finally, we give you some options for engaging specialized teams in the project implementation, while at the same time staying involved in the project.

5.1 Roadmap for a WebSphere Commerce project

WebSphere Commerce project implementations are not all that easy! This is a fact, and anyone who has ever attempted a WebSphere Commerce project would agree with its validity. At the same time, we are not trying to deter you from implementing WebSphere Commerce — quite the contrary — WebSphere Commerce provides a comprehensive set of features and capabilities that is not found in any other equivalent product in the software market today. Perhaps this is one of the reasons that makes it quite complex to use, at least for the first time, but it is also one of the reasons for using WebSphere Commerce. And like everything else, it gets easier with time and experience.

In this section, we give you a roadmap to a successful WebSphere Commerce project implementation. We go through the phases that the project is divided into, highlighting the major milestones of each phase. This should act as an introduction to what lies ahead in your project. It can also be an indicator as you go along of how well the project is progressing and what still needs to be done before you can say that you are finished.

Figure 5-1 shows the various project phases plotted against time and arranged according to the project roles that are involved in each phase. In later sections, we go more into details, focusing on specific parts of the life cycle and the roles involved in them.

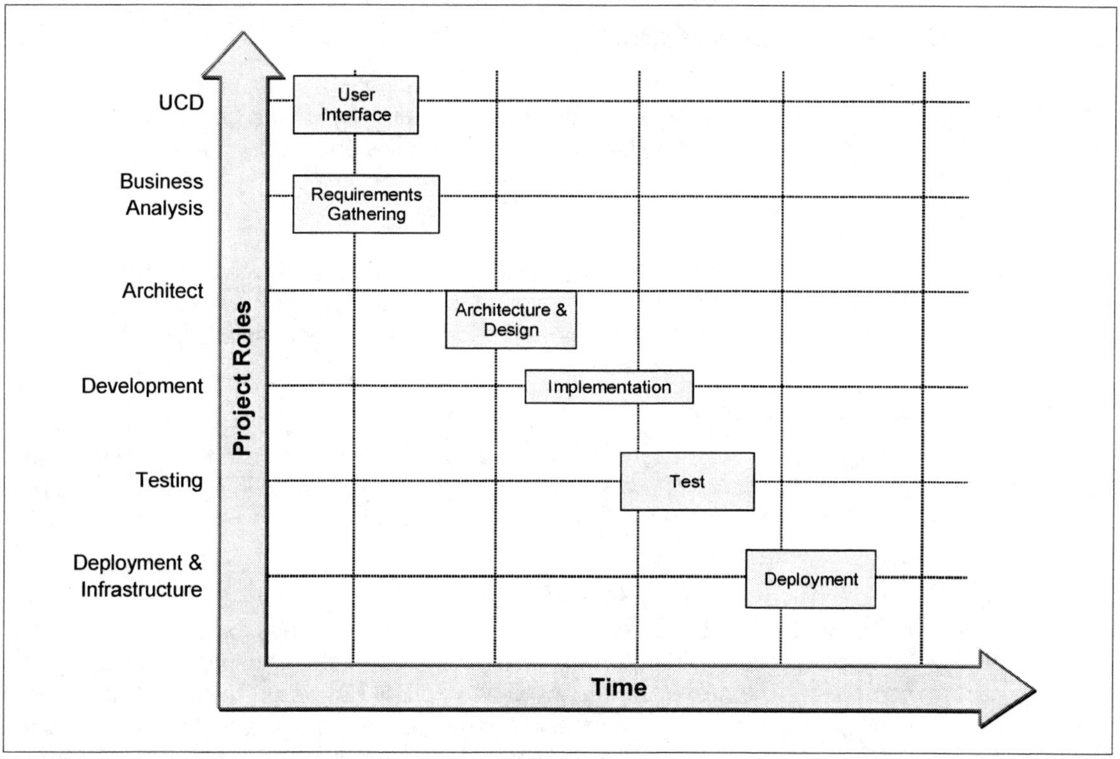

Figure 5-1 Project phases

We are focusing in this book on the overall project life cycle as opposed to the development life cycle, which we include here as part of the overall cycle. For details on the development life cycle and its milestones and artifacts, refer to the Redbooks publication, "*Best Practices and Tools for Creating WebSphere Commerce Sites*", SG24-6699, at:

`http://www.redbooks.ibm.com/redpieces/abstracts/sg246699.html`

5.1.1 Project life cycle phases

The steps you must go through to create an eCommerce site divide into three "engagements," thus called because most WebSphere Commerce deployments involve the engagement of IBM consultants or IBM Business Partners to perform some or all of the work required to build and deploy an eCommerce site. If you are not considering engaging IBM or IBM Business Partners to do at least some of the activities, such as graphic design, it would be unusual.

You follow these steps to create an eCommerce site:

1. Pre-engagement activities:

   Pre-engagement activities start with an initial business proposal (IBP) to develop an eCommerce business and culminate in the decision to go ahead with investing in an eCommerce site and the choice of an eCommerce platform.

2. Engagement activities:

   Engagement activities start with a close scrutiny of the business proposal and turn it into a business and development plan to build the eCommerce business. The engagement step ends with the successful deployment and *Go Live!* of the Web site.

3. Post-engagement activities:

   Post-engagement activities are the most important step in the eCommerce life cycle. Post-engagement activities are led by your business users to maximize the revenue and profit that you can gain from the Web site.

Pre-engagement activities

After your business has made an initial business proposal to consider developing an eCommerce business, you are asked to research eCommerce products to help realize the proposal. You involve IBM, IBM Business Partners, and other suppliers to assess your needs, eCommerce technology, and different paths to take — whether to build the solution in house, to outsource, or a combination.

In the early days of getting to know the market, products, and available software services, you need to familiarize yourself with all the products that perform the functionalities you require. Next, you should start filtering out the products that are not adequate either in functionality, price, or future scalability options. Then, you can compare the remaining products in terms of their features and prices to try to form an idea of the differences between them and what makes each one special. Table 5-1 gives you an idea of how to make such a comparison between the major eCommerce products in the market today.

Table 5-1 Some comparable features of eCommerce software

Features	WebSphere Commerce
Business models	Support for multiple business models; check 2.1, "Business models" on page 22 for details
Infrastructure support	Supports multiple Web servers and databases and has advanced integration capabilities
Development tools	Strong comprehensive development tools based on best practices, supporting different roles in the development process

Features	WebSphere Commerce
Scalability	Support leveraging advanced server capabilities, including clustering, load balancing, fault tolerance, and caching
Skills	Availability of development skills and IBM Business Partners to build the solution

After familiarizing yourself with the features that the key eCommerce products provide, you start the next step in the cycle: choosing which one to go with. In order to do this right, you need to follow four steps:

1. Issue a request for proposal.
2. Look at production Web sites created by the different products, and Web sites of your competitors.
3. Ask for demonstrations of each product.
4. Research all the reading material, including consultants reports, available for each product.

In 5.1.2, "Pre-engagement timeline and milestones" on page 163, we talk about the above steps and organize them in a timeline to help you get a better understanding of the pre-engagement phase.

Engagement activities

Engagement activities can be said to form the development life cycle. During the project development life cycle, you go through many activities, which are grouped into phases that are typical of most Web projects, if not all. These are organized into their Rational Unified Process phases, "RAID", in Table 5-2.

Table 5-2 Engagement phases

RUP	Typical Web project
Inception	**R**equirements gathering
Elaboration	**A**nalysis and design
Construction	**I**mplementation and testing
Transition	**D**eployment

We typically recommend organizing development activities according the to Rational Unified Process development model, and to break a project down into multiple iterations - so called Agile development[1].

[1] See `http://agilemanifesto.org/` for the Agile Manifesto and `http://www.agilealliance.com/library` for many articles and books.

Each iteration delivers some usable and "completed" functionality that should be made available to your customers so you can gain from the marketing and feedback that enables. You might have to limit the deployment because of capacity, geographical, or brand perception issues; there are many examples of firms doing this in a variety of ways.

We can assume that the project development phases are done more or less in sequence in any given project. Therefore, in most projects we begin by gathering requirements, then analyzing them, and then starting on the design. This is followed by implementation, which precedes testing. Finally, when everything found during the testing phase is fixed, we proceed with deploying the project and going live.

> **Note:** In case you are implementing a solution using an iterative or agile approach, the above statement still applies. This is because in any given iteration, the same phases of the project are visited in the same order. The only difference with the iterative approach is that only a subset of the tasks in each phase is performed in each iteration.

Although a WebSphere Commerce project is no different from any other Web project in terms of what phases it is divided into, there are some differences in the composition of the tasks that are carried out in each phase. This is because a WebSphere Commerce implementation is largely a matter of customizing functions that already closely resemble the operation of a real-life store.

As a result, some standard development tasks need not be performed, or are less extensively performed, and some customization tasks that are not done, or are not done so extensively in normal software development have to be added to the plan[2]. In the "Major implementation activities" section, we outline the main tasks to be performed in our project. Where appropriate, we indicate if the task is one that is present in most projects or if it is more characteristic of a WebSphere Commerce solution.

Post-engagement activities

After the successful deployment of your store, there are four main activities you engage in:

1. Regular operational tasks, such as handling user queries, and monitoring the Web site for any operational abnormalities.
2. Updating the business content of the store, adding promotions and marketing spots, and analyzing shopping patterns.

[2] In particular, usability and performance are much more critical than would be the case for software normally constructed by a firm for its own internal use. In this respect, Web site development is much more akin to developing software for consumer use.

3. Troubleshooting and applying software maintenance.
4. Studying usability feedback from users click analysis, and planning enhancements to the store.

We describe these four activities in a little more detail in the next sections.

Regular operational tasks

Operational tasks divide into two types: tasks to keep the software running, and tasks to keep the business running, day to day:

- Software tasks:

  Unless you have decided to outsource your WebSphere Commerce deployment to a hosting company, you require a team on 24x7 coverage to monitor and manage the Web site. Most tasks are routine, such archiving logs and deleting them, and require no additional skills over and above operational staff running WebSphere Application Server. You do, however, need to invest some time and effort into customizing or modifying your existing performance monitoring tools so they can alert your operational team to critical situations.

- Business tasks:

  You have to train and set up your call center to handle custom queries and train them in using the Sales Center, a WebSphere Commerce tool that gives CSRs access to the WebSphere Commerce system ("Sales Center" on page 71)

  Decide how much to train your call center in dealing with user interface problems, both Web site navigation, "How do I get to the kiddies toys page?" and browser or connection problems. Decide which issues they can deal with (cookies being blocked, perhaps) and which need to be forwarded to the IT operations help desk. Do you need to make changes to your customer call center tracking software?

There is more information on operational tasks in Chapter 11, "Running your Web site" on page 325.

Updating the business content of the store

Business users are responsible for performing all the updates to the Web site that keep the business profitable. The tasks include:

- Creating new catalog content and updating the master catalog.
- Creating sales catalogs to support different markets, market segments, brands and seasonal promotions.
- Pricing, tax and shipping cost details.
- Adding and managing relationships with suppliers and resellers.
- Managing payments and fulfillment with suppliers and resellers.

- Creating marketing campaigns and product promotions.
- Analyzing buying patterns

There are a number of tools for business users, which are discussed in other sections. These include:

- "WebSphere Commerce Accelerator" on page 69
- "Management Center" on page 73
- "Staging server data" on page 61
- "Workspaces" on page 62
- "Analytics" on page 115

Maintenance and support

During pre-engagement and proposal evaluation, it is important to consider the maintenance options provided by each solution provider. Does the supplier provide a warranty providing that, within a specified amount of time, any bugs or problems of any sort are fixed by the solution provider at no additional charge? Do you need to purchase a maintenance contract with the supplier, or does the supplier provide source code, build procedures and training for your staff, or a third party?

Are you protected against any possible intellectual property infringements by the supplier? Do you have rights to the source code and any intellectual property it contains? Are you, or another partner, able to extend the code for a future release? Do you, or the IBM Business Partner, have a support contract with IBM in case there are problems with WebSphere Commerce or its tools?

Tackle these issues during the pre-engagement and proposal stages. You do not necessarily have to make a decision about how to support the product then but you want to have options you can exercise when you are more familiar with the solution, and when you have learnt more about the strengths and weaknesses of your team, and the IBM Business Partner. You should plan now; then when you make these decisions, you will get the best package for your business.

There is more information about applying maintenance and troubleshooting in Chapter 11, "Running your Web site" on page 325 and Chapter 12, "Troubleshoot your eCommerce site" on page 359.

Usability feedback and enhancing the store

Even before launch, you are probably already considering further enhancements to the store, features that did not make it to the cut, and were earmarked for the next release. Use the inception phase review (see 5.3.3, "Governance" on page 196) to make sure that real user feedback and analysis of user behavior in the Web site is contributing to the scope of the next iteration.

5.1.2 Pre-engagement timeline and milestones

In this section, we discuss the activities or milestones listed in "Pre-engagement activities" on page 158. Figure 5-2 shows a graph of the activities plotted against the teams involved and time. The points of intersection of teams and time show major milestones during the phase.

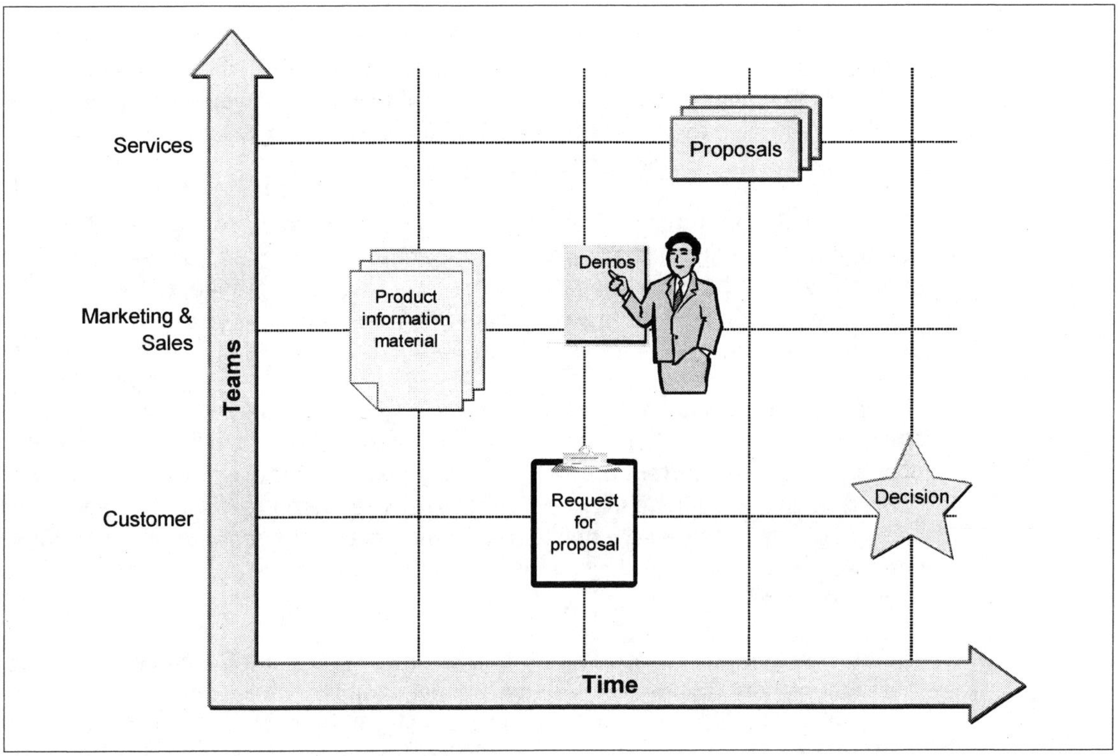

Figure 5-2 Project pre-engagement timeline

Request for proposal

The phrase "Request for Proposal", or RFP, is used in business in the United States, and elsewhere in the world, to describe a document written in a Q&A format designed by the customer, to ask suppliers in a structured way to propose a solution to a business problem. It is an organized way to initiate a bidding process which, unlike a request for quotation (RFQ) invites discussion and not simply the presentation of a priced solution.

When deciding what questions to ask in an RFP, do not limit yourself to technical and contractual questions about building the Web site, instead range widely over many aspects of running an eCommerce business. When describing the features you require in your RFP, include all functionalities you currently require in your online store, as well as support for any features that you might want to add in the future. If you limit yourself to features you require now, you might end up with a solution that is difficult to extend in the future to support your growing needs.

For example, your needs today might well be met by the Express edition of WebSphere Commerce, but if you have plans to take the Web site global, or to add IBM Business Partners among your resellers, then it would be better for you to consider using the Extended Sites model, which is only available in the Enterprise edition of WebSphere Commerce.

Include both your functional and non-functional requirements in an RFP. Even though non-functional requirements are harder to identify and usually need quantification, you must consider them — not just performance, but also availability and recovery. Ask yourself some hard questions about evaluating unlikely contingencies, and how much it is worth spending to manage them.

For example, for a mixed retailer, if your main IT site is taken out by a natural disaster or fire, and you have taken normal precautions of backing up your configuration and current orders, you might be able to lease new facilities and get back up and running in a week. You will suffer some revenue loss and some loss of goodwill. For a sole online trader, the impact will be much more serious, because your online reliability is essential to your brand and consumers' confidence in you.

In addition to getting proposals from IBM for a WebSphere Commerce implementation, or indeed from any product supplier for proposals for customizing their product, ask for proposals from the supplier's Business Partners and from firms that are specialized in certain markets or eCommerce functions. If you request proposals from IBM Business Partners, they will call in to IBM for assistance such as for sizing the hardware and software requirements.

Consider how you are going to evaluate the proposals. It is not going to be just a simple matter of price; proposals are too complex and varied to compare "like for like". You need to prepare a team to do the evaluations, and include people on the team with varied business, financial, legal, and technical perspectives. Some members of the team, at least, should have worked on the original RFP formulation, and considered then, how to evaluate the responses.

Ask the supplier or IBM Business Partner for references that you can talk to as well as having a meeting with them to hear the proposal and discuss its contents.

Demonstrations

Demonstrations (demos) are as close as you can easily get to “kick the tires”. Most eCommerce products on the market today have specialized pre-sales teams that are responsible for performing demos on their products to potential customers at no charge. They, or the IBM Business Partners that you are considering, might be prepared to tailor the demo to your requirements. Include a request for a tailored demo in your RFP. That way, the supplier is going to have to engage some of their technical people to tailor the demo for you, and you should be able to get access to them to ask questions. Use the demo as an opportunity to ask technical questions of the demo team. They should know the product extremely well, and also whether there are unusual aspects to your requirements.

Make sure that your evaluation team are prepared for the demo; they should have some preliminary discussions with the demo teams about what will be demonstrated so the demo can be tailored to your needs. Your evaluation team can get the demos focused on tasks that are important to you and comparable between demos. You could also ask a representative from the development team to be present in the demonstration for technical questions that might arise.

5.1.3 Project implementation timeline

As mentioned before, a WebSphere Commerce project implementation follows the same phases that other project implementations follow. Various teams are involved in those phases, with some joining the project to do a specific job for a limited amount of time and then leaving, after reaching a milestone. There is a flow of activities along the project between teams and phases. In each phase, one or a very few number of teams is the main player, responsible for most tasks and achieving the major milestones of that phase.

As project manager you are responsible for communicating this flow to the team, largely through the project status meeting. The objectives of the team change as the project progresses, and the tasks in the critical path change. The priorities of the whole team change to focus on the changing critical tasks. In subsequent references to this flow, we call it the project timeline.

Figure 5-3 gives a high-level view of the major activities you go through during a typical WebSphere Commerce project, organized by the phases listed in 5.1.1, “Project life cycle phases” on page 157 and project teams responsible.

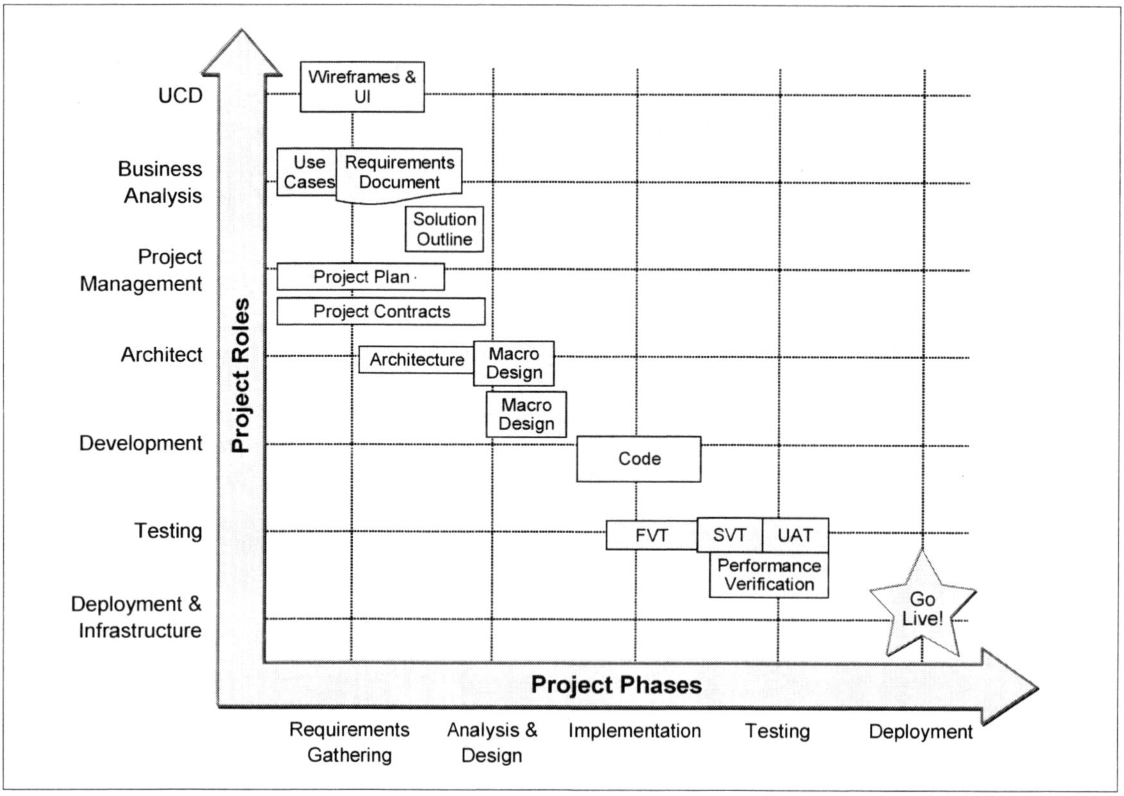

Figure 5-3 Project implementation timeline

Major implementation activities

In this section, we go through all the activities in Figure 5-3, listing the tasks that you need to do.

A useful way to analyze and manage activities is provided by the ETVX model (Figure 5-4), introduced by IBM during the 1980's. The plan for each activity includes a written list of entry and exit conditions, a list of tasks that must be performed, and the verification or validation tests that measure how far the tasks have been done. Weekly status meetings track which activities have started, and how complete they are based on the verification measures.

The software development process is managed like a manufacturing line. Failure of an activity to meet the entry conditions is like a lack of parts at a production station. Applying the ideas of Just In Time or Lean manufacturing, a red light goes on if an activity has not met its entry criteria in time, and (as with software development), rather than carry on with reduced efficiency, the project manager can refocus resources on the step in the critical path that has stalled.

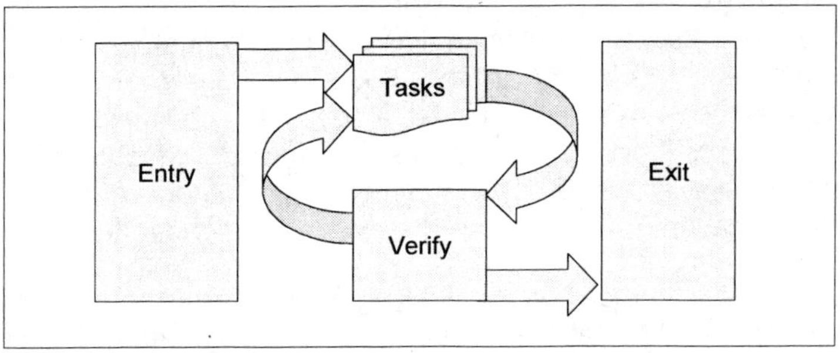

Figure 5-4 ETVX activity model

Use cases

The use case model is one of the earliest milestones in any project and one of the most important. The reason for this is that business users participate in defining the functionality that is being offered to them, and to customers, by the Web site, and it is one of the tried and tested ways that IT teams use to drill down into what functionality users really require. If you can build a Web site mock up to animate the use cases, perhaps by using a story board approach, so much the better (see "Wireframes and user interface" on page 168). Whatever helps transport your team's imagination to visualize how the store will appear also helps to reveal aspects of the design that might be overlooked.

One of the major values of building comprehensive use cases is that although building the use cases is a time consuming business involving a number of people, they are easily changed in response to feedback, and when done, allow specialists with different skills to work in parallel analyzing the use case model.

The use case model serves as a point of departure for thinking about how to customize the Web site, about whether there are going to be performance bottlenecks which could be solved by a different combination of functions on pages, whether there are going to be usability problems with navigating the Web site, and what test cases the test team need to build. These activities continue in the analysis and elaboration phase of the project.

The business analysis team is the owner of the use case model. If the use cases have been prepared by a IBM Business Partner, then the business analyst should be the approver. The use cases should be reviewed by the teams, such as the development team, which depend on them, as being sufficient for their needs. This does not mean that the use cases do not change. On the contrary, use cases are changed throughout the project duration.The project manager should keep use cases under change control from the end of the inception phase, when the use cases are signed off, and evaluate the impact of changes on teams that are dependent upon them.

Wireframes and user interface

The next step, after completing the use case model, is to start working on the wireframes. Wireframes are the click-through paths for your Web site: what your Web site does for users. They are a necessary preliminary to story-boarding how the Web site looks, using graphics. Wireframing, which can be a simple pencil and paper exercise, is one of the most powerful tools to find any problems with the use cases or with the logical flow of operations required by the customer.

At the same time as you are working on wireframing and checking the flow and functionality of the Web site, your graphics design team have started work on the style of the Web pages — the colors, layout, fonts, and styles to be used. The storyboard brings the style and the functionality together and should give everyone a very clear picture of the Web site. Your user centered design team and performance team, in particular, should review the storyboard for problems.

The user centered design specialists[3] are looking in particular at the interaction style of the Web site, and whether users will complete purchasing tasks successfully, or whether they will get lost and perhaps go to a different Web site. The performance team are looking at how the Web page maps to execution paths on different servers. What are the caching challenges? Can you avoid major bottlenecks by small changes to the mapping of function to Web pages?

Requirements document

In conjunction with the use cases being finalized and the user interface and wireframes analysis starting, the business analysis team are writing and managing the requirements document, perhaps with the assistance of a specialized tool such as IBM Rational Requsitepro, or using Lotus Notes®, or some other collaborative document management system. A key part of this activity, as has already been discussed, is phasing requirements into an iterative development plan. This requires the participation of many roles to agree on phasing and to ensure each iteration delivers a meaningful functionality.

The requirements document is divided into two basic parts, one for the functional requirements and the other for the non-functional requirements. Use cases should be linked to requirements (Using Reqpro), or indexed in some fashion, so that you have confidence that each requirement is addressed in the development plan. Each requirement should be allocated "shadow" owners from each development phase to be clear who is responsible for development and testing.

The requirements document is mainly the responsibility of the business analysis team. But, like almost all of the other artifacts of the project, the requirements document is by no means considered final and non-editable. As well as being reviewed at the start of each new iteration, the requirements under development

---

[3] "*useit.com: Jakob Nielsen's Web Site*", found at `http://www.useit.com/` is a good place to look to understand the impact of usability on Web site success.

document can be altered (under change control) during an iteration, if new information warrants it. If you have engaged IBM Business Partners, this might well require a contract amendment.

Solution outline

The solution outline is the statement of the project time frame, solution scope and cost estimate, and is a critical controlled document shared between a customer and solution providers engaged in the customization (see Appendix A, "Solution Outline Template" on page 379). For the solution outline to be complete, the requirements document needs to have been completed, including the use cases section, since these describe the requirements in more detail. There should be at least a 90% complete project plan so that there remain no major uncertainties and risks have been evaluated and mitigation plans understood.

The solution outline is a joint effort between the business analyst, the solution architect and the project manager, with members of other teams contributing to specialized sections. If the solution outline is going to be used as an exhibit in contracts with IBM Business Partners, you also need the approval of the legal department.

Project plan

The project plan plays an essential part in ensuring that the project implementation is done according to the time frame agreed upon by the parties involved and within the budget allocated for it. It lists all the tasks involved in the project categorized according to the activities of which they are a part. For each task, there is a listing of the resources needed to carry it out as well as the duration estimated for it. There are numerous project planning tools to help you document and track a project plan. It takes a good deal of time and experience to use the tools effectively, and to get net benefit from using them. There are free open source project management tools such as OpenProj[4] as well as proprietary software packages such as Microsoft Project.

A practical plan always has a contingency buffer. A planned buffer costs time and money - how much to allow is a matter of experience, and depends on the success the team has had doing estimates in the past, and the number of risks in the plan. The size of the buffer is especially important if you need to meet a particular date for business reasons - as in the case of our ITSO Baby Magic store that is planned to go live immediately after Thanksgiving. Not allowing any contingency usually results in greater costs.

The project manager is the owner of the project plan. Any additional tasks, changes to or deletions of tasks or resources from the project plan require the project manager's approval, and are usually proposed at project status meetings. This is done to ensure the integrity of the plan.

[4] `http://openproj.org/openproj`

Project contracts

Contracts are part of your business relationship with suppliers. They are written to define the work to be done, and to an extent, how it should be done and managed. The contract defines acceptance and completion, and provides a framework to manage risk. Contracts have two purposes, a legal agreement to fall back upon should events go wrong, and to form the basis of a positive business relationship. Unsuccessful projects only focus on the legal framework, which is mainly relevant only when projects fail. Successful projects focus on how the relationship is going to work.

Risks are sometimes formalized into contracts as penalty charges and by putting the project cost up, have the positive effect of building contingency into the plan. However, if penalty charges are written per supplier, they can have the negative effect of pitting suppliers against each other, lowering quality. An alternative approach is to use fixed price contracts and for you, the client, to bear the risk, and only allow a small contingency in supplier contracts. If a supplier runs into trouble, then the supplier loses any profit they would make, but you bear the costs of the overrun.

This approach, which requires active risk management by the client as part of the supplier's project management team, encourages cooperative working and can be allied to a combined bonus paid out of the contingency fund to all suppliers if the project comes in on target.

Ultimately, what type of contracts you write, whether time and materials, fixed price, or including penalty clauses or bonuses, is something that evolves from your business's history of contracting. This includes learning how to work with suppliers effectively, as well as discovering how flexible and capable particular suppliers are to do business in the way you want.

Architecture

The solution architecture is the foundation on which the solution is built. An architecture organizes a system into components and describes the relationship and interaction between components. It is often split into analysis and design, and there is a fuzzy line dividing responsibility for design between the solution architect and the lead designers. The analysis task focuses on how to map requirements to a set of components and interactions that deliver the required functions to the standards required.

The key inputs are business requirements and use cases, the selection of a WebSphere Commerce starter store, IT requirements, and the existing IT infrastructure. The output is a solution architecture document[5], and refinements to the project plan. Architectural design takes the next refinement step and defines data models, such as database schemas for catalogs, and interfaces to components. As you can see, this overlaps with the activities described next in "Macro design".

In WebSphere Commerce project implementations, it is common to have only a short time dedicated to architecture, since a WebSphere Commerce project should not be breaking new architectural grounds, but customizing one of the sample stores that have already been architected. You normally have only a short period of time to deal with any architecture problems that might arise from the integration of the solution.

A WebSphere Commerce project implementation should have a solution architect in responsible for the architecture of the solution. This person needs to have a very good understanding of WebSphere Commerce components and how they interact in order to add new components in a maintainable way. Within an iteration, specification of architectural customizations should be complete before the end of the analysis and design elaboration phase.

Macro design

Macro design is the high-level design of the major system components identified in the architecture. It contains the database design for the entire system, which in case of WebSphere Commerce projects, is not something to be built from scratch, since the system already has a database design. The output from the macro design also affects the project plan, because every time you go deeper into the system details, tasks become more apparent along with the number of resources needed and the level of skills each should have.

The logical owner of the macro design is the solution architect. The data base design and component interfaces have to be stable, and are best thought of as part of the solution architecture. But if, in your organization, the macro design is performed by development teams, then practical ownership should lie with a senior developer who perhaps is not engaged in day to day coding. This person appreciates the importance of interface stability and would withstand the pressure to get code into the next build without sufficient investigation of its consequences.

[5] We do not include a template for a Solution Architect Document (SAD). RUP provides one, or you can visit `http://www.ibm.com/developerworks/rational/library/05/0816_Louis/`, which includes a link to a sample SAD.

Micro design

The micro design focuses on laying out a complete coding framework including all the classes that need to be developed, what methods they contain, and the types of parameters to be used in communication between classes. The inputs to the micro design are the component interfaces and database design, and the requirements and use cases. As parts of the micro design are completed, work can begin on coding, writing test cases, and unit testing. Micro design, coding, and unit testing are most likely all performed by the same people. The micro design should be mentored by development leads with input from the new members of the development team.

Code and unit test

The purpose of the code and unit test phase is, as the name implies, to actually write the code of the application and verify modules meet their specification, based on the system architecture, macro design, and micro design. If those phases are done correctly, then the coding phase can be expected to run smoothly for the most part. Typically, actual coding should take about 10%-20% of the development cycle.

A good way to ensure that the testing phases, which follow this one, run smoothly themselves, is for developers to take part in code inspections[6], to run automated code checking tools, and to write or generate test cases for each part of their code — automating running the test cases as far as possible so that each new build is easily regression tested. Some organizations find it effective to have developers write test cases before coding as part of writing use cases and micro design, as a way prepare to write code and improve the quality of delivered code.

There is a test tool to assist with this in the Rational Development Platform, and there are many other commercially available tools. The importance of unit testing cannot be emphasized enough. Even the most trivial code can and does contain bugs that are overlooked when writing the code, but are immediately obvious when identified by a test tool. Discovering and fixing bugs in unit test saves a great deal of time in later testing phases, when it is very much more difficult to diagnose a problem and identify the failing component.

FVT

Functional verification test (FVT) is conducted by the test team to make sure that each system component functions correctly, using the components' published interfaces. Functional verification test does not test component integration and communication. It ensures that components work as designed.

---

[6] A recent survey of the literature estimated that *formal* code inspections found bugs at one quarter of the cost of unit testing. See Formal Inspections, which can be found at `https://www.goldpractices.com/practices/fi/`

In order for the FVT phase to be executed as efficiently as possible, the testing team should have prepared their test scenarios and test cases, and have reviewed them with the solution architect and developers, before the test phase begins. They should conduct "sniff tests" — running tests against development builds to debug test cases — and they should design and run an acceptance test that needs to be passed before FVT is started. If FVT is started too early, the project team, particularly developers, spend too much time diagnosing and fixing FV problems, rather than engaging in writing and unit testing code. When FVT has started, a regression test should be run against each candidate build. The regression test bucket should grow as problems are fixed, and their verification tests are added to the regression test bucket. If new function is staged into the FV test, then there needs to be mini-acceptance tests for the new function.

SVT

In contrast with the FVT, system verification test (SVT) is conducted to test the integration between the various system components and the overall system functionality.

For projects that have a substantial vendor, or IBM Business Partner component to them, you have to decide whether to duplicate the vendors testing with your own, and whether to participate in aspects of the vendor's process, such as reviewing test cases and attending status meetings. The logical point to run your own independent testing is when vendors' code is integrated with your own IT systems. This is likely to be SVT. The vendor test team might run tests of the whole Web site, against "scaffolded" integration points, and then your own test team can run the final integration tests against your test systems.

Performance test

The performance team need to be involved in design and coding phases, to design performance models to predict throughput and response times, and to do performance profiling of builds to calibrate the performance models, recommend design changes, and recommend where and how to implement caching.

Performance testing is essential at all stages of the project. Performance tests during SVT might identify some unexpected integration problems, but essentially the tests are verifying that the system is performing as expected. You are on the road to perdition if your first performance measurements are made during SVT.

If there is substantial vendor involvement, you need to build early performance involvement into the engagements and have the vendor provide performance measurements during the vendors' testing. Your own performance team should not have to repeat the vendors' measurements, but like your SVT team, measure performance of the system when it is integrated with your own IT components. The performance test team might also be responsible for delivering performance monitoring tools; see "Performance monitoring" on page 329.

UAT

The user acceptance test (UAT), like the performance verification test, should be a verification of all the user centered design activity that has gone into the design and implementation of the solution up to this point. There are normally two classes of users, your customers and business users, and it is important to select users representative of each class. For business users, this should be straightforward, but for your customers it is important that you select people who have not been involved in the solution beforehand, so called "cold users", and the sampled users must be representative of your customer demographics.

Often, the User Acceptance Test has been regarded as a verification that the Web site meets the requirements of its business users and the development team hands responsibility for UAT over to the business users. After all, they are driving sales using the Web site, and think of the Web site as "theirs". The business users might well conduct user trials to verify the Web site — typically by running an online feedback exercise conducted by a market research company. But doing this is to mistake the purpose of the user acceptance test.

The goal of the user acceptance test is to verify that customers have no difficulty in finding the products they want to research, that the promotional and marketing aids the Web site provides to help close the sale, work as designed, and that users can order items and track them confidently. The user acceptance test aims to quantify the success users have performing tasks using the Web site. You do not want to lose customers who cannot navigate the site, and you do want customers to notice promotional and marketing material without losing the sale.

There are many unexpected ways that you can slip up in Web site design, and unforeseen consequences of poor page design which cost you business. The solution is a professional user centered design team which as well as understanding the principles of good Web design, also does systematic testing to measure design changes. The UAT test must be conducted in a repeatable manner, so that changes to the Web site have measurable consequences.

Go Live!

This is the moment everyone has been waiting for. Let us consider what are the components that must be deployed to go live, and what are the ongoing responsibilities of the deployment team. *Go Live!* is not a once-only event.

In order to reach this point, the deployment team has to be involved in setting up the infrastructure, hardware, and software necessary to launch the site; educate business users, CSRs, and IT operational staff; and run any beta program for shoppers, CSRs, and business users. Figure 5-5 shows the five main technical components of a WebSphere Commerce site, and who is responsible for creating these components.

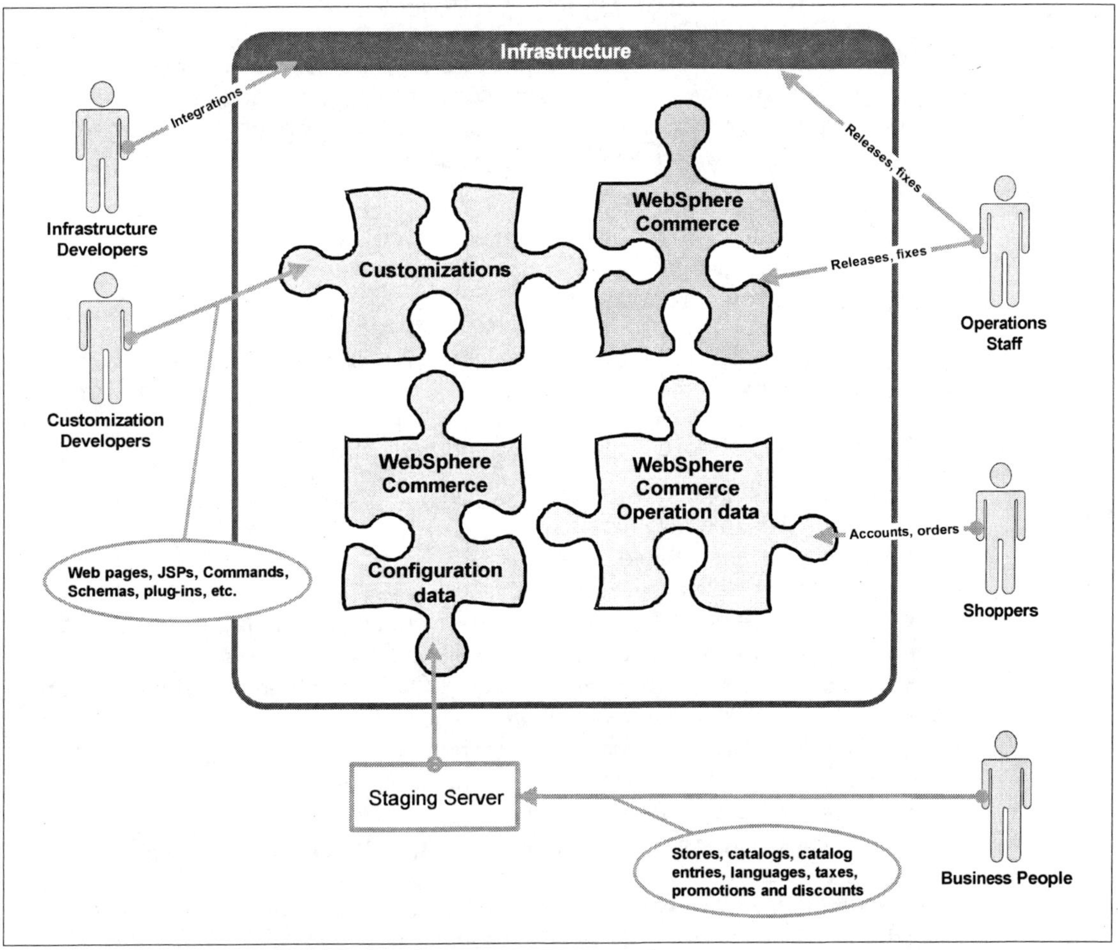

Figure 5-5 Deployment of WebSphere Commerce components

The deployment team is a collaboration between the project implementation team, the business team, and the infrastructure team, managed by the project manager. The goal of the deployment team, in addition to overseeing going live for the first time, is to put itself out of business for the operation and update of the Web site. Future isolated updates to any of the components should be possible without disruption of the other components. Chapter 10, "Development, test, and production environments" on page 307 describes in detail the activities to deploy the WebSphere Commerce Web site.

5.1.4 Agile development and WebSphere Commerce

Agile software development is a software engineering methodology that is being adopted by an increasing number of software engineers and development teams worldwide. It is a response to their experience with changing requirements. The practitioners sought to develop principles based on:

- Close programmer/business person cooperation
- Frequent face-to-face rather than written communication
- Frequent delivery of new function with business value
- Tight, self organized teams

Thus, requirements change became less of a crisis and more of an opportunity to build competitive software that software customers want.

The principles of Agile Software Development[7] are to:

- Deliver valuable software early, continuously, and frequently (within weeks to two months).
- Maintain a sustainable work rate.
- Measure progress by working software.
- Harness changing requirements for competitive advantage.
- Get developers and business people to work together daily.
- Build projects around motivated individuals. Trust them to get the job done.
- Use face-to-face communication.
- Enhance agility with attention to technical excellence and good design.
- Keep it simple: It is essential not to do unnecessary work.
- Organize yourselves around what you need to do.
- Review your progress, and then adjust your behavior accordingly.

The methodology drives software development into having multiple iterations, each of which results in a working piece of the software which has distinct business value that can be tested and delivered to the customer.

The reason behind its increasing popularity with stakeholders is that it focuses on developing leaner, cheaper software more tuned to customers' needs, which makes businesses more competitive. Customer input to functional requirements is more informed by being based on working software, and because it is received earlier, it is therefore acted upon earlier. Having working software earlier increases the trust and confidence of the stakeholders, and reduces the cost and risk of other deployment activities by enabling them to start earlier.

At the beginning of each iteration, a list of requirements and targets to be reached during the iteration are listed in the iteration plan. Normally, the requirements that are expected to be more risky, are included in earlier iterations

[7] Taken from The Agile Manifesto, `http://www.agilemanifesto.org`

to allow their implementation to be tested more thoroughly in all the later iterations. One aspect, which sets the agile development methodology apart from other software development methodologies based on iterations, is that the iteration time for agile development is much shorter, numbering only several weeks or so, and that predetermined duration should not be increased even if the work cannot be finished by the deadline. In that case, the scope of the iteration is is changed by dropping features from the iteration to meet the deadline.

The agile development methodology is considered a good approach to use in WebSphere Commerce projects in general. Unlike developing a solution from scratch, which requires a lot of up-front architectural and design work to build the solution framework, with WebSphere Commerce much of that work is already done, and it is easier to start early delivery of functionally valuable components. WebSphere Commerce Web sites require close ties between developers, business users, and the marketplace to assess how well the Web site is working. It is also relatively easy, compared with other software projects, to stage functionality, adding value incrementally. Even if the project slips its deadline, at least there is a working site with the most important features tested and ready to go live, until the rest of the features are completed.

5.2 Project roles, responsibilities, and skills

In order to carry on with your implementation of your eCommerce Web site, you need to be fully aware of all the roles, their responsibilities, and their associated skill profiles, required to carry out each task in the implementation. This saves you later on from unpleasant surprises, if you discover that there are certain activities in the project that need to be done, with specific focus on skills that are lacking in the implementation team.

There are both technical and non-technical roles involved in an eCommerce project implementation, with different sets of skills for each. The key to a successful implementation is to know the skills required for each role and to assign the right person to it, making them available to the project when needed. In the following sections we list the skills required for each role and the approximate project time when they are needed.

5.2.1 Technical roles

Technical roles are involved in all parts of the project, including pre-engagement, implementation, and post-engagement phases. Some technical roles belong to the solution provider teams, while others are carried out by the customer teams. Not all technical roles, however, require the same levels of skills in all areas of the project. The WebSphere Commerce project needs a diverse set of skills that belong to different people doing different roles throughout the project duration.

Table 5-3 shows the involvement of the technical roles in the various milestones making up the project implementation. In every cell, there is an indication of the role's contribution to the project implementation, either major or minor contribution. In case the role does not contribute to a specific milestone, the corresponding cell is left empty. For more details on the project's main milestones, refer to "Major implementation activities" on page 166.

Table 5-3 Technical Roles and milestones

	Solution outline	**Design**	**Develop**	**FVT SVT**	**UAT**	**Perf'ce**	**Deploy**
Architect	*Major*	*Major*	Minor	Minor	Minor	Minor	Minor
Development		*Major*	*Major*	*Major*	Minor	Minor	Minor
Testing		Minor	*Major*	*Major*	Minor	*Major*	Minor
UCD		*Major*	Minor	Minor	*Major*	Minor	Minor
Performance		*Major*	Minor	Minor	Minor	*Major*	*Major*
Infrastructure	Minor	Minor	Minor	Minor	Minor	Minor	*Major*
Post-engagement							*Major*

In the following sections, we discuss each team involved in the technical parts of the project, including those that are involved in pre-engagement, implementation and post-engagement phases. Moreover, we list each role's main responsibilities in the project activities, as well as the skills needed to carry them out efficiently and successfully.

Architect

The architecture team is usually has architects assigned to work on specific projects, and reporting to the CIO, or a technical strategy group. Being a team that crosses individual project boundaries helps with communication between different projects, and implementing the corporate technical strategy. One of the team should be responsible for the architecture of the WebSphere Commerce project.

Responsibilities

The architect is responsible for designing an eCommerce platform that both realizes the long term eCommerce vision of the business and delivers a Web site within the time and cost constraints of the business plan. Responsibilities are:

- Major technical contributor to the Solution Outline
- Owns and creates the Solution Architecture Document

Skills

- Thorough understanding of WebSphere Commerce architecture
- eCommerce
- J2EE
- Business integration
- Solution architecture

UCD

The design and implementation of a Web site needs a team combining a number of very different skills, and some of the more programming related tasks can be assigned to the development team. All the responsibilities and skills are listed in this section, but you might well have a different team organization.

It is unlikely, unless you are planning a large eCommerce business, for you to have, or wish to retain permanently, all the specialized skills required. Some tasks, such as designing and implementing a graphics style, might well be part of a contract with a specialized design or advertising agency.

Responsibilities

The user interface team is ultimately responsible for the look and feel of the Web site, making the site attractive to visitors, and not losing customers as a result of the Web site being hard to use. Responsibilities are:

- Web page design and navigation:
  - Wire frames, storyboard and Web site prototype
  - Web page design and navigation
  - Graphic design and realization of corporate design standards
  - Accessibility
- User Acceptance test

Skills

- Graphics tools, such as Photoshop® or Corel Draw
- Web usability design
- HTML, JavaScript, style sheets
- Specialized Web technologies being used, such as Flash or AJAX.
- Usability testing

Development team

The development team is a diverse team containing different roles, responsibilities, and skills. They are responsible for the customization of the store, as well as integration with the your IT infrastructure and other applications.

The team is normally made up of people from your own organization and from solution providers, and some parts of the development might be outsourced, delivering components to be integrated into the solution. It is typical to use solution providers to provide technical guidance and to acquire skills from them, as well as using solution providers to fill gaps in your own resource, that you do not need to acquire.

Responsibilities

The overall responsibility of development is to deliver the customized store which is shown in Figure 5-5, "Deployment of WebSphere Commerce components" on page 175. They are also responsible for integration with the infrastructure and other applications. They need to provide the commands, data beans, EJBs, JSPs, and servlets to implement the interfaces required by the user design, and described by the use cases.

- Develop the store features and functions
- Perform unit tests
- Integrate the store with the infrastructure and applications

Skills

- J2EE development, including Java, JSPs, Servlets, and EJBs
- Database design and development
- WebSphere Commerce Developer
- XML technologies

Test teams

There are several testing teams required in the project, in addition to the essential unit testing performed by developers themselves:

- Functional (or component)
- System
- Performance
- User

You could also have a separate integration test team, to test the integration of WebSphere Commerce with other applications, such as Payments. This might be handled by the component test team — but it is advisable to test integration before the system is accepted into System Test.

Some tests might be run by solutions providers as part of their contract; other tests might be performed by your own organization. As a general rule, the solution provider should be responsible for testing the delivery of their components. As part of the solution provider contract, you can stipulate test deliverables as part of your risk management approach.

At the point in the development cycle where you integrate delivery from a solution provider, you should expect to run an acceptance test, supported by the vendor, as part of the ETVX (Figure 5-4 on page 167) approach to project risk management. The acceptance test gives both you and the provider an assessment of the quality of the deliverable, and thus the amount of continued development support the vendor needs to be able to provide until the project goes live.

Responsibilities

Each of the test teams should:

- Provide a test plan, describing test scenarios, test preparation, entry and exit conditions
- Perform acceptance test, stage the tests, and report problems
- Assist developers to recreate problems
- Verify fixes

Skills

- J2EE development, including Java, JSPs, servlets, and EJBs
- WebSphere Commerce developer
- Functional test tools, automated test tools, performance profiling tools
- Software Libraries, problem reporting tools
- Test case design and execution

Infrastructure team

The infrastructure team involves people from both the eCommerce project and people responsible for your IT software and hardware environment. If solution providers are implementing some or all of the eCommerce project, then they need to provide staff to the infrastructure team. As described in Chapter 8, "Best of breed infrastructure" on page 271, best practices are to replicate a cut down environment for testing, and provide a staging environment for new Web site content.

After the infrastructure is built, monitoring software created, and operating procedures are worked out, the infrastructure team needs to be on hand for the first deployment of the Web site.

Depending on how your IT is organized, the infrastructure team might also be responsible for providing an application communication layer, such as a message or service bus, and integrating applications and services with the bus.

Responsibilities

- Install, configure and tune and secure hardware and software.
- Set up environments required by the WebSphere Commerce project.

Skills

- Hardware and software installation, security and configuration management
- Operating systems and TCP/IP networking
- Software stack
  - WebSphere Commerce administration and configuration tools
  - WebSphere Application Server administration and configuration tools
  - Database administration
- Performance tuning, system monitoring tools and troubleshooting

Post engagement

You probably have two or three teams to support the day to day running of the Web site —- typically the operational, maintenance, and support teams. The operational team has permanent full time personnel assigned. Members of the maintenance and support teams might be assigned on rotation from other teams which have the necessary skills.

The operational team performs regular, documented, day to day monitoring and management tasks, following operating procedures planned in advance. The operating procedures are extended to include specific tasks for WebSphere Commerce (see Chapter 11, “Running your Web site” on page 325), and the operators need training, but they are not WebSphere Commerce experts.

You might have a separate maintenance team to apply operating system and software fixes (which do not require redeployment of software). They might also be responsible for migrating new versions the Web site customizations to the production server, as well as new content configurations from the staging server to the production server. If these tasks can be planned and documented — and automated as far as possible — they can be performed by the operations team.

Finally, there is the WebSphere Commerce specific support team, who perform troubleshooting, unplanned fixes and tuning, and provide technical help line support for business users and customers.

These teams are largely involved in the post engagement phase. If the Web site is hosted, then they are part of the hosting support.

Responsibilities

- Operational:
  - Define, test, document, and perform operating procedures
  - Monitor the site, and perform regular maintenance procedures
  - Carry out troubleshooting or recovery actions when instructed
- Maintenance:
  - Plan and perform regular maintenance procedures
  - Migrate new customizations and configurations to the production server

- Support:
  - Troubleshooting and tuning
  - Technical helpline support
  - Support interface to software suppliers

Skills

- Operational:
  - Writing and automating operating procedures
  - Trained in specific hardware and software tasks
  - Performing operating tasks accurately and reliably
- Maintenance:
  - Operating System administration
  - J2EE and WebSphere commerce deployment
  - Database administration
- Support:
  - J2EE development, including Java, JSPs, servlets, and EJBs
  - Database administration
  - WebSphere Performance tuning
  - WebSphere Commerce Developer
  - Web technologies
  - Troubleshooting

5.2.2 Non-technical roles

The non-technical roles include people responsible for establishing and running the project development, and the business people and CSRs who use the eCommerce solution when it is delivered. See Table 5-4.

Table 5-4 Non Technical Roles and milestones

	Pre Engage ment	**Engagement**					**Post Engage ment**
		Design	**Develop**	**Test**	**Perf**	**UAT**	
Acquisition team	*Major*						
Project Sponsor	*Major*	Minor	Minor	Minor	Minor	*Major*	Minor
Project Manager	*Major*	*Major*	*Major*	*Major*	*Major*	*Major*	Minor
Business Analyst		*Major*				Minor	Minor
Business Users	Minor	Minor				*Major*	*Major*

Acquisition team

The acquisition team might formally be run by the procurement department, but it probably works for the project sponsor. Its members include the newly appointed project manager, the Business Analyst, CIO representatives such as Enterprise, Solution, and Infrastructure architects, and possibly representatives of stakeholders who are affected by the eCommerce solution. The acquisition team works with the pre-sales teams from software suppliers and solution providers and works out the details of the business proposal and assessments of options (staff work) for the project sponsor to act on.

Responsibilities

- Pre-engagement documentation
  - Request for Proposal
  - Business Vision
  - Solution outline
  - Outline project plan
- Business case
  - Communication with the rest of the business
- Assess proposals

Skills

- Business re-engineering
- eCommerce
- Financial
- Knowledge of business and customers

Project sponsor

Some of the rationale behind the project sponsor are described in 4.9.1, "Project sponsor responsibilities" on page 146. An eCommerce project involves people from many parts of an organization, and changes many aspects of how a business is run, thus it is very important to have a respected and highly placed project sponsor to oversee the project.

Responsibilities

In addition to the responsibilities covered in 4.9.1, "Project sponsor responsibilities", the project sponsor also has responsibility for:

- Committing funding the project
- Seeding the organization and appointing the project manager
- Making decisions on the use of in house resource, solution providers, and suppliers

Skills

- Executive management
- Experience across the business
- eCommerce

Project manager

The project manager's role and responsibilities are described in 4.9.2, "Project manager responsibilities" on page 146. The project manager is responsible for coordinating the team which produces the WebSphere Commerce implementation, and delivering the project on time, in budget, and to specification — and dealing with the inevitable problems that arise in a large project.

Responsibilities

- Creating and maintaining the project plan
- Ensuring that the project is:
  - Sufficiently resourced
  - Delivered on time
  - Within budget
  - Attains an agreed quality level
- Dependencies on external groups are effectively managed
- Ensuring that legal and corporate requirements are met
- Assessing project risks and reporting unmanaged exposures to the project sponsor

Skills

- Software project management
- eCommerce and WebSphere Commerce architecture
- Understanding of your business

Business analyst

The business analyst is involved from the pre-engagement phase, and creates the business vision and parts of the solution outline document. The business understands how the business works, and plans how to change the business, communicates the changes to the organization for implementation, estimates the costs and benefits of the changes, and monitors and measures the results. The analyst is responsible for requirements — but it is usual to employ a requirements analyst, or at least a requirements coordinator, because managing requirements is so important to controlling the scope of a project.

Responsibilities

- Documentation:
  - Business vision
  - Contribute to solution outline document
  - Business use cases
  - Requirements
- Analyze and model the business and changes required for eCommerce
- Communicate vision, and changes required
- Planning and measuring improvements to business value and reductions in cost.

Skills

- Business analysis and re-engineering, and business modeling
- eCommerce
- WebSphere Commerce features knowledge

Business roles

Business users are largely divided into the same functions as in a bricks and mortar shop, except that many of their activities are carried out online, using tools provided in WebSphere Commerce, or tools you have purchased or built to extend WebSphere Commerce. Each business user performs some, but not all, of these roles and the skills individuals need vary accordingly.

Responsibilities

- Selling: catalog, pricing, information
- Marketing - promotions, e-spots, loyalty programs, newsletters, Web features[8]
- Back office:
  - Orders
  - Payment
  - Shipping
  - Taxes
  - Fulfilment
  - Inventory

[8] Web features is a catch-all term for content on the Web site that is aimed at attracting and retaining customers. This might include content created specifically for the purpose, such as mini-films, or customer content like reviews.

- Customer/Business relations:
  - Accounts
  - Trading Agreements / Contracts
  - CSR Helpdesk

Skills

- WebSphere Commerce tools such as Accelerator, Sales Desk, Management Center, and Workspaces
- Add on tools such as Coremetrics, payment, tax, shipping, and order integration
- Relevant business skills (marketing, payments systems and so on)

5.3 Mentoring a project

It is not advisable to take a WebSphere Commerce course and then start planning and implementing a WebSphere Commerce site. Some experience is essential. In order to gain the most experience with WebSphere Commerce and the related products, it is always best to take part in a real project. Hiring new staff with experience of WebSphere Commerce is one solution, and something you probably want to do anyway.

However, relying on hiring new staff with WebSphere Commerce skills alone is not the best way to go, and we would recommend engaging IBM or an IBM Business Partner specifically to pass on experience with WebSphere Commerce projects for a couple of reasons:

1. Experience:

   Collectively a Business Partner is able to draw upon experience of more WebSphere Commerce projects than newly hired staff, and thus more likely to have had experience of a project similar to yours. In addition, they have had experience of passing on their experience to other clients, and have learned how to make their experience effective for you.

2. Chemistry:

   A Business Partner is, unlike a new hire, not being asked to become an employee in your organization, and should therefore be better placed to communicate to your organization at all management levels.

We term the aspect of the client/Business Partner relationship that involves passing on experience to help client set up their own eCommerce organization, "Mentoring a project."

There are a couple of alternative ways to set up the IBM Business Partner contracts that help to pass on skills to your own organization: vendor managed or client managed.

Vendor managed

You can make IBM or the IBM Business Partner responsible for implementing the project, but with some agreed upon level of involvement with your team.

This way, you can get hands-on experience with the product as well as some best practices on how to use it, but more importantly, you can reduce the risk considerably from undertaking the project on your own. You are the project sponsor, but the vendor is responsible for the project management. You appoint your own project manager to work alongside the vendor, and as well as "learning the trade." Your project manager provides you with risk assessment, and might be responsible for managing the dependencies the project has on other parts of your organization.

Client managed

You decide to take on project management responsibility, perhaps because your project manager has previously managed large scale software projects for you, or because the project manager has managed a WebSphere Commerce project elsewhere. The project manager subcontracts some of the project implementation to IBM or IBM Business Partners, who again work with involvement from your team where later you want to bring the components in house.

For this case, we recommend that you engage consultants from IBM or from an IBM Business Partner to work with your project manager and other leads. ISSW (see "ISSW" on page 190) has a specific mentoring program to help project managers.

In the next sections we discuss the options available to you when taking the project mentoring approach. We discuss the possible teams that can help you in the project implementation as well as some of the tasks — both technical and business — that you can be involved in. We also list some important tasks that you need to be responsible for throughout the project implementation so that you can monitor and review the project status and be aware of any issues that might hinder its progress.

5.3.1 Consultancy options

There are several options to choose from after deciding on project mentoring. If you choose to implement the project with the help from IBM, then you can get consultancy from the GBS team or from the ISSW team. Or, you can choose to use an IBM Business Partner to implement the project. The following sections give brief descriptions about each option available for you to choose from to provide you with more insight when making your decision.

GBS

IBM Global Business Services has different teams of highly skilled consultants specializing in different areas of services. Teams are located all around the globe and have experience in most industries. They deliver an end-to-end project starting at the very beginning when the business goals are still being defined and go all the way to delivery and testing, maintenance and support. The key advantage of using GBS during project implementation is their long list of previous customers and projects that assures you that they have faced it all before. This gives you access to the best experience and helps you build the skills you wish for.

The following Web site provides more details on GBS and how they can help you. You can also check the case studies of the retail industry for further examples of what GBS has to offer:

`http://www.ibm.com/bcs`

IBM Business Partner

An IBM Business Partner provides you with most of what GBS can, but possibly at a smaller scale. IBM Business Partners are mostly involved with small and medium business implementations. Depending on the IBM Business Partner, you can find different levels of skills and previous experience. However, being an IBM Business Partner means that they have access to all the learning material, technical resources, contacts and support IBM produces. In short, you still get all the resources required for your project as well as the participation to get your team experienced in the implementation, but possibly at a lower price. To search for an IBM Business Partner, you can use the IBM PartnerWorld® Web site (Figure 5-6).

```
Using the IBM Find a IBM Business Partner with the following search arguments
yielded 96 hits...

http://d03bphrb.partner.boulder.ibm.com/bpconnections/bpcms.nsf/publicadvancedsearc
h?OpenFrameset&NL=en

IBM Business Partner location (country):
United States

Partner specializes in one or more of these IBM product groups:
WebSphere

Partner holds one or more of these skills and certifications:
WebSphere - Business Portals
IBM Certified Deployment Professional -- WebSphere Commerce Business Edition V5.5
IBM Certified Deployment Professional -- WebSphere Commerce V5.6
IBM Certified Solutions Expert -- IBM WebSphere Commerce Business Edition V5.4
Customization
IBM Certified Solutions Expert -- IBM WebSphere Commerce Suite V4.1 Customization
IBM Certified Specialist -- IBM WebSphere Commerce Business Edition V5.4
Implementation
IBM Certified Specialist -- IBM WebSphere Commerce Suite V 5.1 Implementation
IBM Certified Specialist -- IBM WebSphere Commerce Suite V4.1 Implementation

Partner is qualified under one or more of these partner types:
Service Provider
```

Figure 5-6 Certified Commerce Service Providers

ISSW

IBM Software Services for WebSphere is a team of highly experienced individuals, each having deep knowledge and skills in one or more WebSphere products. ISSW assesses your current team skills and advises you on the skills needed for your project and how to acquire them, whether through courses, training or skill transfer. They also help you set the project scope, review the design, develop an architecture and setup the infrastructure.

Contract ISSW for any of the following options:

- Project planning and sizing:

  This provides you with an expert to be available during pre-sales to help you with gathering requirements, sizing and putting a rough project plan together. Someone from your team shadows the ISSW expert to increase his or her experience and to provide the ISSW with insight into your organization to provide better advice.

- End to end project mentoring:

  In this option, multiple ISSW experts lead the major parts of the project implementation. ISSW provides the following personnel:

  - Solution architect to lead the architecture effort and provide a rough estimate and project plan as well as be responsible for the solution outline and macro design
  - Project executive as a guide for the project manager
  - Installation expert to install software and setup the test environment
  - Data load specialist to be in charge of data loading
  - Senior development team leads as guides to the development team you provide in developing the micro design and the rest of the development effort
  - Test leads to lead the various test efforts, such as functional verification test, system integration and verification tests and performance test

- Expert reviews:

  ISSW reviews the major milestones and documents of your project, such as the project plan, the solution outline document, macro design, use case model, micro design, code and test plans.

- Expert assistance:

  If you have a complex programming requirement that your team is not qualified enough to do on their own, ISSW might have experts to help you. ISSW assists in performance monitoring and tuning tasks, as well as debugging and troubleshooting.

Refer to Table 5-5 and the following Web site for more details on the ISSW team. The table describes the bases for various services ISSW offer. To contact ISSW, click the following URL:

```
http://www.ibm.com/developerworks/WebSphere/s9ervices/
```

Table 5-5 ISSW WebSphere Commerce Services: January 2008

Services	Description
Migration from BroadVision	The WebSphere Commerce Migration from BroadVision application allows you to architect and remodel your existing application assets to our WebSphere Commerce J2EE platform, while taking advantage of new functionality within WebSphere Commerce. IBM works with you to address your current BroadVision environment, the 'to be' WebSphere Commerce solution environment, and the overall platform plan
Migration Program	The WebSphere Commerce Migration Program empowers your development team to use available tooling and employ best practises to design new sites that fully exploit the features and functionality of IBM WebSphere Commerce. IBM has experts to document a migration strategy for your business that allows you to reuse your existing e-commerce assets in the new design.
Center of Excellence	The Center of Excellence services suite for WebSphere Commerce enables your IT staff to accelerate their adoption of this strategic software solution, its tooling and advanced capabilities. The program consists of selected structured workshops, targeted mentoring, and best practices sharing.
Rapid Solution	WebSphere Commerce is designed to address a wide variety of value-chain initiatives, from a basic B2B or B2C online sales channel and strategic sourcing to a completely integrated, multi-tier demand chain - all on a single platform. The WebSphere Commerce Rapid Solutions offering helps you implement a commerce solution quickly and affordably via pre-configured store models that take advantage of the product's rich "out-of-the-box" features.
Application Developer Mentored Workshop	To help you win in a fiercely competitive market, we bring in subject matter experts to deliver the WebSphere Commerce Application Developer Mentored Workshop to your development staff. This hands-on workshop, using WebSphere Commerce Developer enables you to develop commerce applications rapidly that cater to your specific business needs.
Architecture and Design Workshop	Empower your architecture and design teams to develop e-commerce solutions that effectively use IBM WebSphere Commerce's powerful "out-of-the-box" features to quickly position the solutions for implementation. Leverage the deep technical skills and proven experience of IBM architects, developers, and business process experts to perform fit/gap and integration analyses to define a solution, using best practice guidelines, that executes on your business needs.

Commerce ATS team

The Commerce Advanced Technical Services team is part of the WebSphere Commerce Support and Services Organization. The team specializes in configuration, customization, deployment and performance tuning of WebSphere Commerce systems. Billable services are offered both remotely and on-site to help solve system stability issues as well as to offer performance tuning tips and best practices to ensure that you meet your performance targets. The team can also support your highly-scalable WebSphere Commerce system and offer valuable advice on how to monitor and tune it. Discuss WebSphere Commerce ATS services with your WebSphere Commerce sales specialist.

Combining options

Combining options is yet another choice you can make. If you need an affordable solution, there is no IBM Business Partner with the skills and experience required for your specific project, go with the most suitable IBM Business Partner and get an ISSW expert to assist the IBM Business Partner.

Another possibility is to use GBS for the overall project implementation, and hire an IBM Business Partner to carry out well defined activities. This can reduce the price overall, and also give you insight into the different styles of operation of both vendors so that you can adopt what you see best in your future projects.

5.3.2 Client involvement

Now that we have discussed what IBM or an IBM Business Partner does for your project, let us see how you need to be involved to ensure that the project succeeds. Even if you have contracted the management and implementation to a service provider, your input is still essential. There are various teams on your side of the project that are involved in the project implementation depending on the extent to which you have contracted or outsourced the project. Your main players are members of either the business or IT teams. How should they get involved with a WebSphere Commerce project that is largely implemented by service providers?

Business team

Always remember that as the customer and owner of the business, it is in your hands to make or break the project. Here is a list of activities that you need to be involved in throughout the project to ensure its success:

Discuss your requirements

Discuss your requirements, and what you have in mind for the store, with the business analysis team. You have to take time out of your business staff's daily diary to attend these sessions, which are ongoing. Your staff must also be prepared for the sessions, and should expect to do investigation for them. Have your staff read this book to familiarize themselves with the challenges and opportunities of eCommerce, WebSphere Commerce, and its extensions. You have to assist the business analysts by organizing meetings with the major members of your organization to discuss their requirements, and what they need to contribute to the online store.

Work with the UCD team

Work with the UCD team to discuss what you want your online store to look like. Provide them with any images or styles you want included in your online store to match your corporate style. If you already have a real-life store, then it is strongly advisable to give the team a tour of it, and to talk to your corporate design team, to give them an idea of how to design the look-and-feel for the online version.

Reviewing the storyboard

In reviewing the storyboard, and later looking at the site and the results of User Acceptance Testing, think about the success of the project as a whole, and do not get overly bogged down in the appearance and details of each page to the exclusion of the big picture of whether the project has met your customers and business users needs.

The UAT tests should be able to tell you how well users are able to perform tasks using the Web site. Your corporate design staff should review the site's consistency with the corporate brand. Your business users have participated in the UAT and have reported on the fitness for purpose of the Web site, and where they want improvements.

Your main role is to ensure all these roles have approached their assessment of the site in the way you would expect, and they have all contributed to the assessment of the site. If you have your own issues with the site, where it does not meet with your expectations, this is something to work out with the user teams and the implementation teams. Refer any design changes back to the original business vision, requirements and use cases.

IT team

As we mentioned before in 5.2.1, "Technical roles" on page 177, we can expect some involvement of your IT department in the project implementation. There might be integration points as well as hand-over of some functions from the solution provider to your IT team.

Since this is the first time you are using WebSphere Commerce, you should keep the responsibility for the bulk of the implementation with the solution provider team and benefit from members of your team working with them on integration points, or where completed components are to be handed over. Here are a some ideas of technical activities you can work jointly on:

- Development:
  - A shadow or protégé for the solution architect, who works with the solution provider. This helps the solution architect in some tasks and teaches the protégé a lot of skills and knowledge of the product and its underlying architecture and how to extend it.
  - Several junior developers to work under the leadership of a development lead, who works with the solution provider. Again, this shows the developers how to do WebSphere Commerce development and gain experience with the product with guidance from experienced developers.
  - Other development leads to work alongside the development leads provided by the solution provider to learn how to design WebSphere Commerce solutions and how to break tasks down and implement them.
- Infrastructure:
  - Shadow resources for the installation team to see how to install and configure the software stack and setup the development, test, pre-production and production environments.
  - Build specialist to handle builds after being mentored by the build specialist from the solution provider team and being shown how to do build and deploy the code.
- Testing:

  As discussed earlier, it is better practice for the solution provider to test their own deliverables rather than to split effort between development and test. However, if you are going to host the WebSphere Commerce site, and have it integrated it with your IT infrastructure, you must run an acceptance test. This might well be the same test you run before promoting new customizations from the pre-production environment to the production environment. Whether you, or the solution provider are responsible for developing this test, include some of your infrastructure test people on the team

5.3.3 Governance

Choosing to go with any of the consultancy options outlined in 5.3.1, "Consultancy options" on page 189, does not mean that you only get involved at the very end. As described in 4.7.1, "Risk management plan" on page 141, there should be a project status and risk assessment every month, and a phase review before inception, elaboration, construction, and transition — combining these activities where they coincide. The project manager is responsible for orchestrating the reviews. Key decisions, including the count down to *Go Live!* and contract signings and payments can be tied to these reviews.

There are a number of key control documents, that are, in the main, linked to contracts, that you need to approve. You should agree this list of key documents, and their approvers as part of the project plan. That means someone from your organization[9] is involved in the activities that the documents codify. In the main documents are a point in time record of what has been decided, happened, or planned, and are not sufficient, without knowledge of the activities, to understand the project sufficiently to sign off on the documents.

Here is a list of some candidates to be key documents:

- Business Vision
- Solution Outline
- Project Plan
- Requirements - functional and non functional
- Use cases
- Solution Architecture
- Infrastructure Architecture
- Contracts
- Storyboard, or user interface prototype
- Solution Test plan - including final acceptance test for *Go Live!*

In addition, the project has a few "live" documents that get updated for status and project reviews, that are key, including Project Status and Risk Assessment.

[9] The extent of the involvement depends on the confidence you have built up in the business relationship, and the risk you are prepared to take.

6

Challenges and pitfalls

User behavior! Keep this idea at the forefront of your mind as you implement and deploy your WebSphere Commerce site. Internet user behavior is fickle, but it is the foundation on which many a successful online retail store has been built.

If you need to convince yourself, or colleagues in your business, how it is a matter of common sense to spend serious money understanding user behavior to get the most out of your eCommerce site, ask yourself or your colleagues about the research and experience that goes into designing and building a bricks and mortar retail outlet.

The styling, layout, lighting, textures, sounds — even smells — the dress and behavior of assistants, the promotions, the changes, the link up with advertising — so many possibilities: They all go into what makes a store successful. You would expect the same to be true of a Web site; it is a matter of observing consumers using the electronic store.

According to research:

1. When frustrated with an eCommerce site, over a third of Web users simply give up trying to buy an item over the Internet and only one in seven click through to another Web Site and keep searching.
2. Internet users in large numbers abandon sites which are not robust enough, simple enough to navigate (confuse them), or fail to engage them intelligently.

Internet users have little patience for sites that simply do not get the basics right — such as providing fast, secure, easy click-through paths, dependable fulfillment, responsive customer service, and so on. Potential customers will abandon your site for lack of performance and appropriate security, as well as situations where they are frustrated with broken links and broken fulfillment processes.

If the Web site does not adhere to the look and rhythms that Internet shoppers are accustomed to, then you are probably courting disaster — though you might be lucky and establish a new standard — but do not bank on it. Even simple frustrations can cause shoppers to give up. You cannot rely on experienced programmers, or even experienced user interface designers, to get this right every time. You need to measure and test.

For compelling examples of the importance of the user experience, visit Jakon Neilsen's Web site. The highlights are free; you need to pay for the full reports.

`http://www.useit.com/`

For a (free) presentation that selects nine critical success factors for an eCommerce site, and has a useful score sheet to rate your own performance, see Gomez, a leading provider of *"on-demand Web application experience management solutions"*, found at:

`http://www.gomez.com/pdfs/nine_truths.pdf`

In this chapter we look at eight areas of challenge, and finish with our ten top tips.

1. "Requirements"
2. "Hosting challenges"
3. "Performance"
4. "Security issues"
5. "Growth and extensibility"
6. "Quality"
7. "Launch preparation and launch"
8. "Globalization"
9. "Top ten tips"

6.1 Requirements

Understanding your requirements, deciding which ones have to be implemented and which ones need to be satisfied first, implementing them to the satisfaction of your users, and responding quickly to new requirements and requests to modify existing requirements — this is going to determine the success of your eBusiness.

To prioritize your requirements, you need to understand your business, your competitive edge, and your customers; then you can decide which requirements are more important than others and implement them first. All this should be part of your business vision document, so it is clear to the whole team.

The failure of some dot.com firms was in some part a failure to understand eCommerce requirements, and so making the wrong decisions in prioritizing software requirements, whereas companies such as Amazon and Ebay have manifestly made some good trade-offs in deciding how much to invest in their Web site versus the back office. Amazon and Ebay focus much more on what empirical usability research with Internet consumers finds is important, such as clear navigation, good performance, and following well understood conventions.

In this section we discuss what requirements are, in general, and how you should manage them. Then we discuss a couple of particular requirements (Accessibility and Browser compatibility) that are relevant to WebSphere Commerce Web sites, and which you might overlook.

6.1.1 Introduction

Functional requirements define how you want specific aspects of the solution to behave in your WebSphere commerce application. Your goal is to provide designers and developers with sufficient information to design and implement the solution. It is difficult to write good functional requirements to tell developers what you want built for a variety of reasons.

We never fully understand what we want a system to do, and when the system is built, we realize that we did not quite know what we wanted, or the developers did not quite understand us. Also, we see new possibilities when we see the system in concrete form. So it is not surprising that there is uncertainty about how to specify functional requirements, and also confusion about how requirements relate to use cases.

People talk about "extracting" functional requirements from use cases. But the notion of a "functional requirement" is hard to pin down, and what is it that is "extracted" from a use case? The idea of a functional requirement skates between a stakeholder's "feature", and a developer's functional specification. Neither formulation of a requirement is what you want to pass on to developers to start designing a solution.

A feature is too vague, and a functional specification is not a statement of what a normal non-technical user wants from a system. It is very hard, even for a technical person, to visualize how a system will appear to a user from reading a functional specification. Nonetheless, we do want to describe what we want a system to do, and the properties the system should have, and we need functional (and non-functional) requirements to describe what we want to start out with to begin a technical design of the solution.

6.1.2 Capture requirements in use cases

The idea behind use cases is they are a way to describe the behavior users want from a system in a way that users can understand and contribute to. They "capture" functional requirements. There is little point in trying to "extract" and restate the requirements from a use case — developers do this anyway, and their restatement is in prototypes and code that users can test, rather than in another document, which is no easier to understand than a use case, and removes the developer one step further from the description that made sense to users.

A strong recommendation is to write use cases to capture user requirements and review them with users, perhaps using a prototype to visualize the scenario. There are plenty of books to advise you on writing use cases. Perhaps the most important advice, especially for use cases that describe how users interact with the system ("Business Use Cases[1]") is to keep use cases simple — or if you like mnemonics, follow the KISS principle: **K**eep **I**t **S**imple, **S**tupid, which has a proud software heritage[2].

6.1.3 Capture requirements in other ways

Some requirements are best captured in other ways. There are many taxonomies of requirements. Here we have just picked out non-functional, business process, organizational, and technical and IT requirements to illustrate the variety of requirements and the different ways that they are best captured.

1 Sometimes people divide use cases into Business Use Cases and System Use Cases. System Use Cases focus on how components in the system interact to deliver a particular behavior, whereas Business Use Cases focus on the users' interactions with the system as users see it.

2 See `http://en.wikipedia.org/wiki/KISS_principle`

Non-functional requirements

Performance is a good example of a non-functional requirement. Other examples would be availability, and also complying with legislation (such as accessibility or data protection) or company standards (such as security or globalization).

A good rule of thumb is that as far as possible requirements, including non-functional requirements, should be written in terms the stakeholder responsible for the requirement readily understands. Do not restate the requirement in IT terms — you might have misunderstood, and you have made it more difficult for the stakeholder to review.

If the requirement relates to external standards, legal requirements or company standards, then the reference needs to be made clear and available to the developers.

If a requirement is tied to a physically measurable delivery, especially if it will actually be measured, so much the better. For example, capture performance and availability requirements as Service Level Agreements, and Key Performance Indicators (KPI). You can also capture some usability requirements numerically, in terms of the time taken to complete some task — especially valuable if you intend to measure this in user acceptance testing. An example would be the time taken to complete an order, including filling out all the forms required.

Business process requirements

Business process requirements, which describe how business processes operate, who is involved, and what resources are required, can best be described using a business process modelling tool such as WebSphere Business Modeler, or simply in a flow chart using a basic presentation or drawing package.

Organizational requirements

Organizational requirements are also best captured with an organizational modelling tool. There is an organizational modelling tool in WebSphere Business Modeler, and there are wizards in conventional drawing packages such as Visio®.

Technical and IT requirements

Technical and IT requirements include describing constraints on how the solution is to be integrated into the infrastructure, or specifying characteristics of the technology or the implementation that the solution must conform to. Some of these are best expressed using diagrams, such as UML diagrams, and some in conventional words and pictures. Since this is a technical requirement, there is no reason not to state the requirement in technical terms.

Draw UML diagrams in a conventional drawing package, something like Visio. Include UML templates, or use a UML modeling tool, such as IBM Rational Software Modeler. The advantage of UML modeling tools is that when you are familiar with them, they are:

1. Quicker to use:
   - Because you do not have to draw the basic shapes.
2. Are extendible (or refinable):
   - You can add attributes and values to the models.
3. Able to show different views of the same model:
   - You can select what parts of a model you want to include in a picture to show just what you want to communicate, leaving irrelevant and distracting detail off.
4. Team tools:
   - The model is stored in a shared repository.
5. Queriable:
   - You can retrieve information from the models, just like a database, using queries such as "Show me all my application servers".
6. Linked to requirements management tools:
   - You can link requirements in IBM Requisite® Pro to model elements in Rational Software Modeler.
7. Have intelligent auto-completion:
   - These are based on UML rules, and the data you have already entered.
8. Transformable into data, scripts or executable code:
   - Large projects can use UML models as the starting point for generating software artifacts automatically.

6.1.4 Manage requirements

All these different kinds of requirements, captured and represented in different ways, have one characteristic in common, they are all requirements. You want architects, designers, developers, solution providers, deployers and operational staff to implement them. You need to manage requirements so you know what is being implemented, by whom, and in which release.

Managing requirements means identifying them, allocating them to releases, referring to them in contracts, understanding relationships and dependencies between them, having people own them, track their implementation, review them, discuss them, modify them, combine them, break them into smaller parts, feedback to stakeholders about them, test them, and so on. There are a whole number of "life cycle" characteristics of requirements that you need to manage.

Keep track of requirements

The first step to take in managing requirements is to establish a common form for recording requirements and a system for storing and managing requirements. Table 6-1 shows a very simple template for a requirement form.

Table 6-1 Simple requirements form

Name	Name and number of functional requirement
Summary	Brief description of the requirement
Rationale	Brief description of the reason that the requirement is needed
Requirements	Reference to document that fully describes the requirement
References	Other requirements related to this one, and their relationship

Table 6-2 shows an example of using the form.

Table 6-2 Simple requirements form: sample usage

RFQ -1	Enable Request for Quote
Summary	The merchandising process must have an option for the customer to submit a request for a quote on products.
Rationale	Some products might not be priced at all. Others might be priced, but based on the contract a customer has or the quantities they are purchasing, they might qualify for special pricing. Therefore, they should have the option to request a quote on such products.
Requirements	Refer to use case USE-RFQ1
References	OP - 5: Ordering Process

You have probably already thought of additional fields you want to see on the form: When was the requirement written? When was it modified? Who was it written by? What release is it targeted at? Who is responsible for implementing it? What test cases have been written for it? What discussions are there about it? Who is the stakeholder it is written for? And so on. If you want to manage requirements, then you need to capture some of this information in a tool that makes it relatively easy to link information together, share with a team, and build reports.

So the second step to take is to invest in a requirements management tool. There are many. IBM sells Rational RequisitePro, which has the advantage that it links to artifacts in the Rational Application Developer and other tools to improve traceability, and now in Version 7, has a browser interface to make it much easier to deploy to every member of a project. See:

http://www-306.ibm.com/software/awdtools/reqpro/

6.1.5 Stage requirements

Armed with a flexible requirements management system, it is easier to stage requirements into smaller release increments, necessary for Agile development (see 5.1.4, "Agile development and WebSphere Commerce" on page 176). Ship basic functionality to begin with and only elaborate it in response to user requirements. That way it is easier to ship releases quickly, and the extra overhead of shipping more releases is offset by only shipping functionality that has a demonstrable requirement. In the end you hope to gain user satisfaction by responding to user requirements more quickly, and by building a leaner system that is easier to maintain.

6.1.6 Accessibility requirements

Unless your Web site is specifically aimed at customers with physical disabilities, you might not have particular functional requirements for disabled users. However, you have legal and ethical obligations to provide accessibility features.

WebSphere Commerce supports multiple accessibility features, which are those features designed to help users with physical disabilities, such as hearing impairment, visual impairment, or limited mobility to use the product. Some of the features that WebSphere Commerce supports are:

- Magnifying the page if you use Windows as an operating system
- Using screen-reader software to input the text on the screen to a digital speech synthesizer to actually read out all the text on the page
- Operating all the site functions using keyboard or mouse

All WebSphere Commerce starter stores that come with the product have these features enabled. In addition the following accessibility features are provided for the administrators of the site:

- Changing the color scheme of WebSphere Commerce configuration manager to help the color blind or visually impaired.

- Using a silent option when installing the software, which reads the input to the installation program from a predetermined file and prints the output in another file to be viewed later.

If your site needs to support any of these features, make sure that you test them in both the out-of-the-box components and the newly developed or customized components to make sure that they work correctly. Also, you have to keep them in mind during development to make sure that you do not develop new functionality that does not make use of those available features.

6.1.7 Browser requirements

WebSphere Commerce supports many browsers. However, in order for you to access WebSphere Commerce tools, you can only use Internet Explorer® V6.0 or later. Here is a list of browsers supported by WebSphere Commerce for shopping use:

- Internet Explorer 5.5, 6.0. 7.0
- Netscape 7.x
- Mozilla 1.7.7
- Opera 8.0
- Firefox 1.0.8, 2.0

It is important to understand that these supported browsers are for the starter stores and other packaged components of WebSphere Commerce. In order for your customized store to support these same browsers you need to make sure that any new functionality in the user interface part of the store — JSPs, HTMLs, JavaScripts, CSSs — are all supported by all browsers.

Normally, the user-centered design team knows how to design HTML pages with active menus and JavaScript that is supported on more than one browser. But, you still need to make sure they know the browsers you want to support beforehand, so they can design with this in mind. You also need to keep the testing team informed of the decision to support these browsers to make sure they test all their scenarios on all the supported browsers.

6.2 Hosting challenges

WebSphere Commerce provides an infrastructure and architecture to support the Hosting business model. The Hosting business model can be used to support the following business scenarios:

- Hosting of merchants by an Internet Service Provider (ISP).
- Hosting of resellers by a manufacturer.

- Providing unique storefronts for different enterprise customers or for product brands by a seller.

In the first two scenarios, the merchants or resellers are most often independent companies that are provided with hosting facilities or services by a third party that is the hosting company. The third scenario is different in that a single company serves as both merchant or reseller and hosting provider.

For any of these scenarios, the challenges are almost the same. To adopt the best hosting scenario, you should analyze the following considerations:

- High-level business description:
  - A description of the current state of the company
- Business goals
- Assumptions
- Existing environment
- Functional requirements
- Non-functional requirements:
  - Capacity and performance
  - Availability
  - Security
  - Systems management
  - Scalability
  - Maintainability
  - Manageability
  - System Usability
  - Data integrity and failure recovery
- Your company's standards and policies

Note: Refer to Chapter 9, "Size your infrastructure" on page 289 for details on infrastructure requirements.

Based on these requirements, you should be able to determine what kind of hosting services meets your goals.

If you decide to host your site yourself, make sure you have:

- Infrastructure capacity to host the site:
  - Check off the non-functional requirements line-by-line.
- Experienced administration support in-house, or acquire the capacity:
  - Make sure your personnel can support each functional requirement.

On the other hand, if you decide to have your site hosted by a third party, review the following considerations:

- Is the hosting company experienced enough?
  - How many sites are they hosting?
  - What size are the sites?
  - How much traffic are they handling?
- Can you scale your computing capacity according to demand and pay only for what you use?
- Clarify your role and responsibilities
  - Who handles the details of managing the site on a daily basis, including keeping it secure and updated?
- How will the hosting company implement the specification you have identified in your functional requirements document? Is anything left out?
- How does the hosting company demonstrate it can deliver the capacities you have identified in your non-functional requirements document?
- Does the hosting facility provide for training and mentoring?

These are some of the questions you need to ask as you look for a hosting company for your WebSphere Commerce site or you look to host your site yourself. Remember your goal here is to provide an environment for your shoppers where they can easily and comfortably shop without problems. A good shopping experience is more likely to result in purchases.

6.3 Performance

Your eCommerce site will lose revenue if you fail to adequately and correctly address the issues of performance and availability. Speed matters, and in eCommerce it is a fact of life. The faster they can click, the quicker customers move around a site, and when it comes to buying and selling, the more exposure to different purchasing possibilities, the more buying can take place.

As a rule of thumb, human perception of response times fall into three categories (Table 6-3). For measurements of real eCommerce sites, go to:

`http://www.gomez.com/products/viewbenchmark.php?btype=8`

You have to pay for their reports, but if you inspect the free data for the results of an order transaction in retail, you can see the best performers are in the sub 10 second range. This is what you would expect for an order transaction, which is much less frequent than a browse, and perceived by a user as consistent with their perception that they are “waiting for something to happen.”

Table 6-3 Response times

Response time	Perception	Observation
Less than tenth of a second	No delay - instantaneous	No network interaction possible
Less than one second	No interruption to work flow	Gold standard to aim for clicking through
Less than ten seconds	Waiting for something to happen	If the user is expecting something to happen (such as order confirmation) then the wait is consistent with expectation and not a problem. If the user is not waiting for something — for example, they have clicked on a link rather than pressed a button, then the wait is unexpected and a negative experience, which builds frustration with the site, and eventually the customer shops elsewhere. Note that ten seconds is too short a time to display a progress box, or do something else.
More than ten seconds	Do something else	Need to show a progress indicator, and consider another form of interaction to get the shopper's attention; for example, send a payment confirmation e-mail with links back to the site.

6.3.1 Typical pitfalls

These are four functions that have might have poor performance and should be handled carefully:

1. ViewAll:

   Category display pages can offer customers a view of all products on one page. This could potentially be very costly, as the generated page might:

   – Be a very expensive page to generate
   – Have huge memory requirements (EJBs)
   – Create a very large DynaCache object:

   This could pose memory and stability issues when replicating the entry.

2. Remove From Cart:

   Frequently overlooked in load test scenarios, this command is expensive from a CPU perspective and has demanding database locking.

3. Clearance sales categories:

   Several times a year most B2C customers publish a clearance type blanket sales category. Typically this category has all sale products loaded and its execution has similar consequences to ViewAll.

4. Pagination:

   A mistake when implementing the pagination for category and product display pages is overlooking that the URL of the first page is different (it does not contain the pageNum parameter) from the URL if you click the Page 1 link. Having two subtly different pages causes an unnecessary cache miss.

6.3.2 Roadmap for performance testing and tuning

WebSphere Commerce is an enterprise-wide, integrated solution that touches on many components and teams. Any low-performing part of the integrated solution can cause overall performance degradation. You therefore need to have a plan in place to:

- Evaluate the total solution throughput and responsiveness against a predefined set of performance goals.
- Identify the low-performing parts of the system.
- Tune the system to an overall satisfactory performance level.

How do you do all that? There are two good sources of information you should refer to:

1. There is "howto" information in the WebSphere Commerce Infocenter at:

   `http://publib.boulder.ibm.com/infocenter/wchelp/v6r0m0/index.jsp?topic=/com.ibm.commerce.admin.doc/concepts/cpmperformance.htm`

2. The IBM Redbooks publication, *"Mastering DynaCache in WebSphere Commerce"*, SG24-7393, found at:

   `http://www.redbooks.ibm.com/abstracts/sg247393.html`

   This book discusses everything about incorporating DynaCache into your Web site, and also has a lot of project management and architectural information about how to build high performance eCommerce Web sites.

In this chapter we do not repeat all the information about tuning WebSphere Commerce, but cover the main points to bear in mind about planning and testing for performance and highlight some of the challenges and pitfalls.

Overview of benchmarking and tuning

The most important point about performance tuning is that you must do it. Out-of-the-box, WebSphere Commerce is configured so that it runs in any environment — from a 32-way processor "Big Iron" UNIX® machine with 48 GB of RAM to an old Pentium® 3 computer with 1 GB of RAM and a single processor. The initial tuning parameters are set so that, on any hardware, it installs, it can be configured, and you can log onto it.

It is not tuned for large numbers of users, and it is not tuned to take advantage of the powerful hardware that you purchased for it to run on. So it is most important that you set aside several weeks in your deployment schedule for benchmarking and tuning, in addition to all the planning and development work on performance.

It is best if you have a production-like environment set aside specifically for performance tuning, so you can re-run performance tests for later releases.

Before you do any tuning at all, run a performance test, called a benchmark, with all of your WebSphere Commerce code, page layouts, security, and customizations in place. This is termed your *baseline* benchmark[3]. For the benchmark to be meaningful and provide you with predictive information about the behavior of the production Web site, it is important that in addition to building the performance test environment as similar to the production environment as possible, select workload characteristics as similar to the predicted or actual site usage as possible, for example:

- Buy versus browse ratio
- Average size of shopping cart
- Guest versus registered user ratio

Use a workload generator (simulator) to load up the systems with transactions reflecting the normal daily variation in transaction volume[4]. It is important that the simulator is able to repeatedly run the same workload in the same way so that you can do two or three identical runs and check for the consistency of the results. Some parameters in the workload have a major effect on the results, such as the distribution of think times between clicks. If you are using dynacache you need to wait until the cache is "warmed up" (that is, pages are cached); this might take between thirty minutes and an hour. You could devise a cache warm up workload, and use this should you need to warm up the production server.

You should divide your measurements into activity and resource metrics. Activity metrics reflect the system's reaction to workload and can be used to measure business requirement fulfillment and customer satisfaction.

---

[3] Benchmarking WebSphere Commerce is the subject of chapter 9 of "*Mastering DynaCache in WebSphere Commerce*", op. cit.

[4] Basically, a PC repeatedly running a few scripts captured by running though user scenarios.

Examples of activity metrics include:

- Number of Web site hits
- Page response times
- Number of orders placed
- Volume of data transferred

Resource metrics reflect system capacity and are important for predicting system behavior under stress or after long-term operation. Examples are:

- CPU usage
- RAM usage
- VM heap usage
- Hard disk usage

After you have established your baseline benchmark, you are ready to do performance tuning, especially dynacache tuning.

You can then rerun the benchmark and make performance comparisons:

- The size of workload can be used to find the saturation point and study how the system behaves under stress.
- Test any newly-introduced as well as any special-purpose features if you expect them to impact performance or if their impacts are unknown.
- The optimal values of DynaCache parameters depend on a number of aspects, including workload size and type, hardware, and software. Changes to configuration usually require a lot of experimentation. You should keep thorough records of all the changes introduced in each test run in order to get the best tuning.
- Running tests with different hardware configurations (for example, a different number of CPUs or amount of memory) provides important insight into system scalability.
- System performance is bound to change after long-term operation, due, in no small part, to changes to the database and logs. Running a test with a larger database and logs gives you an idea of system performance after extended periods of operation. Copy these from the production system and use them for analysis on the performance system.
- Run benchmark tests between each change to gauge the impact of each parameter as you learn how each one affects your environment.
- Keep an eye on all of your resource metrics for any spikes in resource utilization and resolve any bottlenecks as they appear.

Reference baselines

The baseline you have established should be archived for future use. As well as using the baseline as a way to assess the success of tuning, and the impact of new functionality, you can also use the baseline to verify or "acceptance test" changes to the underlying infrastructure, in addition to its primary use to assess performance, tuning, and changes to the WebSphere Commerce store.

With the intent of building a baseline for the infrastructure, some customers build a baseline using "vanilla" WebSphere Commerce and the "vanilla" Consumer Direct store. There is no direct comparison between the Consumer Direct baseline and your own customized store baseline, but there is value in having two baselines to compare against changes in the infrastructure, or to help diagnose performance problems.

By running both baselines, and by running the customized store on which you might be observing performance problems, you now have a number of data points[5], which might help pinpoint where you should be looking for a performance problem: in the infrastructure, in the customized store, or in interactions between the two. In Table 6-4 A, B and C are historical data you captured from benchmarking. D, E, F, and G are all benchmarks you can measure on the current infrastructure in an effort to isolate the performance problem.

Table 6-4 Five data points

Configuration	Baseline infrastructure	Current Infrastructure
Consumer direct baseline	A	D
Customized store baseline	B	E
Go Live store benchmark	C	F
Current store		G

6.3.3 Performance planning

The following sections outline key best practices, and some common pitfalls, in planning and implementing a successful testing strategy for your WebSphere Commerce implementation.

[5] These are not literally data points, but the complete performance reports for the benchmarks.

Planning tips

Here are some planning tips for your testing strategy:

- Performance testers must have time to gain thorough knowledge of all aspects of the environment and solution.
- Performance testing is of equal importance to development and functional testing when planning and scheduling release cycles.
- Performance testing should start as early as possible, so that testers can give early warning to developers about potential bottlenecks, as well as build up their own skills. Benchmarks, on the other hand, are run after the system has completed solution test.
- Performance testing should be given enough time and resources; testing requires a lot of hardware resources.
- Designate a performance lead for performance testing.
- Designate a performance lead who is responsible for following up with WebSphere Commerce system maintenance after the production site starts operations.
- When there is a performance problem, open a defect and track it as though it were a functional problem.
- Do not use an LPAR (logically partitioned machine) in the performance test environment unless it is also used in the Production environment.
- The solution needs to be fully functional and stable before running benchmark tests — ideally after SVT exit.
- Use scripts to automate basic performance tuning changes to ensure consistency across environments.
- Check the scripts to make sure they cover login, navigational, administrative, public and private pages, reload performance, with realistic think times and login patterns.
- Use an incremental testing approach to execute the performance tests.
- Monitor back end system utilization, and raise concerns if there is an alarming usage of back end resources — even if overall performance results are acceptable.

Hardware and software setup

The goal of benchmarking is to use load generation techniques and measurements to predict the performance behavior of the production environment under various loads. Therefore, the performance testing environment should be an exact replica of the production environment. The hardware and software profiles must be consistent in order to have an accurate prediction of the behavior of your production environment.

In particular, the following specifications should be as close as possible:

- Hardware type (RS/6000®, Sun, iSeries, Intel®).
- CPU speed and architecture (32 bit versus 64 bit, LPAR versus non-LPAR).
- Memory size and speed.
- Software levels (OS, middleware, WebSphere Application Server, and WebSphere Commerce version and patch levels).
- Cluster status of WebSphere Commerce site (clustered versus standalone, horizontal versus vertical clones).

If you are planning to support a large number of users with a large horizontal cluster, it is acceptable to scale back the number of nodes in your performance testing environment. For example, if your infrastructure plan is for a 6-node WebSphere Commerce cluster, you can build a 2-node WebSphere Commerce cluster for the performance testing environment. A performance test run against the performance testing environment with 200 users would predict performance behavior of an actual production load of 600 users:

- Document the hardware for production versus what is going to be used in performance testing.
- Using the manufacturers' information about server performance (such as rperf[6] on pSeries®) you can determine the ratio of the performance environment to the production environment (if they are not equal).
- Locate and document the volumes used to determine the hardware and CPU sizing from the pre-sales team, and check that these match the ones in the production environment. If the numbers are different, this is a project risk that unless rapidly mitigated, will need the attention of the project sponsor.
- When testing is completed, a true hardware sizing can be given.

Establish workload mix and volumes

Establishing workload mix and volumes is the most important element of your testing. You might only have information from the business, and from general industry experience to predict the workload mix and volumes. If you have an existing site, then use data from the Web server logs, or better, if you have previously invested in tools such as Omniture, Coremetrics, or Google analytics, get detailed data. You should pay particular attention to user volumes and when they peak during the day, to the ratio of guest and registered users, the browse to buy ratio, the number of items in a cart, and how often the cart is abandoned. Do not forget to work with predicted volumes, by applying an annual growth rate.

[6] `http://www-03.ibm.com/systems/p/hardware/notices/rperf.html`

Validate non-functional requirements

It is important to define and validate the key non-functional user requirements such as response times and availability, and translate these into the requirements on system components during the design phase. We discuss availability in more depth in "Reliability and availability" on page 293.

Remember, when you build a system out of separate components that work together, the responsiveness seen by a user is the sum of the latencies of the components. One way to increase the responsiveness of the site is to design it so that operations that require "back-end" components, such as transferring an order to a fulfilment system, are buffered, either through messaging, or by collecting orders in a database. The orders are processed by a separate task that reports back to the user via e-mail, or a link to order status on the Web page. That way, even if the back-end systems are slow, the Web site remains responsive.

Use caching

It is also important to consider caching, both within your enterprise by caching static and dynamic pages and page fragments, and also using caches outside the enterprise by enabling pages to be cached in the browser, and to use third party content delivery services such as Akamai and Limelight. Why is caching so important and effective in eCommerce applications?

The reason is that eCommerce architecture is, essentially, a client-server architecture implemented by a network of servers, which are distributed in layers between the customers' browsers and back-end servers and databases (Figure 6-1). In this architecture, the benefits of caching are theoretically delivered in three principal ways:

1. Decrease response times by reducing network latency.

   The number of layers in the network that need to be traversed to satisfy a customer request are reduced. This chiefly improves response times.

   So, for example, if a display of items is created by a search in an EJB, then the second time the display is requested, rather than accessing the application server and the database server to build the EJB, the cached EJB can be served from the Web server.

2. Increase throughput and decrease response times by reducing pathlength.

   In the same example, not having to execute the code in the application server and the database server to build the display of items, reduces the number of CPU cycles that need to be executed. This improves throughput, by freeing up CPU resources, and response time by reducing pathlength.

3. Increase client capacity by funneling resources.

   This is achieved by configuring an increasing of resources (for example, processor threads) to servers as one approaches the client side of the system. The number of threads required to service sudden bunches of client activity would put an overhead on the more CPU intensive back-end servers if the same number of threads was available throughout the system. Resources would be wasted switching between threads which had insufficient time to complete work.

   However, we hope that caching, by satisfying many client requests without recourse to running threads on the application or database server, allows us to rely on the funneling effect, and configure a decreasing number of resources on servers towards the back-end of the system, and so reduce the processor overhead of switching between partially executed threads.

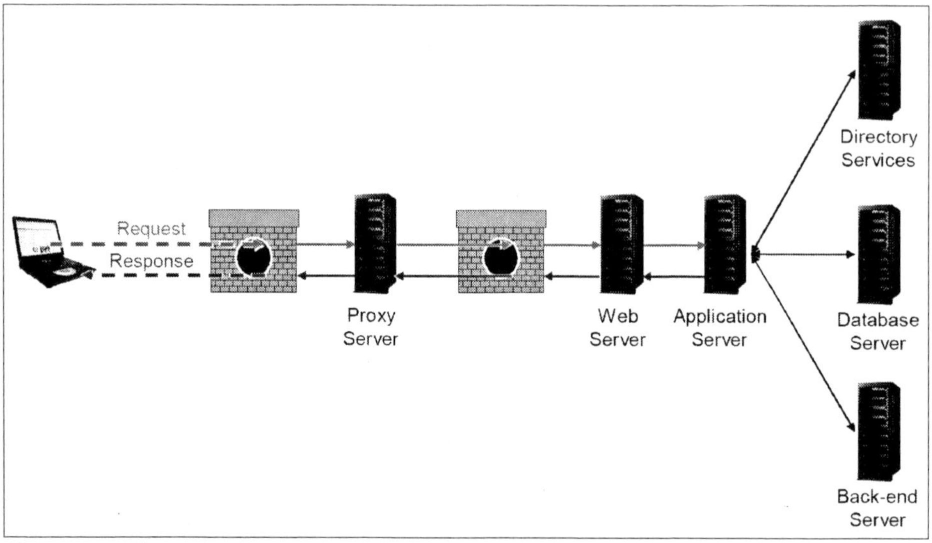

Figure 6-1 Network of servers

Cache planning

Caching needs to have a formal design document, just like any other function on the site. In addition, all design documents must include a caching section to explain the use of caching in every component. The main topics in the design document are:

- Application server caching, Web server caching, content mirroring:
  - Solution wide caching architecture and design
  - Caching methods to be used on the project

- Data replication services:
  - Managing usage of WebSphere Application Server Network Deployment caches
- Invalidation:
  - Policy for flushing (invalidating) stale cache entries
  - Document invalidation methods allowed
- Test plan:
  - Benchmarking
- Deployment:
  - Cache monitoring

6.3.4 Tuning a WebSphere Commerce application

In this section we attempt to explain the various techniques and methods to identify performance problem areas during the design and construction phases of development. Your objective is for performance tuning to be a development task, and not to leave it until just before launch.

At a high level, the tactics are:

1. Have a proactive performance team.

   The performance team must be respected by developers, understand what developers are doing, and train and help them use performance tools, and help develop good practices and communicate them. Developers sometimes mistakenly think of the performance team as, "just another test team". They are not.

   The performance team are responsible for the performance test environment and should use it during development and test to collect performance statistics for developers. With a dedicated environment the performance team can set up workload generators and test scripts, run performance regression tests, and become a center of excellence for running performance tools that would place a big burden on the project if every developer has to be skilled in them.

2. Use evidence.

   Most code is not in a critical performance path, and having developers obsess about performance where it is not necessary wastes resource and can result in poorer design and more bugs.

   Use performance profiling to identify bottlenecks, and concentrate your resources on the bottlenecks.

3. Profile Java code to identify performance hot spots.

   WebSphere Commerce developer includes the Rational performance profiling tools to identify performance hot spots in Java code.

4. Profile SQL using SQL tracing and analysis to isolate and review SQL performance bottlenecks.

   WebSphere Commerce stores all runtime configurations in WebSphere Commerce databases. WebSphere Commerce generates a very large number of DB queries: if there is a bottleneck accessing any of the WebSphere Commerce's underlying databases, it has a significant performance impact. It is well worth understanding how the load is made up. There might be some caching or design changes that would reduce the database load significantly. Analysis of SQL trace reveals:

   – Poorly performing SQL statements
   – Peaks in SQL executions
   – High number of executions for specific SQL statements (such as Inventory fetched repeatedly for all SKUs)
   – Resource usage data to monitor, such as:
     • Sort Time
     • CPU Used
     • Rows Written/Read

5. Monitor DynaCache to ensure that all functionality that can be cached is being accurately and effectively cached.

   – A simple methodology to verify caching implementation is to step through the following for each cachable servlet page:

     i. Clear the cache and access the page once to populate the cache.

     ii. Access the page again, and collect database and java profile traces (as discussed earlier).

     iii. Verify from a database SQL trace that no SQL statements are being executed (except those from "DoNotCache" fragments) and from the Java profile trace no business logic code is being executed (except from "DoNotCache" fragments).

   – Use the cache monitor to see that the page gets cached.

   – Collect cache statistics using the WebSphere Performance Monitoring Interface (PMI) to record cache hits.

6. Design and structure LDAP carefully.

   Connections are made into the LDAP server by the security components of portal frequently for authentication and authorization purposes, especially during the login sequences.

The design and structure of your LDAP server has a significant impact on performance, especially for group memberships. In particular, enabling support for nested groups can impact performance, especially if your LDAP server has a lot of deeply nested groups.

Using dynamic groups or a very large number of groups also has a performance impact unless your LDAP supports (and you configure portal to use) a user attribute to determine group membership rather than spidering group memberships to find the current user (for example, setting the groupMembershipAttributeMap to ibm-allgroups: all in the case of Tivoli Directory Server LDAP).

6.4 Security issues

Privacy is a major concern for all who travel on the Internet superhighways engaged in any kind of commerce or information exchange. For those who shop online, their willingness to provide personal information depends on the extent they trust your eCommerce site. In a US survey reported by the *"Internet Retailer"*, in 2005[7], 67% of Internet users have decided not to register at a Web site or shop online because they have found the privacy policy too complicated or unclear, and 54% have decided not to purchase something from a company because they were uncertain how their personal information would be used.

More recently, in a survey released in January 2008 by the University of Southern California's Center for the Digital Future, reported widely in the press, there has been an increase of 30% in one year from 47% to 61% of people who were very or extremely concerned about the privacy of personal data online[8]. The figures for 2007 contrast with previous years which have shown a nearly steady drop. This concern is greater for people who do not shop online, and for newer Internet users.

The explanation probably lies in the publicity given to the number of identity records compromised last year, reportedly 125,000,000 in 2007 in the US, compared with 20,000,000 reported in the US in 2006[9]. Large scale compromise of identity records is not confined to the US; 25,000,000 child benefits records were lost in one incident in the UK in 2007. Nor are the losses confined to government agencies.

---

[7] `http://www.internetretailer.com/internet/marketing-conference/578566856-vague-online-privacy-policies-are-harming-e-commerce-new-survey-reports.html`

[8] See also response to identity theft question from 2004 to 2006 at: "`http://www.ponemon.org/idtheft.html`

[9] See also `http://www.privacyrights.org/ar/DataBreaches2006-Analysis.htm` which lists 100,000 personal information breaches in 2006. This site is interesting in attempting a breakdown by sector and category of breach.

In looking at security issues, first we look at some of the risks you need to consider, and then at the security best practices for setting up and running a WebSphere Commerce Web site.

6.4.1 Threats

People's attitudes to risk online, if these survey figures are to be believed, do not seem to have affected people's decision to shop online, with the number of people shopping online in the US growing 32% from 50% to 66% between mid 2006 and mid 2007. Given that more people are shopping online anyway, despite the perception of risk increasing, should these survey figures be of particular concern to eCommerce businesses? Probably yes, for two reasons:

- Do the demographics of your customers make them more sensitive to privacy and security issues? Can you gain a relative advantage by addressing consumers' fears?
- If your brand is a major asset in online trading, your brand's reputation is more at risk should there be a security breach, because of the heightened press interest in online security.

How significant are losses associated with eCommerce sites? Although there have been losses of information, such as credit card numbers, associated with eCommerce sites, as often as not these are lapses in security procedures affecting generic IT operations and bricks and mortar commerce as much as they are associated with eCommerce.

Threats to eCommerce sites include:

- Loss of customer confidence in your Web site, or even your brand, due to attacks on customer data, such as identify theft
- Blackmail, or unfair competition using denial of service attacks
- Use of false credentials to order online
- Compromising pages, catalog information, price lists, and other business information
- Employee attacks on IT operations

Customer confidence

Customer confidence in your Web site is strongly influenced by the way your customers' perceive your handling of their personal data, and protecting them when they are interacting with your Web site. There are many ways in which confidence has and can be undermined, and you need make a judgement when procedures that might be perceived as intrusive, such as collecting click behavior, could benefit your business in other ways. You also need to balance usability against confidence. Are your password recovery procedures usable, efficient, and secure?

Your main tools to maintain customer confidence are:

- A privacy policy, clearly stated to your customers, which follows best practices such as laid out in *"Collecting personal information using Web sites"*, Information commissioner, UK Government, found at:

  http://www.ico.gov.uk/upload/documents/library/data_protection/practical_application/collecting_personal_information_from_websites_v1.0.pdf

- Well-run IT and business processes, which we describe in 6.4.2, "Best practices" on page 224.
- Follow practices which are known to improve customer confidence, and avoiding practices which diminish it. These are described next.

What improves or diminishes customer confidence is an empirical matter. In his article, "The Laws of Identity", Kim Cameron lists seven laws, which perhaps you might prefer to think of as hypotheses or observations, that attempt to explain whether people feel more or less confident about sharing personal information online. These observations were made in a wider context, but they are also a useful shorthand way to talk about and test your privacy policy, and the way you plan to handle personal information. If you accept that the Laws of Identity are reasonably grounded by observation, then you can use them to predict how aspects of a Web site will affect consumer confidence in the Web site. However, some features of a Web site might score positively on some of the laws and negatively on others — and then it is difficult to know how your consumers will react to those features.

1. User control and consent:

   We are familiar with the use of opt in/out boxes to extend the usage of identity information gathered during shopping to be used for other purposes, such as passing the information to third parties, and checking agreement to the Web sites privacy policy as a whole.

   You might also consider using opt in / opt out boxes to give users finer grained control over the uses to which their personal data is put.

2. Minimal disclosure for constrained use:

   Sometimes, disclosure can be an inadvertent consequence of a design decision which was not thought as having privacy implications. For example, convenient as an e-mail address is for many people as an easily remembered user name token, it is also a means that user accounts in many domains are more easily cross referenced, and a more complete profile of person built up.

   In a eCommerce context, assuming the shopper has not already saved their credit card information with you, when should you ask for credit card information? Which path retains more buyers, getting the credit card number first, so that finally, when the order price is finalized, it is a single click, or finalizing the order and then taking credit card details? The identity laws would suggest that taking the credit card details last loses fewer shoppers. Asking for identity information when it is actually required, to purchase, is "minimal disclosure".

3. Justifiable parties:

   Making use of third party identity systems, such as the Microsoft Passport system, unless used in the limited context of eCommerce related to Microsoft business, such as through MSN®, reduces the number of shoppers, unless the shopper perceives there to be a legitimate reason for the third party to be involved in their purchases.

4. Directed identity:

   An eCommerce Web site needs to be have an "Omnidirectional" identity — that is, whoever uses the site knows it is your site, and not some other site that has spoofed it by "pharming". There are various anti-pharming measures you can take, but it is a difficult threat to overcome. Using an SSL connection to establish identity, and using the connection from then on, is one measure you might consider taking, but it is going to impact performance. Another is not collecting password information until the user has had an opportunity to verify that they are indeed back into your Web site, for example, by responding to a user name token with pieces of user supplied identify information. This approach is not infallible, but it reduces risk.

   From the other side, your user should be able to choose who knows their identity. So called Unidirectional identity. Unidirectional identity strictly means the identity is only meaningful to one other party. We can use it to mean an person can choose who to make an identity known to. As eCommerce site become more involved with "community" activities, such as hosting chat rooms and providing product reviews, the risk of disclosing identifying information becomes greater.

5. Plural identities:

   Some people desire to keep separate identities, especially separating their cybercitizen, tax, financial, family, private and work identities for example. Requiring people to use government issued identities, such as US Social Security Numbers[10], to sign on to an eCommerce system, is unlikely to win you as many customers as allowing people to choose their own identities.

6. Human integration:

   The interactions between the customer and the Web site to establish and reestablish identity have been called "ceremonies." The point is that everyone knows the part they play, and so they play their part more reliably with fewer mistakes. Login sequences, recalling forgotten passwords, forgotten user

[10] By law, the SSN is not an identity.

names, providing new passwords, pass-phrases, and other secret information are all ceremonies. By deviating from common practices, perhaps with some good security goal in mind, you can end up with a lot of frustrated customers and many more calls to the customer support center.

If the customers' interactions with you are infrequent, then will a customer remember their password or even their username? If the customer cannot change a system generated username or password, it is unlikely. But if you allow too much customization, that also defeats the purpose: Recognition is stronger than recall, so asking someone to make up their own security question is less reliable then giving a fixed selection to choose from. Be sure the fixed selection is appropriate for your demographic.

7. Consistent experience:

   If you offer a number of means of interacting with your store — Web sites in different countries, phone and text, and bricks and mortar outlets — you need to establish common identities across the devices and have a consistent approach to security that matches each device's capabilities and vulnerabilities.

Denial of service

Countermeasures against distributed denial of services attacks are partial, difficult and many require network wide application[11]. You can however mitigate the effects by isolating systems from attacks by a combination of load balancing, throttling, and identifying and routing attack traffic.

False credentials

Depending on your business sector, the importance of false credentials varies considerably. For banks, using false credentials to obtain money is viewed as a major online risk; for a retailer this might not be so significant unless there is a way to turn a product purchase back into cash, or if your agreement with credit card companies makes you liable for fraudulent card purchases. If you are invoicing payments on account, then traditional techniques, such as having preset credit limits, might satisfactorily limit the risk.

Compromised business data

Compromised business data can happen by accident or maliciously. We have all heard those stories of displaced decimal points on the prices of goods offered for sale on the Internet — word gets around remarkably quickly! Your main tools to fight compromised data are access control, audit logs, and reviewing finalized content before it goes live on the production server[12].

[11] See "Distributed Denial of Service: Taxonomies of Attacks, Tools and Countermeasures", Stephen Specht and Ruby Lee, Princeton Architecture Laboratory for Multimedia and Security, found at:
`http://palms.ee.princeton.edu/PALMSopen/DDoS%20Final%20PDCS%20Paper.pdf`

Employee attacks on IT operations

Specific user roles, access controls, and change logging are the main tools to restrict and manage who changes what. WebSphere Commerce has extensive member controls to make it easy to create and assign categories of users to tasks, and Workspaces (see 2.2.9, "Workspaces" on page 62) is an access controlled workspace that enables you to assign specific tasks, such as content management tasks, to users or roles to be carried out.

6.4.2 Best practices

This section describes best practices you can implement to help secure your site.

Industry compliance

WebSphere Commerce version 6.0.0.2 has been validated against a standard known as the VISA Cardholder Information Security Program (CISP) Payment Application Best Practices (PABP). This standard addresses security issues specific to payment applications. Validation against this standard helps to ensure that WebSphere Commerce v6.0.0.2, when installed and configured correctly, enables merchants to certify their sites for PCI compliance. PCI compliance remains solely your responsibility.

You should obtain the detailed IBM technical paper on the PCI DSS from:

http://www.ibm.com/developerworks/WebSphere/library/techarticles/0705_lazaruk/0705_lazaruk.html

You need to understand how PCI compliance relates to WebSphere Commerce, and how ensure customizations of WebSphere Commerce do not comprise PCI compliance.

Policies

A meaningful security and privacy policy well-executed encourages your customers to trust you. This leads to more satisfied customers, increased purchases, and a greater willingness on the part of consumers to provide accurate personal information at your site. It also helps prevent security incidents which could jeopardize the business.

There are many established policies and standards for avoiding security issues. Some basic rules are:

- Never store a user's password in plain text or encrypted text on the system. Instead, use a one-way hashing algorithm to prevent password extraction.

[12] "Workspaces" on page 62, by separating the authoring, approving, and promoting roles requires data to be seen by more than one pair of eyes before it is made public.

- Employ external security consultants (ethical hackers) to analyze your system.
- Standards, such as the Federal Information Processing Standard (FIPS), describe guidelines for implementing features. For example, FIPS makes recommendations on password policies[13].
- Ensure that a sufficiently robust encryption algorithm, such as triple DES or AES, is used to encrypt all confidential information stored on the system.
- When developing third-party software for eCommerce applications, use external auditors to verify that appropriate processes and techniques are being followed.
- Make use of the security features which are specifically designed to handle archiving and transfer of private data from the WebSphere Commerce database to other storage.

Security best practices remain largely an art rather than a science, but there are some good guidelines and standards that all developers of eCommerce software should follow.

Access control

One of the security measures you must focus on in your WebSphere Commerce store is access control. By definition, access control means to check that certain users or groups of users are authorized to access specific resources. WebSphere Commerce implements a set of access control policies that are editable and customizable by the site administration team.

There are two types of policies that WebSphere Commerce implements, command-level and instance-level. In command-level policies, the access manager component of WebSphere Commerce determines if the current user is authorized to call a specific controller command or view, or not. Instance-level access control, on the other hand, is more fine-grained and determines if the current user is authorized to perform a specific action on a specific resource. An example is whether a user can view and modify orders belonging to him or his organization only.

Access control in WebSphere Commerce is not easy to implement or customize. There are bound to be issues with access control and it is better to discover and deal with them sooner rather than later. It is not a good idea to act as though the access control design already done for the sample stores in WebSphere Commerce largely meet your needs. Do not assume anything that does not quite fit will be discovered during testing and fixed with the rest of the bugs. You need to understand the WebSphere Commerce access control model during the design phase and extend it, use it, and test it as you go along.

[13] See the rather dated (1985) `http://www.itl.nist.gov/fipspubs/fip112.htm`

For details on access control policies and mechanisms implemented in WebSphere Commerce, refer to the *WebSphere Commerce Information Center*. The security pages are found at:

```
http://publib.boulder.ibm.com/infocenter/wchelp/v6r0m0/index.jsp?topic=
/com.ibm.commerce.admin.doc/concepts/csesecuritymodel.htm
```

Using cookies the right way or pursuing alternatives

HTTP cookies[14] are parcels of text — some kind of session token — that originates from the Web server but is passed back and forth between the Web server and a Web browser each time the browser accesses that server. Cookies are used for authenticating, tracking, and maintaining specific information about users, but they have been of concern for Internet privacy because they can be used for tracking browsing behavior. As a result, they have been subject to legislation in various countries such as the United States and in the European Union. Cookies have also been criticized because the identification of users they provide is not always accurate and because they could potentially be a target of network attackers.

There are different types of cookies:

- **Temporary cookies:** These cookies are valid only for the lifetime of your current session, and are deleted when you close your browser. These are usually the good type. They are mostly used to keep your session information.
- **Permanent cookies:** These are for a time period, specified by the site, on the shopper's computer. They recall your previous session information.
- **Server-only cookies:** These cookies are usually harmless, and are only used by the server that issued them.
- **Third-party cookies:** These are usually used for tracking purposes by a site other than the one you are visiting. Your browser or a P3P policy can filter these cookies.

> **Note:** A P3P policy is a privacy policy that is understood by computers. It expresses the concepts of a plain-text privacy policy in a predefined XML-based format. A consumer's Web browser (or a special piece of software on the consumer's machine) can download this P3P policy, compare it to a user's privacy preferences, and display the results of this comparison to the user.

[14] Cookies are somewhat overplayed as a security exposure. There is no denying privacy concerns, but contrary to what vendors of anti-spyware might like you to believe, cookies are data, and not active programs.

To blunt the criticism and lower the discomfort with cookies, you could consider using cookies that might not be as intrusive. If you do not want to store cookies, there are other alternatives:

User ID/password on every request

This was popular 5-10 years ago, but now recognized as an insecure technique. The user ID/password flowing under non-SSL is susceptible to attacks. This alternative is not practical for a high volume site. Pages that run under SSL would slow down site performance.

SSL client side authentication

This is the most secure[15], but it is cumbersome for shoppers to install on their browsers. You have to pay for a company to verify who you are and to issue a certificate. The popularity of this technique for client-side authentication has decreased in recent years. It remains very popular on server sites. It is also questionable whether consumers would accept the intrusion to their privacy of having their computer able to identify them to any software running on their computer. This breaks the fourth law of identity. A weaker form of identification — Intel providing a machine readable computer identifier in their processors — was made optional, and not widely accepted for privacy reasons.

URL rewriting

This is a popular alternative to cookies. Each Http link on the page is specially encoded, but it is expensive for the site to implement. It interferes with the performance of the site because the pages cannot be cached and reused for different users. This alternative is susceptible to attack if it is not used under SSL.

Cookies marked as secure

Storing encrypted data and passing to the user only under SSL remains the most popular method of providing a secure online experience.

Your goal is to ensure that the privacy of your patrons is respected and that shoppers trust your site. You need review the drawbacks and advantages for using cookies.

Using threat models to prevent exploits

When architecting and developing a system, it is important to use threat models to identify all possible security threats on the server. Think of the server like your house. It has doors and windows to allow for entry and exit. These are the points that a burglar attacks. A threat model seeks to identify these points in the server and to develop possible attacks.

[15] Actually the security of client side certificates is arguable. If correctly set up, they are very secure, but they need to be set up in a controlled manner for the set up process not to be subverted - one reason they have never caught on with businesses in the uncontrolled environment of eCommerce.

In building a threat model for your Web site, you need to consider all the scenarios that were created as part of the requirements process and understand which user roles are involved, what data is used, and what the use cases are for interacting with the data. You then need to understand what is involved in the implementation of the use cases in the WebSphere Commerce system. What components are involved, what roles are involved and what calls are made to read or modify data. From this, you need to decide if the levels of access are appropriate, or if the design gives rise to vulnerabilities — that is, data accessible to an inappropriate role.

Some of the vulnerable points to consider in a WebSphere Commerce site are:

- Web container security
- Application security
- Web Services massage layer security
- Secure Sockets Layer (SSL)
- Web Services transport security
- Security attribute propagation and CSIv2[16]
- User registries
- Member Groups
- Windows Single Sign On
- Operating system security
- WebSphere Application Server administrative security

Reviewing threat models is particularly important when relying on a third party vendor for all or part of the site's infrastructure. This ensures that the suite of threat models is complete and up-to-date. it is also important to do this work in the design and elaboration phases, as code rework later on to surmount security exposures tends to be expensive.

Responding to security issues

You must prepare an effective overall security strategy to deal with vulnerabilities if they are detected. This also means ensuring that software vendors selected for all or part of the site's infrastructure have proactive and reactive policies for handling security issues. Remember that the weakest link in the chain determines the security of the system.

In the case of WebSphere Commerce, you can form a SWAT team with key developers, testers, and support personnel to deal with security breaches. When an issue arises, this team assumes responsibility to assess the situation determine the cause and develop or implement an immediate fix. In practice, this has meant that an entire Web site has been shut down when a security breach

[16] Part of WebSphere Single Sign-on, see
http://publib.boulder.ibm.com/infocenter/wasinfo/v5r1//index.jsp?topic=/com.ibm.WebSphere.base.doc/info/aes/ae/tsec_enablesecattprop.html

was detected, and the impact was yet unknown. Does your operational team have the initiative and discretion to switch off the site? More commonly, where customers' information have been compromised, a "flash" should be issued to the affected customers to notify them of the problem, the solution, and how to check if they have been exploited.

6.5 Growth and extensibility

WebSphere Commerce implementations should be designed with growth in mind. Here are some considerations:

- Purchase the right WebSphere Commerce product:

  a. WebSphere Commerce Enterprise
  b. WebSphere Commerce Professional
  c. WebSphere Commerce Express

  See 2.4, "Editions" on page 85.

- Consider the Extended Sites model if you plan to customize your site by geography, by market segment, by customer or by brand:

  See 2.1.5, "Extended Sites (eSites)" on page 28.

- Consider using Service Oriented Architecture:

  See 3.1.1, "Service Oriented Architecture (SOA)" on page 90.

- Install a scalable infrastructure to support the future growth of your WebSphere Commerce implementation:

  See Chapter 8, "Best of breed infrastructure" on page 271.

6.6 Quality

You do not want to launch your eCommerce site only to discover that it performs poorly, has application problems, or does not meet customer expectations. According to Forrester Research, nearly 85% of large companies (more than $1 billion in revenue) have reported incidents of significant application performance problems. To avoid such disasters, you need a formal quality methodology both complete with prerequisites for testing and test phases, and production targets defined as measures based on business-defined service level agreements. More important, and key to improving the quality of your site, is to engender a quality assurance culture that assumes that "If you do not test, it does not work." This culture requires testing to be an integral part of the design and development efforts and is supported by efficient code reviews and coding standards.

6.6.1 Have a quality plan

Appoint a quality assurer with responsibility for quality. This person requires the project to implement monitoring tools to be able to measure the quality of the Web site and manage Service Level Agreements (SLA). To improve quality, the quality assurer needs to understand how each team contributes to quality — for example, by writing good quality code, and finding defects. The quality plan documents how each team manages and measures the quality of their deliverable. This provides the foundation for improving the Web site quality, release on release. Quality measures can be part of the ETVX entry and exit criteria (see Figure 5-4 on page 167).

6.6.2 Spread good coding practices

Here we list some recommended coding practices:

1. Break your development effort into iterations and in each iteration specify the use cases to be implemented and the test scripts to adequately test the code.
2. Apply architectural and code analysis and review rules to class library projects, Web site projects, and source code control. Rational Application Developer has a specific view ("Code Review view", rules and tools to help you manage rules and manage code reviews.
    a. Identify the specific errors and warnings that apply during code writing, project builds and code check-ins and review them at each juncture for error and completeness.
    b. Continuously refine strategies that enforce coding standards to improve the quality of your code, while ensuring that inapplicable rules never get in your way.
3. Coding standards significantly reduce opportunities for developers to introduce errors into an application.
    a. For example, use StringBuffer instead of String for non-constant strings. The industry's best resource of coding conventions is found with Sun's Java coding conventions, found at:

       `http://java.sun.com/docs/codeconv/`
    b. Sun also has articles on specific topics, for example, "Servlets and JSP pages Best Practices", found at:

       `http://java.sun.com/developer/technicalArticles/javaserverpages/servlets_jsp/`
    c. Other sources include Doug Lea's[17], "Draft Java Coding Standard", found at:

       `http://g.oswego.edu/dl/html/javaCodingStd.html`

Also see Scott Ambler's[18], "Coding Standards for Java", found at:

http://www.ambysoft.com/essays/javaCodingStandards.html

4. Practice defensive programming techniques.
   a. Anticipate failures and test for errors.
   b. Notify when errors occur and have a standard error recovery procedure.
   c. Validate user input.
   d. Embed debugging support.
   e. Use WebSphere trace support to provide runtime as well as development trace.
5. Perform code inspections[19]. Formal code inspections are estimated to be four times more efficient at finding bugs than unit testing.
   a. When you schedule a WebSphere Commerce customization project, set milestones for the development team to hold formal review checkpoints. These reviews are scheduled within the development cycle and best placed upon unit completion before code is submitted to formal test builds. There is a large literature on code reviews. Experience has shown that the most effective code reviews for removing defects are formal, following a documented process. Code reviews have other benefits:
      - Encourage better, public, coding
      - Programmers learn good practices
      - Enforce and develop good coding standards
      - Discover cross module duplications or misunderstandings
      - Spread knowledge about other areas of the product, enabling developers to be more easily moved from one part of a project to another
      - Provide data to a measurable quality improvement program
6. Prepare and perform unit test (see "Code and unit test" on page 172)

   Going through the process of preparing unit tests during design rather than coding provides a clearer understanding of the solution. Since unit test scripts are created directly from customer use cases, developers are forced to get an intimate understanding of the requirements document and are likely to find oversights in the requirements before coding starts and rework gets more expensive. In IBM service engagements, unit tests are prepared as part of the micro design phase.

---

17 Doug Lea is Professor of computer science of New York at Oswego,

18 Scott Ambler is the Practice Leader Agile Development at IBM Corporation, he consults widely for clients, and is particularly associated with Agile development.

19 An alternative to code review is to adopt "pair programming", advocated by eXtreme Programming (XP) and sometime associated with agile development. It needs to be managed to be effective. See http://www.extremeprogramming.org/index.html

6.7 Launch preparation and launch

There are multiple possibilities that can go wrong at any time during project development, including deployment and launch. This is the most crucial time for the project, and anything that goes wrong here could be potentially catastrophic, as marketing campaigns and inventory stocking might be rolling. At this point, if something goes wrong, there is not much contingency to use up to replan and recover. Accordingly, prepare well for *Go Live!*, including testing all aspects of the launch to know all the issues that can go wrong, and to take them into consideration both for planning and recovery.

In this section, we discuss all the potential risks linked to deployment and launch to prepare you for that crucial phase.

6.7.1 Loading data

Loading data can be started — at least in planning — as early as the project start. However, it is one of the activities that often gets delayed to the deployment phase. It is also often not estimated in the project schedule. Even though it is a simple task — moving some data from the old system to the new — in reality it is not straightforward. Here is a list of common data load problems:

- Data have to be cleaned up significantly before they can be loaded into the WebSphere Commerce database and displayed to the shoppers.
- Data is not in an easily loadable format. Conversion into the right format to load into the WebSphere Commerce database might take a long time.
- Data comes from different systems and must be merged before loading into the WebSphere Commerce database and displayed to the shoppers.
- The data load process is not implemented until the data load task is scheduled to start.
- The data load process is not tested with a sample of real data until the data load task is scheduled to start.
- The time required to load orders and users in addition to catalog items was overlooked.
- Time must be spent ensuring that final versions of catalog entries, prices, inventory levels, and contracts are available for data load.

To mitigate these risks, start working on the data load process early in the project life cycle, treating the data load itself as an operational task, not a development task. The development goal is to have a completely clean operational data load process accepted by the deployment team who have tested the process in readiness for loading the final version of the data for launch.

6.7.2 Down time

If you are upgrading or migrating an existing online store and you are using some of the same hardware, then you need to plan downtime before and during the launch. Unplanned downtime is usually longer, and certainly more disruptive.

If your implementation uses horizontal clustering, then reduce downtime by taking servers out of the cluster during slack periods without disrupting availability. Use the freed up servers for testing. At launch time, build the new system on half the cluster, loading it offline. For launch, switch over to the newly loaded half of the cluster, and the only downtime is the time required to upgrade the database as it is switched from the old to the new half cluster.

If you are not clustering on multiple machines, you need to plan your down time carefully and test the whole deployment on a pre-production server before you can apply it on the production environment to avoid unforeseen problems.

6.7.3 Maintenance and support

As described in "Post-engagement activities" on page 160, when the project gets to the deployment phase you will have decided whether or not to contract a maintenance period from the solution provider for when the store is up and running. Whether and what kind of contract you decide to have with the solution provider for maintenance depends on a number of factors, but not least on how well your development team is gaining the skills and experience in the customized product to take care of technical issues themselves.

Buying WebSphere Commerce entitles you to product support, that covers problems and bugs in the product itself not the customized code. The product support differs in time and level depending on the license and maintenance agreement you have with IBM. You maintenance team needs to plan and test support procedures with IBM.

6.7.4 Post launch

When the site is up and running, your development and infrastructure teams must have the skills and experience to take over the site from any solution providers you only contracted for development. Your teams now manage any problems and handle any extensions you might need in the future. You have to plan their training in WebSphere Commerce development.

For your system administrators and operational team, you need to plan training in WebSphere Commerce, and in the customizations and procedures developed for your site. They also have to plan and test how to apply maintenance and deploy new code in the future.

Similarly, business users need training in how to use the customized system and to have planned and tested the process to update the content on the site.

6.8 Globalization

What does it take to run a eCommerce Web sites globally? There are a lot of business questions to answer. Are you going to run local:

- Product catalogs and price lists?
- Terms and conditions and trading agreements?
- Currencies and payment options?
- Fulfillment?
- CSRs?
- Promotions?
- Accounts?

Table 6-5 lists, by subsystem, some of the customizations that are possible.

Table 6-5 Globalization choices

Subsystem	Globalization impact
Shipping	Define shipping rules and carriers for different areas and jurisdictions.
Taxes	Define tax rules for different areas and jurisdictions.
Payment	Define payment rules for different areas and jurisdictions.
Fulfillment	Define as many fulfillment centers as the store requires. The handling of fulfillment centers is not affected by the language or area that a user selects.
Search	Not affected by language choice.
Catalog	Catalog entries need different names, descriptions, attributes and possibly different images. Use the same master catalog and provide different sales catalogs for different areas.
Integration	Messaging with systems in different countries needs to be sensitive to the codepage of WebSphere Commerce system and the target system. For example, for MIME, set the MIMECHARSET column in the LANGUAGE table to the character encoding value to be used for each language supported by the store.

Subsystem	Globalization impact
Pricing	You can choose to price items differently, as well as price in different currencies, for different countries. Alternatively, choose to define one price in a default currency and provide conversion factors for other currencies. Currencies are not related to the language selected by the user.
Marketing and promotions	You can choose to apply marketing campaigns and promotions to some customers based on their culture or language, or to all customers no matter what their culture is.
Customer Support Representatives	You can choose to provide different CSRs in every language, or you can provide support for all CSRs in multiple languages.

With all these processes to organize, all of which impact the Web site, it begins to look as though you would need to re-implement your Web site for every country you trade in. However, it turns out that this is not the case.

Note: You will see that most global businesses WebSphere Commerce Web sites look remarkably similar in format for the different countries they trade in, although the content is quite different.

If you have implemented your Web site using the extended sites model, many stores within a single WebSphere Commerce system share common parts of the solution and customize only the differences. Even if you used consumer direct, rather than eSites, you can replicate the store, and change just the parts that are different.

These days, where the hardware is located to run the store need have little to do with what country the Web site is used in. It is common to run global stores from only two or three sites world wide. The IT center is located where the skilled staff are, or where you already have facilities. For example, ibm.com runs EMEA, AP, and Americas from three centers, and two are in the US.

From the customer's perspective, and from the point of view of driving revenue, it is not enough to use different languages on Web pages to attract customers from different countries. The site needs to make shoppers feel at home, just like a regular store. WebSphere Commerce supports a lot of features that facilitate multi-cultural stores, and there are ways to even add support for features that are not directly supported by WebSphere Commerce. Here we discuss some of the considerations you need to think about when designing a multi-cultural Web site.

6.8.1 Static and dynamic content

Whenever you talk about building a multi-cultural store that supports different languages, you require a different user-centered design for the pages as well as needing to have different local business centers creating different catalog content, pricing, payment mechanisms, contracts, fulfillment, marketing campaigns and promotions. You could choose to have a single team world wide responsible for the master catalog, and use local teams to create local sales catalogs.

The UCD team is responsible for achieving a look-and-feel for the site that is fitting for the cultures it is targeting. Not all cultures think and behave in the same way and it is important to take this into consideration, when designing a user interface. Here are some issues to keep in mind regarding user interface:

- Not all languages are left-to-right. Some go from right to left, while others are vertical. HTML supports both types of horizontal languages and it is possible for a Web site to actually support both. It is important to keep this in mind when designing the user interface and to use different style-sheets for each language, with a variable to indicate direction of text.
- Unfortunately the effect of left-to-right and right-to-left languages is not limited to the way text is placed on a page. The way we scan a Web page to look for significant content is influenced by the way our language is written. This means that the most viewed portion of a page changes for different cultures, so the positioning of promotions and marketing spots needs to be changed for maximum impact.
- Colors can have radically different meanings in different cultures. If you build your site thinking only about one culture and then try to support others, your shoppers might get offended by the color schemes you use, if they have different meanings in their own culture. Again, when designing the user interface for the site, you need to make sure to include different versions of headers and static images according to the language the user selects. This is possible through storing all static content in properties files for each language to be able to retrieve the right content for the chosen language.
- Just as with colors, you need to store translations for all static text used in the site in properties files for each language to be retrieved according to the language preference chosen by the shopper.
- Categories, products, and items can have different images for each language. It is possible, through using the WebSphere Commerce database to allow for different images, names, descriptions, and attributes of the catalog entries, according to the language preference of the user.

- The site needs to support all the currencies being used by the different cultures it is targeting. Again, WebSphere Commerce supports multiple currencies with the ability to add more unsupported currencies in a few steps. Keep in mind that this also involves converting the price from one currency to another, not just replacing currency symbols. All this is included in the support provided by WebSphere Commerce.
- Numbers can be represented in different ways in different cultures. Some cultures use commas to denote decimal, while others use a period or even an inverted comma to denote this. WebSphere Commerce allows for choosing the number format for each supported language.

6.8.2 Language addition

WebSphere Commerce supports 10 languages out-of-the-box for the software, product documentation, user interfaces and samples. The supported languages are:

- English
- French
- German
- Spanish
- Italian
- Portuguese
- Simplified Chinese
- Traditional Chinese
- Korean
- Japanese

It is also possible to add other languages to the WebSphere Commerce store by following a few steps:

1. Add a new display format for the language, using the Store Profile notebook tool.
2. Translate the properties files content, that are available in all the ten supported languages to your new language. Create a new folder to store the properties files and place it under the storedir folder found in:

   ```
   <WebSphere Commerce Installation folder>/Stores.war/WEB-INF/classes
   ```

   > **Note:** For a non-Latin alphabet, you have to convert the properties files after you translate them into Unicode ASCII representation. This is possible by using the native2ascii utility provided with the JDK™ found under the WebSphere Application Server installation folder.

3. For each entry you add to the catalog, enter the different names, descriptions, attributes, and images of that entry for each supported language.

Refer to the *WebSphere Commerce Information Center* for more information about adding new languages and currencies to your store.

6.9 Top ten tips

This is our list of top ten tips. Each one is expanded upon in the sections that follow. Also look at the list chosen by Gomez, referenced on page 198.

1. Map requirements to out-of-the-box features
2. Get business and technical teams to work closely together.
3. Storyboard and role play the Web site and the business flows
4. Focus on caching for performance
5. Develop well-tuned SQL queries and table indices from the start
6. Understand expected performance early
7. Validate the production environment early
8. Understand how to interpret production monitoring
9. Ensure change control procedures are established and utilized
10. Learn from experienced people

6.9.1 Map requirements to out-of-the-box features

WebSphere Commerce has a lot of out-of-the-box features and best practices. Where features are a close match to your requirements, consider changing your processes and adopting the practices in WebSphere Commerce. After discussion, you might conclude it is better and cheaper to modify your business processes rather than customizing WebSphere Commerce.

1. The first step in implementing WebSphere Commerce is to determine which business model best fits the organization's business plans. Consumer Direct, Business-to-Business, Extended Sites, Partner Relationship Management, Supply Chain, Demand Chain.
2. The second step is to examine the starter store associated with the chosen business model and determine what features can be used, what needs to be removed, and what needs to be added. It is much easier and cheaper to start from one of the starter stores as opposed to starting from scratch. The starter stores have been built as a starting point to accelerate Time-to-Value.
3. The third step is to look at the data load and data mapping early in the project. That is, what out-of-the-box tables match your requirements and what new tables do you need to create? How are you planning to load the tables loaded initially and then incrementally over time? What is the source of the catalog data and is it appropriate for display to customers, or does it need some cleansing or transforming first?

Tip #1: Suggestions:

- Do not reinvent the wheel. Check if the feature is in WebSphere Commerce already.
- Adapt your business processes to the best practices in WebSphere Commerce.

6.9.2 Get business and technical teams to work closely together

Go out of your way to create excellent communication between the business and technical teams. Get them *into* the same open plan and *onto* the same plan!

Ensure that the business and technical teams are involved from the beginning and communicate along the way. It is essential that both the business and technical teams agree on the approach, implementation, schedule, and deployment strategy.

In an eCommerce Web site, like no other, technology is critical to achieving business results. However good the catalog, revenue and margin depend on the success of the technical delivery. Both technical and business people should actively participate in the design of the site. With both parties represented, the technical folks can understand the business drivers and desired results, and the business folks can understand the technical limitations and costs.

Tip #2: Suggestion:

- Involve both technical and business people in both technical and business decisions.

6.9.3 Storyboard and role play the Web site and the business flows

The smallest points can make huge differences in how a Web page is used. Placing links wrongly, coloring wrongly, using words wrongly, creating interaction sequences wrongly — each mistake has measurable consequences in the number of catalog items people view, the time they spend on your site and the amount they spend, irrespective of the catalog you are selling. Conversely excellent features added to the site such as gift centers can add new visitors, or features like "`people who bought this, also considered`", can add to the value of a shopping cart. But they need to be done right for maximum effect.

The closer you can get to your customer, and your customer experience early on in development, the better chance of success. Next we list the critical success factors in getting value out of story-boarding.

Tip #3: Suggestions:

- Make the experience as close to the final site as possible — especially matching the layouts, fonts, colors, graphics and interaction sequences.
- Test subjects must be fresh to the site, and not contaminated by having been involved in the development process — so called "cold users".
- The test subjects' demographics must match the customer segment. If you sell luxury cruises to over 50's, you need to find appropriate test subjects. Over 50's might prefer the keyboard to the mouse, for example.
- As well as testing the Web site business flows, also look at the back office flows.

6.9.4 Focus on caching for performance

A Web site can draw hundreds of thousands of visitors per hour. Each visitor can view tens of pages during their visit. If each page is dynamically generated and accesses the database for information, then the load on the database server is beyond any database's reasonable capacity.

Web surfers are turned off by slowly performing sites. When designing the features of the site and its implementation, one should consider the desired throughput and response rate. A "cool" feature that takes too long to load will not be used by its intended audience, and you might lose a new visitor completely.

WebSphere Application Server comes with a Dynamic Cache (Dynacache) that caches whole pages or parts (fragments) of a page. When storyboarding the site, one should indicate which parts are cachable and which parts are not. Plan the flows with caching in mind. It is very expensive to rework the business flows after the pages are coded.

You should also consider redesigning pages which have dynamic information that cannot be cached — because it is bound to change on each page visit. Sometimes the solution is not obvious — removing the information lessens the value of the page. Usually there is an answer, but it might require some creative thinking. In the end, good performance is essential.

Tip #4: Suggestions:

- Cache dynamic information in dynacache.
- Avoid information that changes on every page hit on high traffic pages.

6.9.5 Understand expected performance early

Performance measures should be established at the beginning of the project (see 6.3.2, "Roadmap for performance testing and tuning" on page 209.) and the performance team should work on how to achieve this performance and help and monitor development along the way. By SVT the performance team should be verifying performance, not redesigning for performance.

It is not all about response times and throughput, it is also about customers completing tasks. Reducing clicks not only reduces overall time to perform a task, but by reducing interactions it increases throughput. Look at the paths through your competitors sites and set that as a baseline to do better.

How many clicks does a shopper expect to make to find a product? How long does a shopper want to spend completing a purchase? How many clicks and how long to find the status an order?

Tip #5: Suggestions:

- Before the site is launched, test to make sure the site performs as expected.

6.9.6 Develop well-tuned SQL queries and table indices from the start

WebSphere Application Server applications typically use a database to store and persist data. SQL queries are used to retrieve information from the database that is used as input to decisions, and then displayed to the Web surfer. These SQL should be reviewed during design for performance. Based on expert review, rewrite the query and add new indices to the database. Possibly modify the original table to increase performance. Performance should be designed into an application, not added as a result of bad performance test results.

Tip #6: Suggestion:

- Consider database performance tuning during design.

6.9.7 Validate the production environment early

Do not leave the planning of the production environment until the last minute. Make sure the production environment infrastructure is working and tested before deploying the test solution — it saves time.

The development environment is not the same as the environment that is used for production. It is highly recommended that your create a pre-production test environment to duplicate the production environment as much as possible — though you can reduce the number of machines or LPARs allocated to clusters to reduce cost.

Since production environments are different from test environments, it is imperative that production environments configuration for launch is not left to the For example, the production environment might use different machine types with different amounts of memory, which means the machine and operating system need to be configured differently. Also, horizontal and vertical cloning can be used in production, but not in test so adequate time needs to be put into the schedule to work through any issues that arise.

Tip #7: Suggestion:

- Configure and test the production environment before deployment.

6.9.8 Understand how to interpret production monitoring

Before deploying the WebSphere Commerce application, operators of the site need to make sure they know how to check the system is running well or if there are problems. You need to build tools and procedures for operators to use, and to test them in the pre-production environment.

Similarly, business users need to understand how business is performing and how to establish comparisons between expected and actual values to detect out of line values. During development and test you should consider testing business reporting.

Tip #8: Suggestions:

- Build operational tools and procedures for operators and run education sessions to verify they can detect out of line situations and intervene correctly.
- Work with business users to build reports they can use to track business results and detect out of line situations, and test the reports.
- Monitoring reports should be generated as soon as the site is launched.

6.9.9 Ensure change control procedures are established and utilized

Uncontrolled change is your worst enemy. It leads to instability, broken schedules and rapidly increasing cost. Business content needs continuous change for your site to remain competitive. Likewise the technical content of your site needs to change to meet changing requirements and maintenance demands. Controlled change is your best friend, without it your Web site at best will not attract much business, and at worst will not work.

You need a change control process that is easy for users to understand and use and puts the right people in charge of managing change.

Technical change is not limited to "scope creep," but includes changes to hardware and software versions, schedules, processes, and people. A totally sound and risk-managed project can be derailed by the best of intentions. Even when an excellent job has been done of requirements gathering and design and architecture of the site, new ideas and perspectives will be found during the project. In the attempt to over achieve, the entire project can be put at risk. It is only too common for a new idea to have unintended consequences. You need a process to manage change, which includes cut-off dates for new features, modifications to features, and even fixes to bugs.

Tip #9: Suggestions:

- Use Workspaces to control business content update.
- Adopting a shorter (agile) increment cycle makes it easier to manage change.
- Cut off dates must be established for all deliverable stages.
- Cost the impact of not changing against the risk of changing at a later point in the current increment. It probably is not worth the risk if the change can be worked into the next increment. The agile rule is "preserve the date, de-scope the increment".

6.9.10 Learn from experienced people

You are not going to succeed on time and in budget without experience. This applies as much to the project manager on their first WebSphere Commerce project, as it does to the development team customizing a starter store. There are plenty of people ready to help, and some help is bundled in "free of charge" as part of service agreements.

IBM has teams such as Business Consulting Services and IBM Software Services for WebSphere who are ready to assist. You also have the choice of many IBM Business Partners. With respect to WebSphere Commerce, typical service engagements include Solution Design Workshops, Migration Workshops, Implementation Services, and Performance Tuning.

The IBM WebSphere Commerce development group also has an Advanced Technical Services team that can be engaged through IBM Software Services for WebSphere. The ATS team can provide guidance with configuring complex environments, capacity planning, and performance tuning.

Tip #10: Suggestions:

- IBM services teams can help to mentor and implement solutions. IBM Business Partners are also able to assist.
- Leverage expert skills for a design workshop, implementation assistance, migration assistance, performance tuning, and so on.

Part 3

Plan your eCommerce infrastructure

This section of the book is more technical, but before any development can get underway, you need to decide what kind of technical infrastructure you are going to use to build your WebSphere Commerce system. So we offer no apologies for looking at IT patterns, and discussing what kind of infrastructure your plan to build. The scale of your infrastructure makes a huge difference to how long it will take to roll out the Web site — from two months for a small infrastructure, to over a year for a large one, and also a large difference in cost (although hardware costs tend to be dwarfed by staff and software costs these days).

In Chapter 7, “Patterns of infrastructure for eCommerce”, we describe different patterns of hardware and software infrastructures to use with WebSphere Commerce. This introduces you to some of the concepts and terminology used in Chapter 8, “Best of breed infrastructure”.

Having selected the topology for your WebSphere Commerce infrastructure, in Chapter 9, “Size your infrastructure”, we offer some help on how to go about sizing your installation. Sizing covers both capacity planning of the hardware, and working out what software products you require, and how many software licenses. We do not aim to provide you with methods to do the sizing yourself; IBM has experts who do that for you using lots of experience, models, and the latest information about hardware models and software performance profiles. Instead, we tell you what information you need to collect to make the sizing more reliable.

Finally in Chapter 10, “Development, test, and production environments”, we discuss what hardware and software environments you need to build to support development and deployment of WebSphere Commerce.

7

Patterns of infrastructure for eCommerce

An infrastructure pattern captures the essential elements of a software architecture. An infrastructure pattern is implemented in countless different ways by different vendors. When you understand the patterns, it is much easier to separate design from implementation, and architecture from the choice of vendor.

In this chapter we explain widely accepted infrastructure patterns for manageability, high availability, integration, performance, and security, and describe how they are implemented for WebSphere Commerce using a variety of products.

7.1 Manageability

There are three infrastructure patterns that improve the manageability of your WebSphere Commerce environment:

- Split the environment into tiers.
- Logically partition the environment using virtualization.
- Outsource management of the site to a hosted environment.

7.1.1 Split the environment into tiers

The software that WebSphere Commerce requires to run is split into three types. The three types are:

Web server Typically this is the IBM HTTP Server (IHS) and the WebSphere Plug-in. However, other supported Web servers include the Microsoft Internet Information Services (IIS) and the Sun Java System Web server.

Application server This is the IBM WebSphere Application Server, the SDK and WebSphere Commerce, itself.

Database server Supported databases are IBM DB2 UDB and Oracle.

Different skills and different tools are required to manage the different application groups, so depending on the size and skills of your IT department, installing each group of applications onto a different set of servers makes your environment more manageable.

1-Tier environment

Attention: A 1-Tier environment will not pass PCI DSS compliance[a] (which is critical for accepting credit card transactions). A client in Australia ran into this problem and was prevented from launching by their legal department. As a minimum, the database must be on a separate server to the server receiving the Web requests.

a. See "Industry compliance" on page 224.

In a 1-Tier environment, the three main software components used by WebSphere Commerce: The Web server, the application server and the database server, are all installed and running on the same physical machine.

A 1-Tier environment has the advantage that it is the only environment supported by Quick install. Quick install configures WebSphere Application Server, IBM HTTP Server, WebSphere Plug-in, and DB2 UDB on a single server.

If you want to use other vendors' Web servers or database servers, you need to use custom install, and install the desired Web server or database server separately.

2-Tier environment

In a 2-Tier environment the Web server, application server, and database server are partitioned across two machines or two groups of machines in tiers (Figure 7-1). The Web server and the application server are installed on the first tier and the database server is installed separately on the second tier.

Quick install does not support a a 2-Tier environment. Instead, to install the Web server and application server, you must use the Custom install method and provide further configuration parameters. The database server is installed separately on the remote machine.

Use of Oracle as the WebSphere Commerce database is only supported in a 2-Tier or 3-Tier environment.

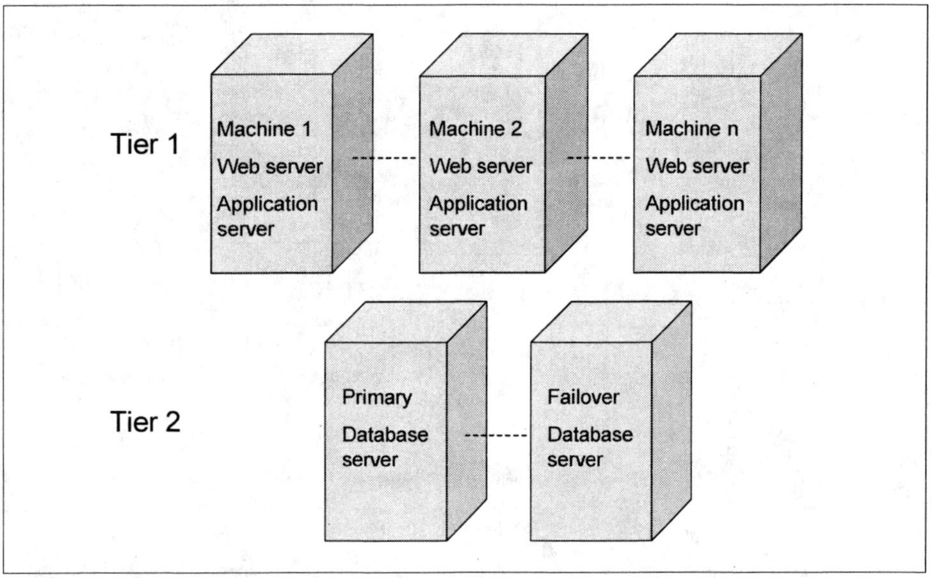

Figure 7-1 2-Tier environment

3-Tier environment

In a 3-Tier environment, the Web server, application server, and database server are each installed on a separate machine or group of machines (Figure 7-2) using custom install. Custom Install is required for 3-Tier environment.

For a 3-Tier installation, an extra step is required to move static content of the Web site (images, property files, HTML) from the application server, where it is deployed, to the Web server, where it should be served from to maximize the performance. This process is often as simple as a script (a Perl script for example) that archives and compresses all of the static content and then copies (using secure copy or FTP) it to the Web server where it is decompressed.

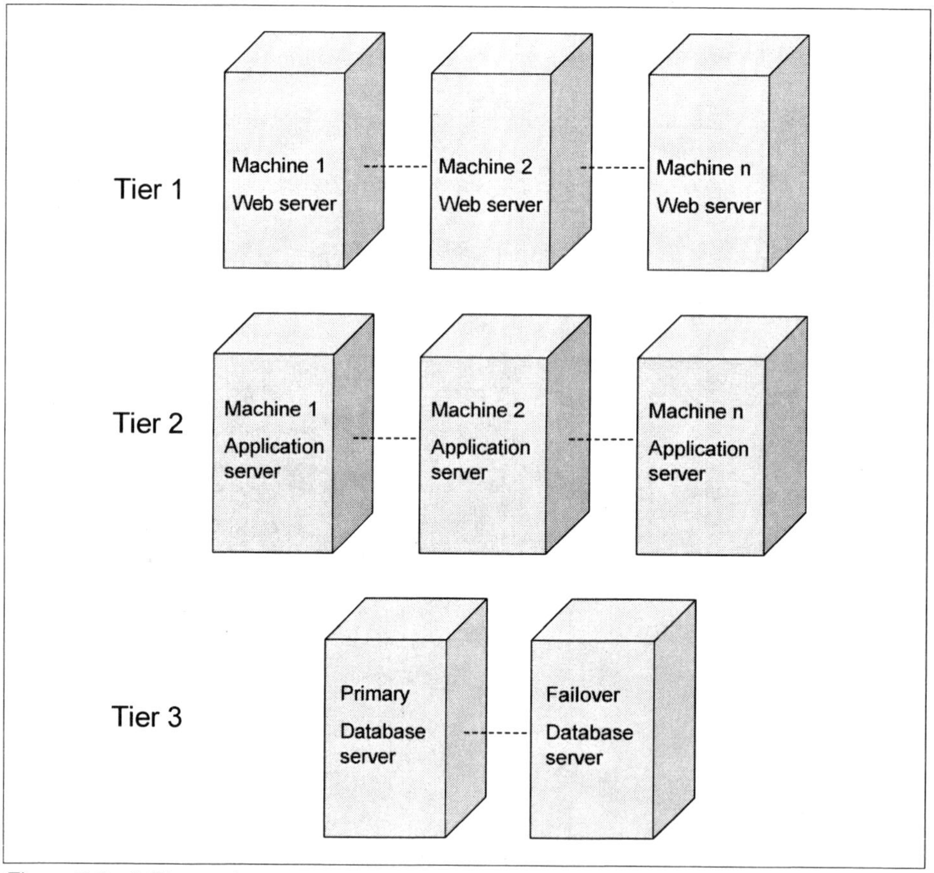

Figure 7-2 3-Tier environment

Three tiers simplify maintenance, are more scalable and offer you more options to improve price/performance.

Simplify maintenance

Physically separating the environment into a 2-Tier or 3-Tier potentially simplifies maintenance by isolating changes (APAR or Fix Pack update) to the operating system, underlying software or the hardware to the machines in that tier. If necessary, to fix a problem with a particular product, changes can be made without necessarily impacting products that are installed on different tiers.

More scalable

Multiple tiers are more scalable. Extra machines can be added to assist Web servers in the first tier without adding machines to the other tiers.

Price/performance

Multiple tiers can be optimized for price, performance, and availability by exploiting platform characteristics best suited to the different characteristics of software and availability on the three tiers. For instance, you might decide to add processor power to tier one by adding lots of blades to a blade server. You might decide to use zLinux machines to optimize database performance and availability[1].

7.1.2 Logically partition the environment using virtualization

With virtualization, you create multiple virtual servers on a single physical server. Each virtual server has its own set of virtual hardware on which an operating system and application are loaded. IBM systems with virtualization prioritize system resources and allocate them on the fly to the virtual servers needing them most at any given time — all based on your business priorities. You can also do the converse, group physical characteristics of smaller machines into a single larger virtual machine.

Virtualization brings a number of advantages such as growing or shrinking hardware resources to match demand, allocating resources to different sites, and sharing resources between production and pre-production environments to perform tests. All of these mean purchasing less hardware, allocating more hardware to test environments, potentially paying less software license fees based on actual hardware usage, and reducing your energy costs and impact on CO^2 emissions, reducing your carbon taxes.

IBM system x, p, i and z provide advanced support for virtualization[2]. See *"IBM Virtualization Infrastructure"*, found at:

`http://www-03.ibm.com/systems/virtualization/infrastructure/server/`

Also see *"Advanced POWER Virtualization on IBM System p5: Introduction and Configuration"*, SG24-7940, found at:

`http://www.redbooks.ibm.com/abstracts/sg247940.html`

---

[1] WebSphere Commerce is supported on both a blade server, running Linux, and on a z-series server running zLinux. But WebSphere Commerce does not support a heterogeneous environment (i.e. not both a blade server running linux and a z-series server running zLinux). The supported environments for WebSphere Commerce require all tiers to be running on the same platform.

[2] WebSphere Commerce has not been tested running under VMWare. It is not an environment that the WebSphere Commerce support team use for problem diagnosis and solution.

7.1.3 Outsource management of the site to a hosted environment

Outsourcing management of your WebSphere Commerce environment to IBM or another hosting provider is another option to consider. In the case of third-party hosting the provider will use either the 2- or 3-tier patterns we have discussed.

There are different types of out-sourcing with varying levels of responsibility for IT support.

1. The hosting site has shared responsibility:

   The hosting site is only responsible for the physical reliability of the machines and you control of operations, maintenance and deployment of software.

2. The hosting site has full responsibility:

   This includes software installation, management of code deployment, hardware and software maintenance and application support in case of problems. Essentially everything except development and testing.

Outsourcing to a hosted site might help contain your costs of daily operations and maintenance. Find IBM IT outsourcing and hosting at:

`http://www-935.ibm.com/services/us/index.wss/itservice/so/a1000414`

7.2 High availability

Your WebSphere Commerce site should operate as close to 100% availability as possible. There are different patterns available that strive to keep the site operational and available in case of unplanned outages. Unplanned outages can be caused by system failure (hardware failure, network failure, operating system failure), application failure and performance degradation. The same patterns that increase availability might also help you to reduce the allowances you need to make for planned outages for deployment and maintenance windows. All of these patterns operate under the paradigm that higher availability is achieved through redundancy.

Options to protect against outages caused by a problem such as application, system or hardware failure and natural disaster are reviewed in the following sections:

- "Clustering" on page 253:
- "Database redundancy" on page 255
- "Network redundancy" on page 257
- "Power supply redundancy" on page 258
- "Site redundancy for disaster recovery" on page 258

7.2.1 Clustering

All of the IBM WebSphere products are *clusterable*. Clusters are groups of servers that are managed together and participate in workload management. A cluster contains nodes or individual application servers. A node is usually a computer system with a distinct host IP address (either physically different or virtualized) that is running one or more applications or software servers, such as WebSphere Commerce, or Internet Http Server. Each of the participating software servers is called a cluster member. With WebSphere Application Server each cluster member appears to the operating system appears as a separate Java Virtual Machine (JVM™).

In order for a cluster to meet the objective of high availability the cluster members must be scaled horizontally across the tier (Web server or application server tier). Horizontal scaling means that the JVMs run on several different machines as opposed to vertical scaling, where several JVMs run on the same machine (Figure 7-3).

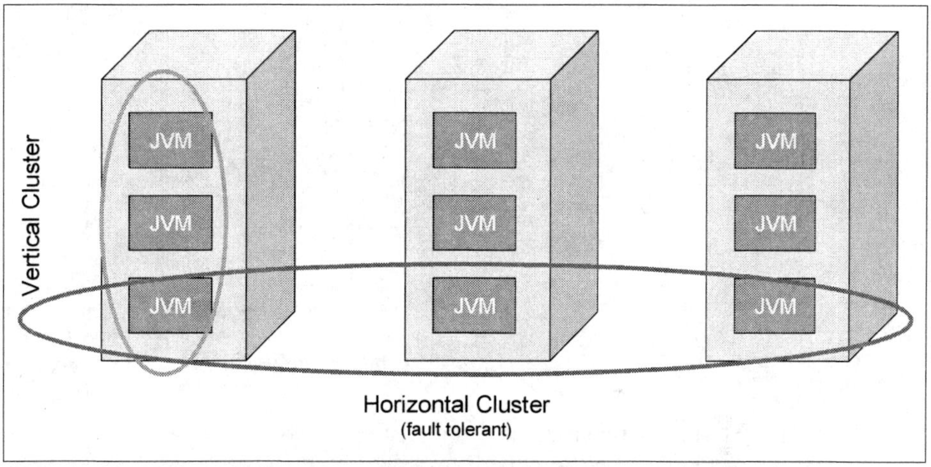

Figure 7-3 Horizontal and vertical clustering

Vertical scaling is sometimes used to optimize resource efficiency and is discussed in 7.4, "Performance" on page 259.

Look at the example of horizontal clustering shown in Figure 7-4.

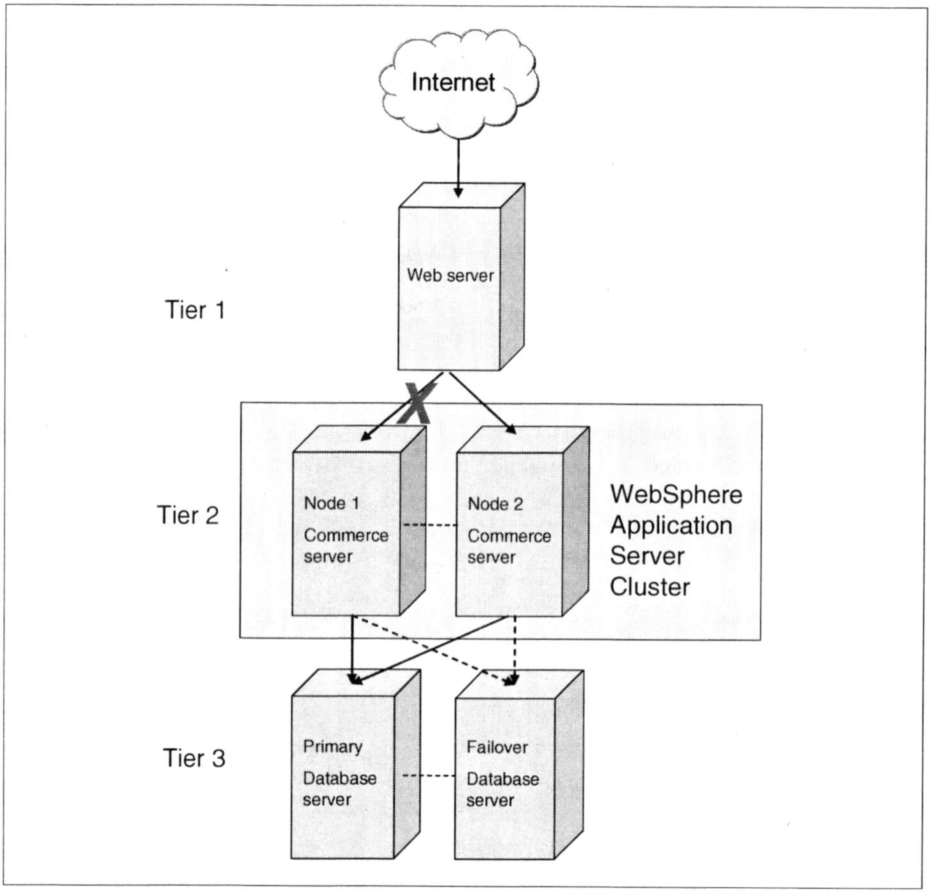

Figure 7-4 3-Tier environment with horizontal clustering on the application server tier

There are two machines in the application server tier. Each machine in the tier is a node within the cluster and each node (labelled node1 and node2) contains at least one cluster member running as a JVM.

The two cluster members are running the same application, WebSphere Commerce, and are sharing data, sessions and so on, across the cluster through the built-in distributed work-load management that WebSphere Application Server provides. In the case of an outage, whether it is planned or unplanned, suppose node1 goes down. In this case, node2 continues to run and assumes the workload of node. The site remains up and running only on node2 until node1 is brought back up to join it. WebSphere Application Server supports more complex failure scenarios too, such as when a portion of the network connecting the members of a cluster fails.

The following WebSphere branded products provider clustering with horizontal scaling across their respective tier.

- WebSphere Application Server
- IBM HTTP Server
- WebSphere Edge Components
  - Caching Proxy
  - Load balancer

For more information, refer to the Information Center, found at:

```
http://publib.boulder.ibm.com/infocenter/wchelp/v6r0m0/index.jsp?topic=
/com.ibm.commerce.admin.doc/tasks/tighorizcluster.htm
```

7.2.2 Database redundancy

Providing redundancy in your database is of vital importance, not only for high availability but for the survival of your eCommerce business. A Web site can always be rebuilt but if your data is lost, it is something that cannot likely be rebuilt easily if at all. The simplest and lowest cost method to protect your data is with periodic backups (hourly, nightly) that are stored on a different machine.

Backups protect your data to some degree but they do not provide high availability. Redundancy assures high availability and is implemented at the disk level, the operating system level and at the application level. In the following sections we look at examples of each of these types of redundancy. You need to use a combination of these techniques to protect different parts of the database server from a variety of failures.

Disk level high availability

Data protection is provided at the disk level by either the RAID and SAN technologies. RAID and SAN are alternative ways of providing redundancy at the disk level, with different performance and failure characteristics.

Redundant Arrays of Inexpensive Disks (RAID)

RAID are multiple hard disk drives in an array that appears to behave as a single large, fast disk. The protection provided by RAID is against disk failure due to operating system misuse, corruption or hardware failure. An example of a RAID system is the IBM RAID products for System x™, found at:

```
http://www-03.ibm.com/systems/storage/product/systemx/scsi_raid.html
```

Storage Area Network (SAN)

SAN is an architecture where different storage devices that can be remote are virtualized such that, to the operating system that is accessing it, they appear to be a local single logical unit. Since different storage devices are dynamically added and removed without any downtime this contributes to higher availability. Also, because the storage devices might be distributed across different geographical boundaries a SAN could be used in conjunction with a disaster recovery plan. Refer to, *"IBM System Storage: Implementing an IBM SAN"*, SG24-6116, found at:

`http://www.redbooks.ibm.com/abstracts/sg246116.html`

Operating system level high availability

Operating system level high availability is provided by having machine level redundancy on at least two separate machines (or separate logical partitions). If one of the machines should fail, the resources required to maintain business operations are transferred to the other machine. The basic configuration is one in which the primary machine performs work while the failover machine acts only as standby. The function provided by the software that operates between the two machines is simply that the failover machine monitors the primary machine. If it detects that the primary machine is down then the failover machine takes over. Table 7-1 is a selection of the available offerings to choose from.

Table 7-1 High availability software products

Product	Description
heartbeat	Open source offering that runs on Linux®.
High Availability Cluster Multiprocessing (HACMP™)	IBM product that runs on AIX®.
IBM Tivoli System Automation for Multiplatforms	IBM product that runs on AIX, Linux and Windows.
Solaris™ Cluster	High availability on Solaris clustered boxes.

Since the redundancy is built in at the operating system level both DB2 UDB and Oracle are supported with all the options. Software failover only provides the monitoring, detection and switch over from the primary to the failover machine, it leaves you the responsibility of keeping the data on the primary and failover machines synchronized. In other words, in a simple configuration, you could use high availability servers to switch the database server if it goes down, and SAN to store the physical database records and protect the database against failure of a disk drive.

Database level high availability

A more integrated and specialized approach is obtainable at the database server level. The DB2 UDB offering is HADR and the Oracle offering is Data Guard.

DB2 High Availability Disaster Recovery (HADR)

HADR is a data replication feature that provides a high availability solution for both partial and complete database server failures (at an application, operating system or hardware level). HADR protects against data loss by replicating data changes from a source database, called the primary, to a target database, called the standby. The communication between the two servers is over TCP/IP, rather than a specific physical connection, to enable splitting the machines across remote geographical locations. HADR requires additional configuration but is a built-in feature in DB2 UDB 8.2. Refer to *"High Availability and Scalability Guide for DB2 on Linux, UNIX, and Windows",* SG24-7363, found at:

```
http://www.redbooks.ibm.com/abstracts/sg247363.html
```

Also see the technical article, *"Improving high availability in WebSphere Commerce using DB2 HADR"*, found at:

```
http://www.ibm.com/developerworks/WebSphere/library/techarticles/0703_w
ang/0703_wang.html
```

Oracle Data Guard

Data Guard is the Oracle equivalent to DB2 HADR. Data Guard is available as a feature of the Enterprise Edition of the Oracle database. It is a software infrastructure that creates, maintains, manages and monitors one or more standby databases to protect enterprise data from failures, disasters, errors, and corruptions. It maintains these standby databases as transactionally consistent copies of the production database. If the production database becomes unavailable because of a planned or an unplanned outage, Data Guard switches a standby database to the production role, thus minimizing the downtime associated with the outage and enabling zero data loss. See an article on Oracle Database High Availability, found at:

```
http://www.oracle.com/technology/deploy/availability/index.html
```

7.2.3 Network redundancy

For a localized network hardware failure there exist several commercial options to create redundancies in the network hardware that employ hot swap modules and virtualized addresses. Hot swap modules are components of the system that are swappable while the rest of the system remains up and running and do not require reconfiguration.

Many commercial routers build in network redundancy based on the open source Virtual Router Redundancy Protocol (VRRP). The standard is defined at:

```
http://www.ietf.org/rfc/rfc3768.txt
```

Likewise, there are many other proprietary solutions such as the Cisco Hot Standby Router Protocol (HSRP) and the Cisco Gateway Load Balancing Protocol (GLBP).

In addition to redundant network routers it is always a good idea to boost the probability of high availability by using redundant network cards as well.

7.2.4 Power supply redundancy

There are many power supplies on the market today with built in redundancy to protect against system failure in the power supply itself. The more common design is to have two power modules. The first is running. If it fails, then the second module detects it and replaces it. A second method is to have the two modules share the load but if either one should fail, the other module automatically carries the full load.

7.2.5 Site redundancy for disaster recovery

You need to think about what you do in the case that you encounter a system wide outage due to a natural disaster. What is your disaster recovery strategy? How long does it take to rebuild your WebSphere Commerce site?

- If the site goes down for a couple of hours or days due to something like a failure in the power grid, how does this affect your short-term and long-term business?
- If the site is destroyed due to a disaster such as a hurricane, earthquake, or fire, how does this affect your short-term and long-term business?

The most straightforward approach for disaster recovery is to have a replica of your site in a different geographic region. Many of the methods described in the previous sections can be used to set-up a disaster recovery environment by splitting the resources into at least two different locations using TCP/IP communications. Full site replication is costly and not all enterprises can afford it. There is certainly a cost versus damage risk assessment that needs to be performed in order to determine how you want to handle disaster recovery.

7.3 Integration

As detailed in Chapter 3., “Complete your eCommerce solution” on page 89, there are many integration points in WebSphere Commerce where you can use third-party software to complete your solution. You might also want to integrate with your back-end systems that perform various tasks such as order management, fulfillment and other business processes.

The infrastructure required to use Web services depends on the communication protocol. If your Web services are transported via Http(s) then you do not need an extra server. However, if you plan to use WebSphere MQ to transport JMS Web service messages then you need to install WebSphere MQ on a separate server[3] If you decide to use WebSphere ESB to attach WebSphere Commerce to a service bus, then you should install WebSphere ESB on the existing WebSphere Commerce cluster members.

7.4 Performance

In this section we describe the capacity, clustering, and caching patterns that significantly affect the performance of the infrastructure.

7.4.1 Capacity

There are many hardware resources that define and determine the capacity of your infrastructure. The most significant hardware resources are the CPU, memory, disk storage, and network bandwidth. These are the hardware components that you must scale up to improve the performance of your infrastructure.

In this section, we define patterns of usage for these components. To size these components to meet the demands of your Web site on a particular infrastructure is not a trivial problem to solve, and the discussion is deferred to Chapter 9, "Size your infrastructure" on page 289.

CPU

The computing power capacity of a server is determined by the type, the speed (or clock frequency), internal cache of the CPU and multi-CPU configurations. Modern servers usually come with multiple CPUs in one machine. For example, the IBM p-series servers, p595 server has 64 CPUs in one machine. These multiple CPU servers allow you to run multi-thread application software like WebSphere Commerce very effectively. This also allows you to vertically scale the system to improve performance of your infrastructure.

[3] We recommend using the standard MQ client to connect commerce to MQ, rather than using the transactional client, or installing a queue manager on the WebSphere Commerce system to recover the message containing the order. If the ND node fails and the session is shifted to a new ND node, a new MQ client session is established. This potentially loses a message, but is easier to write the ordering software to handle this case than having a transaction in doubt with an arbitrarily chosen ND cluster member, or the message potentially reappearing sometime in the future when the node varies online again.

Memory

The capacity of dynamic memory is measured by its size in gigabytes. Insufficient memory degrades performance because your system spends most of its time paging your programs and data to the disk — and disk I/O is slow. To determine the minimum amount of memory you need, you need to estimate the total size of memory needed based on the minimum published memory size requirements for all your software and the number of threads or connections you intend to configure.

Disk storage space

Disk storage space is used for storing database data, local and distributed files, and disk cache spaces. It is measured in gigabytes.

Disk I/O

Disk I/O bandwidth and access time are critical for high performance infrastructure. Disk I/O bandwidth measures the throughput of the I/O and access time measures the response time of the disk storage and is influenced by rotational speed and disk caching. For high traffic Web sites, you might need to consider high throughput and fast access time disk storage supporting fibre optic channel disk technologies such as the one provided by SAN.

Network bandwidth

You might have super fast machines, but make sure that your LAN network is not the bottleneck in your infrastructure. For high volume Web sites, you need to consider a LAN network with gigabit bandwidth capacity supported by your router, network cards and firewall appliances.

7.4.2 Clustering

Vertical scaling is used to make best use of your hardware capacities. In one physical machine, create multiple WebSphere Commerce cluster members to give hardware more processes to service. Each cluster member runs in a separate JVM and the JVM runs on one Unix process.

A single application server running as a single JVM on a single hardware machine with sufficient CPU and memory does not necessarily utilize all the resources effectively and optimally. Creating multiple cluster members creates multiple JVMs. These multiple JVMs run on multiple threads which increases the utilization and consumption of the available hardware capacity. If the capacity is used on user tasks then this improves overall system performance in terms of throughput and response times. If the capacity is used to manage the processes rather than on user tasks, then performance degrades.

The optimal number of cluster members within a physical machine is determined by the number of available CPU(s) and size of memory and disk space within the single machine. There is an optimal number of cluster members you can have for a given hardware system. When you increase the cluster members to a larger number beyond this optimal number, the system management overhead cancels any of your performance gains by vertical scaling with multiple WebSphere Commerce cluster members.

7.4.3 Caching

Caching gives the greatest return on investment for achieving fast response times to user page requests. In this section we discuss the four significant caching mechanisms that you should design and build into your infrastructure:

- Web server caching
- Dynamic caching (dynacache)
- Edge caching
- Content delivery network (e.g. Akamai).

You should optimize response times based on your customers usage patterns of static and dynamic pages and assign cached pages according to the strategy that places cached pages physically closest to your online shoppers.

> **Caching placement strategy:** To achieve the best response times, place your most popular and most frequently accessed pages physically closest to your online shoppers.

Web server caching

From a the perspective of caching content on the Internet there are two classes of content: static content such as pure HTML files, image files, sound files and text files and dynamically generated files or pages. Static content is only changed when the source file containing the content is redeployed. Dynamic content changes depending as a result of browsing the Web site.

The Web server provides a static cache for caching static files such as HTML files and image files. It does not support caching of dynamic contents generated by servlets, JSPs, protected pages, POST method, or any pages over SSL connections.

To enable Web server cache, you need to update the plug-in-cfg.xml file to define the contents you want to cache.

Dynamic caching

Dynamic content typically depends on the values stored in the database and dynamically retrieved using keys such as store identifiers, category identifiers and product identifiers. Pages or files are generated *dynamically* upon request for content since there are almost an infinite number of permutations of pages which could be requested.

Caching dynamic pages is not as simple as caching static pages. WebSphere Commerce uses the Dynacache mechanism in WebSphere Application Server to solve this problem. Dynacache caches both full dynamically created pages and fragments of dynamically created pages. A fragment of a page is defined as any part of the user viewable page such as a sidebar, footer, masthead, mini shopping cart or eMarketing spot, each of which is associated with a separate JSP.

The WebSphere Application Server Dynacache service caches:

- Whole pages or fragments generated by a Servlet or a JSP
- Command objects (typically database queries)
- Dynamic Web pages at the edge of an enterprise network using Edge Side Include (ESI)

Caching is only half the story. The other half is knowing when to “invalidate” a cache item, so that the next request for the item makes a fresh request for the item — by running the actual JSP, for example, and stores the result in the cache. Dynacache provides invalidation support to ensure cached contents are correct and up to date. Invalidation can be rule-based, time-based, group-based, or programmatic.

In a clustered environment, you cannot guarantee the next request for a cached item is received by the cluster member which cached the previous request. There needs to be a replication strategy to make cached items created by one member, available to all the members of the cluster, either by pushing freshly cached fragments and pages, or pulling them, on demand. Dynacache manages replication for you using Data Replication Services (DRS).

Although Dynacache reduces the number of pages that need to be statically cached to cater for every browser page, dynacache still generates a huge number of pages in memory. JVM memory management was never designed to cater for the volumes of dynamically cached pages generated by Dynacache and so the Dynacache implementation includes a disk off-load service to persist cache contents on disk rather than saving them in memory. A side effect of this is that is unnecessary to rebuild the cache contents after a server recycles which reduces the Web site bring up time (that can be a matter or hours).

To implement dynacache, you need to define and specify cache rules in the cachespec.xml file provided by WebSphere Application Server. To automate your cache page updates, you might need to write scripts and create database triggers. These scripts refresh the specific cached pages based on some criteria or events such as after a product has been updated in the database that you want to refresh the corresponding product page in the cache.

For details on how to enable dynamic cache for your WebSphere Commence site, refer to the tutorial: "*Improve WebSphere Commerce performance with dynamic caching*", found at:

```
http://publib.boulder.ibm.com/infocenter/wchelp/v6r0m0/index.jsp?topic=
/com.ibm.commerce.admin.doc/tutorial/tdcperf.htm
```

Also see the Redbooks publication, *"Mastering Dynacache in WebSphere Commerce"*, SG24-7393, found at:

```
http://www.redbooks.ibm.com/abstracts/sg247393.html?Open
```

Edge caching

WebSphere Edge components cache pages closer to the customer. DynaCache's Edge Side Include (ESI) plug-in caches full pages and page fragments at the edge of your enterprise network. Caching on the edge improves response time performance by serving pages immediately at the edge of the Internet. The edge server is closest server to the user under your control and serves pages without having to do any processing on the application server where WebSphere Commerce resides.

To enable the ESI on the edge server, you need to define the cache IDs of your cached pages or fragments in the cachespec.xml file. Using the ESI plug-in, WebSphere Commerce uses the Caching Proxy server to serve pages. The Caching Proxy[4] server is a fundamental building block in a best of breed infrastructure.

The Caching Proxy server is provided as one of the WebSphere Edge Components. It provides highly scalable caching and filtering functions used in receiving requests and serving URLs. It is capable of supporting high cache hit rates. It is programmable via the plug-ins and it caches and invalidates dynamic contents generated by the WebSphere Application Server's dynamic cache.

The Caching Proxy server intercepts data requests from users, retrieves the requested information from content hosting application machines and delivers it back to the users. In this case, when there is cached page hit on the Caching Proxy server, the cached page is returned to the user without having to forward the user request to the application servers, improving response time significantly

[4] The Caching Proxy Server is sometimes called a Reverse Proxy Server in non-IBM literature.

and eliminating the added demand on resources on the application server. For more information about Edge Caching, see:

http://publib.boulder.ibm.com/infocenter/wchelp/v6r0m0/index.jsp?topic=/com.ibm.commerce.admin.doc/concepts/cdc_esi.htm

Content delivery network caching

The most popular caching closest to online shoppers in the industry is Akamai caching. Akamai caching (with the Akamai service called FreeFlow) is a distributed content-caching service that copies your relatively static rich-media Web objects (such as *.jpg, *.gif, *.avi, *.mov files) and files commonly downloaded (such as *.zip, *.pdf and *.exe files) to a cache at the edge of the Internet closest to the online shoppers physical locations.

Note: Akamai caching's FreeFlow is a service not provided by IBM but by Akamai Technologies, Inc.

The Akamai's FreeFlow is a high-performance, fault-tolerant Web content service which is provided by Akamai's network of 12,500 servers located on over 1000 networks around the world. FreeFlow's sophisticated optimization algorithms use up-to-the-second information about the Internet traffic conditions to map every end-user request to the Akamai server that delivers the requested content most quickly.

The Akamai FreeFlow provides you the following benefits:

- Faster page response times and faster downloads for end-users.
- Reduced or eliminated the workload on your application infrastructure.
- Easier for site management and infrastructure scaling.
- Distribute rich-media objects effectively.
- Web Content fault tolerance in the event of a server or network failure.
- Better user experience regardless of the prevailing network conditions.

Perform the following steps to determine if you should Akamaize your Web site:

1. Review all of your files in your Web site and identify the rich-media objects that generate the largest amount of traffic.
2. Remove the dynamic objects from the list because these objects change too frequently. For example, remove those objects that cannot wait for a Time To Live (TTL) of 30 minutes before they expire.
3. If the list of objects or files is significant, determine if you should Akamaize these objects, weighing the benefits against cost and return on investment.

The enablement process for Akamaizing your Web site is relatively straight forward and simple. To obtain more details on how you Akamaize your Web site, refer to the Akamai Web site, found at:

http://www.akamai.com

7.5 Security

There are several patterns to follow to help keep your WebSphere Commerce Web site secure. In this section we discuss splitting your WebSphere Commerce environment into different security zones and connecting the different zones with firewalls. We also look at the impact of using different authentication methods on the infrastructure, as well as the different types of security certificates you need to purchase for your WebSphere Commerce Web site.

7.5.1 Zones

A zone is a network in which the computer devices within the zone have the same level of security trust and risks from external intrusion. Typically a four zone model is used to describe the different security zones in an eCommerce application. Figure 7-5 shows these zones and their corresponding firewalls[5].

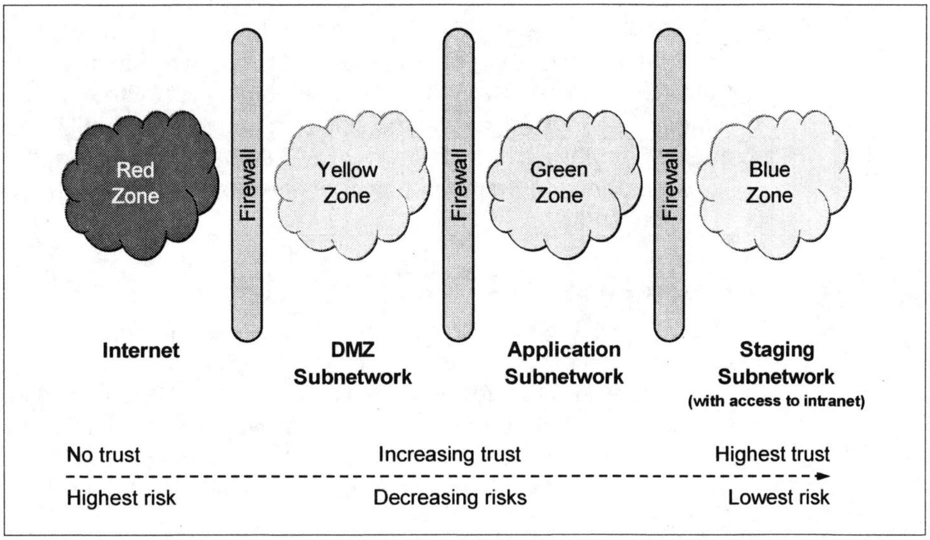

Figure 7-5 Definition of zones and firewalls

[5] We use the term subnetwork to describe the zones as they are commonly implemented using IP subnets.

There is no "perfect" set of zones to secure a Web site. They are not a silver bullet to protect your Web site from Internet attack. You should think of zones as providing rings of defence, and monitor activity in the zones for intrusion. If an attacker breaks through the outer perimeter, and installs software in the DMZ, the damage it can do is limited for a while. The four zone model is a practical compromise between security and efficiency.

The zone color is a widely accepted convention to describe the zones and is used for ease of reference.

Red Zone

The Red Zone is defined as the Internet. It is the most hazardous and highest risk with hackers, viruses and worms. It is the network customer use to access your Web site.

Yellow Zone

The Yellow Zone is also known as the demilitarized zone (DMZ). It is a physical subnetwork that isolates the hazardous Internet from your private network — your Web site. Your WebSphere Proxy Server is hosted in the DMZ, and it is the only server accessible to the Internet users. Users of the public Internet outside your company can only access hosts in the DMZ or Yellow Zone. They cannot access servers in any other zones. The proxy server relays external Internet user to the application servers in the Green Zone.

You should eliminate all but essential software from servers in the DMZ, and close off all ports that are not required except in production. Access to the DMZ from inside your enterprise must be extremely restricted, both in terms of protocols supported, and users able to administer the DMZ servers. The more people and ports that access your DMZ servers, and potentially install rogue software or configure the server wrongly, the more at risk the server is of being compromised.

Green Zone

The Green Zone hosts the application servers and database servers that serve all the customer requests and functions of your Web site. It is protected by the firewall between the Yellow Zone (DMZ) and the Green Zone from requests coming from the Internet except on specific ports to specific applications. The DMZ does not protect the Green zone from poorly written Web site programs which accept a compromising request on a valid port.

You should be careful about requests being routed to generic services rather than Web pages. Where do you check authentication and authorization to use the service? Consider filtering requests against a known set of valid requests the service has been tested against using an XML firewall. A traditional DMZ only protects you from unplanned requests routed to unknown applications, it does not protect you from unplanned requests routed to a known application.

The green zone is also protected from applications running in the blue zone. As few people need to access the green zone, except through defined programs you should minimize the software installed in the green zone, and minimize the number of people given general access. This reduces the chance that the zone is comprised accidently or deliberately by an employee or contractor. If you give your employees wider Internet access through different zone set ups, or they bring mobile computers to work and connect them to your blue network, the green/blue firewall helps prevent ingress of unauthorized software via that route.

Blue Zone

The Blue Zone is the subnetwork where you host your pre-production build and the staging area for daily content changes and updates. Normally, after you have made the changes and updates of your contents in the Blue Zone staging area, you do a data propagation and file propagation to the Green Zone for production.

The Blue Zone has direct connection, normally through a router, to your company's corporate intranet where your content management staff access to the tools in the Blue Zone staging servers for content changes and updates. It is also used to interface your company's systems to the Web site.

7.5.2 Firewalls

A firewall is special software which is installed between two networks to connect zones with different levels of trust. The theory is that rules in the firewall promote only trusted traffic from the zone of lower trust to the zone of higher trust, allowing only trusted traffic from a less trusted zone into a more trusted zone. But how effective are the rules? How much do you trust them?

A firewall is often installed in the router, but it can also be a general purpose computer. It filters traffic between two networks using a relatively simple set of rules, and rejects traffic that is not configured to enter the Web site.

The normal mode of operation is to inspect network traffic passing through it, deny some messages and pass through other messages, all based on the pass-deny rules that you set up for the firewall. These pass-deny rules act like filters that determine what data you specified are allowed to go through and what data you specified are not allowed to go through.

Firewalls come in a limited number of types, mainly categorized by the degree of intelligence or level in the network protocol stack that they operate on. We shall split our discussion into two, non-XML (Packet, TCP/IP and Http) and XML firewalls.

Packet, TCP/IP, Http firewalls

These are the basic type of firewall, and are essential to protect a Web site. They protect against harmful commands being sneaked in at all levels of a TCP/IP stack, up to the level of Http commands.

Depending on your requirements and the level of protections for the firewall, your pass-deny rules can be based on a long list of possible criteria or attributes for filtering, including:

- Source IP address
- Source port number
- Destination IP address
- Source port number
- Protocols such as TCP, UDP, FTP, Telnet, FTP, WWW
- Domain names
- URLs
- Application data packets

The firewall also can provide network address translation (NAT) and physical address translation (PAT) for your machines between the adjacent ones. This is useful to maintain constant IP or DNS names for your Web site even though the way the Web site is mapped to physical servers changes.

As shown in the Figure 7-5 on page 265, you need to define the different pass-deny rules for the firewall between the:

- Red Zone and the Yellow Zone (DMZ)
- Yellow Zone and the Green Zone
- Green Zone and the Blue Zone

Since your pass-deny rules are dependent on the security requirements of your Web site and on your company corporate security standards, you need to define the exact firewall rules for each of these firewalls between the zones of your Web site.

XML firewall

XML firewalls are relatively new, and began to appear only after XML started to be seriously used as a communication protocol, after the invention of SOAP in the late 1990's. Unlike the preceding generation of firewalls, which could look for the misuse of known commands, what XML means is programmable, hence XML firewalls are general purpose programmable XML processors. Firewall vendors always include GUI tooling to assist with the creation of context sensitive filtering rules.

If you are hosting XML based services directly, you should consider adding an XML firewall to filter out unplanned service requests, such as the IBM DataPower series, found at:

```
http://www-306.ibm.com/software/integration/datapower/
```

A comprehensive family of firewall appliance products that might suit your needs is from Cisco:

```
http://www.cisco.com/en/US/products/ps5708/Products_Sub_Category_Home.h
tml
```

7.5.3 Authentication

Authentication verifies identity. Authentication is verified through different methods at various entry points into WebSphere Commerce. Authentication to login to WebSphere Commerce as a user is accomplished either through the built in database mechanism or using Lightweight Directory Access Protocol (LDAP).

Certificates

IBM WebSphere Commerce serves both Http and Https content. The Secure Sockets Layer (SSL) protocol provides transport layer security including authenticity, data signing, and data encryption to ensure that data transfer between a client and a server remains private and secure. The foundation technology for SSL is public key cryptography, which provides asymmetric encryption and decryption using a private and public key. The server publishes its registered public key to everyone, which clients use to encrypt private data. The data can then be decrypted only by a server which knows the private key

Production Web servers must use a signed certificate purchased from any X.509 compliant Certificate Authority (CA) that supports IBM HTTP Server such as VeriSign or Thawte. Similarly, if you are planning to use Web services as part of your commerce solution you also need to acquire a certificate for authentication.

Single sign-on

If your WebSphere Commerce Web site is part of a large enterprise Web site or set of Web sites then you should be interested in implementing Single sign-on (SSO). In WebSphere Commerce, registered users are prompted for their LogonId and password when attempting to login to a WebSphere Commerce store. If you have several stores or sites within your main Web page that also require login it avoids user frustration to implement SSO. The goal of SSO is to avoid prompting the user multiple times for security credentials within a given trust domain that includes:

- Cooperating but disparate WebSphere Application Server servers.
- Cooperating LDAP servers such as IBM Directory Server.

In a SSO scenario, an Http cookie is used to propagate a user's authentication information to disparate Web servers relieving the user from entering authentication information for every new client-server session.

WebSphere Commerce provides documentation for how to implement SSO with WebSphere Portal. In order to enable single sign-on in your WebSphere Commerce enabled WebSphere Portal the prerequisite is an installed and configured LDAP server.

Information about configuring directory services (LDAP) with WebSphere Commerce is found at:

```
http://publib.boulder.ibm.com/infocenter/wchelp/v6r0m0/index.jsp?topic=
/com.ibm.commerce.admin.doc/tasks/tmsenablemmwc.htm
```

There is more information about enabling single sign-on with WebSphere Commerce at:

```
http://publib.boulder.ibm.com/infocenter/wchelp/v6r0m0/index.jsp?topic=
/com.ibm.commerce.admin.doc/tasks/tsesso.htm
```

It is possible to enable SSO with other applications. However, WebSphere Commerce provides no documentation on how to do so. This would be a custom configuration scenario that would most likely require custom code to handle the SSO.

8

Best of breed infrastructure

In this chapter we describe the characteristics of an infrastructure that make it the best of breed for small, medium, and large implementations. By best of breed we mean a class of solutions that can be considered as the top or best in its category, depending on many individual project requirements and constraints. We focus on the characteristics that contribute to making a Web site the best of breed.

We provide an example of a best of breed infrastructure for each of the small, medium, and large implementations. However, keep in mind that these are examples. The Web site for your business might be different, depending on your project requirements and constraints.

8.1 Characteristics of best of breed infrastructures

What qualifies an infrastructure to be best of breed? The best of breed infrastructure balances the following attributes of a good Web site and satisfies project cost and schedule constraints:

- Scalability
- High availability
- Manageability
- Topology
- Secured with zones
- Secured with firewalls
- Staging contents
- Sophisticated caching
- Database redundancy
- Failover
- Network redundancy
- Disaster recovery
- Virtualization
- Legacy systems
- Integration with external applications
- Support SOA
- SSO
- Operating Systems
- WebSphere Commerce Editions
- Customizability and configurability
- Sophistication
- Maintenance requirements
- Project staffing
- Length to launch

We begin the discussion with the best of breed characteristics described in Table 8-1.

Table 8-1 Characteristics of a best of breed infrastructure for each class

Characteristics	**Small**	**Medium**	**Large**
Scalability	Scale vertically with multiple Commerce cluster members within one server; Add more memory and disk space.	Scale horizontally with multiple servers in clusters and vertically with multiple Commerce cluster members and more memory and disk space.	Scale horizontally with multiple application and Web servers in clusters. Vertically with multiple Commerce cluster members and more memory and disk space.

Characteristics	Small	Medium	Large
Highly availability	None	Clustering WebSphere Caching proxy servers, backup ND servers, clustering application server. hot standby DB server. RAID DB, Vertical WebSphere Commerce clustering	Clustering WebSphere Caching proxy, IHS, WebSphere Application Servers, hot standby DB server, RAID/SAN DB, backup ND servers. Vertical WebSphere Commerce clustering
Manageability	1 tier for simplicity of maintenance and cost.	2 tiers with separation of DB server for ease of maintenance of data.	3 tiers with separation of Web servers, application servers and database servers for ease of maintenance of the three servers independently
Topology	1 tier	2 tiers	2 tiers or 3 tiers
Secured with zones	Secured by zoning: Red, Yellow, Green and Blue zones	Secured by zoning: Red, Yellow, Green and Blue zones	Secured by zoning: Red, Yellow, Green and Blue zones
Secured with firewalls	Secured by firewall protection between all zones.	Secured by firewall protection between all zones.	Secured by firewall protection between all zones.
Staging contents	Yes	Yes. Separate staging DB server	Yes. Separate staging DB server
Sophisticated caching	Dynamic page and fragments caching by Dynacache at WebSphere Application Server	Static whole page and some dynamic page and fragments caching at WebSphere Caching proxy. Dynamic page and fragments caching by Dynacache at WebSphere Application Server	Static whole page and some dynamic page and fragments caching at WebSphere Caching proxy. Dynamic page and fragments caching by Dynacache at WebSphere Application Server. Rich-media caching by Akamai edge server.
Database redundancy	Database on RAID disks. Frequent database back ups.	Database on RAID/SAN disks. Frequent database back ups	Database on RAID/SAN disks. Frequent database back ups
Failover DB server	None	Duplicated DB server hot standby with HADR. Database failover.	Duplicated DB server hot standby with HADR. Database failover
Network redundancy	Duplicated network cards to each server	Duplicated network cards to each server	Duplicated network cards to each server

Characteristics	Small	Medium	Large
Disaster recovery	DR Plan.	DR plan.	DR plan.
Virtualization	Optionally virtualize all machines in leased space in third party deployment center	Optionally virtualize all machines in deployment center leased or owned.	Greatest benefits from virtuality all servers with AIX on p5 series or Linux on z series machines in large deployment center leased or owned.
Back-end systems	Likely no back-end systems	Possibly a few back-end systems to integrate with	Large number of back-end systems to integrate with.
Integration with external applications	Likely none.	Few. Use Web Services, MQ	Many. Use MQ, Web Services, ESB, Integration Message Broker
Support SOA	Not ready.	Yes Web Services, XML	Yes. Web Services, XML, ESB
Single Sign On	Likely not required	Likely not required	Likely required
Operating systems	Windows, Linux, AIX, Solaris,i5/OS®	Windows, Linux, AIX, Solaris, i5/OS	AIX, Linux, Solaris, i5/OS, Windows, zLinux
WebSphere Commerce Edition	Express, Professional	Professional, Enterprise	Enterprise
Customizability and configurability	Use mostly out-of-the-box (OOB) with little customization required	Some customization and configuration efforts	Major customization and configuration efforts
Sophistication	Simplicity	Moderate	Complex implementation for long term future. Leader in industry
Maintenance requirements	Very minimal maintenance expected	Moderate level of maintenance expected. Many tools can be home grown	Sophisticated maintenance tools required such as Tivoli network management tools.
Project staffing	1 to 2 IT developers	Small inhouse development and IT team and experienced DBA.	Skilled and experienced development and IT team e.g. DBA, Legacy systems developers
Time to launch	1-3 months	around 6 months	around 1 year

How do small, medium and large class of Web sites achieve best of breed infrastructure by implementing these best of breed characteristics?

Scalability

As your business grows, your infrastructure needs to grow without redesign to handle the additional load.

If you start off with a small infrastructure, grow your capacity by vertical scaling. Add more CPU power, memory, disk space, and create additional WebSphere Commerce cluster members. For medium and large infrastructures, apply the same vertical scaling techniques and extend the tiers horizontally by adding more servers.

Highly availability

For a small infrastructure with only one server, adding WebSphere Commerce cluster members only protects you against a software failure in one of the members and not against hardware failure. You should consider moving to a medium infrastructure to achieve higher availability.

For medium and large infrastructures, the high availability is achieved by clustering your WebSphere caching proxy servers, WebSphere Commerce servers, hot standby WebSphere Application ND servers, and failover database servers in additional to increasing the number of WebSphere Commerce cluster members.

Manageability and topology

For a small business with a small infrastructure, use a one tier topology for simplicity of maintenance.

For medium and large businesses, choose two tiers with separation of the database server for ease of maintenance or choose three tiers to separate the Web server, application server and database server for ease of maintenance and performance turning.

Secured with zones

Regardless of the size of your business and infrastructure implementation, your infrastructure must be secure and organized into security zones for ease of security management: Yellow Zone (DMZ), Green Zone, and Blue Zone. This is done by placing your content staging servers with pre-production contents and non-customer facing servers in the Blue Zone, all your customer facing application production servers in the Green Zone, and the caching proxy server in the Yellow Zone.

Secured with firewalls

Your security zones must be insulated by firewalls with specific pass-deny rules which you need to define and specify to meet your business requirements.

Staging contents

Regardless of the size of your infrastructure, you need to stage your contents before production. Contents mean all your application data in the database (Figure 5-5 on page 175). Your staging machines must be placed in the Blue Zone staging area. You should prepare your pre-production contents in the staging area and perform necessary testing before propagate your data to the production servers. You should never update contents to the production servers directly without staging and pre-production testing.

Sophisticated caching

For all sizes of infrastructure, you should cache your dynamic pages and page fragments using Dynacache. For the middle and large size infrastructures cache full static pages, session independent dynamic pages and fragments in the WebSphere Caching Proxy server.

For large infrastructure, in addition to caching your pages in the Dynacache and WebSphere Caching Proxy cache, consider optimizing cached page creation by using the Data Replicator Service (DRS) working with Dynacache in the application server cluster. The DRS makes caching more efficient by replicating copies of the cached pages from one application server to another. You might also consider caching media rich files closer to your customers. This is usually done by paying Akamai for the service of placing your files in an Akamai edge server cache in a physical location closest to your customers.

Database redundancy

For any size of infrastructure, data and files are the most precious and most valuable assets in your infrastructure. You must make sure that you do not lose them by accident or any failure in your infrastructure. You data and files must be hosted on redundant disks using RAID or SAN. In addition, frequently backup your database and transfer copies to a remote location.

For medium and large infrastructure, consider the Storage Area Network (SAN) technology and products from IBM for improving your database reliability.

Failover

For medium and large infrastructures, having a hot standby failover database improves database server reliability. HADR synchronizes the failover DB2 database server with the primary database server and transfers database server functions from the primary to the failover server when the primary fails.

Network redundancy

A network card is a single point of failure. Improve the reliability of your network by adding a redundant network card to each of your critical servers such as Database servers, WebSphere Application Servers, Web servers, WebSphere Caching proxy servers and network dispatcher servers.

Disaster recovery

Do you need a plan to deal with a disaster such as flood, fire, earthquake, war, or terrorism?

Disaster recovery (DR) can be very expensive. Small businesses are potentially better placed — for a small business and small infrastructure, you might be able to recreate your infrastructure within a few weeks using off the shelf parts and generically skilled staff, since you have only a few servers to deal with. Your main responsibility is to keep off site copies of all the software and data you need to reload, and documentation how to rebuild and run the system.

But for a medium, and large implementation with sophisticated infrastructure, DR is very expensive and it is also difficult to verify if the DR plan works. Depending on the nature of your business, you need to make a business decision on how much to actually implement and test your DR plan.

Our recommendation is that you should least have a DR plan, and have thought through various contingencies. Because buying extra equipment, renting a site, and testing the DR plan can be difficult and expensive, you have to weigh your plan against cost, feasibility and testability. An alternative to owning the equipment is to contract with a DR specialist, and decide where, between having a hot standby, and building your infrastructure from software and hardware at the recovery site, you want to plan your DR.

Virtualization

You can take advantage of the virtualization technology available in AIX, and z/OS® to improve the flexibility, speed to launch, and cost of implementing your infrastructure.

For a small infrastructure, you can lease logical partitions (LPARS) from a third party hosting center for deploying your servers and networks. Because staff costs for operating and maintaining a site exceed the hardware costs, leasing LPARs is highly recommended as it reduces operating and maintenance costs by sharing IT support resources in the third party hosting center.

For medium and large infrastructures, if you own the infrastructure hardware with virtualization capabilities such as AIX and z/OS, you can consolidate and virtualize your servers in LPARS and share CPUs, memory, disk I/O and network I/O to best utilize these resources, and to be able to repartition the hardware between production and pre-production systems to reflect changing workload at peak times, and thus reduce the total cost of operation of your infrastructure.

Existing systems

For medium and large implementations, there are back-end systems to integrate with WebSphere Commerce to exchange product, account or sales information. There are various solutions for integrating systems that are recommended for WebSphere commerce, using messaging or services including WebSphere Message Broker, WebSphere MQ and WebSphere Enterprise Service Bus. Alternatively you can integrate using traditional batch oriented techniques such as file transfer or data base replication.

Integration with external applications

For medium and large infrastructures, you might need to integrate services from external applications such as portal servers, single sign on (SSO) Web identity system, configuration servers, payment systems, tax systems, order fulfillment systems, and order status servers. The recommended method of integration is through Web services. Other integration technologies can be considered are WebSphere Message Broker, WebSphere Enterprise Service Bus and WebSphere MQ servers.

Support SOA

A best of breed infrastructure supports the implementation of Service Oriented Architecture. SOA promises re-use of services, shortened the development cycle time and reduced cost for development. A successful SOA goes beyond designing a service integration bus, and focuses attention on managing service development and deployment to promote reuse.

SSO

If your application needs to redirect customers from one application to another without asking users to log on again, your infrastructure needs to support Single Sign On. SSO requires an LDAP server and configuring WebSphere Commerce.

Operating systems

For small and medium infrastructures, recommended operating systems are Windows, Linux, AIX, i5/OS, or Solaris.

For a large infrastructures, you might also consider running Linux on z-Series.

Sophistication

The sophistication of an implementation is closely tied to the time to deploy, the cost of deployment, and the skills you need to find to do the deployment. The payback comes in long run savings in management, operating and maintenance costs for larger sites. You should look very closely at whether very sophisticated plans for a small Web site are going to give you good returns, as well as whether an unsophisticated implementation for a large site or a large organization will be able to meet all the requirements and demands made upon it.

Maintenance requirements

Maintenance for a small infrastructure is either outsourced to a hosting site, or is a minimal collection of scripts to clean up logs, compact databases, and to check that the site is operational. The scripts would be run manually or as a scheduled jobs using the appropriate operating system task scheduler.

For a medium infrastructure, regular maintenance should definitely be automated, and you should consider writing scripts or buying tools to track the performance of the site.

For a large infrastructure, you expect sophisticated maintenance tools such as Tivoli network management tools to integrate maintenance with other IT systems you manage to reduce operating costs.

Project staffing

A small infrastructure requires 1or 2 developers to perform all IT functions. Or you might choose to outsource to hosting centers.

Typically, for a medium infrastructure, you would support a small inhouse development and operations team.

A large infrastructure requires various skilled and experienced development and IT teams.

Length to launch

These are typical time frames required to launch:

- Small infrastructure: Around one to three months
- Medium infrastructure: Around six months
- Large infrastructure: Around one year

8.2 Examples of best of breed infrastructures

This section has examples of the small, medium, and large infrastructures. These are examples, not fixed patterns to follow religiously. No one infrastructure pattern is going to meet the requirements of all businesses. In this section, we give a reasonable, workable, and representative infrastructure for each of the small, medium, and large sites, which can be called best of breed in each class.

To simplify our descriptions, we use IBM products in our examples as much as possible. However, using other supported non-IBM products is equally valid as long as they are documented in the online documentation, found at:

`http://www-1.ibm.com/support/docview.wss?rs=3046&uid=swg21243500`

8.2.1 Small infrastructure

Figure 8-1 shows an example of a small infrastructure.

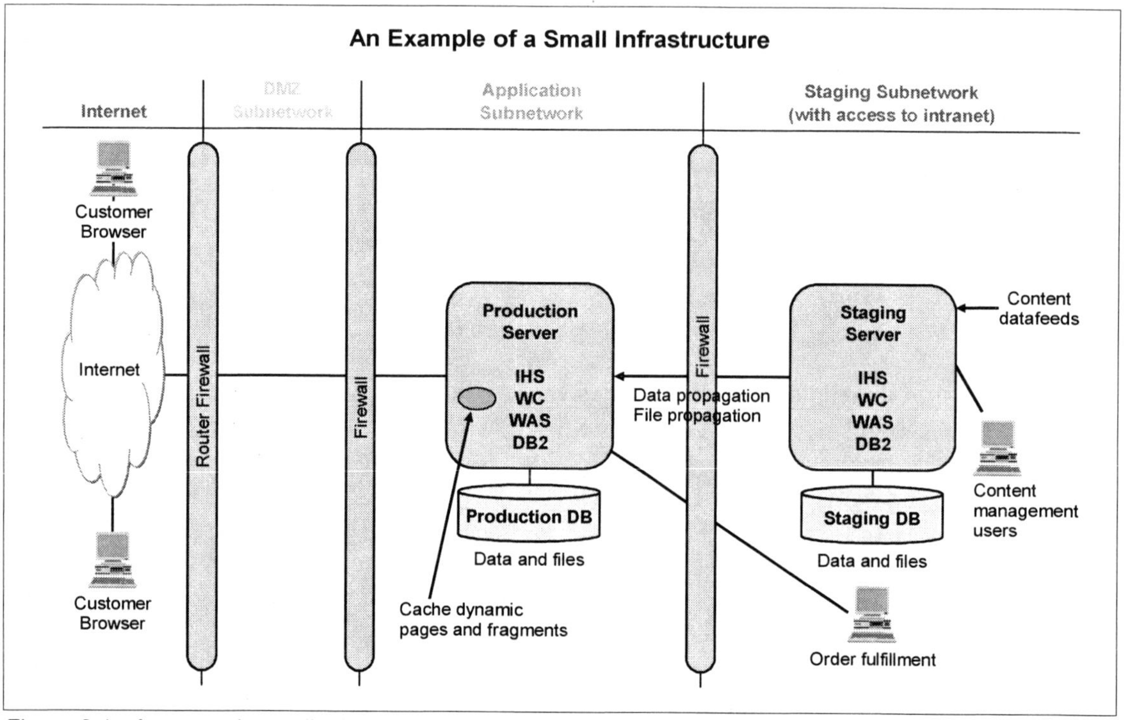

Figure 8-1 An example small infrastructure

This infrastructure consists of one production application server located in the Green Zone, one staging server in the Blue Zone, a firewall between the Blue Zone and the Green Zone, and another combined firewall between the Green Zone and the Yellow/Red Zones. In this example, we do not use a WebSphere Caching Proxy server in the Yellow Zone. However, you can have a general purpose proxy in the Yellow Zone, perhaps just even a router with twin firewalls, which intercepts IP connections in a restricted environment that is difficult to compromise.

All the application software that serves customer facing functions is hosted within a single application server machine in the Green Zone. In this example, the software installed in this application server includes a Web server, WebSphere Commerce, WebSphere Application Server and the database server. The production database and all system and application files are stored in the local system hard disk space.

Pre-production servers

All application software that provides staging content functions are hosted within a single staging server machine in the Blue Zone. The software in this staging server include the Web server, WebSphere Commerce, WebSphere Application Server and a staging database. The same server is used in pre-production to verify new software releases and maintenance. The staging database and all system and application files are stored in the local system hard disk space.

Staging

The staging server connects directly to content data feeds directly. These contents are information about catalog, product, pricing data, and product availability information changes. The business content management users can also update the contents using the WebSphere Commerce Accelerator in the staging area.

Payment

For payment, it depends on the size of the number of orders. If your business has hundreds of orders in a day, you need to consider implementing an online connection to financial institutions such as Visa and Mastercard for synchronous online payment. If your business expects only a few dozen orders a day, you can choose to handle this manually with the assistance of the WebSphere Commerce Accelerator tool.

Order fulfillment

If you have an automated fulfillment system, you must automate the transmission of the order information to your fulfillment system. Otherwise orders are fulfilled manually, with the help of the WebSphere Commerce Accelerator tool.

Caching

In a small infrastructure, static pages are cached in the Web server and the category and product pages in the application server's Dynamic Cache.

An example software installation for this small infrastructure is shown in Table 8-2 based on Windows on Intel hardware platform.

Table 8-2 An example software installation for a small infrastructure

Physical Server	Software	Edition/Version
Production Server in the Green Zone (GZ) and Staging Server in the Blue Zone (BZ)	Windows Server® 2003	Standard Edition
	IBM HTTP Server	6.0.2
	WebSphere Commerce	Express Edition
	WebSphere Application Server	Express Edition
	DB2 Universal Database	Express Edition 8.2 FP3

A slightly more powerful small infrastructure example based on the IBM AIX platform is shown in Table 8-3.

Table 8-3 Another example software installation for a small infrastructure

Server	Software	Edition/Version
Production Server in the Green Zone (GZ) and Staging Server in the Blue Zone (BZ)	AIX 5L™	5.3
	IBM HTTP Server	6.0.2
	WebSphere Commerce	Professional Edition
	WebSphere Application Server	Professional Edition
	DB2 Universal Database	Enterprise Edition 8.2 FP3

Choose other combinations of software from the officially supported list found at:

`http://www-1.ibm.com/support/docview.wss?rs=3046&uid=swg21243500`

The hardware sizes, such as CPU size and configurations, memory size, disk space and network size are omitted because they all depend on your traffic and workload requirements.

8.2.2 Medium infrastructure

Figure 8-2 shows an example of a medium infrastructure.

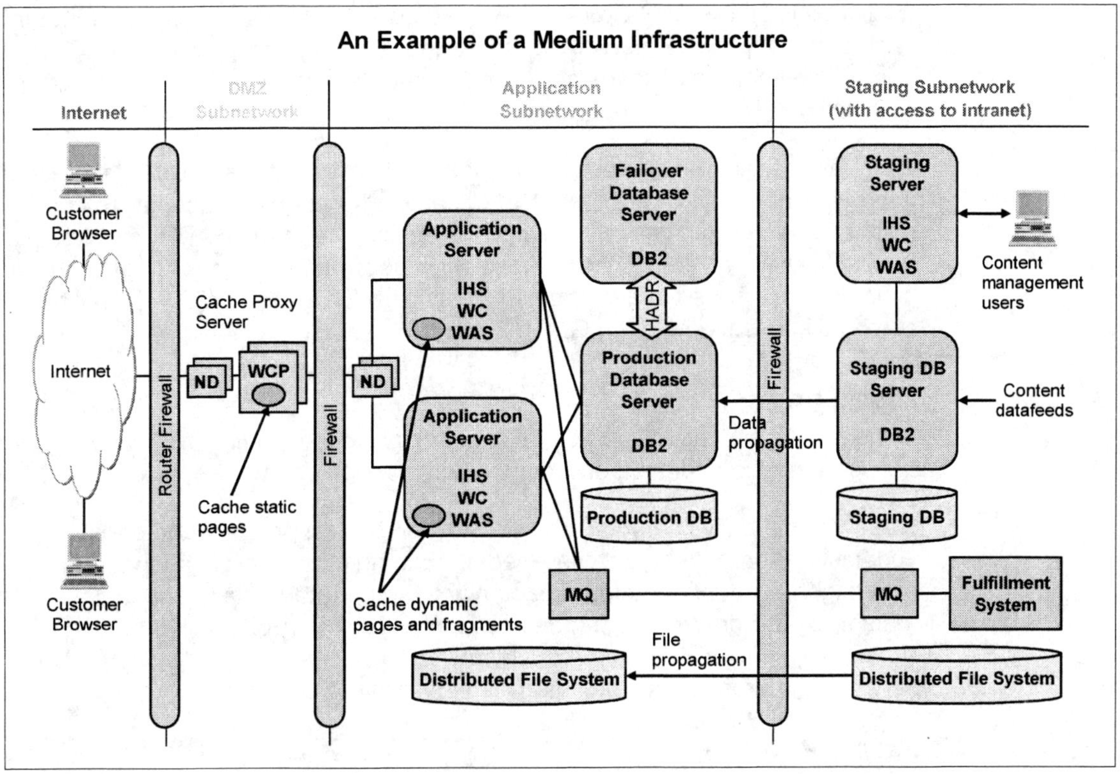

Figure 8-2 An example medium infrastructure

The infrastructure is deployed in three zones secured by firewalls.

Yellow Zone

In the Yellow Zone there is a cluster of two WebSphere Caching Proxy servers which provide proxy addresses for user requests and cache selected full pages and fragments. There are two proxy servers to improve reliability. The WebSphere Caching Proxy is load balanced with a Network Dispatcher. The Network Dispatcher is duplicated by a backup Network Dispatcher to remove the single point of failure in the infrastructure.

Green Zone

In the Green Zone there is a cluster of two application servers for better reliability and performance. IBM HTTP Server (IHS), WebSphere Commerce, and WebSphere Application Server and DB2 Client are installed in each of the application servers. WebSphere Commerce is installed as a cluster member in each of the application servers for improving reliability and performance. The application server workloads are evenly distributed by the Network Dispatcher. The Network Dispatcher has a backup for reliability.

There are separate physical servers for the primary production DB2 database to improve availability. The primary DB2 database server has a hot-standby database server and can failover with the assistance of the HADR. To eliminate the duplication flat files and to improve efficiency and maintainability, only one set of flat files are stored in a distributed file system (DCE/DFS) which is shared among all the servers in the Green Zone.

Blue Zone

In the Blue Zone, the staging database server and the staging application server are separated to improve performance and manageability.

Large volume daily content updates, such as catalog, product, and price updates, are processed by mass loaders running on the staging server and updating the staging database. Each night, the updated data changes are “dataprop'ed” from the staging database server to the production database server while the file changes are “fileprop'ed” from the staging distributed file server to the production distributed file server in the Green Zone.

Payment

For a medium size implementation, the daily order volume is likely to be in the thousands and requires automated payment processing. In this example, we use Web services to connect to financial institutions such as Visa and Mastercard for synchronous online payment.

Order fulfillment

The example shows WebSphere MQ used to integrate WebSphere Commerce with a fulfilment system. When an order has been completed in WebSphere Commerce, the order is transmitted reliably to the order fulfillment system.

Caching

Store dependent category and product pages and page fragments are stored the application server's Dynamic Cache. Some store independent category and product pages and page fragments are cached in the Caching Proxy Server, together with all the static content.

Table 8-4 shows an example software installation based on IBM AIX platform.

Table 8-4 An example software installation for medium infrastructure

Server	Software	Version
(YZ) Network Dispatcher	IBM Load Balancer	6.0
(YZ) Caching Proxy Server	IBM Caching Proxy	6.0
(GZ) Network Dispatcher	IBM Load Balancer	6.0
(GZ) Application server (BZ) Staging Server	AIX 5L	5.3
	IBM HTTP Server	6.0.2
	WebSphere Commerce	Professional Edition
	WebSphere Application Server	Network Deployment 6.0.2.5
	MQ Client	5.3
(GZ) Database Server (BZ) Staging DB Server	IBM DB2 Universal Database	Enterprise Edition 8.2 FP3
(GZ) MQ server	MQ server	5.3

8.2.3 Large infrastructure

Figure 8-3 shows a diagram of a large infrastructure.

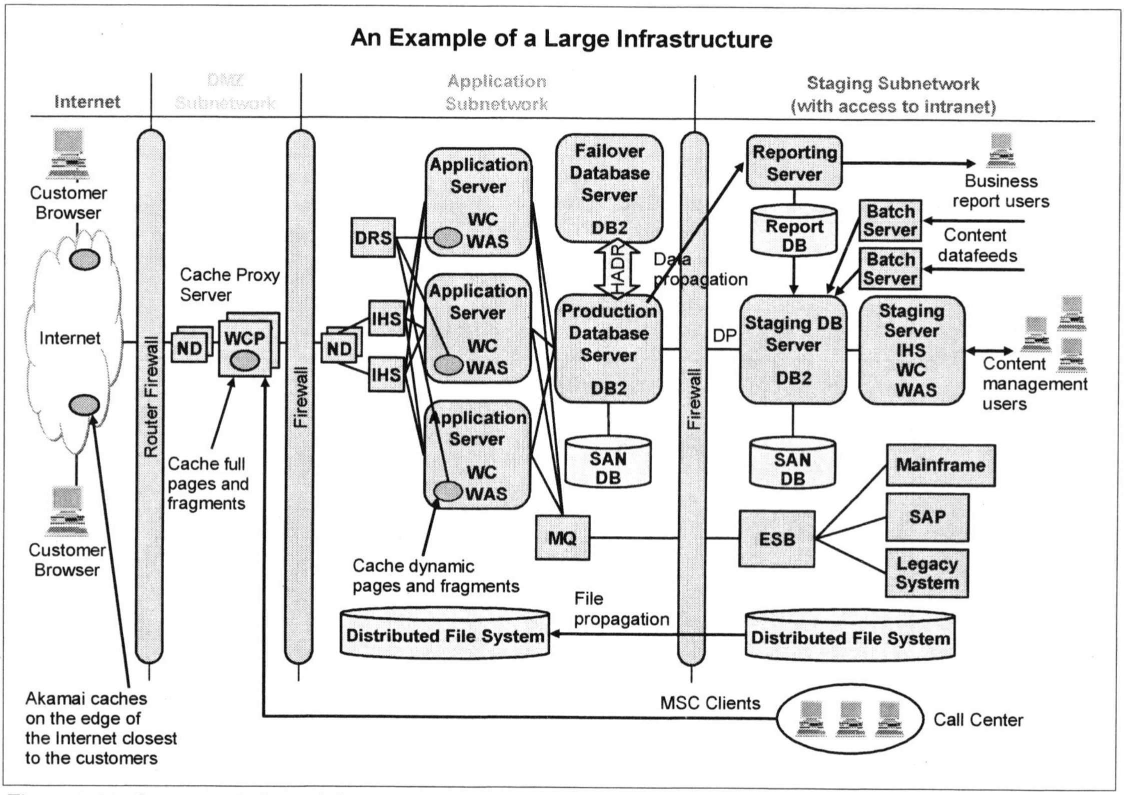

Figure 8-3 An example large infrastructure

It is similar to the medium infrastructure, but is more sophisticated and has more capabilities. The infrastructure is deployed in three zones secured by firewalls.

Green Zone

In the Green Zone, to support a higher volume of customer requests, there are more cluster members in the application server cluster. In this example there are three application servers in the cluster. A three tier topology improves manageability and availability for this size of deployment. The Web servers (IHS) are installed onto two separate physical IHS servers. The user traffic is evenly distributed by the Network Dispatcher. The Network Dispatcher is configurable to distribute workloads using either a round-robin algorithm or a random algorithm to the Web server cluster members. These in turn distribute load to the application server cluster.

There is a failover database server to back up the primary production database with the assistance of a HADR. In this large infrastructure the database is implemented using SAN disks connected through a very high speed fiber optics which improves disk throughput and response time as demanded by a very large Web sites as this one.

Not shown in the diagram, there are a number of Web services interfaces to externally integrated applications performing eCommerce functions such as portal, SSO, pricing, address verification, tax calculation, payment and order status.

Blue Zone

The Blue Zone configuration for the staging application and database servers is similar to the medium infrastructure. In this example, the database is implemented using SAN disks connected to a high speed fibre optics channel rather than connected to a RAID array.

There are ten of thousands of daily changes in the Web site contents such as categories, products, parts, prices, currency exchange rates, contracts, stores and product availabilities. Multiple batch servers mass load the data feeds in parallel to make sure that the loads are completed within the data propagation window at night.

Using either a WebSphere Enterprise Serve Bus or WebSphere MQ, the back-end systems, such as CICS® or SAP systems, are connected to WebSphere Commerce for order fulfillment.

A reporting server is used to keep a copy of the production database synchronized using the Dataprop utility. The database in the Reporting Server provides the basis for business reporting using tools such as Brio Reports or Coremetrics. We use a duplicate database for reporting rather than using the production database server because report processing is very CPU and I/O intensive.

A WebSphere commerce Sales Center call center is integrated providing a call center for CSRs who use the WebSphere Commerce Multi-Sales Center clients to connect to Green Zone application servers.

In this large example infrastructure, we implement and optimize caching at multiple levels:

- Dynamic Cache at the application server
- Caching Proxy cache at the WebSphere Caching Proxy server
- Data Replicator Service (DRS)
- Content delivery cache (Akamai)

The DRS is used to replicate cached pages and fragments between the application server dynamic caches optimize response time and minimize the load on the application server.

The Akamai cache service is used in this large infrastructure to deliver a large amount of rich-media objects such as pdf , audio , video and image files. The files are deployed using Akamai FreeFlow caching facilities.

Table 8-5 shows a software installation for this large infrastructure based on the IBM AIX platform.

Table 8-5 An example software installation for medium infrastructure

Server	Software	Version
(YZ) Network Dispatcher	IBM Load Balancer	6.0
(YZ) Caching Proxy Server	IBM Caching Proxy	6.0
(GZ) Network Dispatcher	IBM Load Balancer	6.0
(GZ) Web server	IBM HTTP Server	6.0.2
(GZ) Application server (BZ) Staging Server	AIX 5L	5.3
	WebSphere Commerce	Enterprise Edition
	WebSphere Application Server	Network Deployment 6.0.2.21
	MQ Client	5.3
(GZ) Database Server (BZ) Staging DB Server	IBM DB2 Universal Database	Enterprise Edition 8.2 FP3
(GZ) MQ server	MQ server	5.3
(BZ) Reporting Server	IBM DB2 Universal Database	Enterprise Edition 8.2 FP3

9

Size your infrastructure

Sizing the correct infrastructure to meet your business needs is one of the most important tasks to plan your Web site. Often it is very difficult to size exactly the capacity you need at any given time, but it is always a good guiding principle to oversize your infrastructure than undersize it.

Guiding principle for sizing: It is better to oversize your infrastructure than to undersize it. Undersizing it could cause system outages or even system failures, while oversizing provides a safety margin for unexpected traffic bursts.

Sizing infrastructure involves two steps:

1. Approximate:

   Collect your business objectives and non-functional requirements. Provide these data as input for expert consultation. An expert will give you an approximate estimate of the hardware and software resources you need.

2. Validate and fine-tune:

   The performance team conducts performance and other non-functional tests of the infrastructures as you proceed through development and test. You might need to modify the initial configuration and perhaps obtain more servers, network capacity, memory, or disk sooner than you planned to meet initial performance objectives.

The outcome of these steps determines the type and amount of size of resources for your infrastructure:

- Infrastructure topology and architecture
- Hardware capacities for each server:
  - CPU
  - Memory
  - Disk I/O
  - Disk storage
  - Network bandwidth
- Software stack and application software

In this chapter, we focus on the first step of estimating and sizing. Performance testing and tuning is discussed in the Information Center.

You can find details at:

```
http://publib.boulder.ibm.com/infocenter/wchelp/v6r0m0/index.jsp?topic=
/com.ibm.commerce.admin.doc/concepts/cpmperformance.htm
```

Refer also to the Redbooks publication, *"Mastering DynaCache in WebSphere Commerce"*, SG24-7393-00, found at:

```
http://www.redbooks.ibm.com/abstracts/sg247393.html?Open
```

In the second part of the chapter we discuss how to get the best expert advice.

9.1 Sizing

One of the most important tasks in defining your business objectives is defining the performance objectives of your Web site. Customers expect Web pages to respond quickly to mouse clicks — if they do not, you can be sure that a competitor's will. Whether you have a good catalog or not, no one will want to know if your Web site performance is poor.

9.1.1 Performance objectives

You need to define the following performance objectives in order to size the correct infrastructure:

User online response time

The user online response time is defined as the time duration after the user submits a request by clicking the mouse on a button or a link to a page, and the display of the page with all the information requested. This is also called the latency. Classify the response time objective for each of the transaction categories such as log on, browsing catalog, browsing products, add to cart, checkout, and order status pages. Time is usually stated in fractions of a second, for example, 1.25 seconds.

Batch turnaround time

Batch turnaround time is measured as the *elapsed* time from the start of a batch job to its completion. The batch turnaround time is an important performance measurement because, as in the example of currency data feeds, data needs to be updated by a specific time to accurately compute prices in a local currency at the correct exchange rate for customer orders.

Some batch jobs, such as daily catalog and price feeds to the staging server, are large and need to be completed by certain time of the day or night before data propagation can begin to move data from the staging server to the production server.

The data propagation job is another important example. In most WebSphere Commerce applications, the data propagation batch job is performed at night, publishing data from the staging database to the production database server. The data propagation has to be completed before the beginning of your next business day.

List each batch job, and define its required turnaround time. Time is measured to to an accuracy of minutes.

Throughput

Online thoughput is measured by the number of customer pages served per hour. A more refined measure is to split throughput into the number of browsed pages and checkout pages served per hour.

Batch thoughput is measured by the number of records processed per hour.

Data volume

Data volume measures the amount of database and total file space required for the database server and file server. They are quoted separately in gigabytes.

Operational hours

Specify the days and hours of operation of your Web site throughout the year, including holiday seasons. Many Web sites are operated twenty four hours a day, three hundred and sixty five days a year, with no breaks. Often call centers and chat response lines are open for shorter hours.

Scheduled maintenance windows

During the year, Web sites are upgraded with new features, new or replacement hardware, and maintenance fixes. Define a maintenance window to apply these changes to your production Web site in a planned and scheduled manner.

Maintenance windows can result in some system downtime, depending on the nature of the maintenance tasks to be performed. Scheduled maintenance windows are usually planned during low traffic hours of the week, typically on early Sunday morning. You need to specify the exact range of hours of the day. Some Web sites plan a monthly or yearly break for maintenance. Holidays are a favorite time to do major maintenance tasks.

z/OS systems are rarely booted, with a frequency of less than a year. Some sites plan an annual reboot (often Christmas day). Reboot can reveal dormant issues, so this should be planned as a significant maintenance event.

Growth projection

You hope your business grows and so you need to project traffic growth over the year. Specify growth in percentage (%) of your Web site traffic per year. Your sizing should be based on the expected year end volume of traffic.

9.1.2 Other non-functional requirements

You need to consider the non-functional requirements that significantly affect the architecture and therefore the cost of your infrastructure.

Reliability and availability

You have to specify the total reliability of your Web site, including all other dependent applications that make up the end-to-user transactions. We measure reliability of the Web site in terms of availability. Availability of the entire Web site is defined as the percentage (%) of total system up time of the Web site performing end-to-user transactions. The availability % is calculated by the following formula.

> **Availability formula:** Web site availability % = Total system up time in hours divided by (total number of hours in a measured period - scheduled maintenance hours in that same measured period)
>
> **Alternatively:** Web site availability % = 1 - (total system downtime in hours) divided by the (total number of hours in a measured period - scheduled maintenance hours in that same measured period)

Keep in mind that if your Web site has two dependent components A and B, your total Web site availability is the product of the two availabilities. For example, if availability of A is 99.5% and B is 99.5%, then your Web site availability is (99.5%)x(99.5%) = 99.0% which is less than each of the individual availability

Figure 9-1 shows the effect of adding component redundancy to a Web site by duplicating each component. The vertical axis shows the availability of the overall system, and the horizontal axis the number of components that need to be online simultaneously for the whole system to be available. In this theoretical example, availability has no units. In practice availability is quoted for a specific time period, or as mean time between failures (MTBF).

As the number of components that are required to be online goes up, so the availability goes down. But the simple expedient of duplicating components improves availability remarkably. It is probable that spending money on installing redundant components is a much more economic way to get better availability than spending money on extremely reliable components. Even a tenfold increase in each individual component's reliability still leaves a larger than acceptable chance of failure.

For a complete discussion of the application of redundancy techniques to enterprise software availability see the developerWorks article, *"Planning for Availability in the Enterprise"*, by Rick Robinson and Alexandre Polozoff, found at:

`http://www.ibm.com/developerworks/websphere/techjournal/0312_polozoff/polozoff.html`

This article also includes a useful availability calculator.

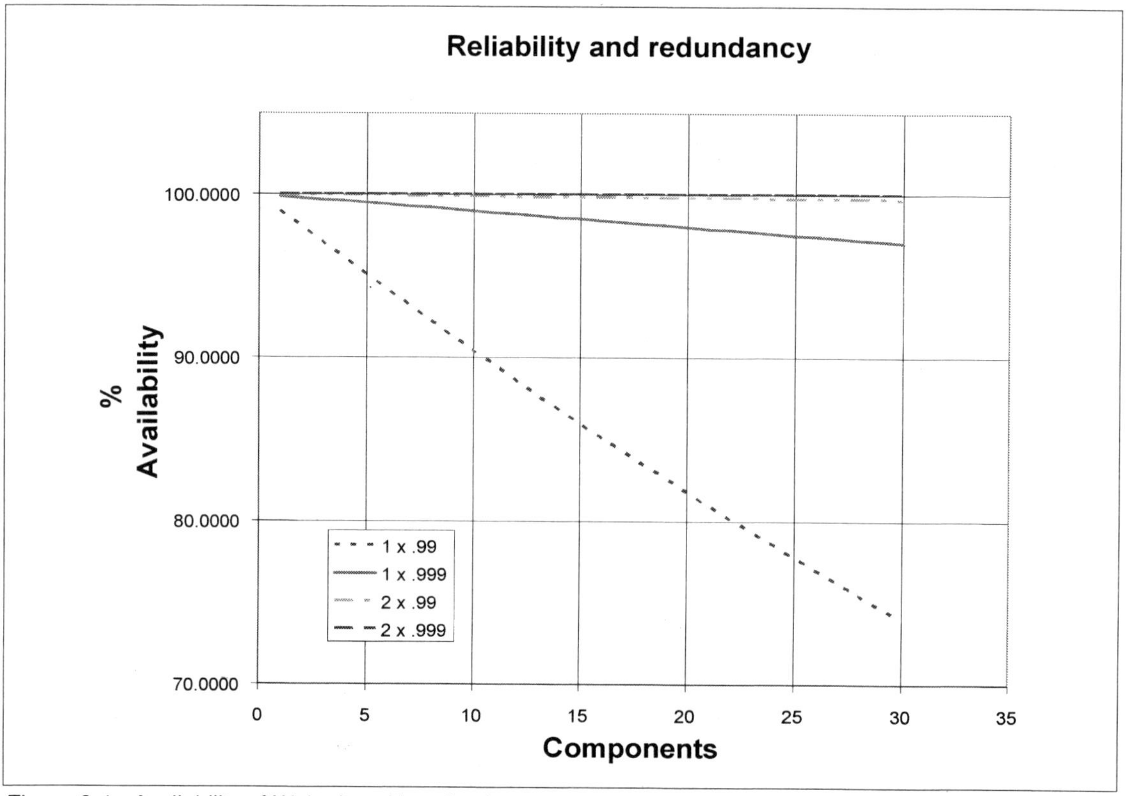

Figure 9-1 Availability of Web site with redundant components

To meet the availability requirements of your Web site, maximize redundancy of your infrastructure components by using the scalable capabilities of WebSphere Commerce. Use WebSphere Commerce horizontal clustering by adding separate servers to improve availability. Using vertical clustering of WebSphere Commerce within the same application server reduces the effect of software failure in some components, but does not protect you against the operating system or the server failing. Consider improving your overall system availability by duplicating or clustering the following components in your infrastructure:

- Duplicated routers coming from the Internet to your Web site infrastructure
- Duplicated network dispatcher in the DMZ
- Clustering WebSphere Caching Proxy Server in the DMZ
- Duplicated network dispatcher in the Green Zone
- Clustering Web servers
- Clustering application servers
- Hot standby Database Server
- RAID (Redundant Array of Independent Drives) disk storage
- Duplicated network cards between LAN and each server

Scalability

Your infrastructure needs to scale up with your business. Chapter 7, "Patterns of infrastructure for eCommerce" on page 247 shows some of the ways of scaling different sizes of infrastructure. Allow contingency in your investments for the addition of more equipment, software, and staff at a later date.

Security

Identify what data needs to be protected, what the threats are, and what measures you are going to take to combat the threats, and to increase customer confidence in the security of their data at your Web site.

The baseline is to secure your infrastructure with firewalls and to maintain access controls and security logs:

- Firewall between the Internet (Red Zone) and the DMZ (Yellow Zone).
- Firewall between the DMZ (Yellow Zone) and the Green Zone
- Firewall between the Green Zone and the Blue Zone

These firewalls are computers with special security software and scripts that filter the desired and predefined transactions to cross the firewall boundaries and block all illegal unexpected transactions crossing the firewall boundaries in both directions. You need to plan for the implementation and operation of these firewalls.

If Single Sign On (SSO) is a requirement, then you need to plan to implement the SSO mechanism on your Web site infrastructure.

System interface to external application or existing systems

Consider the interfaces to external application or existing systems to connect to the Web site. Some external system interfaces influence the architecture of your infrastructure. For example, if you have a fulfillment system connected using a message or service bus then these components need to be incorporated into the architecture of the site infrastructure.

You might also have program to program communications over other technologies to consider such as TCP/IP sockets, VPN, Http, FTP, and many others. You probably also need connections to e-mail and fax.

Backup, recovery, and retention

To secure your data in the database server and files in your file servers, you must plan for resources to back the data up and transfer it to store in a safe place at a regular time interval. Most security breaches occur in the transport of data, so you need to be especially vigilant in planning how backed up data is secured, tracked and logged.

You need to specify data and file retention policy and time frames. With these in mind you can work out how much data and file space you need to back up the systems.

To comply with the Payment Card Industry Data (PCI) security standard, a Key Locator Framework (KLF) has been introduced that allows the encryption key (for example, the merchant key and Payments instance password) to be stored and retrieved from a configurable location such as from an external, more secure, device.

Disaster recovery

For planning disaster recovery, you need to specify the risks you want to protect against and your disaster recovery goals. The main goal is the time it takes to get the site up and running again. But you also should also consider what the priorities are in getting the system running again. Maybe it is more important to handle existing orders before accepting new ones.

9.2 Analyze and design your hardware infrastructure

With business objectives and non-functional requirements well defined, you are ready to analyse them and design the hardware infrastructure.

Analyzing and designing an infrastructure that meets your business objectives and non-functional requirements is a complicated task. Get assistance from an expert who has extensive knowledge and experience, and has access to models and tools to architect and design your infrastructure. IBM Techline supports you and the sales team during the sales process. To help you get the best results from Techline, the following two sections describe what the Techline staff do, and what you need to do to assist them.

9.2.1 Consult the experts: Techline

Techline is the pre-sales, technical support organization for IBM sales and IBM Business Partners. Techline staff are available to assist you, or your solution provider, in designing, sizing your hardware and infrastructure, configuring, and proposing solutions based on IBM products and services. However, Techline cannot help you with project sizing, in terms of man-hours or people required.

You and your solution providers have full access to the technical sales support from Techline to help you to design your infrastructure, even if you are not contracting services from IBM to implement and operate your Web site.

Techline services include:

- Solution design
- IBM server sizing for IBM software and for selected software vendors
- Configuration, validation, and assistance
- Technical product information, including:
  - Interoperability and compatibility
  - Versions and release positioning
  - Performance and benchmark information
- Education sources
- Solution assurance information
- For IBM Business Partners, Techline also provide assistance in competitive situations

The sizing estimate from Techline is an approximation of the hardware resources needed for your Web site. It is based on the information you provide, benchmark performance data and expert knowledge of the consultants who have sized comparable Web sites. As the implementation proceeds you need to review both your sizing assumptions, and conduct continuous performance design and tests before going live.

9.2.2 Prepare your input

Provide the following input data for the Techline consultation. If you do not have actual data, give estimates, and the bases for the estimates:

1. Preferred hardware platform to run WebSphere Commerce?
2. B2C or B2B solution, or both?
3. One, two, or three tier architecture?
4. How many user transactions on average (or user clicks for a page) per user session (visit)?
5. How many total user transactions (Web page hits) per hour in your Web site, for both average and peak hours.
6. What is the average think time?

   Think time is the average time your visitor takes to view a page.
7. What is the browse to buy ratio?

   For example, a 19:1 ratio means out of one hundred user visits, five visits result in placing a buy order.

8. How many orders are processed in the peak hour?

   You need to provide figures for the peak hour in holiday seasons too.

9. On average, how long does a visitor spend at the Web site?
10. Do you plan to have a staging area with a staging server and staging database?
11. How many hours per day is your site active?
12. What is the expected average traffic to the site (page views per day)?
13. What portion of the pages served during a visit are dynamic pages?
14. What is the desired peak CPU utilization (%)?
15. How many products or items are in the catalog?
16. How many specific product items do your customers browse per visit?
17. How many items do your customers place in the shopping cart per visit?
18. Do pages have frames? Is there 1 dynamic request per page ?
19. What is the ratio of the peak to average load on this Web site?

    For example, a ratio of 2 to 1 means that peak load is twice as large as the average load. Measure or estimate the peak load on high season traffic.

20. How many searches per visit to the site?
21. What is the expected network traffic into the site from the Internet? (MByte/second)
22. When and how long is the scheduled maintenance window?

    You also need to provide data to the following questions to estimate physical storage sizing. The physical disk storage estimate is provided on an annual basis, and is a gross figure. For example, if you have a catalog containing one thousand items, and you change all the items once in a year, then the answer is two thousand.

23. How many of these items over one year? Provide a point in time figure for the start of the year, the total over the year, and the point in time figure for the end of the year:
    - Products or items in the database
    - Categories of these items
    - Registered customers
    - Orders
24. What is your data retention policy?
    - Registered users, order history in day or months, years?
    - Do you prune your database? How and when?

9.3 Estimate your software costs

As a project manager, you need to budget for the total cost of your software. You need to plan for software licenses, eCommerce customization, training, and necessary services and support.

9.3.1 Software licenses

There are three categories of software to consider in configuring an operational eCommerce platform:

- WebSphere Commerce
- OS/platform
- Supporting software

You also need to consider additional copies of software to run on servers in the non-production environments shown in column 2 of Table 9-1.

Note: A complete list of WebSphere Commerce system requirements can be found at:

`http://www-1.ibm.com/support/docview.wss?rs=3046&uid=swg27007501`

We recommend that you use the IBM supported platforms and software versions for the best support and services. If you depart from the list, you might not be able to get support from IBM. The service teams might not have experience with or access to the software you are using.

The following sections guide you through the steps needed to make a sizing of the software you need to acquire. Select software from each category to come up with combinations per server environment.

Table 9-1 Software categorization

Category I WC Suite	Category II Environment	Category III Platform	Category IV Supporting Software
► Express ► Professional ► Enterprise ► WC Developer ► Sales Center ► Gift Center	► Development ► Test ► Staging ► Production ► DB Server	► AIX ► i5/OS ► Linux Intel ► Linux iSeries ► Linux pSeries ► Linux zSeries® ► Solaris ► Windows	► Version Control ► Test ► Operation ► Analytics ► WebSphere MQ ► Mail Server ► Content management ► Database (non UDB) ► Development

Category I: Commerce Suite

The license for WebSphere Commerce in any edition covers the underlying WebSphere Application Server and DB2 (which is bundled to be used only with WebSphere Commerce).

For Professional and Enterprise editions, staging and production are considered separate licenses. For the Express edition, there is no separate license for staging. However, the Express edition has other limitations to prevent you from scaling it into large clusters.

For licensed servers (such as staging and production) with multiple CPU's, the license numbers are calculated per 100 value units that measure the power of the processor. For example, a powerful dual-core processor requires two licenses, while a weaker dual-core requires only one license.

> **Note:** Processor Value Unit is a measurement IBM uses to calculate the number of software licenses. Refer to:
>
> `https://www-112.ibm.com/software/howtobuy/passportadvantage/valueunitcalculator/vucalc.wss`
>
> Or, you can ask your IBM sales team for assistance.

In addition to the core WebSphere Commerce platform, there are other WebSphere Commerce family products you might require that are priced separately.

WebSphere Commerce Developer

This is the packaged Open Development Environment (ODE) for WebSphere Commerce development. It contains everything you need for your store customization, including starter store front assets, sample data in a Cloudscape database, comprehensive help and tutorial support, and the built-in runtime test environment. You must match the ODE edition to the same edition of the WebSphere Commerce platform you plan to purchase.

Sales Center

Sales Center for WebSphere Commerce provides call-center representatives with the richer functionality they need to respond to customers requests and to provide shoppers with advice and guidance.

Gift Center

Gift Center for WebSphere Commerce is a multi-channel gift registry. It operates either as a Web-only front end integrated into an existing gift registry system, or as a stand alone, centralized, cross-channel solution.

Category II: Servers

Chapter 10, "Development, test, and production environments" on page 307 describes the details you need to build best of breed environments for development, test and production. Table 9-2 is a brief summary.

Table 9-2 Hardware and software requirements

Servers	Description
Development	Windows based development platforms are required - the number you need depends on the size of the development team. A separate development server installs on Windows 2000 or 2003 server. Install Windows XP SP2 to run the development environment on a workstation.
Test	For functional, integration, system, performance and user acceptance testing
Staging	For production content preparation and validation. The configuration should be close to the production server, if not the same, to perform pre-production verification
Production	To do eCommerce business. Scalability is essential.
Database	For eCommerce data storage and management. Where IBM DB2 or Oracle resides
Build	To perform builds for all the environments
Configuration management	Runs the source configuration management software, such as Clear case or CVS, provides version control to manage software at different release levels and in the process of development and testing.

Category III: Platform

WebSphere Commerce runs on the following operating systems and hardware:

- AIX
- Solaris
- Linux Intel
- Linux iSeries
- Linux pSeries
- Linux zSeries
- i5/OS
- Windows

For details consult the Web pages from Table 9-3.

Table 9-3 Hardware and software requirements

Edition	Software and hardware requirements
Enterprise	http://www-306.ibm.com/software/genservers/commerce/wcbe/requirements/
Professional	http://www-306.ibm.com/software/genservers/commerce/wcpe/requirements/
Express	http://www-306.ibm.com/software/genservers/commerce/express/requirements/

Category IV: Supporting software

The following are examples of typical software to help develop or run a WebSphere Commerce system.

Table 9-4 Supporting software

Category	Product	Description and reference
Configuration management	CVS	Concurrent Versions System is a version control system, a component of Source Configuration Management (SCM). CVS is a popular choice in WebSphere Commerce development community. See: `http://www.nongnu.org/cvs/`
	Rational Clearcase	Rational ClearCase® offers complete software configuration management. It is an industry-leading solution that provides sophisticated version control, workspace management, parallel development support and build auditing to improve productivity. Refer to: `http://www-306.ibm.com/software/awdtools/clearcase/`
	Rational Clearquest	Rational ClearQuest® offers comprehensive software change management. It provides defect tracking, process automation, reporting and life cycle traceability for better visibility and control of the software development life cycle. Refer to: `http://www-306.ibm.com/software/awdtools/clearquest/`
Project management	Rational RequisitePro	Rational Requisitepro is a requirements management system for all kinds of requirement documentation, such as vision documents, use cases and requirements requests. See: `http://www-306.ibm.com/software/awdtools/reqpro/`
	Rational Portfolio Manager	Rational Portfolio Manager helps you to manage releases, and align IT expenditure with business objectives and cost controls. See: `http://www-306.ibm.com/software/awdtools/portfolio/index.html`
	OpenProj	OpenProj is an open source project management tool which helps you create product time lines and manage project resources. See: `http://openproj.org/`
Modeling	Rational Software Modeler	Rational Software Modeler and Rational Data Architect are available as a single package to model your IT architecture and data. Rational Data Architect has extensive import and integration capabilities to capture existing data and data models. If you are using Rational Application Developer v.7 you can combine all these products in the same development environment. See: `http://www-306.ibm.com/software/awdtools/modelbundle/index.html`
	Rational Data Architect	
	WebSphere Business Modeler	WebSphere Business Modeler is a business or process analysts tool you can use to model and document your business processes. See:

Category	Product	Description and reference
Testing	Rational Functional Tester	Rational Functional tester automates function and regression testing, including testing of web-apps. See: `http://www-306.ibm.com/software/awdtools/tester/functional/index.html`
	Rational Performance Tester	Rational Performance Tester is a multi-user load testing and performance testing tool for validating Web application scalability. See: `http://www-306.ibm.com/software/awdtools/tester/performance/index.html`
Content management	WebSphere Product Center	WebSphere Product Center is a product information management solution for building a consistent central repository. It delivers rich product information to Web sites and eCommerce applications, printed documents and marketing collateral, kiosks and mobile devices as well as directly to customers and trading partners through various access points. Refer to: `http://www-306.ibm.com/software/data/masterdata/product-info/`
	IBM Workplace Web Content Management	IBM Workplace Web Content Management software offers end-to-end Web content management. It assists with content creation, life cycle and publication, and ensures a consistent, professional look and feel across multiple sites. Refer to: `http://publib.boulder.ibm.com/infocenter/ieduasst/lotv1r0/index.jsp?topic=/com.ibm.iea.wwcm/wwcm/5.1/Overview.html`
	Interwoven TeamSite	Interwoven TeamSite is a content management platform. Refer to: `http://www.interwoven.com/components/page.jsp?topic=PRODUCT::TEAMSITE`
Run time Extensions	Likeminds	WebSphere Commerce contains an optional, dynamic recommendation system powered by LikeMinds. LikeMinds is a collaborative filtering engine that analyzes user interactions that occur on your Web site and generates real time predictions and recommendations to your Web site users, which are displayed using Web activities. Likeminds has been imbedded into WebSphere Commerce for no additional cost under the defined usage. Refer to: `http://publib.boulder.ibm.com/infocenter/wpdoc/v510/topic/com.ibm.wp.zos.doc/pzn/pzn_intro_likeminds.html`
	Coremetrics	The Coremetrics enhanced Web analytics for WebSphere Commerce provides tools to simplify setting up your site to take advantage of the industry leading hosted Web analytics solution. To take advantage of Coremetrics for IBM WebSphere Commerce, install Coremetrics enhanced Web analytics for WebSphere Commerce (no additional cost), and contract with Coremetrics (with additional cost) to collect your data, and to generate and host the resulting reports. Refer to: `http://www.coremetrics.com`
	Endeca information access	Endeca information access platform works with a customized WebSphere Commerce providing high speed multi-dimensional catalog search. Refer to: `http://endeca.com/`
	Akamai	Akamai offers edge of network content distribution and high speed search engine optimization. Refer to: `http://www.akamai.com/`

9.3.2 Estimate your software development and training costs

Software development is the main cost component of your eCommerce solution. The key elements to consider for cost estimation are listed in Table 9-5.

Table 9-5 High level view of your software development cost

Element	Description
Software training	For the most current WebSphere Commerce training and certification refer to `http://www-306.ibm.com/software/genservers/commerce/education/`
Solution Design	Solution, Macro, and Micro Design
Install/Config software	Varies with complexity (number of tiers, clustering, other software such as LDAP, Portal, etc.)
Data Load	Varies with number of systems where data comes from, and what data is loaded (such as catalog, inventory, price, contracts, users, orders)
Code & unit test for out-of-the-box	Configuring and loading data for out-of-the-box functionality with changes limited to look-and-feel
Code & unit test for customization	Leveraging the WebSphere Commerce programming model and overriding or extending exit points (task commands). Adapting WC Processes.
Code & unit test for integration	Integration with ISVs or back-end systems through web-services and WebSphere MQ
Code & unit test for new functionality	New capability built using the WebSphere Commerce programming model.
Test	Functional, Integration, System, Performance, and assisting with User Acceptance Tests.
Launch	Production install and setup, training business users and site administration, and post-deployment support.
Project Management	Full- or part-time project management to cover IBM, customer, and remote project resources.

9.3.3 Estimate service and support costs

This book has encouraged you to look at using solution providers, IBM and partners, to assist you in the development, operation and hosting of WebSphere Commerce, depending on your circumstances. In our experience, some part of your development effort will benefit from working with a solution provider, at least until your developers have picked up sufficient skills.

Within IBM, Global Services provide specialized technical and business services for retail, as well as IT services for building, deploying and operating eCommerce sites.

IBM Software Services for WebSphere (ISSW) provide specialized services aimed at WebSphere Commerce clients. The commerce team are headquartered in Toronto, along with the WebSphere Commerce development team, and so you get the benefit of the cross fertilization of personnel moving between development and services.

With their long history of working with WebSphere Commerce, ISSW have built up a portfolio of service assets which help to make the team more efficient and effective when working on a WebSphere Commerce engagement. Some of the assets they have developed to use in engagements are:

- Solution Scoping Questionnaire
- Ballpark Sizing Spreadsheet
- Non-Functional Requirements Template
- Project Plan Template
- How to Plan and Organize a Solution Design Phase
- v6.0 HTML Starter Stores
- Solution/Macro/Micro Design Document Templates
- Use Case Template
- FVT Test Plan Template
- Business Object Load Utility
- Systems integration patterns and assets

In addition they have more than two dozen system integration design patterns and implementation assets available including ones for:

- SAP
- Yantra
- Taxware

These assets are available only to the ISSW consultants working on engagements with clients. The tools help clients build solutions more quickly and cheaply.

10

Development, test, and production environments

In this chapter we describe the environments that are needed to program, test, and deploy WebSphere Commerce.

Figure 10-1 shows an overview of four different environments:

- Development
- Function tests
- System tests
- Production tasks

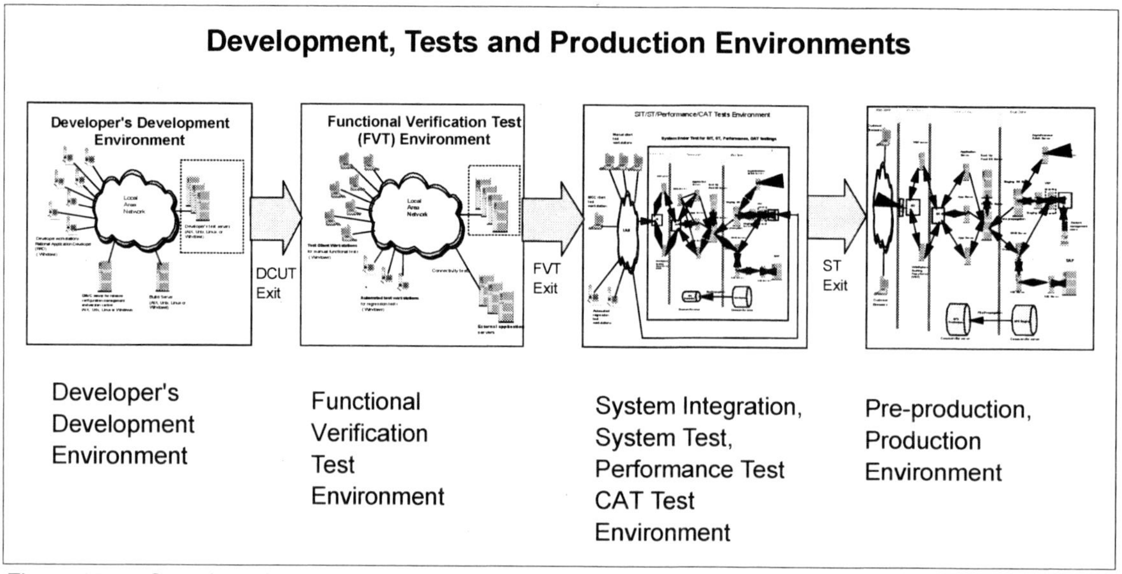

Figure 10-1 Overview of development, test and deployment environments

A WebSphere Commerce site typically maintains four different types of WebSphere Commerce environments for development, function test, system test, and production tasks. There can be multiple instances of the different types of environment to support different tasks. The environments differ in a number of ways, including the hardware used, whether they are connected to other applications, and whether there are multiple instances of the environment.

The following sections describe the characteristics of each environment, including special considerations to be aware of when planning what resources are needed to build and manage the environments.

10.1 Development environments

In this section, we describe the basic development environment that programmers use to design, code, and unit test (DCUT) their deliverables for DCUT exit. Figure 10-2 shows a typical development environment, which consists of the following basic components connected in a LAN environment:

- Laptop and desktop computers with Windows
- Configuration management and version control server
- Build server

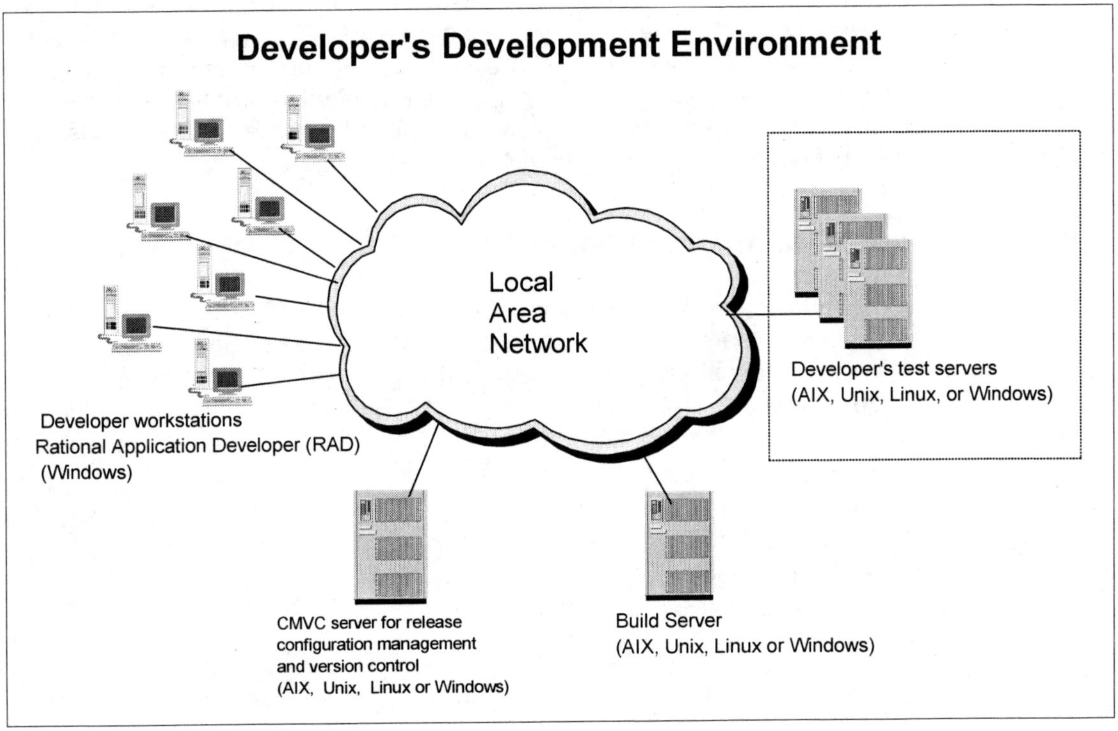

Figure 10-2 Development environment

10.1.1 Mobile or desktop workstation

The mobile computer or desktop workstation is the primary tool for each developer to perform basic tasks such as design, documentation, code, and unit test. The workstation should have at least 2 GB of memory and a speed of 2 GHz. A typical workstation installation includes the following software:

- Windows
- WebSphere Commerce Developer or Rational Application Developer (RAD)
- Database with a copy of the application database

RAD is an Eclipse based software development tool that provides a rich plug-in for WebSphere Commerce programming development. It gives the developer an efficient environment for code editing, code generation, compiling, building, integration, debugging, and unit test. You either need WebSphere Commerce Developer, for developers who are working with commerce customizations, or the normal RAD for developers who are developing generic software.

10.1.2 Configuration management and version control server

A configuration management and version control (CMVC) server provides the development team with a secure repository for source code and artifacts, and a mechanism to manage and control versioning of source files, build levels and software releases. The CMVC server typically contains the following source files that developers check in and out:

- JSP files
- XML files
- Java files
- Jar files
- Shell script files such as ksh files
- Text files
- Image files

Figure 10-3 shows the source file repository, build, and distribution process of release artifacts for testing and deployment.

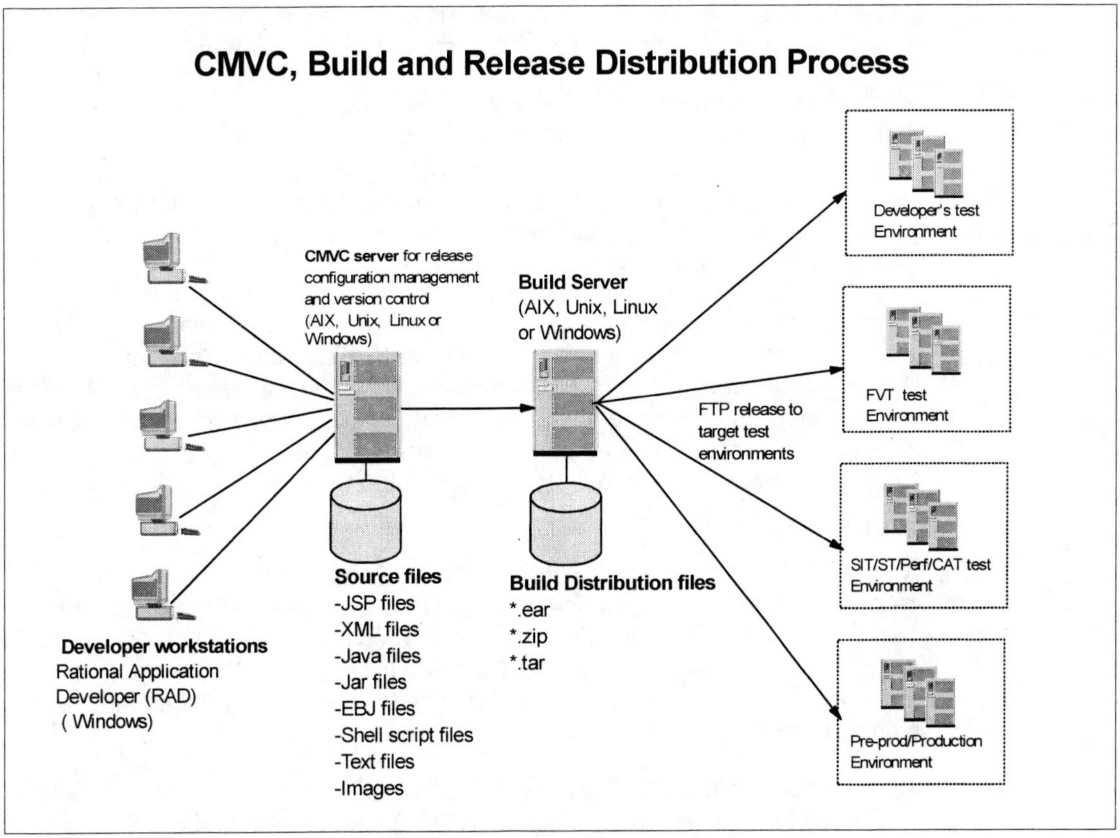

Figure 10-3 Software repository, release build, and distribution process

The CMVC and build servers manage different source and build streams. Developers can simultaneously work on fixes for a production system, and can be fixing problems in different build levels that are progressing through test systems, as well as working on the current public development build, and their own private builds that are made public some time in the future.

For code development, a controlled process is required, to define new source files to the build system and the CMVC system. To develop and fix code, developers check out their files from the CMVC server and work on the checked-out files on their personal workstations. After they finish their code changes and unit testing, they check in their completed files into the correct build stream on the CMVC server.

Some build systems work on a delta system - changes are saved as deltas (effectively edits) to a base line source file, and some work with a file as the lowest unit of change. From the developers perspective it makes little difference, except delta systems are able to support multiple changes to the same source file simultaneously and merge them back together (unless the same lines of code have been changed). There is no guarantee that the changes are consistent of course!

Many CMVC systems allow forked and merged code paths. Figure 10-4 shows a relatively simple example of using a CMVC system to manage releases and fixes. The solid outlined documents are released builds, and the solid arrows show how each build is derived from a previous build, with updates added. In the example, the 1.2 dot release, and the new release 2, are developed in parallel to fixing activities on previously released software.

At a some stage in their release cycles, a manual merge has to take place to incorporate fixes that postdate the base-lining of the new release. The merge requires manual review — because even if the changed source files are not in conflict, the changes that have been made might be inconsistent. A good CMVC system with change tracking helps considerably in this process.

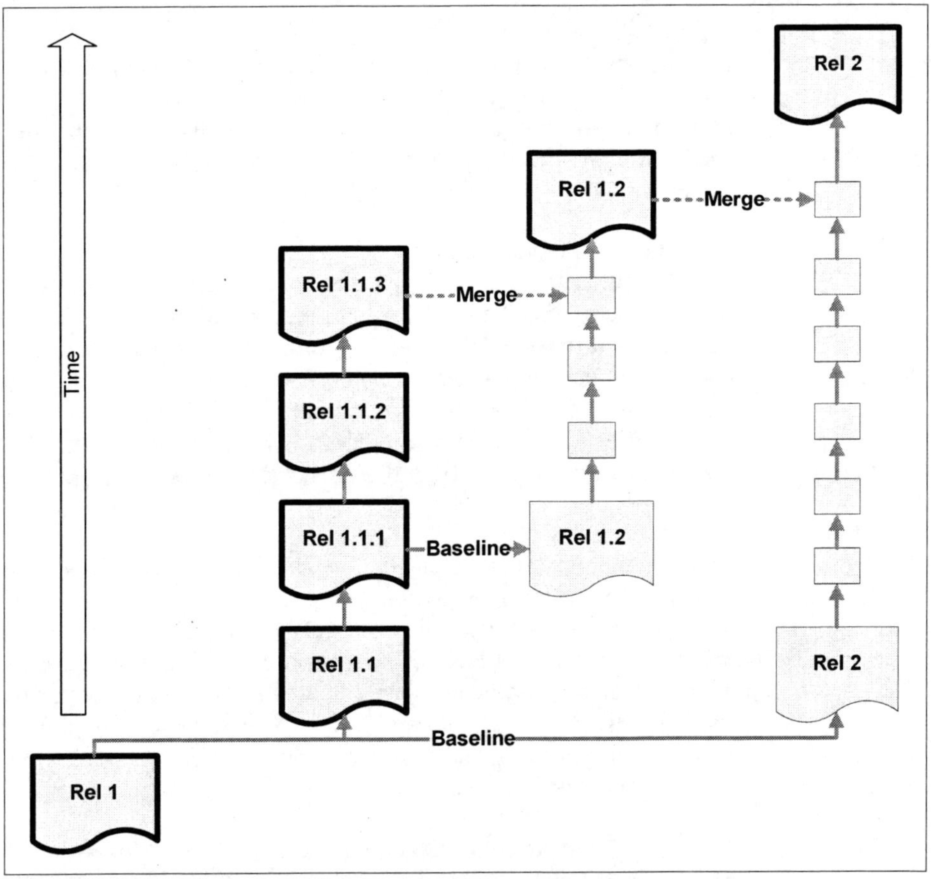

Figure 10-4 Example of parallel development streams

If you are using a system such as ClearQuest, then code changes can be flagged with a change number, a change history maintained and correlated with a problem identifier or a new requirement. This is very useful for code maintenance.

It is critically important that have a configuration management and version control server to protect and control your source code regardless of the size of the project and the scale of the production site you are developing.

There are many commercially available tools which provide you the configuration management and version control functions. Among the tools at the top of the list is the IBM Rational ClearCase set of tools. To explore more information about the Rational ClearCase set of products, refer to:

http://www-306.ibm.com/software/rational/sw-atoz/indexC.html

10.1.3 Build server

The purpose of the build server is to take in all the source code targeted for a specific build level and compile it into deployable files for a target machine. The target machine might be a Windows server, a UNIX server, or a Linux server, all running with WebSphere Commerce. Figure 10-3 on page 311 shows the build process and the release artifacts distributed to different environments.

To optimize the build, distribution and deployment process, you need build scripts to automate the build process, and scripts to automate the deployment and verification test. The build script takes the source files at a specific build level and stream from the CMVC server, compiles them and produces deployable objects such as ear files and zip files.The zip files can contain text files such as property files, XML files, and configuration files. They are compressed or zipped for ease of distribution. The completed build product files are deposited in a specific directory identified for the particular release and build level on the build machine.

When the build is successfully built, a Build Verification Test is performed on a development server. This is a “sanity test” composed of a minimal set of selected test cases to check if the build has really completed correctly and is ready for further testing such as FVT, ST, UAT and pre-production tests. In the BVT You aim to detect if a cleanly compiled build is bootable and perform a simple set of regression tests. You should add to the tests as more function is completed, but keep the number of test small, as you aim to perform the test in a matter of minutes not hours.

Upon the completion of the build and release, you issue a Release Note about this particular release and either distribute it to the target environments or issue instructions on how to transfer or FTP the release files to the target environments.

The build server must be consistent with the target machine. If the target server is a Windows server, then the build server should be a Windows based computer with a consistent software stack installed. If the target server is UNIX based, the build server should be a comparable UNIX server. If the target server is Linux based, the build server should be a comparable Linux server.

10.2 Test environments

In this section, we describe the functional verification, system integration, system test, performance, and user acceptance test environments.

10.2.1 Functional verification test environment

The functional verification test (FVT) environment is set of servers connected a controlled LAN to allow the FVT test team to verify the functionality of the software deliverables. A typical FVT environment is shown in Figure 10-5. It consists of the following components:

- Application server
- Database server
- Connections to external application systems, or to scaffolded test stubs
- Manual test client workstations running on Windows with browsers installed
- Automated test workstations
- FV testers' workstations for developing FV and administering tests

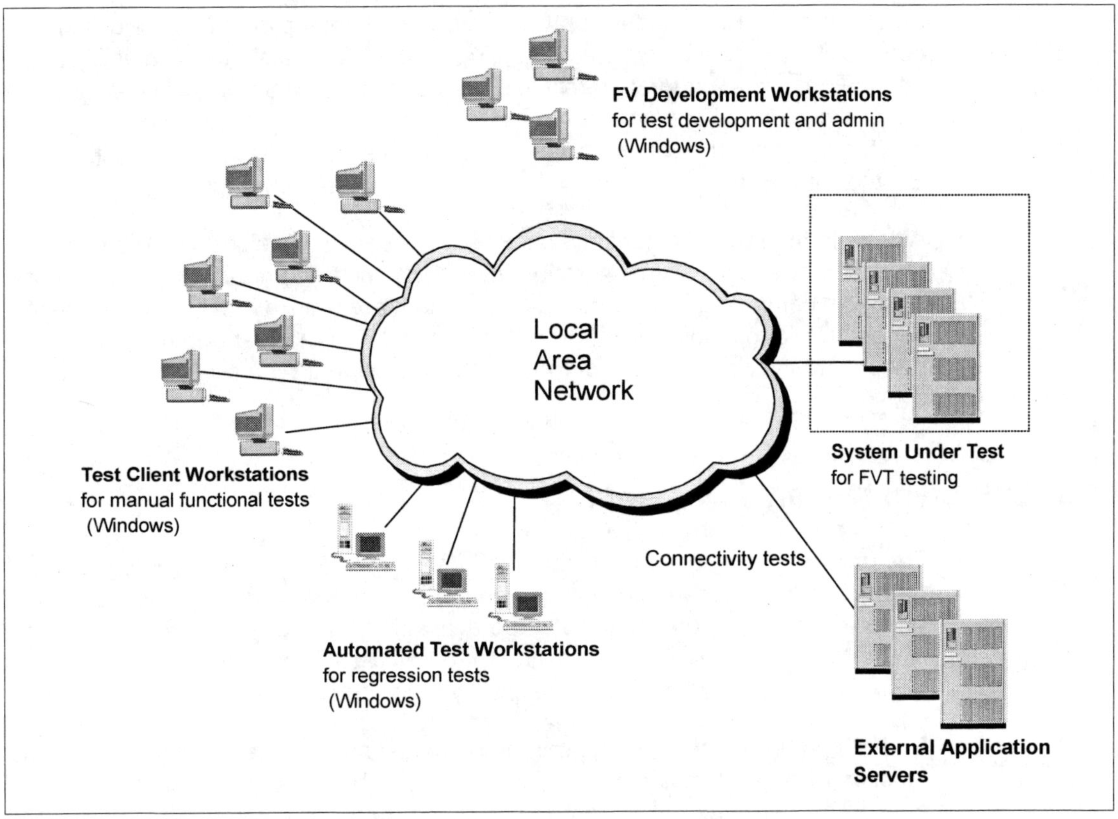

Figure 10-5 Functional Verification Test (FVT) environment

The application server under test must have installed an identical software stack as for the target system for production launch.

The database contains as much production data as possible. If this is not possible, use data with the same data definition and format.

If the Web site connects to external applications such as a payment system, or a fulfillment system, you need to decide whether integration specialists should develop the connections as part of the normal pre-FVT customization development effort. All the components in the system are then tested together as part of FVT.

Alternatively, for logistical or schedule reasons, you might decide to perform a separate integration test after FVT, and to schedule integration development in parallel with FVT. The latter approach is frequently adopted, because of the complexity and cost of integration testing, and the difficulty of debugging integration errors. Integration test is more economically performed when most of the components of the system have been shown to be working correctly. Whichever approach you adopt, external connectivity must work before the System Test Entry or else no end-to-end test system cases can begin.

Automate the regression test cases as much as possible since these tasks are repeated for each FVT test iteration after each build. There are reasonably good test tools commercially available. Among them are the Rational Function Tester set of tools, and also WinRunner is widely used. For more about the IBM Rational Function Tester set of tools, visit the Rational Web site at:

`http://www-306.ibm.com/software/rational/sw-atoz/indexF.html`

10.2.2 System test environment

The primary purpose of the system test environment (Figure 10-6) is to provide a production-like environment for running the end-to-end system verification test. The same environment should also be available for running preliminary system integration tests, and for other testing that requires a near-production system, such as performance verification, security tests, and user acceptance testing.

End-to-end tests include both user interface testing and interconnected system function testing. All major system functions must be represented in this environment so they can be tested and proven working before going to the production environment. The rationale for having all major system functions represented and tested in this environment is so that there are no surprises when moving the release into the pre-production or production environment.

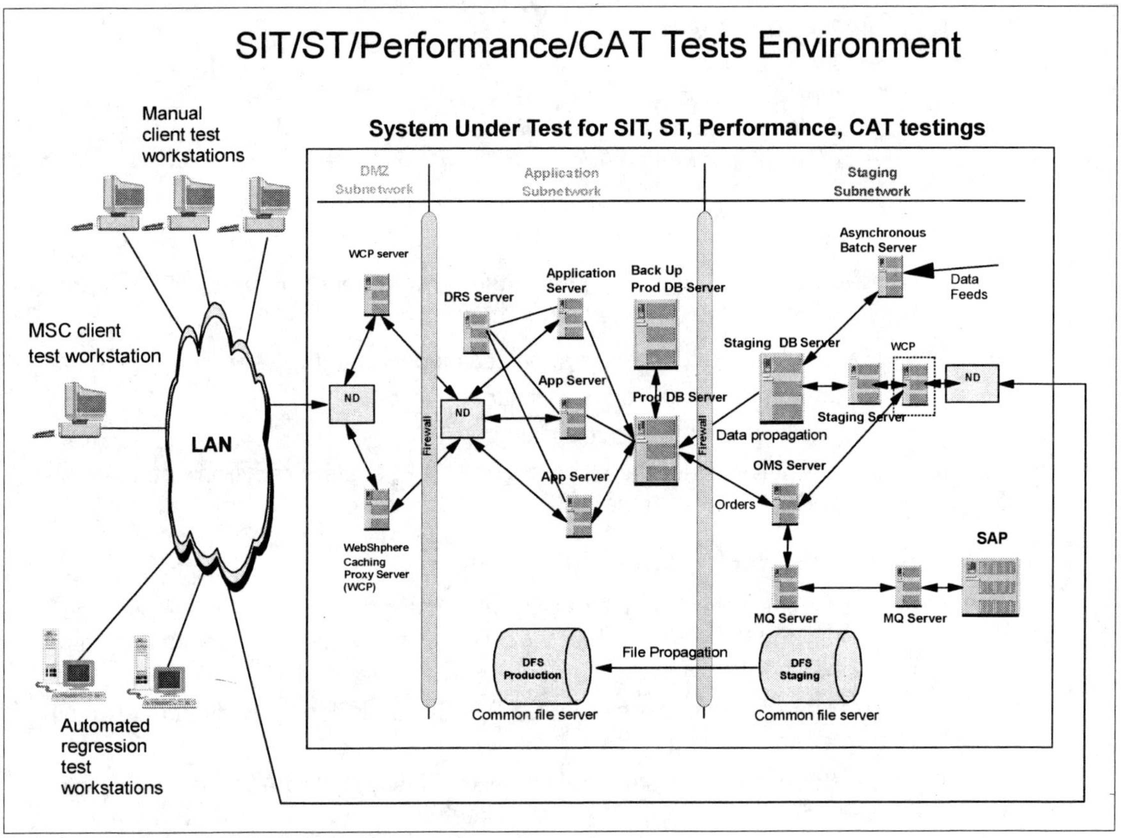

Figure 10-6 Typical system integration and system test environment

In the "system under test" in Figure 10-6, there are the following components:

- Interfacing Red Zone
  - Router
- In the DMZ (Yellow Zone):
  - Network dispatcher
  - WebSphere caching proxy cluster
- In the Green Zone:
  - Network dispatcher
  - Application servers cluster
  - Database server
  - Database backup server
  - Shared file system

- In the Blue Zone:
  - Staging server
  - Staging database server
  - Asynchronous batch server
  - Order management server
  - WebSphere MQ server
  - Shared file system
  - Proxy server

To develop, run, and manage tests, the environment is connected to a controlled LAN, which has the following equipment:

- Manual system test workstations (Windows with browser)
- Automated test tools on workstations
- System test scripts and test cases
- If the MultiChannel Sale Center (MSC) is a system requirement, there should be workstations with the MSC client installed.

System test typically focuses on four areas:

- User facing interfaces: This tests all the components in the Yellow Zone (DMZ) and the Green Zone, including any external application systems connected.
- User interfaces in the staging area in the Blue Zone: This tests the staging server and staging database server.
- Datafeed and data propagation tasks: This tests the Asynchronous Batch Server (ABS) server, the staging database server, and data propagation to update from the staging database to the production database.
- Fulfillment channels: This tests all components that deliver orders to fulfillment systems using integration servers such as WebSphere MQ.

In addition, if the solution incorporates connections to Akamai and Coremetrics, then you should include testing those components in the system test plan.

If the system integration and system testing environment does not include performance and availability testing activities, for budget reasons, then the production-like environment can be simplified by reducing the redundancy of servers.

10.2.3 Performance test environment

The performance test team requires a test environment to measure performance during development and to verify that response time, throughput, and future growth objectives are met during system verification test. To verify performance, you need to test on a production-like infrastructure.

There are two scenarios to consider:

1. New Web site:

   If the Web site is launching for the first time, then construct a pre-production environment that is switched to being the production environment when it meets its performance objectives and is ready to be launched.

2. Software release on an existing infrastructure:

   Since you cannot perform the performance test on the production hardware infrastructure, perform the tests on the System Test Environment instead.

   Upgrade your system test infrastructure to match the production infrastructure as closely as you can, including server clustering, and redundancies, so that the performance results match the actual performance you expect to see on the production Web site.

Set up the following tools for performance measurements:

- Automated load simulation tools and workstations such as LoadRunner or Rational Performance Tester which provide a simulated workload.
- User interface performance profiling tool such as Rational Performance Tester or WinRunner which provides a timing breakdown of performance measurements for a user page response time at the user browser.

10.2.4 User acceptance testing

You need to perform User Acceptance Tests (UATs). These can be conducted in the system test environment or in the pre-production environment if it is planned. For this test, you need to prepare and set up the exact data to be tested in the database and with the final version of application software release.

10.3 Pre-production environment

The pre-production environment is literally the production environment before it is launched. After all the development and testing of the Web site, you need to build the actual Web site that will go live on the machines that run the production site. If you are releasing a significant change, there is almost certain to be some down time. You aim to minimize the downtime by building the new Web site offline, and doing the minimum work necessary to switch from the existing site to the new site.

There are three scenarios to consider:

- First time launch on new infrastructure
- New software release on new infrastructure
- New major software release on existing infrastructure

10.3.1 First time launch on new infrastructure

The pre-production infrastructure has the exact production hardware, network and software planned for launch. Figure 10-7 shows an example of a pre-production infrastructure.

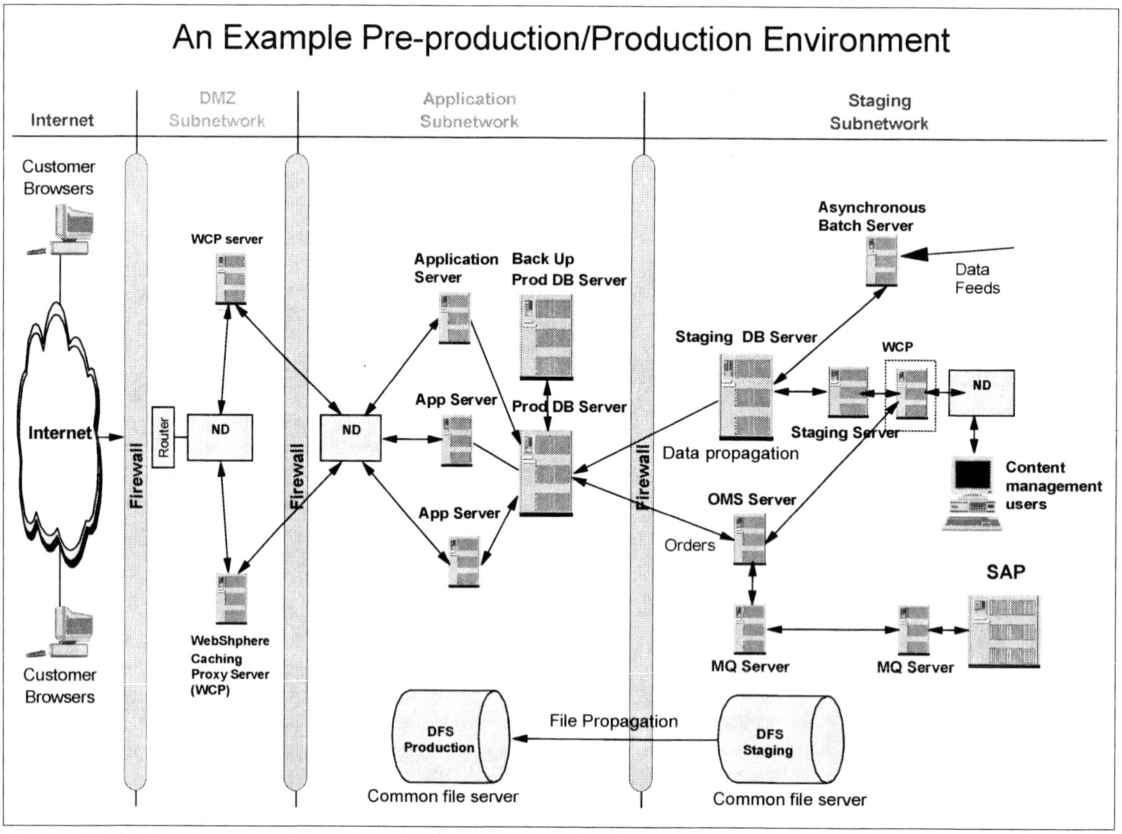

Figure 10-7 An example of a pre-production or production infrastructure

The primary purpose of the pre-production environment is to set up all the hardware, network connectivity, software stack with the application software. and all necessary data for the final round of testing in a truly to-be production environment before launch.

When the pre-production environment is set up, the following round of testing is performed:

- System connectivity tests
- End to user function test
- User Acceptance Test is sometimes performed in this environment[1]

When these tests are successfully completed, you should go through your launch procedure to turn your pre-production environment into a live production site.

10.3.2 New software release on new infrastructure

Another scenario where you need to construct your pre-production environment is when hardware, software, and infrastructure are being significantly upgraded. You do not want to disturb the production system with such large changes, and probably cause significant system downtime. Treat this scale of change the same as building a wholly new Web site and build a complete pre-production system to switch over with the production environment.

10.3.3 New major software release on existing infrastructure

This scenario is the hardest to arrange. Because you are not planning on changing hardware, you might not have enough hardware to build a parallel pre-production environment.

The tricky procedure that is followed is to release some machines from the production Web site, and start building up the new pre-production environment in parallel. When you have transferred half the production site over to the pre-production site, you can then switch the live Web site to the pre-production environment. The switch over requires you shut down the live site, do a last minute dynamic data migration from the old to the new database, and then bring up the new Web site. You can then continue to add servers to the new Web site after you have migrated the new software onto them.

If you can recycle some hardware (perhaps from the test systems) during the changeover, then it reduces the risk of running with lower capacity.

[1] This should only be verification of known points, perhaps some wording or graphics changes; it is too late in the development cycle to react to major problems in UAT at this stage.

Part 4

Keep on running

Now, here, you see, it takes all the running you can do, to keep in the same place. If you want to get somewhere else, you must run at least twice as fast as that![1]

When your Web site is up, what must you plan to do to keep it running? Chapter 11 discusses five different kinds of activities you should plan for to keep your Web site running.

But sometimes expectations do go wrong, and you have to plan for those too. It is not enough to sign all the right support contracts, you should plan to do troubleshooting as well. Chapter 12 describes troubleshooting procedures.

1 *"Through the looking glass"*, Lewis Carroll

11

Running your Web site

When your site is operational, there are quite a few tasks that must be completed on a regular basis in order to keep the content fresh and the site operating at peak efficiency. This chapter describes these tasks and should help you define some solutions and procedures that fit your particular needs.

We discuss these topics:

- "Maintaining the Web site"
- "Managing business content"
- "Protecting the Web site"
- "Solving customer problems"
- "Applying software updates"

11.1 Maintaining the Web site

The responsibility of maintaining your Web site on a day to day basis falls to your operations team as described in "Business roles" on page 186. Alternatively, you might choose to have the site hosted. If this is the case, many of these tasks fall to the hosting company. In either case, you should have some level of operational staff in-house that either perform the tasks described in this section or oversee the hosting company as they perform the tasks. The tasks described in this section include:

- "Administering the Web site"
- "Monitoring"
- "Managing logs"
- "Maintaining the database"

11.1.1 Administering the Web site

Your Web site should be administered by someone in-house, regardless of whether or nor your site is hosted elsewhere. The Site Administrator installs, configures, and maintains WebSphere Commerce and the associated software and hardware. The Administrator responds to system warnings, alerts, and errors, and diagnoses and resolves system problems. This role typically controls access and authorization (creating and assigning members to the appropriate role), manages the Web site, monitors performance, and manages load balancing tasks.

The Site Administrator might also be responsible for establishing and maintaining several server configurations for different stages of development such as testing, staging, and production. This role also handles critical system backups and resolves performance problems.

A WebSphere Commerce Site Administrator must have the following skills:

- Database administration skills
- Web server administration skills
- WebSphere Application Server administration skills
- Basic XML skills
- General familiarity with WebSphere Commerce
- Appropriate operating system skills

For an in-depth discussion of what the Site Administrator should know about WebSphere Commerce, refer to:

`http://publib.boulder.ibm.com/infocenter/wchelp/v6r0m0/topic/com.ibm.commerce.base.doc/concepts/covunderstanding.htm`

The administration task can be subdivided into routine and non-routine tasks. Routine tasks can either be automated, or written up in procedures to be followed by and delegated to System Operators. The Site Administrator is responsible for defining the routine activities, handling non-routine tasks, and keeping records of all changes to the site.

Attention: Keeping accurate logs, with precise date and time stamps, of all activity at the site is very important. To make this a matter of routine, all standard procedures, manual or automatic, should be designed to include logging when they are performed, who by, and the outcome. The information is invaluable when problems need to be debugged.

11.1.2 Monitoring

The question is not whether to monitor your Web site, but rather what and how often. Nothing damages the reputation of an eCommerce site worse than an extended, unplanned outage except perhaps a very public security breach. Security breaches are discussed in 11.3.3, "Monitoring for security threats and breaches" on page 348.

The key objective of monitoring is to be the first to find a problem — even to predict a problem — before your customers find it and start leaving the site or bombarding you with e-mails and calls. There are several types of monitoring that are discussed in this section:

- "Up/down monitoring"
- "Feature and function monitoring"
- "Performance monitoring"

Up/down monitoring

This type of monitoring is just like it sounds: determine whether a key component of the infrastructure is up or down. It is the simplest type of monitoring and should be done on every site. The only question is how often the components are checked. Every hosting company should include this type of monitoring.

The first level of checks should be at the computer system level. This can be accomplished by simply pinging the devices on a periodic schedule from a central monitoring point. If one of the devices does not respond in a preset time frame, raise an alert.

The devices might be operating but one or more of the software components might have stopped. A way of determining whether or not key software components are running is to check for the existence of running processes.

Identify all the key processes that should be running during normal operations in each of the servers, such as these:

- Web server
- Application server
- Database server
- Mail server

Execute a script on each servers where these processes should be running and check if they indeed are running. Raise an alert if one is missing.

> **Note:** It is easy enough to write simple scripts to check if processes are running. It is harder to get the results of these scripts to one central place where operators are alerted and corrective scripts are initiated. The whole process of monitoring and automating management of systems is called autonomic computing, and you should investigate using products from Tivoli or other vendors as a platform to grow automation for your Web site. See the Redbooks publication, *"IBM Tivoli Monitoring: Implementation and Performance Optimization for Large Scale Environments"*, SG24-7443, at:
>
> `http://www.redbooks.ibm.com/abstracts/sg247443.html?Open`

The final up/down monitor that should be in place checks the status of your primary URL. Can you get to the store? This should be done from the Internet rather than the intranet so that you are accessing the storefront as a typical customer would. If a customer tries to access your store and fails, chances are he does not come back.

Feature and function monitoring

The next level of monitoring is at the feature or function level. The store might be running but your search engine is not. It is possible that the application is running but a bug in the code causes a particular function of the store to fail each time a customer hits it. Again, you do not want a call from a customer to be the way you find out about these problems.

A solution would be to create a script that walks through your store mimicking a customer. This script could attempt to execute a set of key functions. If one of the functions fails, raise an alert. This should be done on a regular schedule that does not put too much load on the server.

Think of this as an extension of your normal regression testing. Except this time you run the scripts against the production server not a test server. There are many automated testing tools available for this job. The following list contains a few that you might want to look into further.

- Borland:

  http://www.borland.com/index.html
  - SilkTest
  - SilkPerformer

- IBM:

  http://www-306.ibm.com/software/rational/offerings/testing.html
  - IBM Rational Functional Tester
  - IBM Rational Performance Tester

- HP:

  https://h10078.www1.hp.com/cda/hpms/display/main/hpms_content.jsp?zn=bto&cp=1-11-15-24%5E1074_4000_100__&jumpid=reg_R1002_USEN
  - HP WinRunner software
  - HP LoadRunner software

- Tsung (open-source):

  http://tsung.erlang-projects.org/

- Other open source automated tools: look under the performance tab:

  http://www.opensourcetesting.org/functional.php

Performance monitoring

A final type of monitoring is to check for performance degradation over time. You start by creating a script similar to the one described above only this time, it records timestamps after each activity. Record the time it takes to:

- Login
- Perform a search
- Bring up a product page
- Add a product to the shopping cart
- Checkout

The script does not need to be run very often — perhaps create a schedule to run it every four hours during the day. Log the date and time of each execution of the script and then once a month, graph the results. You are looking for downward trends in performance for each of the functions over time. This indicates whether investigation is required and if corrective action should be taken.

Corrective action in this case should to look at the code for problems as well as the database tables and queries being used at the time. Many problems in the performance of WebSphere Commerce sites can be traced back to poor database maintenance. See "Maintaining the database" on page 332.

11.1.3 Managing logs

WebSphere Commerce generates a lot of log entries. Keep this sharply in mind — these log entries accumulate over time and if left unchecked exhaust your available storage space. Devise a plan to manage the logs.

Look at each set of logs and determine how long it should remain on the system for troubleshooting or audit purposes. After this has been determined, you need to develop scripts to automatically roll the logs to off-line storage.

Examining logs is error prone and time consuming. System management tools come with tools to filter logs to identify classes of messages. It is a simple matter to write your own scripts to scan logs. There are a lot of good tips in this recent series of articles for AIX:

`http://www.ibm.com/developerworks/views/aix/libraryview.jsp?search_by=System+Administration+Toolkit`

Application server log files

When starting and stopping an application server, a number of log files are generated. After starting or stopping an application server check the log files to ensure that both the application server and the applications that run inside the application server started or stopped successfully. These logs are configured with a maximum size so that as the as the maximum size is reached, a new log file is created automatically.

The application server log files (Example 11-1) are in the following directory:

```
WC_profiledir/logs/server_name
(e.g. /opt/IBM/WebSphere/AppServer/profiles/demo/logs/server1)
```

Example 11-1 Application server log files

```
trace_07.11.30_13.25.53.log
trace.log
```

The following log files should be examined after starting or stopping an application server:

- startServer.log

  This log file contains messages generated when the application server was starting. The application server started successfully if this log file contains the text Server server_name open for e-business, where server_name is the name of the application server that was started.

Note: The successful start of an application server does not necessarily indicate that the application that runs inside the application server started successfully. For that information, examine the SystemOut.log file.

- stopServer.log

  This log file contains messages generated when the application server was stopping. The application server stopped successfully if this log file contains the text, Server server_name stop completed, where server_name is the name of the application server that was stopped.

- SystemErr.log

  This log file contains Java exceptions and stack traces. These exceptions are caught by enterprise applications and their associated application servers.

  An empty SystemErr.log file does not necessarily indicate success since not all error messages generated by an application are considered to be error messages by the operating system. You must also examine the contents of the SystemOut.log file.

- SystemOut.log

  This log file contains messages generated when the applications running inside the application server are being started or stopped. This log file does not contain error messages — such messages appear in the SystemErr.log file. However, this log file does contain errors that the operating system does not see as error messages.

  Both this log file and the SystemErr.log file should be checked after starting an application server to confirm that the applications inside the application server being started have also started successfully.

- trace.log

  The log file contains the components trace messages while the service is running, if the trace is enabled in the server. Trace logs get very large very fast. Trace should only be enabled when actively troubleshooting a problem.

- Loading utilities log files

  `http://publib.boulder.ibm.com/infocenter/wchelp/v6r0m0/topic/com.ibm.commerce.data.doc/refs/rml_logs.htm?resultof=%22%6c%6f%67%22%20%22%66%69%6c%65%73%22%20%22%66%69%6c%65%22%20`

- Store publish log files

  `http://publib.boulder.ibm.com/infocenter/wchelp/v6r0m0/topic/com.ibm.commerce.admin.doc/concepts/clspblg.htm?resultof=%22%6c%6f%67%22%20%22%66%69%6c%65%73%22%20%22%66%69%6c%65%22%20`

Web server log files

Each Web server machine contains a set of logs for each active instance of a Web server. They are normally stored in the directory:

`WC_installdir/instances/<instanceName>/httplogs/.`

The log files include:

- Access_log
- Error_log
- Admin_access_log
- Admin_error_log

These logs do not have a maximum size configuration unlike the application server logs. You need to create your own process to rotate them.

An additional log file that is stored on Web server machines is the Web server plug-in log. This log is relatively small unless tracing is enabled. The default location is

Plugin_installdir/logs/*webserver_name*
(such as: /opt/IBM/WebSphere/Plugins/logs/webserver1/http_plugin.log)

Database server log files

DB2 stores the database activity logs under the instance name. The default location is

`/home/db2inst1/db2inst1/NODE0000/SQL00001/SQLOGDIR`

Where db2inst1 is the name of the instance owner. In this example, there is a single node on the database server and a single database has been created within the node. You can create multiple nodes and multiple databases. The size and number of log files is configurable from within the DB2 Control Center.

11.1.4 Maintaining the database

WebSphere Commerce is a database application and suffers significant performance degradation if the database is not properly maintained. An experienced DBA should be on your staff to manage the WebSphere Commerce database. WebSphere Commerce supports both DB2 and Oracle, but the examples in this section are for DB2 as it is the database that ships with WebSphere Commerce. See Oracle documentation to understand how to perform database management tasks on an Oracle database.

A good data retention plan must be devised prior to the launch of your WebSphere Commerce site. You should determine what data should be kept in the database and for how long. Unnecessary data in the database only slows down performance. As part of site planning, make a list of the major objects in the WebSphere Commerce database and determine how long each should be kept in the database. When you are ready to implement this plan, following these steps:

- "DBClean"
- "RUNSTATS"
- "REORGCHK"
- "REORG"
- "REBIND"

Note: Database maintenance should be performed when the traffic to the WebSphere Commerce site is minimal, as there will be some performance degradation and additional locking with these tasks are being executed.

DBClean

WebSphere Commerce includes a Database Cleanup Utility that is used to delete records marked for delete and obsolete data. You might want to do this if you have changed a lot of information in your database and have unused tables or rows.

When the Database Cleanup utility deletes an object, the records in the object's tables are deleted to preserve the referential integrity of the database. The Database Cleanup utility deletes records in child tables based on the delete rule of the referential integrity definition in the database schema. You can set the delete rule to on delete cascade, on delete set null, or on delete restrict. If you add new tables, ensure that the referential integrity and delete rule is properly defined. Otherwise, the Database Cleanup utility cannot work with your new tables.

For more information about the Database Cleanup Utility, refer to:

`http://publib.boulder.ibm.com/infocenter/wchelp/v5r6/topic/com.ibm.commerce.admin.doc/refs/rdcucommand.htm`

RUNSTATS

The RUNSTATS command updates the statistics that are used by the optimizer when determining access paths to the data. If the statistics are not up to date, the system suffers performance degradation.

Most WebSphere Commerce sites update statistics on a daily or weekly basis (generally over the weekend). You should also consider updating the statistics after schema changes or massive update or load (such as refreshing the catalog). Remember to run db2rbind after RUNSTATS so the static packages can take advantage of the new statistics.

For more information about the DB2 RUNSTATS command, refer to:

http://publib.boulder.ibm.com/infocenter/db2luw/v8/topic/com.ibm.db2.udb.doc/core/r0001980.htm

REORGCHK

The REORGCHK command outputs a table listing all the table and indexes objects. An asterisk (*) on the REORG column indicates that the calculated results exceed the set bounds of its corresponding formula, and that the table might need to be reorganized. Unless you use the "CURRENT STATISTICS" specifier, the REORGCHK command updates the statistics for all the objects on the database. If you are running REORGCHK after RUNSTATS, you can use the "CURRENT STATISTICS" specifier to avoid updating the statics twice.

For more information about the DB2 REORGCHK command, refer to:

http://publib.boulder.ibm.com/infocenter/db2luw/v8/topic/com.ibm.db2.udb.doc/core/r0001971.htm

REORG

After the tables or indexes to be reorganized have been identified using the REORGCHK command, the REORG command has to be explicitly invoked for each object. DB2 does not offer a way to automatically reorganize all the tables or indexes that were identified by REORGCHK.

Table reorganization is commonly performed in any one of the following ways:

- DBA to run REORG for each table identified by REORGCHK
- Explicitly executing REORG for the tables and indexes that are most likely to need a reorganization (for example, the USER table after using DBClean to delete guest shoppers)
- Implementing a script to select the tables or indexes that contain an asterisk (*) on the REORG column, and invoke the REORG command for each of them (not recommended)

A standard (offline) REORG locks for write the tables being reorganized. If you need to allow updates to the tables, Online table reorganization can be used instead.

For more information about the DB2 REORG INDEXES/TABLE command, refer to:

http://publib.boulder.ibm.com/infocenter/db2luw/v8/topic/com.ibm.db2.udb.doc/core/r0001966.htm

REBIND

Static packages need to be rebound after executing RUNSTATS to make use of updated statistics. Packages can be rebound one by one using the REBIND command or all at once by using the **db2rbind - Rebind all Packages** Command.

WebSphere Commerce includes sixteen out-of-the-box stored procedures that benefit from rebind.

Note: The command does not rebind a package that is in use.

For more information about the DB2 db2rbind command, see:

`http://publib.boulder.ibm.com/infocenter/db2luw/v8/index.jsp?topic=/com.ibm.db2.udb.doc/core/r0001995.htm`

11.2 Managing business content

The quality of the content on your Web site is what brings customers back. The responsibility for this should rest with business team. The primary roles include:

- Marketing Manager
- Merchandising (or Product) Manager
- Category Manager
- Operations Manager
- Workspace Manager

The last role in the list is unique to WebSphere Commerce. Workspaces are available in WebSphere Commerce Professional and Enterprise editions only. Workspaces are described in “Workspaces” on page 62.

Business content takes a number of different forms; each of them is equally important to the success of you site. The tasks described in this section include:

- “Managing online catalogs”
- “Managing the product life cycle”
- “Managing promotions”

Note: Much of 11.2, “Managing business content” is also discussed in Chapter 2 and Chapter 3 in the context of describing the tools and extensions to WebSphere Commerce used to manage business content. In this section we focus on what business user can do with the tools to keep a Web site competitive and up to date.

11.2.1 Managing online catalogs

The category manager is responsible for the financial success of a category of products by organizing the products and services offered by the store and how they are organized into product categories. The category manager is responsible for managing products, expected inventory records, vendor information, inventory, and return reasons within each category and modifying the category hierarchy by creating, modifying, and deleting categories.

There are two types of catalogs in a WebSphere Commerce system: master and sales. The master catalog is the central location to manage all your store's merchandise and services and a sales catalog is a subset of the merchandise and services found in the master catalog used to present products in an organized way to your customers.

Master catalog

The master catalog is the central location to manage your store's merchandise. Everything you need in your store is contained within the master catalog. It is the single catalog containing all products, items, relationships, and standard prices for everything that is for sale in your store. You use the Product Management tools in the WebSphere Commerce Accelerator to view and manage your master catalog.

Every store in the WebSphere Commerce system must have a master catalog. You can share the master catalog across stores and define as many stores as needed. There are important structural restrictions for the master catalog:

- The master catalog must be a proper tree, which means that there are no cycles. You must avoid the following type of scenario: The parent category A has a subcategory B. It is important that B and any of B's subcategories are not the parent category of A.
- A product cannot belong to more than one category. To place a product in more than one category, use a sales catalog.
- The Product Management tools only work with products that are associated with a master catalog.

Sales catalog

Every store in the WebSphere Commerce system must have a master catalog. Only one master catalog can exist at a time, and multiple stores can share a master catalog. However, you can create one or more sales catalogs for customer display purposes. A sales catalog has a flexible display structure that allows you to associate products to more than one category, to suit the requirements of your store.

Sales catalogs allow you to maintain an unlimited number of catalog hierarchies and place products in any number of locations within a single sales catalog structure. Sales catalogs can be used to create unique hierarchies and product assortments for seasonal purposes, targeting specific customer segments or business customers. For example, you could have a Spring sales catalog and a Fall sales catalog, as well as a Gold-rated Customer sales catalog.

You manage your sales catalog with the WebSphere Commerce Accelerator. Typical tasks are:

- Create, change, or delete sales catalogs. You can create sales catalogs based on segments of your master catalog, or choose to create one from scratch.
- Create, change, find, or remove categories. Select new parent categories and rearrange the category tree structure for a new look.
- Link a category. Take a category from one sales catalog to another sales catalog. That category, and all its catalog entries, are then be displayed in both (or more) sales catalogs.
- Duplicate the structure of a category. From your master or sales catalog, you can duplicate a section of categories and subcategories to preserve a similar structure.
- Assign, find, or remove catalog entries from different categories.

Sales catalogs are used in conjunction with the master catalog and contracts to control which products display for a particular customer. If a customer is not entitled to see a subset of the products in the master catalog, the contract system makes sure that customer does not see those products in the WebSphere Commerce store. The sales catalog is used to organize the products that the customer is entitled to see and purchase in a more meaningful way.

For example, customers can buy products to support a business project. Instead of organizing products by department and sub-department, it might be easier for the customer to find products if the products are arranged in a manner that matches the components of their project. In this scenario, a top level category might be titled Network Replacement Project and the subcategories in the sales catalog would be Hardware and Software.

Merchandising associations

Merchandising associations suggest additional, different, or replacement products based on a selected catalog entry. The merchandising associations are used as product recommendations to increase store sales. In addition to promotional associations such as cross-selling, up-selling, and suggested accessories, key words highlight extra semantic information of merchandising relationships, such as `requires` and `comes with`.

The behavior of these semantics is determined by your store's specific business requirements. It does not perform any business logic by default — that needs to be added. For example, one store might decide that `require` automatically adds a product to the shopping cart, while another simply displays a message to the customer.

For each merchandising association there is a source catalog entry and a target catalog entry. For example, if a shirt has a tie as an accessory, the shirt is the source entry and the tie is the target entry. A source catalog entry can have multiple associations with different target entries. Continuing the previous example, the shirt can have both a tie and cuff links as accessories. In this case the shirt is the source entry, and the tie and cuff links are each target entries. After a merchandising association is created, from the source catalog entry you determine its associated target catalog entries.

Merchandising associations are either static, which is a fixed relationship, or dynamic, which uses customized rules and queries to form personalized associations. Table 11-1shows the static merchandising associations you can create.

Table 11-1 Merchandising associations

Association	Description
cross-sell	A merchant suggests other catalog entries based on an already chosen catalog entry. For example, a merchant suggests a high-resolution color printer when a digital camera is purchased, or a particular type of batteries when a flashlight is purchased.
up-sell	A merchant suggests a better catalog entry based on the one selected. For example, a merchant can suggest a higher quality television when a low-end model is selected.
accessory	A merchant suggests an accessory that complements the selected catalog entry. For example, a merchant can suggest an extra game controller when a video game system is selected.
replacement	A merchant indicates that the relationship between two catalog entries is considered equivalent. Replacement is only valid when two catalog entries are of the same catalog entry type: product, package, bundle or dynamic kit. For example, if one type of brand name battery is sold out, a merchant can suggest a different brand name battery, as long as both batteries are products.
custom	A merchant can create custom merchandising association types based on specific requirements. For example, a merchant might want to offer a down-sell merchandising association to suggest lower-priced catalog entries based on the selected catalog entry.

11.2.2 Managing the product life cycle

The Product Manager traces customer purchases, suggests promotions, and determines the best way to display, price, and sell products in the online store. In performing his job, the Product Manager uses the Product Management tools in WebSphere Commerce to create:

- Catalog entries
  - Products
  - SKUs
  - Bundles and kits
- Attributes
- Pricing

Products

Products act as templates for SKUs, the individual pieces of merchandise which are ultimately sold to a customer. The product wizard allows you to create new products for your catalog. Use the product notebook to view or change product details, such as names, descriptions, and images, or delete products from your catalog. You can update product taxes, discounts, and shipping categories, and add shipping measurements for each product. You can also customize fulfillment options for your product, such as tracking inventory or back ordering a product for an order.

SKUs

When you have created your product, you create SKUs to represent each orderable item of merchandise for sale. All SKUs related to a particular product exhibit the same set of attributes and are distinguished by defining their attribute values. Create SKUs using the SKU wizard. Or you can automatically generate SKUs for a product, after you have created all required product attributes. The SKU notebook allows you to view or change SKU details, such as names, descriptions, and images, and delete SKUs from your catalog. You can update sales tax, discounts, and shipping categories, and add shipping measurements for each SKU.

Bundles and kits

Bundles and kits are groupings of catalog entries. Used for promotional purposes, the catalog entries in bundles and kits are grouped in such a way to attract customers.

Table 11-2 Kits and bundles

Kit/Bundle	Description
Prebuilt kit	A prebuilt kit is a collection of catalog entries that are not sold separately. For example, a computer prebuilt kit might contain a specific central processing unit, monitor, and hard drive. A prebuilt kit has its own price and can be added to the shopping cart. After being added to the shopping cart, the prebuilt kit contents cannot be changed. A prebuilt kit has descriptive attributes just like a product. Inventory for a prebuilt kit is independent of the inventory of its component parts. For example, selling a computer prebuilt kit does not affect the inventory of the central processing unit, monitor, and hard drive that the prebuilt kit contains.
Dynamic kit	A dynamic kit is a group of products that are ordered as a unit. The information about the products contained in a dynamic kit is controlled by an external configurator and supplied at order entry time. The definition of the components that make up the kit is not known until the kit is configured, hence the name dynamic kit. The individual components of a dynamic kit cannot be modified in the order, but they can be reconfigured by the configurator. The entire configuration must be fulfilled together.
Static kit	A static kit is also a group of products that are ordered as a unit. The information about the products contained in a static kit is predefined and controlled within WebSphere Commerce. The individual components within the order cannot be modified and must be fulfilled together. A static kit back orders if any of its components are unavailable. While a static kit cannot be viewed with the Product Management dynamic tools, it can be viewed as a prebuilt kit. A static kit has no inventory of its own. When a static kit is purchased, the inventory of its component parts is lowered. For example, if a computer is sold as a static kit and not a prebuilt kit, the inventory amounts for the central processing unit, monitor, and hard drive are be decreased when the computer is sold.
Bundle	Unlike kits, a bundle is a collection of catalog entries which customers buy with one click, as a convenience for the shopper. When a bundle is placed into the shopping cart, the cart contains the individual items, which can the customer can remove or change individually. For example, when a bundle for a computer system is a computer, a monitor, a printer, and a scanner, the bundle components can be sold separately. A bundle's price is composed by its different catalog entries. A bundle cannot be purchased directly.

Attributes

There are two types of attributes, Defining attributes and Descriptive attributes.

Defining attributes are properties of SKUs in an online store, such as color or size. Attribute values are the property of an attribute such as a specific color (blue or yellow) or size (medium). Define the attribute values of attributes before assigning them to SKUs. Each possible combination of attributes and attribute values defines a new SKU. After creating attributes and their values, you can update information such as name, description, and type (text, whole numbers, or decimal numbers). Defining attributes are also used for SKU resolution.

Descriptive attributes are simply additional descriptions. For example, some pieces of clothing should only be dry cleaned, never wash. A descriptive attribute can specify the dry clean only condition. Or if electronics equipment uses AA or AAA batteries. Descriptive attributes are not used for SKU resolution.

Pricing

You can create, list, and change pricing associated with a product or SKU. Pricing of a product or SKU is more flexible than simply setting a single price. A different price can be set for different currencies, and you can also define pricing conditions, typically quantity ranges (for example, 1 to 5, 6 or more), which must be satisfied in order to use the price.

11.2.3 Managing promotions

The Marketing Manager, often with input from the Product Manager, is responsible for the management of promotions. Promotions allow you to offer customers incentives to purchase. WebSphere Commerce supports numerous types of promotions such as price promotions including simple discounts; merchandise specials such as gifts with purchase and buy one, get one free, and service promotions including reduced shipping costs.

Promotion groups

Promotion groups, as the name implies, group promotions according to their type. These groups have no hierarchical structure, or priority. By default, each store has three promotion groups. Promotion groups serve the following two purposes:

1. All of the promotions within a group share a common set of promotion policies.
2. Promotion groups are one factor that determines the order in which promotions are evaluated to determine whether they apply to the current shopping cart or order. By default, promotions are evaluated according to their promotion group in the following order:
    a. ProductLevel group
    b. OrderLevel group
    c. Shipping group

Table 11-3 lists the promotion groups, and the promotion types that make up each group that are available with WebSphere Commerce:

Table 11-3 Promotions

Group	Type
Product-level promotions	Percentage off catalog entry X
	Fixed amount off each catalog entry X
	Fixed amount off the subtotal of all catalog entry X
	Buy catalog entry X, get catalog entry Y free
	Buy catalog entry X, get additional catalog entry X at a discount
	Percentage off product X
	Fixed amount off each SKU of product X
	Fixed amount off subtotal of product X
	Buy catalog entry from category X, get catalog entry Y free
	Buy catalog entry from category X, get additional catalog entries from category X at a discount
	Percentage off catalog entries from category X
	Fixed amount off per catalog entry from category X
	Fixed amount off on subtotal of catalog entries from category X
	Buy catalog entry X, get percentage discount off catalog entry Y
Order-level promotions	Percentage off
	Percentage off
	Free gift with purchase
Shipping promotions	Free shipping
	Discounted shipping for an order using a selected ship mode
	Discounted shipping for all items using a selected ship mode
	Discounted shipping per item using a selected ship mode

Redemption methods

You can select the redemption method associated with any promotion. The choices include:

- Qualifying purchases
- Promotion codes
- Coupons

Using these methods, you can specify how customers qualify for and apply the promotions to their orders. These options help you determine whether a customer has only to add the necessary items to their shopping cart, or whether they must know a promotion code or possess a virtual coupon. You use promotion codes and coupons to raise promotion awareness.

Exclusivity

Each promotion has an exclusivity setting. It governs how the promotion should be evaluated with respect to other promotions. For instance, you can configure a promotion so that it has one of the settings in Table 11-4.

Table 11-4 Promotion exclusivity

Setting	Resulting implementations
Combine with other promotions	The promotion is not exclusive.
Exclusive within selected groups	If the promotion is applied, no other promotions from the same group can be applied.
Exclusive within all groups	The promotion is globally exclusive, so that if the promotion is applied, no other promotion can be applied to the order.

Note that specifying an order level or shipping promotion as exclusive within the selected group effectively does nothing. By default, both of these promotion groups only allow a single promotion within the group to be applied to a single order. However, promotions in the order group are not exclusive of promotions in the shipping group, by default. The same is true for shipping promotions; they are not exclusive of promotions in the order group. This means that a customer can receive both an order level promotion, and a shipping promotion, if they qualify.

Promotion status

Promotions that are current can be in one of two states; namely Active or Inactive. New promotions are inactive by default when created. Promotions can be activated at any time. Likewise, an active promotion can be deactivated at any time.

Storefront availability

To determine whether a promotion is available, the system checks its status. If the promotion is currently in the Active state, then the evaluation continues. If the promotion is Inactive, it is considered unavailable, and is not evaluated.

The next consideration is a promotion's schedule. When a promotion is created you must define availability dates, which act as boundaries. Furthermore, when you create a promotion, you might optionally specify that the promotion is only available on one or more specific days of the week. In the same manner, you have the ability to define a promotion such that it is only available within a certain time period, such as between noon and 5:00 PM. If the current time stamp (according to the WebSphere Commerce Server) falls between the two availability dates, and meets the other optional scheduling criteria, it is considered available. Otherwise, the promotion is considered unavailable, and the promotion is not evaluated further.

Applicability to customers and shopping carts

After a promotion is determined to be available, it is evaluated to determine whether it is applicable to the current shopping cart. You can target specific customers by selecting one or more customer segments to either target or exclude during promotion creation. If the current customer is not a member of the target segment, or is a member of an excluded customer segment, then the promotion is not applicable.

You must define purchase conditions during promotion creation. These conditions can be at either the product level or the order level. For instance, if you want to offer a 10% price reduction on a product, the purchase condition would require that the customer's shopping cart contains the specific product. In the same manner, if you wanted to offer free shipping on orders totaling over $100, the purchase condition would require that the shopping cart total exceed $100.

Applicability limits

You can impose limits on your promotions' applicability in three different ways:

1. Maximum number of times that the promotion can be applied

   This limits the total number of times the promotion can be applied by all customers. For example, if you wanted to reduce inventory on some item, you might set this application limit to match the amount of the item that you have in inventory, to ensure that no one can use the promotion after the item has been cleared out.

2. Maximum number of times that the promotion can be applied to a particular qualifying order.

   If you define a value for this, it limits the total number of times that a customer can take advantage of a promotional offer at one time.

3. Maximum number of times that the promotion can be applied by a particular customer

   If you define a value for this, it limits the total number of times that a customer can take advantage of a promotional offer.

For example, if you had a gift with purchase promotion that offered a free tie when a customer buys two dress shirts, you might only want to allow a customer to apply this promotion once on any given order. Otherwise, a customer buying ten shirts might qualify for five ties. Note that by default, this application limit has no effect on order level and shipping promotions.

Applicability limits are often communicated to customers so that there are no surprises. For example, some promotions are communicated as being in effect, "While supplies last," while other limits are communicated directly, such as "Limit, two per customer." If you impose application limits on a promotion, consider including this information in any advertising messages to ensure accurate customer expectations.

Discount ranges

If required, you can define multiple discount ranges for a single promotion, which increases the amount, or percentage of a discount as the volume of the order grows. For example, when creating a percentage discount on a total order, you might create a promotion that offers a 5% discount on an order that totals less than $100, but offers a 10% discount on orders that total $100 or more. Another example might give $5 off shipping on orders that total $50, $10 off shipping for orders between $50 and $100, and free shipping on orders that total $50 or more. There is no limit on the number of ranges that can be defined for a given promotion.

Advertising your promotions

You can advertise promotions using the marketing tools in the Management Center. To do so, create content which supports the promotion, and select the content when you are assigning the advertisement to a particular eMarketing Spot. The content you create can range from simple flat text describing the promotion, to images with actions defined for how to respond when a customer clicks on them.

11.3 Protecting the Web site

Protecting your Web site from both external and internal threats is a job that must be taken very seriously. Customers must be assured that their data is safe and will not be used for purposes other than those that they approve.

Tasks described in this section include:

- "Defining security practices"
- "Managing a privacy policy"
- "Monitoring for security threats and breaches"
- "Security audits and ethical hacking"

11.3.1 Defining security practices

WebSphere Commerce provides multiple ways to make your site more secure. It is important that you know about these capabilities and utilize those that fit your particular business needs.

Authentication policies

An authentication policy is a set of rules that are applied to the authentication process and to the verification of authentication data by WebSphere Commerce. WebSphere Commerce supports account policies and other authentication-related policies, as described in the following subsections.

An account policy defines the account-related policies such as password and account lockout policies.

An account lockout policy disables a user account if malicious actions are launched against that account in order to reduce the chances that the actions compromise the account. An account lockout policy enforces the following items:

- The account lockout threshold. This is the number of invalid logon attempts before the account is disabled.
- Consecutive unsuccessful login delay. This is the time period for which the user is not allowed to login, after two failed attempts to login. The delay increments by the configured time delay value (for example, 10 seconds) with every consecutive login failure.

A password policy defines characteristics with which user passwords must comply. A password policy enforces the following conditions:

- Whether the user ID and password can match.
- Maximum occurrence of consecutive characters.
- Maximum instances of any character.

- Maximum lifetime of the passwords.
- Minimum number of alphabetic characters.
- Minimum number of numeric characters.
- Minimum length of password.
- Whether the user's previous password can be reused.
- Number of previous passwords to check against when the user selects a new password.

WebSphere Commerce ships with two default account policies: shoppers and administrators. The Site Administrator has the ability to modify those policies or create new ones.

Additional authentication-related policies that are included with WebSphere Commerce include:

- Password invalidation

  When enabled, password invalidation requires WebSphere Commerce users to change their password if the user's password has expired. In that case, the user is redirected to a page where they are required to change their password. Users are not able to access any secure pages on the site until they have changed their password.

- Password protected commands

  When the password protected commands feature is enabled, WebSphere Commerce requires registered users who are logged onto WebSphere Commerce to enter their password before continuing a request that runs designated WebSphere Commerce commands.

  Caution: When you configure the password protected commands, some of the commands shown in the command selection list can be executed by generic or guest users. Configuring such commands as password protected restricts generic and guest users from running them.

- Login time-out

  With the login time-out policy, WebSphere Commerce will log off a user that is inactive for an extended period and request they log back on to the system using the Login Timeout node. This enhancement is invoked through the WebSphere Commerce Configuration Manager and is described in detail in Enabling login timeout.

Storing sensitive data

The WebSphere Commerce database holds a quite a bit of sensitive personal information that must be safeguarded. This is usually in the form of passwords but can also contain data such as credit card numbers as well. All of this information should be stored in encrypted format. The encryption is managed by a merchant key that is defined when the instance is created. It is a 16-character hexadecimal number that is basically a big password. If this password becomes known to unscrupulous individuals, all encrypted data stored within the database is at risk.

WebSphere Commerce provides a utility that allows you to change the merchant key and thus re-encrypt all encrypted data within the database. You should use this utility on a regular basis; refer to:

```
http://publib.boulder.ibm.com/infocenter/wchelp/v6r0m0/topic/com.ibm.co
mmerce.admin.doc/tasks/tsedbupdate.htm
```

There is also a utility to store payment key information on an external, more secure device using the Key Locator Framework, refer to:

```
http://publib.boulder.ibm.com/infocenter/wchelp/v6r0m0/topic/com.ibm.co
mmerce.admin.doc/concepts/csekeylocframework.htm?resultof=%22%4b%4c%46%
22%20%22%6b%6c%66%22%20
```

11.3.2 Managing a privacy policy

Every eCommerce site should have a well defined and publicly accessible privacy policy. This is a statement to your customers of what information you ask of them, what you do with it and how you protect it. If you do not have a privacy policy that customers can read, they might not want to shop at your site.

The privacy policy should contain:

- What information you collect at what points
- If you use cookies, define what is stored in the cookies and why
- What information is shared and with whom
- Methods to "opt-in" or "opt-out" of direct mail or telemarketing campaigns
- Overview of security and encryption procedures
- Contact information so customers can report potential violations of the privacy policy
- Applicable laws governing how your store does business

11.3.3 Monitoring for security threats and breaches

The use of a good intrusion detection system (IDS) is a worth while investment if you plan to run your site yourself. If your site is to be hosted, you should talk to potential hosting companies about their investment in this technology. An intrusion detection system is used to detect several types of malicious behaviors that can compromise the security and trust of a computing platform. This includes attacks against vulnerable services, data-driven attacks on applications, host-based attacks, unauthorized Logins, and malware (viruses, trojan horses, and worms).

An IDS is comprised of several key elements:

- Sensors which detect events and post alerts
- A console to monitor alerts
- An engine that logs the alerts and contains a set of rules to categorize each alert for review on the Console

11.3.4 Security audits and ethical hacking

Other means of ensuring the security of your Web site include performing regular security audits and hiring security firms to conduct ethical hacking of your site. A security audit is a systematic technical assessment of your overall security policy to ensure that all standards, policies, and procedures are being met and followed. This should be done, possibly with the aid of an outside organization, on an annual basis. Here are some security issues that an auditor looks for:

- Are passwords difficult to crack?
- Are there access control lists in place on network devices?
- Are there audit logs in place?
- Are the security settings on operating systems in accordance with industry standards?
- Have all unnecessary applications and services been removed from all devices?
- Are the operating system, database management system, application server, Web server patched to current levels?
- Is there a disaster recovery plan in place and has it been tested?

An ethical hack or penetration test is usually conducted by an outside firm and is designed to attempt to circumvent your security protocols. While a security audit is performed with the full knowledge of all your IT staff, the penetration test is geared to gauge their reaction to external attempts to gain access to sensitive aspects of your site.

11.4 Solving customer problems

It is inevitable that some customers have problems either navigating or using your Web site. If the customer cannot successfully find or purchase their desired products, they most likely do not return.

11.4.1 Planning and training

Determine what type of customer support that you want to provide for your site. Live chat sessions are implemented by "Customer care" or a similar product as described in "Customer care" on page 350 or you can include a customer hot-line and provide remote phone support or a combination of the two.

Remote phone support operators at a call center use a product like Sales Center as described in "Sales Center" on page 351 or WebSphere Commerce Accelerator to access WebSphere commerce on behalf of customers who call in.

Sales Center provides a wide array of features for your customer service representatives (CSRs), to assist customers and Accelerator provides the following functions:

- Create new customer
- Find customer
- Find order
- Place customer order

When a customer record has been created or found, the CSR can:

- Reset the password
- Change customer profile information
- Place an order
- Modify an order
- Create a return
- Process a return

It is important to consider what types of support you want to provide and how many customer support representative you need to handle the load. When you have determined the number of people and the tools that they are to use, make sure that your staff are properly trained. You need to ensure that each customer is responded to as quickly as possible and that their concerns are resolved just as quickly.

11.4.2 Customer care

An optional feature that is available for the Professional and Enterprise editions of WebSphere Commerce is called Customer care. The customer care feature provides real-time customer service support by way of a synchronous text interface using the Lotus Sametime server. A customer entering the site can click a link titled **Live Chat with Customer Representative** in the Left Panel of the Store Page to connect to a Customer Service Representative (CSR). The two parties then chat over the Internet.

A CSR accesses the customer care interface through the WebSphere Commerce Accelerator. In addition, the CSR can view the store page where the customer needs assistance, and retrieve shopping cart and profile information.

To speed up communication with your customers, customer care supports the use of predefined lists of URLs, and topics. After creating these lists, they are available during conversations so that CSRs have accessible lists of the most commonly referenced store pages, and answers to the most commonly asked questions.

Customer care also supports multiple queues so that customers looking for help can be routed to the most appropriate queue, monitored by CSRs qualified to answer their questions. You can also configure custom messages for your waiting customers. This interface also allows the CSR to chat with other CSRs. Prior to use, Sametime must be installed and configured for use with WebSphere Commerce.

11.4.3 Sales Center

Another optional feature for the Professional and Enterprise editions of WebSphere Commerce is Sales Center. The IBM Sales Center for WebSphere Commerce manages stores, customers, organizations, orders, quotes, and payment information. The IBM Sales Center is a rich client interface which is installed on CSRs' systems.

The IBM Sales Center offers the following features for CSRs:

- Interact with WebSphere Commerce. The same store can receive orders from both the Web and an inbound call center.
- Complete the following customer service tasks:
  - Select and remove stores
  - Create, find, edit, and delete customers
  - Create, find, edit, cancel, prepare, save, submit, and view orders
  - Create, find, edit, copy, and cancel quotes
  - Add and view shipping instructions for orders
  - Add, remove, and edit payment instructions and methods for orders and quotes
  - Find, compare, and view products
  - Add products, prebuilt kits, dynamic kits, and merchandising associations
- Accomplish customer service tasks more easily and efficiently with the user interface:
  - Data fields are pre-populated with default values.
  - Dialog boxes are directly accessible from any area in the user interface.

- Dialog boxes contain concise information.
- Search results are sorted to quickly find required information.

An application developer can customize, extend, and reconfigure parts of the IBM Sales Center (such as panels, views, and dialog boxes) to meet the unique business needs of the company. The system administrator can update the IBM Sales Center automatically, and manually to apply any necessary fixes or to install updated features and plug-ins.

In addition, WebSphere Commerce provides reports on CSR performance and activities, including revenue, sales, orders, price overrides, performance ranking, profit, quotations, customer organizations, and customer territories. These reports are available for individual Customer Service Representatives or a CSR team. You can access these reports in the WebSphere Commerce Accelerator.

11.5 Applying software updates

Only an experienced Configuration manager should apply software updates. It should be done with standardized scripts according to set procedures to ensure that it is done correctly, repeatably, and with minimal disruption of operations. Applying software updates to a WebSphere Commerce implementation can take several forms:

- "Managing the software stack"
- "Applying WebSphere Commerce Feature Packs"
- "Customizing WebSphere Commerce"

11.5.1 Managing the software stack

The release of any software has the potential of introducing bugs. You, or your hosting company, need standardized procedures to successfully identify and deploy fixes to components of the software stack.

Components of the software stack

Fixes might be required at any level within the software stack; for example:

- Operating system
- Database management system
- Web server
- Application server
- Application server plug-in
- WebSphere Commerce

Identifying fixes

Fixes are applied in a proactive or reactive manner. If you have identified a problem in the site's operation, you should follow standard troubleshooting procedures to determine whether a fix is required. For more information about troubleshooting a WebSphere Commerce implementation, see Chapter 12, "Troubleshoot your eCommerce site" on page 359. You should also check for new fixes being made available on a periodic basis in order to avoid potential downtime on your site.

To locate new fixes that are available for IBM HTTP Server, refer to:

`http://www-306.ibm.com/software/webservers/httpservers/support/`

To locate new fixes that are available for WebSphere Application Server, refer to:

`http://www-306.ibm.com/software/webservers/appserv/was/support/`

To locate new fixes that are available for WebSphere Commerce, refer to:

`http://www-306.ibm.com/software/genservers/commerce/wcbe/support/`

To locate new fixes that are available for DB2, refer to:

`http://www-1.ibm.com/support/docview.wss?rs=71&uid=swg21256235`

You can also subscribe to IBM Software Support RSS feeds in order to actively monitor the release of software fixes for IBM products, refer to:

`http://www-306.ibm.com/software/support/rss/`

Deploying fixes

When deploying fixes, be sure to deploy them to a test environment before they are deployed to your production environment. Fixes have been known to introduce new problems as well as correcting existing ones. Always read the Readme file that accompanies each fix. It provides valuable information about what is fixed and the proper procedure for installing the fix. Define a procedure for introducing new fixes and continually revise it as needed.

1. Identify a problem or potential problem.
2. Download the fix or fix pack.
3. Read all materials available.
4. Backup your test environment.
5. Deploy the fix to a test environment that mirrors your production environment.
6. Test to ensure that the problem has been corrected.
7. Perform a full regression test to ensure that no new problems have been introduced.

8. Schedule a time of minimal traffic to your site to deploy the fix.

   Depending upon the scope of the fix, you might need to take your site off-line.
9. Ensure that you have a back out plan in case the fix does not work or causes new problems.
10. At the appointed time, backup your production environment.
11. Deploy the fix to production.
12. Test the fix.
13. Perform a regression test.

If the testing is successful, resume normal operations. If the testing fails, implement your back out plan.

11.5.2 Applying WebSphere Commerce Feature Packs

With the announcement of WebSphere Commerce v6.0, IBM has extended the major release cycle. In between major releases, IBM releases occasional Feature Packs. As of this writing, IBM has released three feature packs for v6.0.

A feature pack contains one or more new components that customers can choose to add to their existing implementations. This is new functionality, as opposed to the corrections that are included in fix packs. While IBM recommends that customers load all fix packs, customers are free to load feature packs or individual components of feature packs as needed.

The Feature Packs that have been released to date include these:

- WebSphere Commerce Feature Pack 1 version 1.0
  - Coremetrics enhanced Web analytics
  - JCA Connectors for Web Services
- WebSphere Commerce Feature Pack 2 version 1.0
  - Component services
  - Coremetrics e-mail analytics for WebSphere Commerce
  - Coremetrics analytics for WebSphere Commerce Sales Center
  - WebSphere Portal integration
  - Enabling Sitemaps integration
  - Paymentech plug-in
- WebSphere Commerce Feature Pack 3 version 3.0
  - IBM Management center for WebSphere Commerce
  - A sample catalog that features baby and children's clothing, showcasing the following pre-loaded sample Web activities:
    - Recommend the catalog's top category on the store's home page

    - Recommend some of the catalog's best selling items on the store's home page
    - Advertise a "Buy X and get Y free" promotion
    - Advertise a "Buy X and then recommend Y in the shopping cart page" promotion
    - Advertise a "20% off a category" promotion
  - eMarketing Spot JSP snippets for displaying Web activities created using the Management Center
- WebSphere Commerce Feature Pack 3 version 3.0.1
  - Customization of Management Center

To check for the release of new Feature Packs, go to the following URL:

`http://www-1.ibm.com/support/docview.wss?uid=swg24013534`

11.5.3 Customizing WebSphere Commerce

Most WebSphere Commerce implementations contain custom code. The platform is designed to make customizations easy. As business requirements change over time, there might be a need to create more customizations to the base code of WebSphere Commerce.

WebSphere Commerce is a Java and J2EE compliant application. To successfully customize WebSphere Commerce you should have knowledge and skills in the following: programming SQL, Java, JavaScript, HTML, XML. You should also be familiar with developing and deploying Java servlets and JavaServer Pages in dynamic Web applications. In addition, you should have a basic understanding of Rational Application Developer.

Developing customizations

There are a great many ways to customize a WebSphere Commerce implementation. You can develop custom:

- Data assets
- Store pages
- Store business logic
- Integrations with back-end and external systems

You can also customize WebSphere Commerce tools like these:

- Loading utilities
- Promotions engine
- Accelerator
- Gift Center
- Sales Center

Deploying customizations

When you deploy customized assets for WebSphere Commerce, there are two stages: packaging and deploying.

1. Package:

   The first stage is twofold: compiling and then packaging:

   - Compiling involves taking source from your source code management system, and building or compiling it into the binaries that are required by the target server environment. For example, you can take your .java files and compile them into .class files.
   - Packaging involves taking the output of the build process and creating deployment packages for your target environment. For J2EE assets, the format of your packaging varies depending on the type of objects: a single file, a partial application, or an entire module.

2. Deploy:

   In this stage, the deployment packages are actually copied to the target server environment. This process makes the assets created in the build process ready to be executed in the target environment. Each target environment has a set of tools that are used to deploy of the packages.

WebSphere Commerce deployment checklist

The WebSphere Commerce deployment checklist is based on lessons learned from IBM internal groups, external customers and IBM Business Partners deploying WebSphere Commerce-based solutions.

- Access control:
  - Is access control on commands and on JSP pages applied appropriately?
  - Is access to administration tools (WebSphere Commerce Accelerator, Administration Console and Organization Administration Console) outside the firewall properly configured, or disabled?
  - Are the right subset of roles assigned to the right set of administrators? Do any passwords need to be reset?
- Database:
  - Is the production database free from test data, or erroneous data?
  - Are the database statistics up-to-date?
  - Are the database configuration and tuning parameters signed off by the Database Administrator (DBA)?
- Caching:
  - Is the cachespec.xml file set up appropriately for caching and invalidation?

- Are the caches primed (pre-populated) to maximize response times?
- Is the Web server cache and edge server cache configured and properly loaded?

- Integration:
  - If a back-end system is unavailable, or too slow to respond, is there a alternative solution in place?
- Store pages:
  - Is the final artwork and store JSP pages approved?
  - Are the error JSP pages meaningful and helpful for the customer?
- Initial data load:
  - Are the final catalog updates loaded and verified?
  - Are the final prices and inventory levels loaded and verified?
  - Are the right set of contracts deployed?
- Campaigns:
  - Are the right set of campaign activities Active?
- Site monitoring:
  - Are the system administrators aware of how to tell if the site is working well or if the site is experiencing problems?
  - Is there a plan to monitor resource utilization (CPU, disk, memory)?
  - As traffic increases, is the site's expected breaking point known?
  - Are the right WebSphere Application Server logs turned on?
  - Is an appropriate level of WebSphere Commerce logging turned on?
- Reporting:
  - Is there a need to turn on the User Traffic Log?
  - Is there a need to turn on the Marketing Event Monitors?
  - Are the right Web server logs turned on?
- Backup and recovery:
  - Is there an available backup of the production site database, customized code, and configuration parameters?
  - Is a disaster recovery plan in place?
  - Is there a plan for how the site will be managed in the case where the site needs to be brought down temporarily or for an extended period of time?

- Upgrades and fixes:
  - Is a regular maintenance window planned?
  - Is there a plan for how upgrades and fixes will be applied to the site?
  - Is there a plan for how emergency updates will be made to the catalog (products or prices)?
- Development, test, staging and production:
  - Have you confirmed that key functionality, scripts, processes work the same way in the production environment as they did in the test environment?

12

Troubleshoot your eCommerce site

This chapter provides guidance with troubleshooting problems on your WebSphere Commerce site. The first step is to localize the problem. When the source of the problem has been identified, there are various paths to follow to identify a solution.

There are few articles on approaches to debugging, but there is a good one in IBM developerWorks by Terrence Parr, Professor of Computer Science, University of San Francisco, *"Learn the essentials of debugging. Systematically take on mysterious errors with confidence"*, found at:

`http://www.ibm.com/developerworks/web/library/wa-debug.html`

Professor Parr concludes that there are six essential elements to debugging:

- Reproducibility:

  Find a way to reproduce a problem reliably.
- Reduction:

  Reduce a problem to its essence.
- Deduction:

  What can you deduce from reliably reproducing the problem?

- Experimentation:

  Test whether your deductions are necessary and sufficient.

- Experience:

  There is no substitute for experience, not only generic professional experience doing debugging, but also knowing the history of the Web site, and tapping into experience of colleagues working on the Web site.

- Tenacity:

  It is very rare to be faced with a solution to a software problem and not think *"If only I had tried ..."*

In "Define the problem!" on page 364, we shall look at an example, and see how these elements help you work through a problem.

12.1 Problem symptoms

There are many different symptoms for problems that are encountered on a WebSphere Commerce site. Often times a symptom does not lead to the source of the problem in a straightforward manner. Here are some examples of problem symptoms:

- General site-wide slow performance
- Localized slow performance
- Site-wide lack of response
- Lack of response on a particular URL
- Incorrect content displayed on site
- Content updates not being correctly displayed
- Functionality such as promotions, taxes, shipping, order totals not calculated correctly
- Exceptions or warnings in the log files

Upon encountering the problem symptoms, the next step is to gather the appropriate data for problem determination.

12.2 Data to gather

If you have encountered problem symptoms but are not sure what is causing the problem the first place to look is the SystemOut.log:

```
WebSphere/AppServer/profiles/profileName/logs/server1/SystemOut.log
```

Open the SystemOut.log in a text editor. Scan down through the log. Errors are easily found by searching in the text editor with the string ' E '.

The end of the start-up sequence is indicated by this message:

```
Server server1 open for e-business
```

There are a couple of exceptions that appear in the start-up sequence of the SystemOut.log that can safely be ignored:

```
WebApp E Error while adding servlet mapping.
```

and

```
MetaDataLoade E loadWebContainerPorts could not find any http or https
ports
```

If there are any other errors in the server start-up before reaching the 'server1 open for e-business' message that is a sign that the server did not start-up properly. All of these errors should be addressed first before investigating any exceptions that occur later on in the SystemOut.log. In this case proceed to 12.3, "Analyzing data" on page 363.

12.2.1 Functional problem

If there are no exceptions in the SystemOut.log and it is a functional problem particular to one of the WebSphere Commerce components such as tax calculation, first take a look at the WebSphere Commerce *Must gather* documentation to see if the problematic component is covered.

Must gather: Read first for all WebSphere Commerce products

`http://www-1.ibm.com/support/docview.wss?uid=swg21206092`

If the problematic component is not covered in the WebSphere Commerce Must gather document then it is probably a good idea to enable some additional tracing for that component and reproduce the problem.

Enabling tracing

`http://publib.boulder.ibm.com/infocenter/wchelp/v6r0m0/index.jsp?topic=/com.ibm.commerce.payments.doc/tasks/tvvenabtrace.htm`

Trace components

`http://publib.boulder.ibm.com/infocenter/wchelp/v6r0m0/index.jsp?topic=/com.ibm.commerce.admin.doc/refs/rlslogging.htm`

Do not turn on all of the tracing components at once. This creates way too much data for it to be useful for analysis. Instead, focus on the component that you need more information about. The only trace component that it is useful to have enabled in conjunction with the component specific trace is the WC_SERVER trace because this shows all requests that are being processed. When you have done this, collect these two logs:

```
WebSphere/AppServer/profiles/profileName/logs/server1/SystemOut.log
WebSphere/AppServer/profiles/profileName/logs/server1/trace.log
```

Then proceed to 12.3, "Analyzing data" on page 363

12.2.2 Non-functional problem

If there are no exceptions in the SystemOut.log and it is a non-functional problem such as performance degradation or site-wide outage then the next step is to review the WebSphere Application Server *Must gather* document:

Must gather: Read first for all WebSphere Application Server products:

`http://www-1.ibm.com/support/docview.wss?uid=swg21145599`

The WebSphere Application Server *Must gather* document gives you instructions about which trace to enable and which logs to gather in order to debug problems in different WebSphere Application Server components. The types of logs that you gather following the *Must gathe*r instructions help you to identify if the problem is in the Web server tier, application server tier (WebSphere Application Server or the application itself, WebSphere Commerce) or the database tier. When the problem is better localized, you might need to collect different traces and logs. These steps are detailed in the *Must gather* documents.

12.3 Analyzing data

When you have collected the appropriate logs while the problem is occurring, you can open a PMR and send the data to IBM support for analysis. This is covered in 12.4, "WebSphere Commerce support". However, if you are interested in trying to resolve the problem on your own first, here are some tips on the problem determination process and tools that you can use.

12.3.1 Background questions

After you have encountered a problem in your system, there are some questions to ask yourself.

What has changed?

> **Note:** It is important to keep track of any and all changes made on the site. Even if they do not appear to be related to the problem that is occurring do not dismiss their importance.

For any problem that appears to have just started that did not exist before, or for any problems that are intermittent, look for what changed to the site and might have caused or exposed the problem. If you have kept logs of all activity (see 11.1.1, "Administering the Web site" on page 326) this is very much easier. Try and correlate the problem appearance with an unusual event, or recurring events in the log.

- Code push?
- Fix Pack or APAR update to any of the software on the site?
- Hardware change?
- Business content update?
- Particular time of day?

Are there any jobs (chron jobs, data loads, stage prop, DBClean, communications with external systems, or scheduled jobs) that are running simultaneous with when the problem occurs that might be creating or adding to the problem?

Can developers or testers help?

Ask developers and testers whether the problem "rings any bells". Were there any test cases or problems outstanding at the end of test? In the case of a functional problem, was this scenario properly tested before putting it on production? Even if the answer is yes, was some new function added or changed which might be related to the problem. Perhaps the problem suggests a test scenario that was not tried.

Can you reproduce the problem on a test system?

Does the same exception or behavior occur on your development, testing and staging environment? If not, what is different? Do the databases contain the same data as the production database?

Performance beyond specification?

For a performance problem, do the current volumes fall within your predicted capacity based on your performance tests?

Define the problem!

How many times have you exhausted all avenues of solving a bug by yourself, and decided to take a break, gone to visit the coffee machine and met a colleague there. You start to describe the problem, and before you are half way through (and the colleague has said nothing) you say, oh! I know ... and you make another step forward.

Possibly by relaxing, you unlocked other areas of your brain to work on the problem (there is evidence for this). However, and just as important, you have stepped back from the details and looked again at the bigger picture, questioned your assumptions, and organized your observations and thoughts to describe the problem to someone else.

Consider these two imperatives:

1. Look at the bigger picture. What else is going on, what does this problem remind me of?
2. Define the problem carefully. Be very precise about what you definitely know, why you think you know it, and what you are guessing at or interpolating from the known facts.

These two imperatives are the two poles of debugging; as you triangulate between them, you hope to net down to the problem.

Problem definition example

Let us look at an example of how to properly define a problem using the debugging elements suggested by Professor Parr. For example, a definition of a problem might be:

```
We have created a promotion and it does not behave as expected. The
problem is repeatable for each promotion we create.
```

Reproducible

Deduction

Experience

Reduction

The problem is reproducible - that is a very good start. What can we deduce from it? One deduction is that there is some kind of defect in the promotion creation code in WebSphere Commerce Accelerator. Is that really likely? No, WebSphere Commerce Accelerator does create promotions successfully - we must have tested it too, but perhaps we applied a bad fix or perhaps we are not running the copy of WebSphere Commerce Accelerator we think we are. It is a worth a quick scan and an ask-around to see if there is a chance something is awry with WebSphere Commerce Accelerator, Did we test it? If nothing turns up quickly, we would be better spending our time trying to reduce the problem to identify what we are doing differently. What is it about our way of creating promotions that is specific?

Let us get away from the details and think about the bigger picture. What else is going on here? What else is involved in creating these promotions and displaying them on the Web site that is specific to these promotions, but might have nothing to do with the actual task of creating them? In our example it turns out that these are not simple "out-of-the-box" promotions, but have been customized.

```
The promotions are customized promotions that are being loaded manually
into the database.
```

Deduction

With this background information it seems less likely that WebSphere Commerce Accelerator is the problem and it seems more likely that the promotions data being loaded is the source of the problem.

Experimentation

Now try creating "out-of-the-box" promotions and see if they work. If they do, it looks a lot more likely the problem is to do with loading customized promotions into the database. Perhaps that was never tested?

There is still a lot to do in this problem definition, and in the end it might turn out to be a bug in IBM code rather than in operating procedures, user input, or customized code. But the time you have spent defining the problem is not wasted — IBM support might well guide you through the same procedure anyhow, and the information you are able to provide is likely to be more valuable to the support engineers than say a trace of the "Create promotion" task, when the problem actually lay in a quite different piece of code you might not have traced.

The time to call for support is when you have successfully reduced the problem to an interface with WebSphere Commerce by a process of elimination or reduction, or the evidence (such as a trace) is pointing at IBM code, or you are unable to make any more headway. But there is one more possibility to try before calling support. The IBM Support Assistant.

12.3.2 IBM Support Assistant (ISA)

ISA is a thick client based on the open source Eclipse platform. It is a free workbench that consolidates many tools and utilities to assist you with problem solving. These are the same resources used by IBM support to troubleshoot problems. There are plug-ins available for many IBM products which are installable at any time. ISA allows you to:

- Search for an answer to your question or problem in many different locations at the same time (that is, Technotes, InfoCenter, developerWorks, Redbooks, Google search).
- Get speedy access to critical product information.
- Run free troubleshooting and diagnostic tools on your problematic application.
- Shorten the amount of time it takes to resolve your problem with automated data gathering and submission.

Download the IBM Support Assistant from:

`http://www-306.ibm.com/software/support/isa/`

After you have installed ISA, you need to add the WebSphere Commerce plug-in to access the product specific resources. From the main page on ISA (Figure 12-1) install product specific resources by clicking **Updater**.

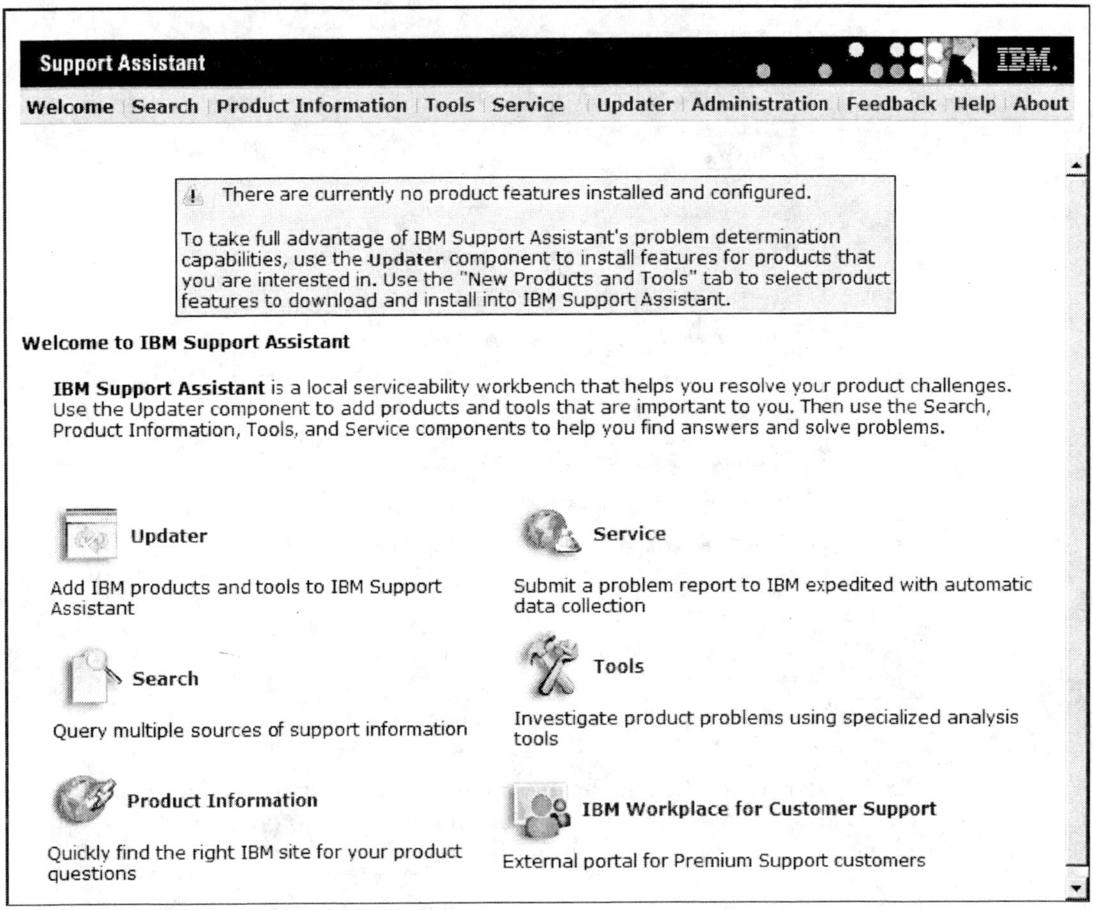

Figure 12-1 IBM Support Assistant main menu

On the **Updater** page, click the **New Plug-ins** tab. On the **New Plug-ins** panel select and install the plug-ins for products that you're working with, especially:

- WebSphere:
  - WebSphere Application Server V6.0
  - WebSphere Commerce Server
- Common Component Tools:
  - IBM Guided Activity Assistant (IGAA)
  - IBM Pattern Modeling and Analysis Tool for Java Garbage Collector
  - Memory Dump Diagnostic for Java (MDD4J)
  - ThreadAnalyzer

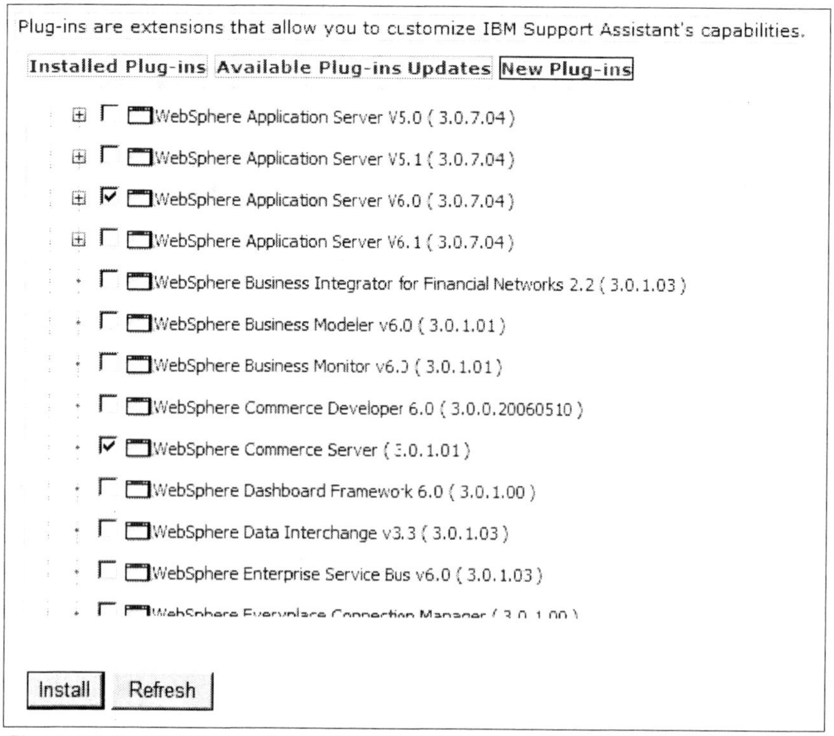

Figure 12-2 IBM Support Assistant New Plug-ins panel

Downloading and installing these plug-ins might take a bit of time, so it is a good idea to install and configure ISA before you run into a problem. That way when you need to access information ISA is ready and waiting to help you.

Let us go through an example of solving a problem using ISA.

Problem definition

While trying to create a category level promotion in WebSphere Commerce Accelerator (Figure 12-3) we get an error that says: "*The categories listed below are being removed because they do not match with the categories in the current database. Click search to find valid categories. Salt.*" as shown in Figure 12-4.

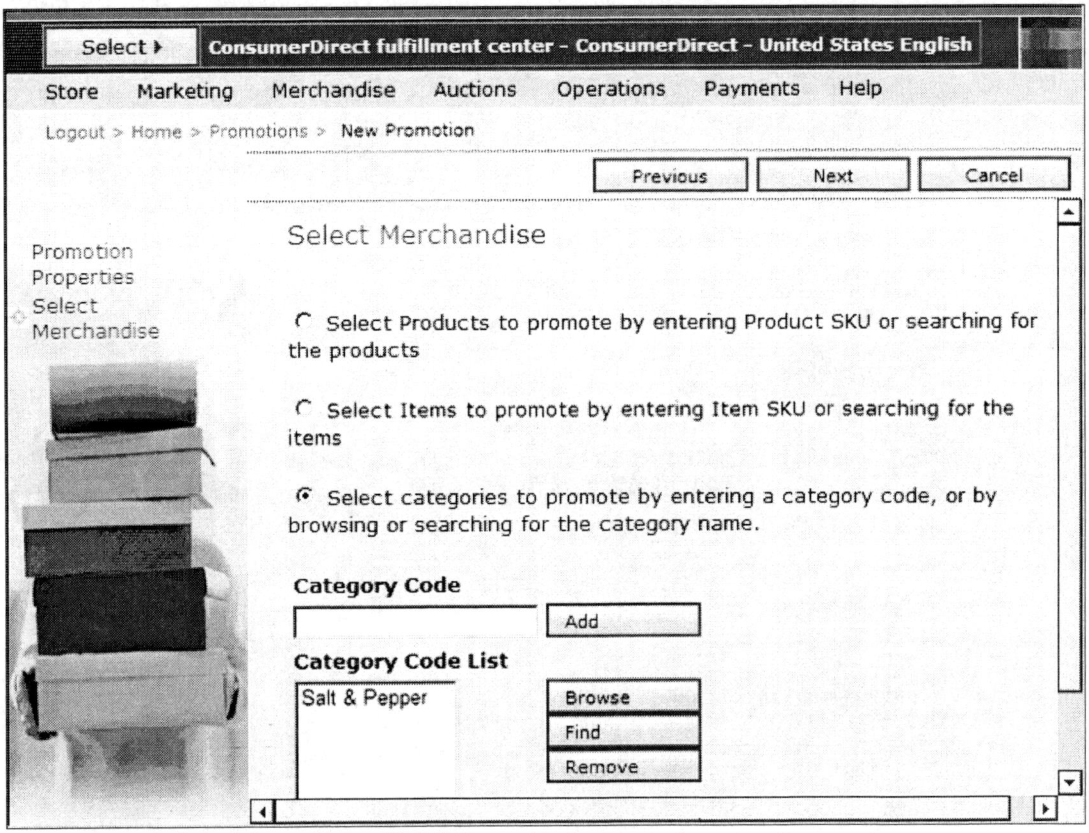

Figure 12-3 Selected the category 'Salt & Pepper' to feature in the promotion

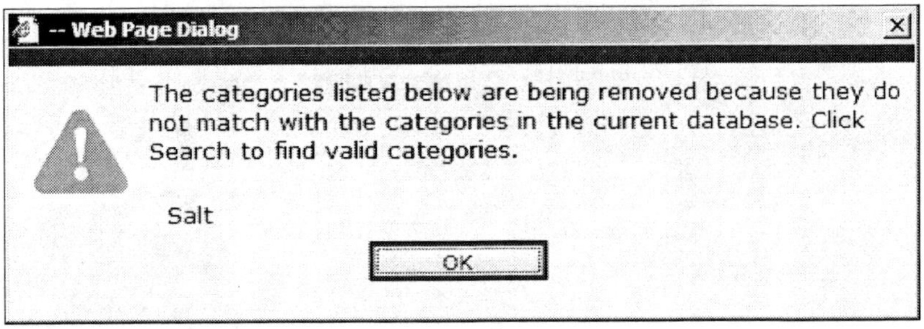

Figure 12-4 Example promotions exception

Reduction

Notice here that WebSphere Commerce Accelerator thinks that the category is named *Salt* but it is named *Salt & Pepper*. The category name is being truncated somewhere. Perhaps there is a problem with the spaces in the category name, or else maybe the ampersand character (&) is the problem.

Experience

In ISA open up the **Search** tab. Since we got an exception while trying to create a promotion we search on the term *promotion* and click **Select All**. Without specifying any limits this returns 940 results. We get better results when we use the filter. As shown in Figure 12-5 on page 370, for the search locations select only:

- IBM Software Support Documents
  - specific document type
    - IBM Technotes

To limit the products under which we search, under **Limit search by products** select only:

- WebSphere Commerce
  - specific versions
    - 6.0

When searching with these filters ISA now narrows down the results returned to three technotes (Figure 12-6).

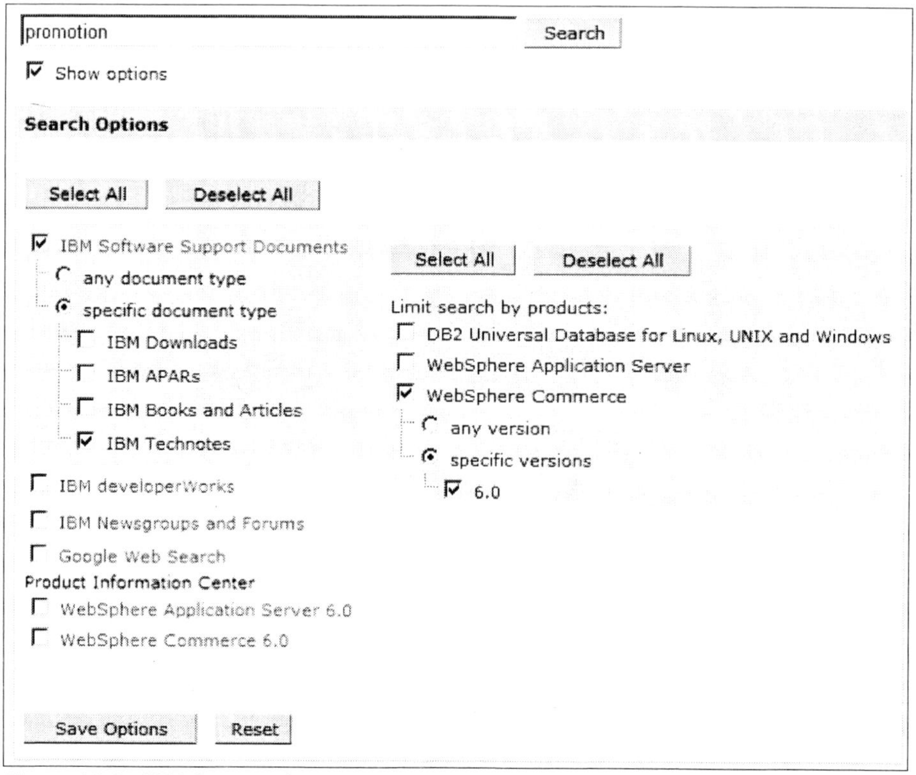

Figure 12-5 IBM Support Assistant search options

Clicking through them ,the first and third technotes do not seem relevant to solving our problem. However, the second Technote does seem relevant: *"Creating a promotion fails for categories if the category name contains special characters"*.

`http://www-1.ibm.com/support/docview.wss?uid=swg21266916`

Experiment

Based on the above technote it looks like there is a reasonably good chance that APAR JR25944 resolves our problem. We can further test this assumption by eliminating the special character. If this proves positive we can choose to apply the fix. We can either contact WebSphere Commerce Support to get the APAR or we can upgrade our WebSphere Commerce installation to Fix Pack 6.0.0.3 or higher to resolve our problem.

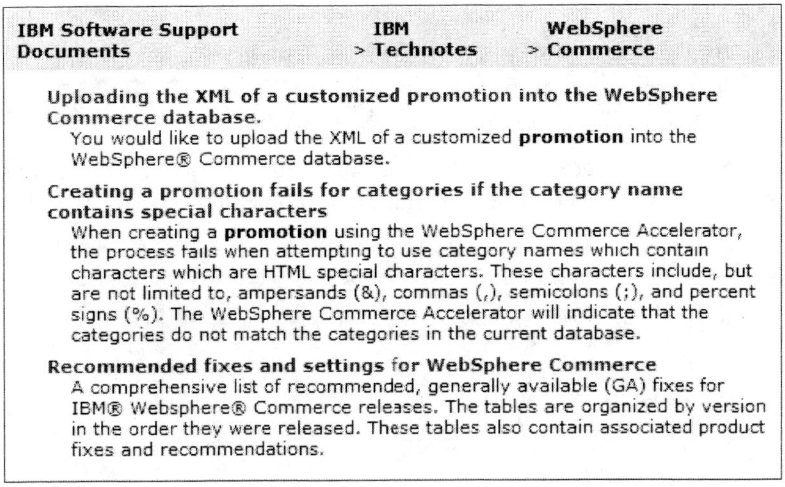

IBM Software Support Documents **IBM > Technotes** **WebSphere > Commerce**

Uploading the XML of a customized promotion into the WebSphere Commerce database.
You would like to upload the XML of a customized **promotion** into the WebSphere® Commerce database.

Creating a promotion fails for categories if the category name contains special characters
When creating a **promotion** using the WebSphere Commerce Accelerator, the process fails when attempting to use category names which contain characters which are HTML special characters. These characters include, but are not limited to, ampersands (&), commas (,), semicolons (;), and percent signs (%). The WebSphere Commerce Accelerator will indicate that the categories do not match the categories in the current database.

Recommended fixes and settings for WebSphere Commerce
A comprehensive list of recommended, generally available (GA) fixes for IBM® Websphere® Commerce releases. The tables are organized by version in the order they were released. These tables also contain associated product fixes and recommendations.

Figure 12-6 ISA filtered search results

In addition to the advanced search capabilities that ISA provides, ISA also provides access to a lot of useful tools and information:

- Debugging tools that can be used to solve performance scenarios such as hangs, crashes and Out of memory.
- Access to IBM Education Assistant (IEA). IEA is a collection of multimedia educational modules designed to help you gain a better understanding of IBM software products. There are many tutorials that provide step by step guidance on how to debug many common issues.
- Access to Electronic Service Request (ESR) to be able to open, update and manage your PMRs online. More on this in 12.4.2, "Electronic Service Request (ESR)".

Try to make use of these resources to learn about the product and how to debug and resolve problems yourself. IBM Support is fast and effective. However, you will find as you become more competent with WebSphere Commerce that it can be even faster if you resolve the problem yourself.

12.4 WebSphere Commerce support

You have a detailed problem description. You have gathered the logs. You have tried resolving the problem yourself using the many resources available to you, such as the IBM Support Assistant. However, so far you have been unsuccessful. It sounds like it is time to open a Problem Management Record (PMR) with IBM support.

IBM has prepared a document that provides guidelines and reference materials that are useful when receiving assistance from IBM service and support. This handbook has been produced with the following objectives in mind:

- To introduce you to IBM Software Support, including our operating systems and software divisions of DB2, Lotus, Rational, Tivoli, and WebSphere.
- Provide information about the support services currently available from IBM, including definitions of programs, policies, and procedures.
- Help you to effectively utilize IBM Software Support.
- Explain how you can enhance your IBM Software Support with additional services to meet your needs.
- Introduce you to the people of IBM Software Support.

Find the IBM Software Support Handbook at:

`http://techsupport.services.ibm.com/guides/handbook.html`

12.4.1 Before you open a PMR

There a couple of actions that you can take before opening a PMR that speed up the time it takes for IBM to resolve your problem.

- Take down a detailed problem description with background information, as described in 12.3, "Analyzing data" on page 363. This can include a document containing steps to reproduce the problem illustrated with screen shots.
- Identify the appropriate severity for the PMR. The WebSphere Commerce support team prioritizes PMRs based on your assigned severity. Opening all PMRs as severity 1 does not win you friends on the support team.

The severity definitions used by IBM are listed in Table 12-1. Here are some example classifications:

Severity 1	Unable to start production WebSphere Commerce server.
Severity 2	Problems loading new products into the catalog.
Severity 3	Assistance with custom command implementation
Severity 4	How to plan for a WebSphere Commerce migration?

- Provide detailed system information including:
  - WebSphere Commerce version and Fix Pack level
  - Operating System
  - Database type, version and Fix Pack level
  - WebSphere Application Server version and Fix Pack level
  - List of existing APARs applied to WebSphere Commerce and WebSphere Application Server
  - Details of any related customizations including source code
- If you have been following a *Must gather* document, then gather up all of the tracing and logs that you have generated when reproducing the problem.

PMRs can be opened the traditional way by calling the IBM 1-800 number. However, many customers are quickly adopting the new PMR management tool called ESR. Another tool that is fast becoming the tool of choice for remote assistance is IBM Assist On-site (AOS). We review both in the following sections.

When you talk to the IBM support specialist, tell them:

- If you are under business deadline pressure
- Your availability (that is, when you will be available to work with IBM Software Support)
- Whether you can be reached at more than one phone number
- A knowledgeable alternate contact with whom we can speak
- If you have other open problems (PMRs/Incidents) with IBM regarding this service request
- If you are participating in an early support program
- That you have researched this situation prior to calling IBM and have detailed information or documentation to provide for the problem

Severity levels and goals

Table 12-1 lists the severity levels and response time goals for problems raised with IBM. IBM will use commercially reasonable efforts to respond to service calls from your authorized callers within two hours during normal country business hours. Our initial response might result in resolution of your request, or it will form the basis for determining what additional actions might be required to achieve technical resolution of your request.

Table 12-1 Severity definitions and goals.

Severity	Impact	Response goal
1	Critical	Within two hours
2	Significant	Within two business hours
3	Some	Within two business hours
4	Minimum	Within two business hours

12.4.2 Electronic Service Request (ESR)

ESR is an IBM online tool that you can use to submit and manage PMRs. It is free and very handy.

- You are given the opportunity to provide detailed problem description, problem severity and upload files to your PMR. This can help speed up problem resolution.
- You can specify your preferred method of communication: phone, email or via ESR updates.
- You can makes updates to the PMR at any time and be notified by email when updates are made to your PMR.
- You can view updates made to the PMR by the support analyst working your PMR.

If you have already installed ISA then you already have quick access to ESR by clicking on the **Service** tab on the main ISA page. In fact, ISA provides the additional assistance of automated, product specific, collection of data that is convenient to upload to a newly created PMR.

If you are not using ISA you can still access ESR independently online. Whether accessing ESR through ISA or directly online you need to set-up your ESR account before being able to use it. The following link provides details for accessing ESR, setting up your ESR account and using ESR.

`http://www-306.ibm.com/software/support/probsub.html`

12.4.3 IBM Assist On-site (AOS)

AOS is a secure application that is installed temporarily and allows an IBM support analyst to view your desktop and share control of your mouse and keyboard. The support analyst working your PMR might ask you for remote access to your system using this tool because for certain problems it can eliminate communication inefficiencies and can drastically speed up problem resolution. IBM Assist On-site is found at,

`http://www-1.ibm.com/support/assistonsite/`

Part 5

Appendixes

A

Solution Outline Template

The solution outline template described here is a customized working document used by the IBM Software Services for WebSphere (ISSW) and IBM Global Business Services (GBS) consulting organizations to describe the outline of a WebSphere Commerce solution as input to the solution architecture and project plan. In terms of the Rational Unified Process, it is customized from the Software Development Plan and the Software Architecture Document.

1. Document Control
    a. Document Source
    b. Approval
    c. Distribution
    d. Structure of this document
    e. Acknowledgements
2. Introduction
    a. Document Goals
    b. Project Design and Development Methodology
    c. Project Milestones
        i. Solution Outline Phase
        ii. Macro Design Phase
        iii. Micro Design Phase
        iv. Build/Development Phase
        v. Deployment Phase
        vi. Evaluation Phase

d. Project Skills Requirements
    i. WebSphere Commerce developer
    ii. Project Manager
    iii. IT Technical Lead (Customer
    iv. Business Process Lead (Customer)
    v. Service Catalog Owner (Customer)
    vi. Server Installer
    vii. Performance Analyst
    viii. Application Software Installer
    ix. Database Administrator
    x. Web Designer
    xi. Network Administrator
    xii. Other Integration Specialist
    xiii. Security Analyst
    xiv. Build/Deploy Specialist
    xv. Test Automation Specialist
    xvi. Web Services Specialist

3. Project Requirements
    a. Customer Requirements
    b. Out of Scope Requirements
4. System Context Diagram
5. Solution Architecture Overview
    a. Business Model
    b. Storyboards
    c. Store Flow
    d. Administrative Tool
    e. Key Architectural Decisions and Development Components
    f. System Integration Components
6. Operational Model
    a. Production Environment
    b. Staging/QA Environment
    c. Development Environment
7. Non-Functional Requirements
    a. Reference documents
    b. Browser supported
    c. Performance guideline
    d. Storage requirement
    e. Security requirement
    f. Availability
    g. Monitoring the application
    h. Database maintenance requirements

i. Backup and recovery strategy
j. Testing tools

B

Business Vision Template

The Business Vision document captures very high-level objectives of a business development effort. It provides input to the project-approval and requirements process. It communicates the fundamental "why and what" related to the project, and is a gauge against which all future decisions should be validated. The Business Vision document is to be read by managers, funding authorities, business analysts, and developers in general.

The Business Vision Template is part of the Rational Unified Process, and a Microsoft Word version of the full template is shipped with Rational Method Composer v7.2.

We have summarized the contents of the template in Table B-1, but encourage you to find out more about using Rational Method Composer to document your software development process, and to have access to all the method descriptions which are available help you customize your process.

Table B-1 Business vision template

Section	Sub-section	Example content
Introduction	Purpose	What is the vision aiming to achieve?
	Scope	What projects are affected
	Summary	What is in the document
	Definitions	Unfamiliar and specialized terms, acronyms

Section	Sub-section	Example content
Opportunity	Description	Brief description of the opportunity
	Problems being tackled (multiple)	Description
		Who is affected
		What is the impact
		Benefits of solution
	Position to other channels (multiple)	For (customer segment)
		Need or Opportunity
		Benefit
		Overlap/differentiation
	Stakeholder and Customer descriptions	Relationship to company
		Description
		Main interest in solution
		Success criteria
		Deliverables required
Objective	List objectives	Description
Priorities	List of priorities	Define priorities of different objectives
Other requirements	Development objectives	Time / Cost
		Outsourcing
	Applicable standards	Corporate / Brand
		Accessibility
		Privacy and security
	Project Objectives	Availability
		Throughput
		Response times
	Financial objectives	Browse/Buy ration
		Visitors
		Revenue / Profit / Return

Related publications

The publications listed in this section are considered particularly suitable for a more detailed discussion of the topics covered in this book.

WebSphere Commerce

- WebSphere Commerce Product Information:

  http://www-306.ibm.com/software/info1/WebSphere/index.jsp?tab=products/commerce
- WebSphere Commerce v6 Documentation (InfoCenter):

  http://publib.boulder.ibm.com/infocenter/wchelp/v6r0m0/index.jsp
- WebSphere Commerce v6 Supported Stack:

  http://www-1.ibm.com/support/docview.wss?rs=3046&uid=swg21243500
- WebSphere Commerce Document Library:

  http://www-306.ibm.com/software/genservers/commerce/wcbe/library/lit-tech-general-en.html
- *"Best practices and tools for creating WebSphere Commerce sites"*, SG24-6699

  http://www.redbooks.ibm.com/abstracts/sg246699.html
- *"Mastering DynaCache in WebSphere Commerce"*, SG24-7393:

  http://www.redbooks.ibm.com/abstracts/sg247393.html
- *"Improve WebSphere Commerce performance with dynamic caching"*

  http://www-128.ibm.com/developerworks/WebSphere/library/tutorials/0507_crick/0507_crick_reg.html
- *"IBM Sales Center With Computer Telephony Integration"*, REDP-4315-00:

  http://www.redbooks.ibm.com/abstracts/redp4315.html?Open
- *"Getting Started with Commerce Module for OmniFind Discovery Edition Customization 101"*, SG24-7358-00:

  http://www.redbooks.ibm.com/abstracts/sg247358.html?Open

- *"Deploying and Customizing IBM Sales Center for WebSphere Commerce V6"*, SG24-7249-00:

  http://www.redbooks.ibm.com/abstracts/sg247249.html?Open"

- *"Remodeling a Standard Store into the Extended Sites Model With WebSphere Commerce Business Edition V5.6.1"*, REDP-4091-00:

  http://www.redbooks.ibm.com/abstracts/redp4091.html?Open

- *"Shipping Simplified: Integrating WebSphere Commerce with Third-party Shipping Providers"*, REDP-3910-00:

  http://www.redbooks.ibm.com/abstracts/redp3910.html?Open

- developerWorks WebSphere Commerce zone:

  http://www.ibm.com/developerworks/WebSphere/zones/commerce/

- WebSphere Commerce discussion forums:

  http://www.ibm.com/developerworks/forums/forum.jspa?forumID=284

- *"Optimizing your WebSphere Commerce online store for Apple iPhone browser clients":*

  http://www.ibm.com/developerworks/WebSphere/library/techarticles/0709_mckegney/0709_mckegney.html

- *"Customizing the e-mail template to add dynamic tags in WebSphere Commerce":*

  http://www.ibm.com/developerworks/WebSphere/library/tutorials/0708_mittal/0708_mittal.html

- *"Implementing WebSphere Commerce operational reports with Crystal Reports":*

  http://www.ibm.com/developerworks/WebSphere/library/tutorials/0707_zhou/0707_zhou.html

- *"Customizing WebSphere Commerce Accelerator":*

  http://www.ibm.com/developerworks/WebSphere/library/tutorials/0707_mittal/0707_mittal.html

- *"Improving high availability in WebSphere Commerce using DB2 HADR":*

  http://www.ibm.com/developerworks/WebSphere/library/techarticles/0703_wang/0703_wang.html

- *"Shipping Simplified: Integrating WebSphere Commerce with Third-party Shipping Providers"*, REDP-3910:

  http://www.redbooks.ibm.com/abstracts/redp3910.html?Open

WebSphere Application Server

- WebSphere Application Server Product Information:

  http://www-306.ibm.com/software/webservers/appserv/was/
- WebSphere Application Server v6 Documentation (InfoCenter):

  http://publib.boulder.ibm.com/infocenter/wasinfo/v6r0/index.jsp
- WebSphere Application Server V6 Scalability and Performance Handbook:

  http://www.redbooks.ibm.com/abstracts/sg246392.html
- Redbooks publication: WebSphere V5.1 Performance, Scalability, and High Availability WebSphere Handbook Series:

  http://www.redbooks.ibm.com/abstracts/sg246198.html

DB2

- DB2 Product Information:

  http://www-306.ibm.com/software/data/db2/udb/
- DB2 v8 Documentation (InfoCenter):

  http://publib.boulder.ibm.com/infocenter/db2luw/v8//index.jsp

IBM HTTP Server

- IBM HTTP Server Product Information:

  http://www-306.ibm.com/software/webservers/httpservers/
- IBM HTTP Server v6 Documentation (InfoCenter):

  http://publib.boulder.ibm.com/infocenter/wasinfo/v6r0/index.jsp?topic=/com.ibm.WebSphere.ihs.doc/info/welcome_ihs.html

SOA

- *"Migrating WebSphere Commerce to the SOA foundation tooling":*

  http://www.ibm.com/developerworks/WebSphere/library/techarticles/0611_mohan/0611_mohan.html

- *"IBM SOA Foundation - An Architectural Introduction and Overview":*

  http://download.boulder.ibm.com/ibmdl/pub/software/dw/webservices/ws-soa-whitepaper.pdf

  and

  http://www.ibm.com/developerworks/WebSphere/newtosoa/index.html

- *"SOA Logical Architecture and WebSphere Commerce back-office integration":*

  http://publib.boulder.ibm.com/infocenter/wchelp/v6r0m0/index.jsp?topic=/com.ibm.commerce.developer.doc/concepts/csdsoasoi.htm

- *"Connecting Enterprise Applications to WebSphere Enterprise Service Bus"*, SG24-7406:

  http://www.redbooks.ibm.com/abstracts/sg247406.html

- *"Using IBM WebSphere Message Broker as an ESB with WebSphere Process Server"*, SG24-7527:

  http://www.redbooks.ibm.com/abstracts/sg247527.html?Open"

- *"Patterns: SOA Design Using WebSphere Message Broker and WebSphere ESB"*, SG24-7369:

  http://www.redbooks.ibm.com/abstracts/sg247369.html?Open

- *"IBM WebSphere DataPower SOA Appliances Part I: Overview and Getting Started"*, REDP-4327:

  http://www.redbooks.ibm.com/redpieces/abstracts/redp4327.html?Open

Security references and information

- Learn about social factors in computer security. Schneier, Bruce:

  Secrets and Lies: Digital Security In A Networked World, John Wiley and Sons, Inc., 2000.

- A good introduction to computer security:

  Pfleeger, Charles P., Security in Computing, Second Edition, Prentice-Hall, Inc., 1996.

- Low level tips for writing secure code:

  Howard, Michael and LeBland, David, Writing Secure Code, Second Edition, Microsoft Press, 2003.

- Denial of service:

  Internet Denial of Service: Attack and Defense Mechanisms, by Jelena Mirkovic, Sven Dietrich, David Dittrich and Peter Reiher, Prentice Hall PTR, ISBN 0131475738

- An example of a denial of service attack:

  Yahoo on Trail of Site Hackers, Reuters News Service, February 8, 2000.

  http://www.wired.com/techbiz/media/news/2000/02/34221

- *"Distributed Denial of Service: Taxonomies of Attacks, Tools and Countermeasures"*, Stephen Specht and Ruby Lee, Princeton Architecture Laboratory for Multimedia and Security:

  http://palms.ee.princeton.edu/PALMSopen/DDoS%20Final%20PDCS%20Paper.pdf

- Ernst & Young, P3P Dashboard Report, January 2004. This is the most recent version of Ernst & Young's report, measuring the adoption rate of P3P on the most popular domains:

  https://www.privacyassociation.org/docs/sum04/1-4Tretick3.pdf

- P3P v1.0 Specification. The official specification of the P3P standard, which includes detailed descriptions of all P3P elements as well as DTDs and XSDs:

  http://www.w3.org/TR/P3P/

- Increase consumer trust in your WebSphere Commerce site by deploying a P3P policy:

  http://www.ibm.com/developerworks/websphere/library/techarticles/0511_smit/0511_smit.html

- Data: Lost, Stolen or Strayed. A news article on credit card data being lost or stolen:

  http://www.computerworld.com/printthis/2005/0,4814,103541,00.html

- Consumer confidence:

  http://www.internetretailer.com/internet/marketing-conference/578566856-vague-online-privacy-policies-are-harming-e-commerce-new-survey-reports.html
  http://www.ponemon.org/idtheft.html

- Security breaches:

  http://www.privacyrights.org/ar/DataBreaches2006-Analysis.htm

- *"Collecting personal information using Web sites"*, Information commissioner, UK Government:

  http://www.ico.gov.uk/upload/documents/library/data_protection/practical_application/collecting_personal_information_from_websites_v1.0.pdf

- Federal Information Processing Standard:

  http://www.itl.nist.gov/fipspubs/fip112.htm

Usability research and tips

- A useful summary of usability pluses and minuses:

  http://www.smashingmagazine.com/2008/01/31/10-principles-of-effective-web-design/
  http://www.smashingmagazine.com/2007/09/27/10-usability-nightmares-you-should-be-aware-of/
  http://www.smashingmagazine.com/2007/10/09/30-usability-issues-to-be-aware-of

- useit.com: Jakob Nielsen's Web Site:

  http://www.useit.com/

- *"On-demand web application experience management solutions"*:

  http://www.gomez.com/pdfs/nine_truths.pdf

Project and risk management

- Software acquisition risk analysis:

  http://www.stsc.hill.af.mil/resources/tech_docs/gsam3/chap6.pdf

- *"Risk reduction with the RUP phase plan"*, Mark Akred, DeveloperWorks, November 2003, found at:

  http://www.ibm.com/developerworks/rational/library/1826.html

- Agile development:

  http://agilemanifesto.org/
  http://www.agilealliance.com/library

- *"Project management at Heathrow Terminal 5"*, Public Finance, April 22 2005:

  http://www.christianwolmar.co.uk/articles/pubfinance/apr22,05.shtml

- OpenProj project management tool:

  http://openproj.org/

Coding standards and debugging

- Sun's Java coding conventions:

  http://java.sun.com/docs/codeconv/
- "Servlets and JSP pages Best Practices":

  http://java.sun.com/developer/technicalArticles/javaserverpages/servlets_jsp/
- "Draft Java Coding Standard", Doug Lea:

  http://g.oswego.edu/dl/html/javaCodingStd.html
- *"Coding Standards for Java"*, Scott Ambler:

  http://www.ambysoft.com/essays/javaCodingStandards.html
- *"Learn the essentials of debugging. Systematically take on mysterious errors with confidence"*, Terrence Parr:

  http://www.ibm.com/developerworks/web/library/wa-debug.html

Virtualization

- IBM Virtualization Infrastructure:

  http://www-03.ibm.com/systems/virtualization/infrastructure/server/
- Redbooks publication: Advanced POWER™ Virtualization on IBM System p5: Introduction and Configuration:

  http://www.redbooks.ibm.com/abstracts/sg247940.html

Redundancy

- *"Planning for Availability in the Enterprise"*, by Rick Robinson and Alexandre Polozoff:

  http://www.ibm.com/developerworks/websphere/techjournal/0312_polozoff/polozoff.html

- IBM RAID products for System x:

  http://www-03.ibm.com/systems/storage/product/systemx/scsi_raid.html

- "IBM System Storage: Implementing an IBM SAN", SG24-6116:

  http://www.redbooks.ibm.com/abstracts/sg246116.html

- "High Availability and Scalability Guide for DB2 on Linux, UNIX, and Windows", SG24-7363:

  http://www.redbooks.ibm.com/abstracts/sg247363.html

- Oracle Database High Availability:

  http://www.oracle.com/technology/deploy/availability/index.html

- Virtual Router Redundancy Protocol (VRRP):

  http://www.ietf.org/rfc/rfc3768.txt

Services engagements

- IBM IT outsourcing and hosting:

  http://www-935.ibm.com/services/us/index.wss/itservice/so/a1000414

- IBM Global Business Services has to offer:

  http://www.ibm.com/bcs

- IBM Software Services for WebSphere:

  http://www.ibm.com/developerworks/WebSphere/services/

- Find an IBM Business Partner:

  http://www-304.ibm.com/jct09002c/gsdod/showcase.do?

How to get Redbooks

You can search for, view, or download Redbooks, Redpapers, Technotes, draft publications and Additional materials, as well as order hardcopy Redbooks, at this Web site:

ibm.com/redbooks

Help from IBM

IBM Support and downloads

ibm.com/support

IBM Global Services

ibm.com/services

Index

A

B

E

F

Q

R

S

T

U

V

W

X

Y